Politics in

THE
MIDDLE
EAST

*The Little, Brown Series
in Comparative Politics*

Under the Editorship of
GABRIEL A. ALMOND
JAMES S. COLEMAN
LUCIAN W. PYE

Politics in

THE
MIDDLE
EAST

James A. Bill
Carl Leiden

University of Texas, Austin

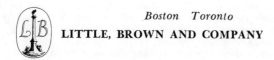

Boston   Toronto

LITTLE, BROWN AND COMPANY

TO HASSAN ALAVI, RICHARD WARE, AND HEDAYATOLLAH HAKIM-ELAHI

LIBRARY OF CONGRESS CATALOG CARD NO.: 78-70455

ISBN 0-316-095052

9 8 7 6 5 4

ALP
*Published simultaneously in Canada
by Little, Brown & Company (Canada) Limited*

PRINTED IN THE UNITED STATES OF AMERICA

Portions of this book appeared in different form in *The Middle East: Politics and Power* (Boston: Allyn and Bacon, 1974).

The following authors and publishers have granted permission to include material from their publications. Page numbers for specific citations appear in the footnotes.

A. J. Arberry. From A. J. Arberry, ed., *Religion in the Middle East,* Vols. I and II, 1969. Reprinted by permission of the publisher, Cambridge University Press.

N. J. Coulson. From N. J. Coulson, *A History of Islamic Law.* Repro-duced by kind permission of Edinburgh University Press, 22 George Square, Edinburgh, Scotland.

Lord Kinross. From Lord Kinross, *Ataturk: The Rebirth of a Nation.* Reprinted by permission of the publishers, George Weidenfeld & Nicolson Ltd. and William Morrow & Company, Inc.

Bernard Lewis. From *The Emergence of Modern Turkey,* 2nd ed., © Royal Institute of International Affairs 1968, by permission of Oxford University Press.

John Sewell. Reprinted with permission of John Sewell and the Staff of the Overseas Development Council. *The United States and World Development: Agenda 1977* (New York: Praeger Publishers, 1977), © 1977 by the Overseas Development Council.

United Nations. From *United Nations Statistical Yearbook 1975,* pp. 845–867. Reproduced by permission.

precious wealth has ignited a process of exploration that has led to the discovery of other resources; it is catapulting the area into a position as the world's new international heartland. The ancient lands of pyramids, pharaohs, prophets, and poets is in the midst of a remarkable renaissance. The area's blinding transformations carry an international impact.

If it would only "stand still!" is a familiar reaction of every traveller to the Middle East. If he repeats his visit in a year or so — or perhaps only in a few months — he will discern the incredible and dizzying process of change. What leaps to the eye at first are the physical changes that today are both massive and frightening. But more important, though less obvious, are the changes in habits, manners, and behaviors. An example of the constant change in the area is the fact that as this book was going to press, the Iranian monarchy collapsed. Still, there is much that is permanent in the Middle East. The analysis of the Iranian monarchy explains much about both traditional political patterns and politics in Iran today.

This book is based on an earlier study entitled *The Middle East: Politics and Power* (1974). That book was received favorably by students and faculty alike. In preparing this volume, we have attempted to retain the flavor of the earlier book; yet this is a substantially different study. The important introductory chapter on the related issues of modernization and political development is quite different from its predecessor. All the other chapters have been subjected to significant revisions. Chapter III, for example, contains a new section on the power of women in Middle Eastern history and politics. In Chapter V, Turkey's Kemal Atatürk and Ismet Inönü as well as Egypt's Gamal Abdel Nasser and Anwar Sadat are compared and contrasted as political leaders. Many other significant changes have been made throughout the book.

We have deleted the chapter on bureaucracy that appeared in the earlier work and have added two new chapters: one on the Arab-Israeli dispute and another on the politics of Middle Eastern oil. The inclusion of these chapters can be justified on the grounds of their pertinence and relevance alone. Indeed, many students and colleagues had questioned our earlier exclusion of these topics. As one undergraduate argued: "You owe it to those of us who read your book to include a bit more spice now and then!" If anything, the subject of Arabs, Israelis, and oil does this. More importantly, the Arab-Israeli dispute and the ever evolving aspects of oil politics profoundly affect the many facets of domestic political processes that are our chief concern.

This book is topically organized. It does not take the reader on a country-by-country tour of the area, but rather focuses on problems and patterns. This organizational format was well received in our earlier venture and therefore is retained.

The system of transliteration in this study generally follows the format used by the *International Journal of Middle East Studies*. We have decided to delete all diacritical marks with the exception of the *ayn* (') and the *hamza* (') when they appear in the middle of a word. This decision may upset a number of careful scholars of Middle Eastern history and linguistics. It is done, however, to assist students and non-area specialists who have expressed their reluctance to plow through numerous dots and dashes which to them appear randomly sprinkled over the pages of the text. (It should even merit an enthusiastic hurrah from the typesetters.) Arabic, Persian, or Turkish words commonly used in English are spelled as they appear in *Webster's Third International Dictionary* or in *Webster's Geographical Dictionary*. Well-known proper names are presented as they appear in the English literature or as they have been transliterated by the individuals themselves (e.g., Gamal Abdel Nasser, Anwar Sadat, Muhammad Reza Shah Pahlavi, King Farouk, Nuri al-Said, Kemal Atatürk). This approach, of course, leads to occasional inconsistencies. In response, we quote T. E. Lawrence who in the preface of his *Seven Pillars of Wisdom* writes that, "Arabic names won't go into English, exactly, for their consonants are not the same as ours and their vowels, like ours, vary from district to district. There are some 'scientific systems' of transliteration, helpful to people who know enough Arabic not to need helping, but a wash-out for the world."

There are many friends, colleagues, and students who helped us critique our 1974 volume and have also contributed to this one. Our students at the University of Texas, undergraduates at Dartmouth, Pennsylvania State, and Portland State have had input into this book. Their reactions to our 1974 study were carefully collected and relayed to us by their professors, Gene Garthwaite, Arthur Goldschmidt, Jr., and John Damis respectively. Ervand Abrahamian, Dale Eickelman, Manfred Halpern, Mike Hillmann, Malcolm Kerr, George Lenczowski, David Long, Phoebe Marr, Rouhollah Ramazani, and Frank Tachau encouraged us with their kind words and comments. We are especially appreciative of both the substantive suggestions and the help provided by Nazar Al-Hasso, Salman Al-Khalifa, John Duke Anthony, Hossein Askari, John Cummings, Harvey, Goldberg, Peter Gran, Metin Heper, Bill Hickman, J. C. Hurewitz, Arnold Leder, Jerry Obermeyer, Jim Piscatori, John Voll, and Robert Springborg.

Twelve enthusiastic professors from colleges around the country spent the summer of 1977 with us at the University of Texas where they participated in a seminar sponsored by the National Endowment of the Humanities on Middle Eastern political systems. These twelve not only critically analyzed our 1974 book but also subjected our new ideas to careful inspection and dissection. Many opinions were questioned at this seminar, pet theories were scuttled and intuitive insights mangled. But much that was new and positive came out of our marathon sessions; some of which is presented in the pages of this volume. For this and more, we thank Charley Barber, Bruce Borthwick, Sandy Danforth, Gabor Galantai, Mike Germaine, Jared Graber, Tom Harlach, Donn Kurtz, Phil Mikesell, Larry Schulz, Sandy Wurth-Hough, and Hoda Zaki. Others who joined us at various times during that eventful summer were Jacob Landau, Halim Barakat, Ed Sheehan, Elizabeth Fernea, and John Duke Anthony, Manfred Halpern, and Arnold Leder who are mentioned above.

Morris David Morris of the University of Washington and the Overseas Development Council personally assisted us with his new conceptual tool, the Physical Quality of Life Index, which we use in Chapter I. Our colleague, Neil Richardson, analyzed and tested this newly developed instrument for us and made a number of helpful suggestions for using it. Geologist Samuel P. Ellison has helped us interpret the confusing and sometimes inconsistent data on petroleum reserves.

In addition, the strong support of Paul English, Director of the Center for Middle Eastern Studies at the University of Texas at Austin, is noted with appreciation. Robert Stookey, longtime foreign service officer in the Middle East and a leading scholar of Arabs and things Arabic, has been a constant resource whom we have called upon again and again. Gabriel Almond has been an unusually active and helpful editor. We would also like to thank Bob Ellis of Time-Life Books and Rick Boyer and especially Gregory Franklin of Little, Brown for their encouraging assistance. Tina Samaha, the book editor, and Barbara Poetter, the copyeditor, did superb jobs. Both of us acknowledge the continuing support of the Earhart Foundation. We also thank Munther Dajani, Tim Dickey, Blake Dominguez, David Fink, and especially Pamela Kress for their research assistance. Beverly Bowman, Wanda Franklin, and Patti Willey were more than generous in their important help in typing and retyping portions of the manuscript.

We save the best for last: our wives, Ann and Mary, who have coddled us, humored us, and supported us through one more project. In the meantime, they put up with piles of manuscripts and open books, frayed nerves, and irregular schedules. This book is as much their production as it is ours. In this sense, their names should go on the cover alongside ours.

No book goes out into the world of readers without its flaws. We do not deny our responsibility for these but we do hope that this study will find favorable reception on the part of both students and specialists alike, *insha'allah* . . .

J.A.B.
C.L.

Contents

Chapter I

Political Development and
the Challenge of Modernization   *1*

> *The challenge of modernization. The concept
> of political development. The dialectics of
> modernization and political development.
> Modernization in the Middle East. Political
> development in the Middle East.*

Chapter II

Islam and Politics   *38*

> *Islam. The contemporary role of religion.
> Religious reform. Religious reaction. Islam
> and modernization. Judaism in the Middle
> East. Other Middle Eastern religious forces.*

Chapter III

The Genes of Politics:
Groups, Classes, and Families   *75*

> *Group structure: vertical stratification. Class
> structure: horizontal stratification.*

Chapter IV

The Politics of Patrimonial Leadership   *134*

*Muhammad: the politics of a prophet.   Patterns
of patrimonialism in the Middle East.*

Chapter V

The Politics of Leaders and Change   *178*

*Twentieth-century traditional leaders.
Atatürk: the revolutionary father of Turkey.
Muhammad Reza Shah Pahlavi: the
traditionalism of a modernizing monarch.
Gamal Abdel Nasser: patrimonialism and
transformation.   Anwar Sadat: the return of
traditional patrimonialism.   Leaders and
change: a concluding perspective.*

Chapter VI

Violence and the Military   *237*

*The tradition of violence.   The Middle Eastern
military.   Patterns of violence and coercion:
conclusion.*

Chapter VII

The Imprint of Ideology   *280*

*The need for legitimation.   The nature of
ideology.   Ideology in the Middle East.   The
patina of religion.   Nationalism.
Communism.   Neutralism.   Summary.*

Chapter VIII

The Arab-Israeli Connection 318

The political dimensions. The Arab-Israeli wars. The negotiations. The prospects for a general settlement.

Chapter IX

The Power of Petroleum 360

The pool of petroleum power. The major oil companies and the traditional international power structure. The politics of OPEC. The political consequences of petroleum power. Concluding thoughts.

Bibliography 405

Index 412

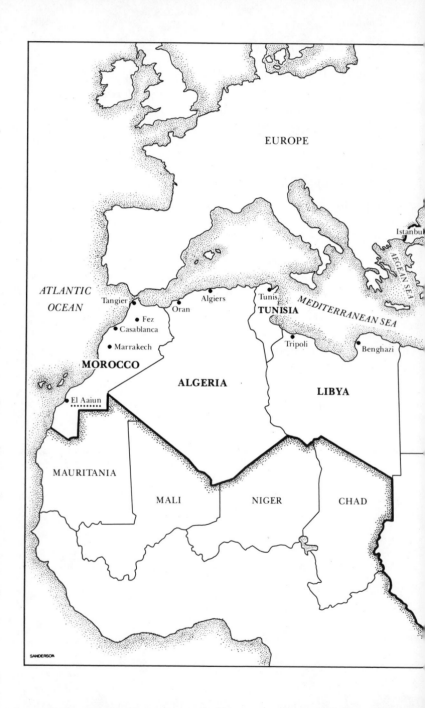

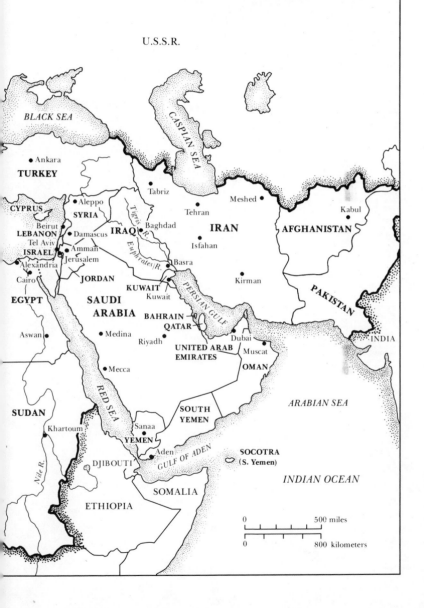

The Middle East

CHAPTER I

Political Development and
the Challenge of Modernization

As WE MOVE well into the last quarter of the twentieth century, the Middle East is a part of the world greatly torn by the turbulence of change. The symptoms are present everywhere. Old human relationships and social structures are crumbling, while new patterns and systems remain to be formed. Economic crisis, political upheaval, and human violence dominate a situation in which individuals, families, and nations struggle to achieve their goals.

In the Middle East, lavish wealth exists alongside of abject poverty, both between and within societies. Politically, absolute monarchs and revolutionary command councils live side by side, and no form of government seems immune to coups and countercoups. Internal violence sparked by sociopolitical dissatisfaction and interregional warfare dominated by the persisting Arab-Israeli conflict have become an integral part of the scene. The effects of the developmental challenge in the Middle East extend far beyond the borders of the area itself. Economically, the oil embargo of late 1973 remains a vivid example of this fact. Politically, the unprecedented violent disruption of the Olympic games in Munich by Palestinian guerrillas in 1972 and the Israeli commando raid on Entebbe in Uganda in 1975 are only two of dozens of dramatic cases in point. The world has also been involved in one way or another in the civil wars that have been fought in Sudan, Oman, Iraq, and Lebanon — all in the 1970s.

At the level of everyday living, change is highly evident, for ancient customs and lifeways are under heavy seige. This is particularly true with respect to the related areas of occupation, transportation, recreation, and education. Stenographers and typists are rapidly replacing calligraphers and scribes; the carpet and metal industries have been transformed by the machine; and factories and assembly lines are taking the place of town workshops and cottage industry. In the realm of transportation, donkeys and camels have already lost their centuries-long domination to automobiles and trucks. Airplanes and airports are omnipresent. Throughout the Middle East, herdsmen and shepherds listen to transistor radios, and television sets now adorn village teahouses. The urban young increasingly flock to movie houses, dance halls, bowling alleys, pool halls, and ski resorts. The patterns of dress are also in a stage of interesting transition. Veiled women go about their shopping in tennis shoes, and street cleaners ply their trade in reasonable facsimiles of sport coats. In addition the family and religious institutions that dominated education for centuries have given way to modern secular schools, colleges, and universities.

Social change in the Middle East is currently marked by a curious and even bizarre blend of tradition and modernity. The jagged course of change has left in its wake a number of imbalances, inconsistencies, inequalities, and enigmas. Heart transplant centers and nuclear engineering and aerospace programs exist in Iran — a society with an acute shortage of physicians and with infant mortality rates that hover in the area of 130–140 per thousand live births. In the shaykhdom of Abu Dhabi, which now boasts the highest per capita income in the world, the population literally moved directly from mud huts into modern, air-conditioned houses and apartment buildings. In Saudi Arabia, a society which by itself possesses over 20 percent of the world's petroleum reserves, water remains scarce and is often still transported in bottles by mule or is delivered to private homes in small tanks.

Central to the entire problem of change as it is manifested

in the Middle East are the related issues of modernization and political development. The revolution of modernization and the politics of development are two of the most critical problems confronting Middle Eastern peoples and cultures. It is here that they are caught in a grim struggle for survival, justice, and happiness. The extraordinary importance of these issues is perhaps matched only by the great difficulty involved in coming to grips intellectually with them. The following section will present some of the definitions and distinctions essential to any serious analysis of the processes of modernization and political development in the Middle East.

THE CHALLENGE OF MODERNIZATION

C. E. Black defines modernization as "the process by which historically evolved institutions are adapted to the rapidly changing functions that reflect the unprecedented increase in man's knowledge, permitting control over his environment, that accompanied the scientific revolution."[1] Dankwart Rustow writes that modernization is a process of "rapidly widening control over nature through closer cooperation among men."[2] And Marion J. Levy, in a major hypothesis in his work, asserts that "the greater the ratio of inanimate to animate sources of power and the greater the multiplication of effort as the effect of applications of tools, the greater is the degree of modernization."[3] Modernization is most concisely defined as the process by which man increasingly gains control over his environment.

The process of modernization has, of course, always occurred in every society. In the past, the wide variety of responses to environmental challenges produced some very disparate results; this legacy is evident today in much of the developing world, including the Middle East. In the twentieth century, rapid communication not only facilitates the discov-

---

[1] C. E. Black, *The Dynamics of Modernization* (New York: Harper and Row, 1966) , p. 7.

[2] Dankwart A. Rustow, *A World of Nations: Problems of Political Modernization* (Washintgon, D.C.: The Brookings Institution, 1967) , p. 3.

[3] Marion J. Levy, Jr., *Modernization and the Structure of Societies* (Princeton, N.J.: Princeton University Press, 1966) , p. 35.

ery that stages of modernization other than one's own are possible, but also enables the tools and techniques of certain cultures to be transmitted to others.

Perhaps the most dramatic dimension of modernization is the technological revolution, which carries with it impressive trends in the areas of industrialization, economic development, and communication. In the Middle East, the constant physical transformations that seem to occur everywhere are outward evidence of technological development. Skyscrapers, highway grids, airports, hotels, dams, and steel mills continually sprout throughout the area. One author refers to this rapid change in the economic and material aspects of life as the "Edifice Complex."[4] Spurred by the discovery and exploitation of petroleum and natural gas, these economic and technological factors provide the driving force of modernization.

Closely related to technological advancement are the strides that have been made in education. The grip in which the clerics traditionally held education in Muslim societies has been broken. Literacy programs multiply in the area, while the sheer numbers of school buildings and educational facilities increase at an amazing rate. The result of all this activity has been a heightened consciousness and an expanded scientific and technical knowledge. Acting as a catalyst to all this, of course, are technological forces, such as advances in communications and the mass media that provide the means by which information can be transmitted more quickly, effectively, and universally.

The developments in the Middle East in technology and education have a number of organizational and psychological implications. Organization is becoming more elaborate and specialized, and formal institutions are beginning to replace informal, personal administration. As values and expectations become more secular, important shifts in attitudes are occurring. Traditional emphasis on the spiritual and magical is waning.

The patterns that constitute the modernization syndrome

---

4 Norman Jacobs, *The Sociology of Development: Iran as an Asian Case Study* (New York: Frederick A. Praeger, 1966), p. 74.

are mutually reinforcing. This reinforcement accelerates modernization even in societies in which resources are scarce and in which the population largely continues to follow traditional lifestyles. Technological progress promotes educational advancement, which in turn influences attitudes and values that are reflected in organizational settings. Moreover, value systems and organizational styles that are in a state of transformation are highly supportive of continuing and deepening technological and educational change. It is easy to see why modernization is a major obsession of the peoples of the Middle East.

Modernization is inevitable and omnipresent. In the words of Marion Levy, it is a "universal social solvent."[5] Those societies that are relatively more modernized have tended to be located in the West, and hence the process has sometimes been unfortunately referred to as Westernization. The inevitability and universality of modernization are products of the increasingly interdependent world in which we live. Although the societies in the Middle East will all struggle in one way or another to modernize, not all will succeed to the same degree. The unevenness of the success of modernization in the various Middle Eastern societies is in itself a source of tension and conflict. Robert L. Hardgrave, Jr. has written that "seeking the fulfillment of their aspirations for independence, the nationalist elites of the new states have committed themselves to rapid economic growth and social transformation. . . . The aspiration for modernity is almost universal: Few leaders are willing to relegate their nations to ethnographic museums — fewer still have the choice."[6]

Modernization is an unsettling, disruptive, painful process. The comforts of traditional habits are lost as these habits are uprooted. In modernizing societies, new processes and institutions seem always to be trapped in a state of becoming, and, as a result, the expected uncertainties of the past have given way

[5] Marion J. Levy, Jr., *Modernization: Latecomers and Survivors* (New York and London: Basic Books, 1972).

[6] James A. Bill and Robert L. Hardgrave, Jr., *Comparative Politics: The Quest for Theory* (Columbus: Charles E. Merrill, 1973), p. 64.

to the more frightful and unknown insecurities of the present. In the Middle East, where most of the societies have seriously begun to modernize, any slowing or reversal of the process causes unprecedented stress. Yet the uneven supply of national resources, the shortage of technical skills, and the weakness of political leadership are all severe impediments to continuing modernization. Modernization is a process in which expectations necessarily race beyond their satisfaction. However, satisfaction must never lag too far behind. In most Middle Eastern societies, the gap between sharpened aspirations and their attainment threatens to become a chasm. The consequent frustrations directly promote social upheaval and political unrest.

The direction and depth of the drive for modernization are determined largely within the political system. The political elites of the various Middle Eastern societies make the basic decisions that shape the strategies and programs of modernization. Much of the responsibility for the success and failure of policies of modernization resides in the political arena. Modernization in turn affects the capacity of the political system to respond to political challenges. For reasons such as these, the important issue of political development is closely interwoven with the problem of modernization.

THE CONCEPT OF POLITICAL DEVELOPMENT

One survey of the literature on development tallies ten different definitions of political development.[7] There is much confusion about the relationships between the concept of modernization and that of political development. Often the terms are treated as synonymous. In other instances, they are sharply distinguished from each other. In this study, we view the two processes as analytically distinct but actually interrelated. It is in this sense that we will study them in the Middle East.

Alfred Diamant writes that "political development is a

[7] Lucian W. Pye, *Aspects of Political Development* (Boston: Little, Brown and Co., 1966), pp. 33–45. For a penetrating analysis of the major intellectual attempts to confront the issue of development, see Leonard Binder's chapter, "The Crises of Political Development," in Leonard Binder et al., *Crises and Sequences in Political Development* (Princeton, N.J.: Princeton University Press, 1971), pp. 3–72.

process by which a political system acquires an increased capacity to sustain successfully and continuously new types of goals and demands and the creation of new types of organizations."[8] S. N. Eisenstadt provides a similar definition when he discusses a political system's ability to meet changing demands and then "to absorb them in terms of policy-making and to assure its own continuity in the face of continuous new demands and new forms of political organization."[9] Eisenstadt goes on to state that "the ability to deal with continuous changes in political demands is the crucial test of such sustained political development."[10] This concern for the capacity of a political system to meet new challenges is also evident in the Social Science Research Council Committee's work on development. The developmental capacity of politics "is a capacity not only to overcome the divisions and manage the tensions created by increased differentiation, but to respond to or contain the participatory and distributive demands generated by the imperatives of equality. It is also a capacity to innovate and manage continuous change."[11]

The last sentence above introduces a central dimension of our conceptualization of political development. The political system is not only a responsive, reactive mechanism in which demands and challenges are absorbed and digested. The political system is preeminently a system with a primacy and an autonomy that permit the introduction and generation of change. It is the political system that leads, guides, and directs. And it is in this system that the demands and programs of tomorrow often originate.[12] Manfred Halpern therefore de-

[8] Alfred Diamant, "The Nature of Political Development," in *Political Development and Social Change,* ed. Jason L. Finkle and Richard W. Gable (New York: John Wiley and Sons, 1966) , p. 92.

[9] S. N. Eisenstadt, "Initial Institutional Patterns of Political Mobilization," *Civilizations* 12 (1962) , reprinted in *Political Modernization,* ed. Claude E. Welch, Jr. (Belmont, Calif.: Wadsworth, 1967) , p. 252.

[10] Ibid.

[11] James S. Coleman's words in Binder et al., *Crises and Sequences,* p. 78.

[12] This emphasis upon the political is especially critical in studying development in the Middle East. The Middle Eastern perception of change is oriented more to politics than to economics. In making this important point, C. A. O. van Nieuwenhuijze writes: "Intriguingly, the most conspicuous aspect in the Middle East is not the one that has virtually undisputed primacy in the Western perception of change, namely the economic aspects

fines political development as the "enduring capacity to generate and absorb persistent transformation."[13] Political development as it is discussed in this study involves the capacity of Middle Eastern political systems to initiate, absorb, and sustain continuous transformation.

Among the most important of the demands that the political system must foster and satisfy are the demands for equality of opportunity, political participation, and social justice.[14] These demands are much more difficult to meet than those derived directly from the economic and technological facets of life. The process of political development includes the capacity to provide more and more individuals with the power to improve their own positions in society on the basis of personal merit rather than personal connections. New groups and classes continually appear in society and must be brought effectively into the political process. Political development is a "process of admitting all groups and all interests, including newly recognized interests, and new generations, into full political participation without disrupting the efficient working of the political system and without limiting the ability of the system to choose and pursue policy goals."[15] Finally, the rewards and priorities of the society need to be allocated and reallocated in a way that permits all to expect and receive rationally based and evenhanded treatment.

By defining political development in terms of a capacity to stimulate demands and to solve problems, one is able to avoid a number of ethnocentric problems that have long haunted

---

of material well-being. As it happens, this discrepancy in orientations has resulted in endless confusion and misunderstanding between on the one hand Middle Easterners with their development needs and on the other hand Western experts and observers with their development aid and advice. The two are, so to speak, on different wavelengths." See van Nieuwenhuijze, *Sociology of the Middle East: A Stocktaking and Interpretation* (Leiden: E. J. Brill, 1971), pp. 773–74.

13 Manfred Halpern, "The Rate and Costs of Political Development," *Annals* 358 (March 1965) :22.

14 For a recent study of the politics of the Arab world that focuses on the concept of participation, see Michael C. Hudson, *Arab Politics: The Search for Legitimacy* (New Haven: Yale University Press, 1978).

15 This is Leonard Binder's view of the manner in which most liberal democrats in the West define political development. See Binder et al., *Crises and Sequences,* p. 68.

developmental studies. The proclivity to define political development in terms of a Western-oriented view of democracy is one example of this ethnocentricity. Many "democratic" systems may not succeed in political development because of their inability to effectively absorb the changes occurring in the contemporary world. In the Middle East, Lebanon is a tragic case in point. It is also possible that an authoritarian system that is able to overcome its inherent weaknesses concerning the issue of participation may succeed in political development. Using this definition of political development, it is possible to account for the developmental process as it existed in many ancient and traditional systems. Indeed, certain traditional Islamic societies were perhaps more highly developed politically than some contemporary Middle Eastern societies. This need not be surprising, since these traditional systems undoubtedly had much more limited demands placed upon them. To speak of political development as if it were something rare and unique to our modern age hinders our ability to understand the dynamics of change, since it distorts important historical patterns and trends.

The contemporary era, however, is fundamentally different from any earlier time, because scientific advances and technological revolution have wrought unprecedented change. Modernization, or man's increasing control over his environment, races onward at a breakneck pace. The impact of this modernization on the patterns of political development has been profound. Modernization and political development must be analyzed together.

THE DIALECTICS OF MODERNIZATION AND POLITICAL DEVELOPMENT

Partly to maximize their own power and authority, political elites may seek to generate and accelerate the processes of modernization within their societies. Although such efforts enlarge capacities to meet new challenges, they also help improve the standing of particular societies in the world of nations.[16] The

---

[16] J. P. Nettl and Roland Robertson go so far as to define modernization in terms of the search for technological equivalence among nation-states. See J. P. Nettl and Roland Robertson, *International System and the Modernization of Societies* (New York: Basic Books, 1968).

unleashed forces of modernization meanwhile influence the behavior and policies of the elites. Leonard Binder writes that in Europe "the overwhelmingly accepted view was that politics was essentially a response to the historical forces of modernization. Outside of Europe, the prevailing view has been the opposite. Politics is not a response to modernity, it must rather be the cause of modernity if modernity is to be achieved."[17] In this discussion, we view the processes as mutually interactive. Political elites forge modernization policies that strongly affect their future decision-making capacities.

Once modernization has begun, it tends to become a pervasive, irreversible process. As a result, the political group that stimulated and encouraged the modernizing movement often loses its ability to control and regulate the process. Demands increase and outstrip any capacity to cope with them. It is for this reason that political development is a highly problematic process. It cannot be assumed that because "modernization is taking place, political development also must be taking place."[18] It *can* be assumed that there will always be a gap between the demands that accompany modernization and the political system's ability to satisfy these demands. In this sense, it is easier to generate change than to absorb it.

Changes occasioned by the forces of modernization usually occur in the physical environment and are most dramatically evident in the areas of technology and economics. Impressive change here, however, does not necessarily signal basic alteration in the sociopolitical system. Traditional patterns of power and authority tend to resist fundamental change. Personal equality, political participation, and social justice are usually the last issues to be confronted. Political elites have vested interests in preserving ongoing political patterns. Yet if political development is to take place, it must involve a capacity for continuous change *especially* with respect to these social and political issues. No matter how much technological and economic progress may occur, there can be no political development without accompanying change in the power and authority structures.

17 Binder et al., *Crises and Sequences,* pp. 15–16.
18 Samuel P. Huntington, "Political Development and Political Decay," *World Politics* 17 (April 1965) :391.

FIGURE I.1 *The Development Process*

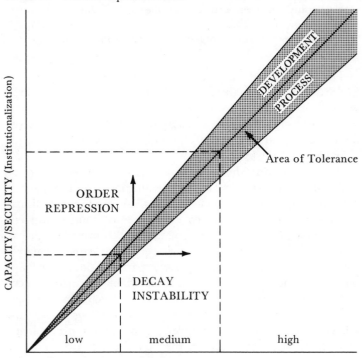

DEMANDS/LIBERTY (Participation)

The developmental process is driven by a dialectical dynamic that marks the relationship between demands and capacity. In more conventional terms, the struggle is one for both liberty and security. Figure I.1 provides a diagrammatic view of this process. In their recent study of comparative politics, Gabriel Almond and G. Bingham Powell identify liberty and security as two basic political goods that societies must provide. They point out that the provision of both of these goods has long been the classic dilemma of politics.

> At the logical extremes, at least, there seem to be negative trade-offs between liberty and security, and no ready ethical answer dictates the most appropriate balance between them. . . . At some point, liberty for some individuals threatens the security of others. The logical and ethical dilemma does not, however,

obviate some very important empirical questions about the relationships between security and liberty. . . . For part of the problem of liberty concerns the use that citizens wish to make of it, and part of the problem of security concerns who shall enforce it.[19]

The increasing demand for liberty and related values, such as participation, equality, and justice, must in today's world be confronted. There must be either an enhanced capacity to satisfy these demands or a capacity to repress them. The satisfaction of demands is usually provided by increasing institutionalization and by effective new methods and style of rule. This often means the centralization and concentration of authority as ongoing relations are uprooted and new ones created. The forces of modernization, by providing political elites with more sophisticated techniques of control, can enhance their capacity to meet demands and to provide security. They also, however, can permit elites to stifle demands through repressive means. Calls for participation, equal opportunity, and justice can be smothered by "security" forces superbly equipped with the most modern technology. When this occurs, demands are confined and bottled up — they are not satisfied. Security through repression is often a harbinger of violence and upheaval. On the other side of the coin is a situation in which anarchy and chaos reign supreme. Here, the society explodes into fragments in the absence of effective institutions and guiding authority.

Almond and Powell investigate some of the conditions for a tradeoff between liberty and security by constructing a three-part typology of societies.[20] Society A is one in which the citizens enjoy substantial amounts of both liberty and security. Such a society is usually culturally homogeneous and lacks deep and divisive ethnic or religious cleavages. Although these societies are characterized by relatively low tension levels, there are short, pendulum-like movements between an emphasis on liberty and an emphasis on security in these societies.

[19] Gabriel A. Almond and G. Bingham Powell, Jr., *Comparative Politics: System, Process, and Policy*, 2d ed. (Boston: Little, Brown and Co., 1978), pp. 411–12.
[20] Ibid., pp. 412–15.

In the Middle East, countries that tend to fall into this category include Egypt, Turkey, Israel, Tunisia, Libya, and Algeria. Boumedienne's Algeria and Qaddafi's Libya tilt more strongly in the direction of security, while Sadat's Egypt and Bourguiba's Tunisia place a relatively greater stress on liberty.

Society B is one in which both ethnic and class tensions are so deep that the pendulum swings away from security, back through liberty, and ultimately into anarchy. "After a substantial amount of liberty appears, the society collapses at lease temporarily into civil war, and security vanishes completely. Moreover, even with very great sacrifices of liberty, it may be impossible to attain high amounts of security."[21] The prototype of Society B is Lebanon, a society torn both vertically and horizontally by religious and class strife. Other Middle Eastern candidates for Society B status include Sudan, Syria, and Iraq. In the case of Iraq, the constant specter of violent anarchy has caused successive regimes to become preoccupied with security. This, then, brings us to the third type of society.

Society C is one in which coercion and repression are dominant. In its most extreme forms, "the massive application of terror tactics — against even high-level officials in the government, not to mention millions of citizens — and a context of constant police and party intervention, complete censorship, and travel control destroy liberty, but provide little security. The uncontrolled actions of the regime itself undermine any security for its citizens."[22] Iran and Iraq are the Middle Eastern societies that most closely approximate the Society C type. Although there are fundamental differences in the political and ideological structures of these two countries, the leadership of both has opted to sacrifice liberty for tight and complete control from the center. Other examples in descending order of applicability include among the monarchies, Saudi Arabia, Oman, Jordan, and Morocco, and among the modern authoritarian systems, Sudan and Syria.

The push and pull between the demands of the regime for

21 Ibid., p. 413.
22 Ibid.

control and the demands of the populace for freedom and participation is in a state of constant change. Societies move from one type to another. Algeria, for instance, was an extreme example of Society C when central control was enforced by the French, an outside power. After the revolution, it moved through a short chaotic Society B period, beginning when Ben Bella was unable to consolidate control and continuing through the rule of Houari Boumedienne, whose regime delicately balanced popular demands and central authority. Although there is no doubt that control by the regime takes precedence over personal liberty in Algeria, there is nonetheless considerable emphasis on mass political participation, education, and social justice in the country.

There is also a continual shifting of emphasis within each type of society. In Iran under the rule of the present Shah, periods of crushing oppression are interspersed with times of relative freedom. For example, the repressive police-state control that dominated the country between 1964 and 1976 was bounded by periods of relative enlightenment and reform from 1961 to 1963, in 1977, and in 1978 prior to the institution of martial law. In Egypt, both Nasser and Sadat alternately tightened and relaxed their control in response to exigencies of domestic and international politics.

These examples indicate the delicate dialectic that lies at the core of the process of political development. Its outcome is shaped, however, within the larger field of modernization. It is this latter dynamic that can either retard or promote political development. Dramatic economic and technological growth increases the needs felt by the population. At the same time, such advancement strengthens the capacity of the political elite to exert influence and control. In order to muster the strength necessary to exploit scarce resources and to initiate effective planning programs, Middle Eastern elites have often relied upon authoritarian political methods. When they do this, they risk sliding into repressive and oppressive modes of behavior that fatally weaken their capacities for political development. Centralization and institutionalization may take complete precedence over participation. On the other hand, if the elites govern loosely and decentralization reigns supreme, they may also forfeit their developmental capacities as society breaks down into competing and conflicting ethnic, regional, and class-based cliques. As Figure I.1 indicates, the developmental process is a wobbly path between repressive rule and anarchical instability. The process is a delicate balance of capacity and demands. Increasing demands require an enhanced capacity to meet them. Development involves a constant push and pull between the two sides of this dialectic. Meanwhile, the fires of modernization continue to crackle. This complicates the developmental process by constantly altering and shifting balances, demands, responses, and capacities.

Any assessment of political development is made difficult by the accompanying processes of modernization that tend initially to suggest fundamental change. In fact, many traditional political systems are able to foster modernization while maintaining ongoing political patterns. In such systems, however, the basic sociopolitical demands usually outstrip the capacity to meet them, ultimately giving rise to revolutionary upheaval. A fundamental difficulty of Middle Eastern politics is the expanding gap between political demands for increased participation and justice, and the ability to satisfy such demands. This situation is sometimes partially alleviated by a greater capacity to satisfy material demands, which are also vital to the population. In this arena, modernization plays a temporarily stabilizing role. In the long run, however, there must be an enduring capacity to satisfy continually and effectively the social and political needs of all groups and classes in the society.[23]

MODERNIZATION IN THE MIDDLE EAST

Nowhere in the world are the forces of modernization moving more rapidly than in the Middle East. Technological growth, industrial development, and the dramatic expansion of transportation, communication, and housing facilities are

[23] We note here the extreme difficulty of developing an operational concept of political development. The assessment of capacity to generate and absorb change is obviously more complex than the accumulation and interpretation of modernization data. Nevertheless, we do have some measures of this capacity, although perhaps crude ones. These include the analysis of power structures, authority relations, and political programs and policies.

evident throughout the area. Another visible sign of the modernizing process is the growth of military capacity in the area. Countries such as Israel, Iran, and Saudi Arabia are now among the world leaders in expenditures on arms. They are gathering the most sophisticated weapons that modern technology can produce. In terms of per capita military expenditure, Israel spends three times more than any other country in the world.[24]

Quantitatively, gigantic advances have also been made in the social fields of health and education. Thousands of new school buildings, clinics, and hospitals have sprouted up throughout the countries of the Middle East. The number of students enrolled in primary, secondary, and higher education in sixteen selected Middle Eastern countries was less than 5 million in 1950; by 1965, this figure had more than tripled to over 16 million; and in 1973, the number approached 27 million. By 1978, the figure for these countries was an estimated 40 million — an eightfold increase since 1950 (see Table I.1 for the detailed figures).

The modernization boom has accelerated sharply since 1974 when a fourfold increase in the price of oil suddenly provided a huge pool of the resources essential to fuel modernization. In 1970, the petroleum revenues of the eight major Middle Eastern oil-producing countries were less than $6 billion. By 1974, the figure had ballooned to more than $82 billion. National Bank of Chicago studies reported in 1977 that the collective foreign assets of Kuwait, Qatar, the United Arab Emirates, and Saudi Arabia during 1977–1981 would be approximately $229 billion. Saudi Arabia's income from its foreign assets alone rose from $59 million to $3,800 million in 1976. It is estimated that by 1981, its income on these assets will be a staggering $10 billion.[25] This is the kind of wealth that pro-

24 John W. Sewell et al., *The United States and World Development: Agenda 1977*, published for the Overseas Development Council (New York and London: Praeger Publishers, 1977), pp. 218–19.

25 See Odeh Aburdene's two papers, "The Collective Current Account Surplus of Kuwait, Qatar, Saudi Arabia and the United Arab Emirates for the 1977–1981 Period" and "Saudi Arabia's Earnings from its Foreign Assets." These papers were written in September and June 1977 respectively for The First National Bank of Chicago.

TABLE I.1   *Enrollment in Primary, Secondary, and Tertiary Levels of Education (thousands), 1965 and 1973*

Country	Primary level		Secondary level		Tertiary level	
	1965	1973	1965	1973	1965	1973
Afghanistan	358	621	34	170	3.5	9.4
Algeria	1,358	2,409	95	384	8.1	30.1
Egypt	3,450	4,097	819	1,710	177.1	351.5
Iran	2,412	3,646	637	1,778	36.7	123.1
Iraq	978	1,409	241	405	28.4	65.5
Israel	450	527	66	149	35.9	70.4
Jordan	295	353	99	126	3.2	8.2
Kuwait	50	94	29	60a	.4	5.3
Lebanon	354	498	82	174	20.3	44.3
Libya	190	489	23	107	1.9	9.6
Morocco	1,116	1,506	195	433	9.0	25.5
Saudi Arabia	261	571	24	148	1.9	14.9
Sudan	427	1,083	90	231	7.7	20.0
Syria	707	1,103	183	408	32.7	51.8
Tunisia	734	910	104	197	6.2	9.2
Yemen	69	179	2	14		1.0
Totals	13,209	19,495	2,723	6,494	373.0	839.8

Note: For detailed explanations of the data contained in this table, see the two sources from which the data are drawn.

a Tentative estimate.

Sources: United Nations, Department of Economic and Social Affairs, *World Economic Survey, 1969–1970* (E/4942, ST/ECA/141), pp. 206–8; United Nations, *Statistical Yearbook 1975* (New York: United Nations, 1976), pp. 845–67.

vides the capacity to import wholesale the fruits of modernization. Natural wealth will continue to propel Middle Eastern modernization for many, many years to come.

It is sometimes not realized that the Middle East is very rich in resources other than petroleum. Iran, for example, has the second largest reserves of natural gas in the world. Only the Soviet Union has more. Algeria and Saudi Arabia also possess huge reserves of this important resource. One of the world's richest deposits of copper has recently been discovered in Iran. Turkey is the international leader in wolfram production and the second largest producer of chrome. Both Turkey and Iraq have very large deposits of lignite and iron ore. Morocco accounts for more than 90 percent of the exports of phosphates in the world. Tunisia and Jordan also have substantial phosphate reserves. As the oil revenues pour in, they will be used for the exploration and production of other valuable resources. Rapid modernization will be one of the persisting effects of this wealth of resources.

When one examines aggregate data and gross statistical indices, such as annual per capita gross national product (GNP) figures, the conclusions concerning modernization are somewhat distorted. Abu Dhabi of the United Arab Emirates, for example, has a per capita GNP that is three times that of the United States. The per capita GNP of Kuwait is nearly five times that of the Soviet Union. In the early 1950s, Libya's per capita GNP was about forty dollars; by 1974, that figure was approaching $5,000. Iran's per capita GNP rose from less than $300 in 1960 to nearly $2,000 in 1978. Yet, in all these societies the benefits of this wealth are very unevenly distributed. Quantitative measurements, no matter how impressive they may be, indicate very little about the qualitative effects of wealth and resources. In short, they do not address Harold Lasswell's fundamental question: Who gets what, when, and how? Surely, in any study of the modernization of society and politics, it is necessary to get some sense of how these benefits affect the society at large.

During the last few years, a group of scholars associated with the Overseas Development Council has been developing a new index designed to measure more than quantitative growth. Headed by Morris David Morris, a development economist with long experience in South Asian studies, this group has taken a significant step away from the emphasis on GNP. In discussing the need for this new measure, Dr. Morris writes:

> The traditional measure of national economic progress — the gross national product (GNP) and its component elements — cannot very satisfactorily measure the extent to which the human needs of individuals are being met, nor should it be expected to do so. There is no automatic policy relationship between any particular level or rate of growth of GNP and improvement in such indicators as life expectancy, death rates,

infant mortality, literacy, etc. A nation's economic product at any particular level may be allocated in a variety of ways, both among areas of activities and among social groups; or national policies may emphasize the growth of military power and of sectors of the economy that do not contribute in any obvious way to improving the health and physical well-being of that country's people. Nor does the growth of average per capita GNP or personal disposable income necessarily improve the well-being of large portions of a country's population since that income may flow to social groups in very unequal proportions. The very poorest groups of the society may not benefit much, if at all, from rising incomes and some may even suffer declines in real income. Moreover, even if rising incomes are shared with the poorest groups, there is no guarantee that these increases in income will be spent in ways that improve physical well-being.[26]

In response to these difficulties, Morris and his colleagues at the Overseas Development Council have carefully and conservatively constructed a new index known as the Physical Quality of Life Index (PQLI). This new measure is a composite of three indicators — life expectancy, infant mortality, and literacy rate. Each indicator is weighted equally, and all the problems of monetary measurement are avoided. The new index is also resistant to charges of ethnocentrism, since its major assumption — that people everywhere desire improvements in life expectancy, infant mortality, and literacy — does not in any way specify how these goals ought to be sought. Finally, the three indicators "do reflect distributional characteristics within countries, for countries cannot achieve high national averages of literacy, life expectancy, and infant mortality unless majorities of their populations are receiving the benefits of progress in each of these areas."[27] The theoretical range of the PQLI is 0–100.

[26] Sewell et al., *Agenda 1977,* p. 147.

[27] Ibid., p. 152. Pages 147–152 of this book will provide the reader with an introductory discussion of how the PQLI was constructed. A 1976 working paper explains the rationale and procedure in much more detail (see Morris David Morris, "A Physical Quality of Life Index," mimeographed, [Washington, D.C.: Overseas Development Council, December 1976]). Our colleague, Neil Richardson, has helped us check the operational soundness

Table I.2 presents the per capita GNP and PQLI for twenty-two Middle Eastern countries. It also indicates the mid-1976 population figures for each country, as well as the specific statistics that were used in calculating the PQLI: life expectancy at birth, infant mortality per thousand live births, and literacy rate. The data are instructive. The ten leading countries on the basis of per capita GNP standing are, in descending order, Kuwait, the United Arab Emirates, Qatar, Libya, Israel, Saudi Arabia, Bahrain, Iran, Iraq, and Lebanon. Using the PQLI as the standard, the ranking is quite different: Israel, Lebanon, Kuwait, Bahrain, Turkey, Syria, Jordan, Egypt, Iraq, and Tunisia. Only five countries that rank in the top ten on the GNP scale also appear among the PQLI leaders. The five that do not have done relatively poorly in the important area of resource redistribution.

The United Arab Emirates, which is second in per capita GNP, ranks only fifteenth on the PQLI. Qatar, which is third in the former, places eighteenth in the latter. Two important countries, Saudi Arabia and Iran, also have very weak records in the distribution of the fruits of modernization. Saudi Arabia, which is sixth in per capita GNP, is nineteenth in PQLI; only the two Yemens and Afghanistan have weaker PQLIs. Iran, eighth in per capita GNP, ranks fourteenth according to the PQLI.

If one takes the major Middle Eastern countries in terms of resources, geographic size, and population, then Turkey, Syria, Egypt, and Iraq have done the best according to the PQLI.[28] As we shall see later, Turkey was the first Middle Eastern country to undergo deep social and political reforms, and

---

of the PQLI by running some dummy data through the outlined procedure. The index appears to be conceptually and operationally sound. It is worth repeating, however, two points made by Morris David Morris. First, the PQLI is a limited measure that does not pretend to address the question of the social or psychological characteristics usually suggested by the phrase "quality of life." Second, the data upon which the index is based are not good. They are, however, the best that are available. This difficulty is surely not unique to these formulations. The quality of data is a problem that plagues all attempts at cross-national analysis.

28 Our arbitrary cutoff point here is a population figure of at least 7 million persons.

TABLE I.2 *Modernization Indicators for Middle East Countries*

Country	Population mid-1976 (millions)	Per capita GNP, 1974 ($)	Physical Quality of Life Index (PQLI)	Life expectancy at birth	Infant mortality per 1,000 live births	Literacy (%)
Afghanistan	19.5	110	19	40	182	8
Algeria	17.3	710	42	53	126	26
Bahrain	.2	2,330a	60	61	78	40
Egypt	38.1	280	46	52	98	26
Iran	34.1	1,250	38	51	139	23
Iraq	11.4	1,160	46	53	99	26
Israel	3.5	3,460	90	71	23	84
Jordan	2.8	430	48	53	97	32
Kuwait	1.1	11,770	76	69	44	55
Lebanon	2.7	1,070a	80	63	59	86
Libya	2.5	4,640	42	53	130	27
Morocco	17.9	430	40	53	130	21
Pakistan	72.5	130	37	50	124	16
Qatar	.1	8,560	32	47	152	15
Saudi Arabia	6.4	2,870	29	47	138	10–15
Sudan	18.2	230	33	49	41	10–15
Syria	7.6	560	52	54	93	40
Tunisia	5.9	650	44	54	128	32
Turkey	40.2	750	54	57	119	51
United Arab Emirates	.2	11,710	34	47	138	20
Yemen Arab Republic	6.9	180	27	45	152	10
Yemen, Peoples Republic	1.7	220	27	45	152	10

a Tentative estimate.

Source: Adapted from John W. Sewell et al., *The United States and World Development: Agenda 1977* (New York: Praeger Publishers, 1977), pp. 160–71.

Syria, Egypt, and Iraq have now had at least two decades of authoritarian leadership dedicated to distributive and mobilizational goals. And of these four countries, only Iraq has had the huge petroleum reserves that are easily transformable to rich financial resources.

In comparing particular Middle Eastern countries with those of similar population size in other parts of the world on the basis of PQLI, we note the following results. Iraq has a PQLI of forty-six, while Chile's is seventy-seven; despite this, Chile's per capita GNP is less than that of Iraq ($830 compared with $1,160). Turkey and Thailand, with respective per capita GNPs of $750 and $310, have PQLIs of fifty-four and seventy. Even more dramatic is the comparison of Iran with the Republic of Korea. Iran's PQLI (thirty-eight) is less than half that of Korea (eighty); yet the per capita GNP figures are $1,250 and $480 for Iran and Korea, respectively.

The Middle Eastern PQLI figures are higher than those of the countries of Black Africa. Ghana, for example, with a population similar to that of Iraq and of Chile, has a PQLI of only thirty-one. Ethiopia's PQLI of sixteen falls far below that of either Iran or South Korea, countries roughly equivalent to Ethiopia in population. At the same time, however, the per capita GNP figures of these African countries are also very low. For Ghana and Ethiopia, the numbers are $430 and $100, respectively.

The patterns indicated in these comparisons of specific countries are also evident when we analyze per capita GNP and PQLI data for four regions of the Third World. Table I.3 presents the results of these regional comparisons, which are based on the average of individual country indices. The Middle East, with far and away the largest average per capita GNP, ranks a distant third behind South/Southeast Asia and Latin America in average PQLI. Only Africa has a lower PQLI than the Middle East. Yet Africa also has a very low average per capita GNP. In order to compare the gap between per capita GNP and PQLI for the four regions, we have constructed what we term a Per Capita GNP-PQLI Ratio. This ratio is designed to give us a general idea of the comparative regional standing with respect to resource distributon.

TABLE I.3   *Per Capita GNP and Physical Quality of life Ratios:*
The Third World

	Average per capita GNP ($)	Average PQLI	Per capita GNP-PQLI ratio
South/Southeast Asia	469	60	8
Latin America	816	71	11
Africa	328	25	13
The Middle East	2,431	45	53

Note: The data contained in this table have been calculated on the basis of information provided in John W. Sewell et al., *The United States and World Development: Agenda 1977* (New York: Praeger Publishers, 1977), pp. 160–71. The figures refer to sixteen South/Southeast Asian countries, nineteen Central and South American states (including Mexico but excluding Cuba), and thirty-six African countries (all states excluding those in North Africa are herein considered part of the Middle East).

The outstanding feature of Table I.3 is the extraordinary size of the gap between per capita GNP and PQLI in the Middle Eastern countries. The anomalies in the data presented here are so great when figured both linearly and curvilinearly that they can only suggest that for the year of record (1974) the Middle Eastern countries trail far behind the rest of the Third World in the distribution of key resources. The huge size of this gap is partially explained by time factors and lags, since it is to be expected that time is required before improvements can be registered in such PQLI indicators as life expectancy and literacy. The huge GNP gains in the Middle East have been recent, and it is of course much too soon to expect any noticeable increase in the PQLI. On the other hand, the infant mortality index should reflect improvement much sooner. In this case, the Middle Eastern countries still trail significantly behind both the South/Southeast Asian and Latin American countries. The figures for infant mortality per thousand live births are 115, 85, and 71 for the Middle East, South/Southeast Asia, and Latin America respectively.

The gross data that measure modernization are very impressive indeed for the Middle East. This is particularly true of economic modernization, as our study of the per capita

GNP data indicates. With respect to quantitative and qualitative progress in such areas of social modernization as health and education, the record is much less imposing. And within this context, quantitative progress far outstrips qualitative change. Education is a case in point. The sharp increases in school enrollment and the dramatic new availability of modern facilities and buildings have not been matched by equivalent progress in educational content. The principal conclusion of Joseph Szyliowicz's major study on education and modernization in the Middle East is precisely that the educational enterprise in Egypt, Turkey, and Iran "has demonstrated a remarkable ability to withstand efforts at reform and to absorb the impact of major external forces without changing."[29]

The bridge between modernization and political development concerns the problems of distribution, which themselves must be solved before quantitative growth can be transformed into qualitative progress. As the analysis of Physical Quality of Life Indices has indicated, the countries of the Middle East have not yet successfully met this challenge — a challenge which is above all else political in nature.

POLITICAL DEVELOPMENT IN THE MIDDLE EAST

Processes of modernization run far ahead of advances in political development in the Middle East. The capacity to generate and absorb persistent transformation varies widely from society to society. In all cases, however, the ability to fundamentally transform the basic power configurations has been the rarest form of political change. Even when nations have occasionally sought to do so, they have tended to lack the capacity in the face of a resistant and resilient tradition. Transformations in the economic system have come easiest, followed by alterations in the social system. Political development in the Middle East lags conspicuously.

Spurred by economic modernization and especially by social modernization, the capacity to *generate* change in the

[29] Joseph S. Szyliowicz, *Education and Modernization in the Middle East* (Ithaca, N.Y.: Cornell University Press, 1973), p. 454.

political realm has been increasing. By sponsoring advancements in the related fields of education and technology, Middle Eastern elites have been indirectly responsible for the burgeoning growth of indigenous professional middle classes. The members of these middle classes possess the loudest of the voices clamoring for deep political change. In failing to address these demands, the political elites exhibit their unwillingness to absorb and institutionalize political transformation. This begets a situation in which expanding gaps, like bubbles, burst into one another. The gap between socioeconomic modernization and political development is increased by the capacity to generate transformation and the failure to absorb it.

Change dominates the history of Middle Eastern political systems. Transformation, or radical alteration of the underlying power and authority structure, has been considerably less in evidence.[30] The legitimating authority structure and the fundamental power patterns have consistently weathered changes involving rulers, elites, and dynasties. The traditional political patterns of the Islamic Middle East survived by being in a state of constant movement. Continual modification and piecemeal revision effectively deterred system transformation. Political elites in the Middle East carefully implemented policies of both co-operation and coercion. Selective mobility and sporadic repression ensured the preservation of ongoing political patterns by introducing carefully apportioned doses of modifying change. These tactics and techniques still persist to a large degree in the contemporary Middle East. They remain sporadically in evidence even in societies such as Egypt, Turkey, and Kuwait, which have been relatively successful in the business of political development. One leading political scholar in the Arab world writes, therefore, that "the Arabs have not yet experienced a political revolution under nationalism, i.e., a

[30] Transforming change is fundamental, radical change — change at the very roots of relationships and institutions. Modifying change, in contrast, is a reforming and revising process in which adjustments are continually made, leaving basic patterns unaltered. For a detailed discussion of these concepts and their relationship to political power and violence, see James A. Bill, "Political Violence and Political Change: A Conceptual Commentary," in *Violence as Politics: A Series of Original Essays,* eds. H. Hirsch and D. C. Perry (New York: Harper and Row, 1973), pp. 220–31.

fundamental change that produced a new principle of authority, political organization and style of political life."[31]

Perhaps the most critical dimension of political development is participation. The demands of the population for an effective voice in important matters that affect their lives need to be confronted and satisfied. The literature on political development generally argues that participation is furthered by institutionalization and that formal institutions, such as political parties and parliaments, are the most effective instruments for building participation. The Middle Eastern experience provides some differing insights on this issue.

Political institutionalization has never been absent in the Middle East. Masses and elites were bound together by a number of important linkage structures, which included elaborate networks of intermediaries and middlemen composed of messengers, adjutants, clerics, overseers, bureaucrats, and secret police. This kind of personalized institutionalization resulted in numerous lines of communication through the society. These provided channels through which demands and grievances moved upward to the political elite, while orders and policies poured downward to the middle and lower classes. This was the quality of political participation in traditional Middle Eastern politics. Grievances could often be aired and demands could be heard. The political elite, however, enjoyed the prerogative of action and redress. The petitioners lacked the institutional organization that could guarantee the satisfaction of their demands.

The coming of political parties and parliaments has seldom changed this form of participation. If anything, these instruments have served more as barriers to communication than as channels of communication. Parties have often existed as loose collections of personal cliques that have penetrated little beyond the upper crust of society. In the upper crust, they have served largely as the instruments of powerful individuals and small elites. This has been true even in Tunisia, whose Neo-Destour party is the most effective mass party organized at the

31 P. J. Vatikiotis, *Conflict in the Middle East* (London: George Allen and Unwin, 1971) , p. 25.

grassroots level in the Islamic world. Like political parties, Middle Eastern legislatures tend to exist as Western-style institutions grafted to Middle Eastern political systems. In the legislatures, however, participation is even less advanced than it is in the political parties. The legislatures often promote underrepresentation, pseudorepresentation, and misrepresentation.[32] In fact, they tend to extend participation little beyond the confines of the parliamentary body itself.

Political participation is a process whereby individuals engage in activity that impinges directly upon the national power and authority structure of society. This activity can be system-challenging or system-supportive. System-supportive participation exists when large numbers of individuals come to support an authority structure to which they have meaningful access and which represents their interests. As the process of participation develops and matures, the masses of people are continually brought into the decision-making process, primarily at the grassroots of society. Increasing social and political demands emanating from the lower and middle classes accompany this entire movement. The political elite will persistently both encourage and meet these demands for expanding representation. In the Middle East, the first important break with the past signaling the serious advance of political participation was the overthrow of a number of traditional semifeudal regimes. Turkey and Egypt are the two most dramatic early examples of this kind of revolution. The transformation of the class structure is usually a sign of new patterns of political participation. Where there has been no such change, even the existence of political parties and parliaments does not indicate effective patterns of participation.

Yet a revolutionary act such as the Egyptian revolution does not guarantee the institutionalization of political participation, nor does it necessarily represent the beginning of political development. Traditional patterns and power resist change and persist. Capacity is weakened by a lack of resources. Cru-

---

32 For an excellent analysis of voting behavior in three Middle Eastern societies where legislatures have been relatively more meaningful, see Frank Tachau, Ergun Özbudun, and Jacob Landau, eds., *Electoral Politics in the Middle East: Issues, Voters and Elites*, publication forthcoming.

cial resources that do exist are drained away in emotion-charged international adventures. The festering Arab-Israeli issue has profoundly stunted the growth of political development in the Middle East. Shattered morale, helpless frustration, and political disillusionment have severely hampered developmental capacities. This has been true in the Arab Middle East ever since the 1940s. Since the October war of 1973, the issue has also seriously damaged the Israeli developmental effort. The need to live in a state of constant crisis has taken an increasingly noticeable social and political toll. This "siege mentality" is accompanied by a central political establishment that is more and more often plagued by doubt and indecision. The Israeli government is best defined as "a patchwork coalition of ideological opposites that includes doves and hawks, religious conservatives and secular liberals, capitalists and socialists, and, on the sensitive issue of occupied Arab territories, maximalists and minimalists."[33] It was partly in response to this situation that Menahem Begin of the extreme right-wing Likud bloc slipped into power in May of 1977.

The delicate dialectic between demands and capacity to meet them, between anarchy and repression, between participation and institutionalization, between liberty and security, is a particularly important issue in the Middle East. Demands increase dramatically as larger and larger groups of people seek political participation. Harried elites threatened by serious domestic and international problems struggle to maintain their own authority, while at the same time striving to modernize their societies. Moderate authoritarianism begins to move in the direction of harsh repression as these elites gradually stifle demands. In the footrace between modernization and political development in the Middle East, modernization always runs out ahead. Manfred Halpern's "authoritarian road to democracy"[34] is a narrow path fraught with peril and false exits. George Lenczowski correctly warns that the price of

[33] Terence Smith, "Reflections on a Troubled People — Israel Journal: 1972–1976," *Saturday Review* (5 February 1977), p. 13.

[34] Manfred Halpern, *The Politics of Social Change in the Middle East and North Africa* (Princeton, N.J.: Princeton University Press, 1963), pp. 223–26.

modernizing progress is sometimes high, because "the erosion of democratic institutions and the centralization of power in the hands of those who control the means of coercion, i.e., the army, the police, and the revolutionary militia, have caused the states to fall into a virtually preinstitutional era of the law of the jungle."[35] On the other side are anarchy and incoherence, which in some Middle Eastern societies have "resulted in a series of coups, counter-coups, and purges which have taken a heavy social toll by eliminating group after group of intelligentsia from constructive work for the society and by producing a climate of uncertaintly and violence."[36] Between these two alternatives runs a narrow path indeed.

Middle Eastern societies have adopted various and differing strategies for political development. The countries fall into five different categories on the basis of their policies of political development: popular-participatory, authoritarian-technocratic-traditional, authoritarian-technocratic-distributive, authoritarian-technocratic-mobilizational, and traditional.[37] Table I.4 provides an inventory of the Middle Eastern countries according to this classificatory scheme.

The popular-participatory path of development stresses liberal democratic political values and provides relatively open participation through such institutions as parties, parliaments, and elections. Systems in this category are in wide retreat throughout the world, and the Middle East is no exception. Israel's relative success with this form of government stems partly from its ability to import a set of social and political patterns wholesale. Turkey's participatory style has survived

---

[35] George Lenczowski, "Democracy, Development, and Political Integration in the Arab World: A Search for a Comprehensive Formula," *The Conflict of Traditionalism and Modernism in the Muslim Middle East*, ed. Carl Leiden (Austin: University of Texas Press, 1966), p. 61.

[36] Ibid. Also see Lenczowski's article, "Changing Patterns of Political Organization in the Twentieth-Century Middle East," *Western Political Quarterly* 18 (September 1965):660–88.

[37] This taxonomy of political systems according to developmental strategies is a slight variation of that presented in Almond and Powell, *Comparative Politics*, pp. 372–90. The five Almond and Powell developmental strategies are termed democratic populist, authoritarian-technocratic, authoritarian-technocratic-equalitarian, authoritarian-technocratic-mobilizational, and neo-traditional.

TABLE I.4   *Middle Eastern Developmental Strategies: A Typology*

Popular-partici-patory	Authoritarian-technocratic-traditional	Authoritarian-technocratic-distributive	Authoritarian-technocratic-mobilizational	Traditional
Israel	Iran	Bahrain	Algeria	Afghanistan
Lebanon	Jordan	Kuwait	Egypt	Yemen
Turkey	Morocco	Qatar	Iraq	Sudan
	Oman	U.A.E.	Libya	
	Saudi Arabia		Syria	
			Tunisia	

through extraordinary measures, including military intervention in 1960, when the army overthrew the repressive regime of Adnan Menderes. In 1971, leaders of the armed forces issued a public communique that again toppled the government in a time of political crisis. The difficulties of the Turkish political system were seen again as a result of the elections in 1977, when neither major party could gain a clear mandate to govern. But the apparent irrelevance of the popular-participatory strategy to the countries of the Middle East is best illustrated by the collapse of Lebanon in 1975. Here a feeble central government stood by helplessly as religious and class tensions erupted into a bitter and bloody civil war.

In the authoritarian-technocratic-traditional political system, "emphasis is placed on increasing the order-maintaining and economic-growth-facilitating capacities of the government."[38] Rule is of the most conservative traditional mode, and although economic dynamism is often dramatically present, the benefits tend to coagulate at the top. The five monarchies of Iran, Jordan, Morocco, Oman, and Saudi Arabia are the Middle Eastern examples of this kind of system. Security for the ruling house is the overwhelming obsession of the political strategists who direct these governments. The precariousness of these systems is evident in the attempted assassinations, popular unrest, aborted military plots and coup attempts that dot the recent history of these countries. Saudi Arabia, with an estimated population of six million, an annual income from

[38] Ibid., p. 376.

petroleum royalties alone of close to $30 billion, and foreign monetary reserves second only to those of West Germany in the world, continues to be plagued by problems of instability. The major plots uncovered in 1969 were followed by the assassination of King Faisal in 1975; in July 1977, an extensive conspiracy against the regime was uncovered, resulting in the arrest of some 1,300 persons, including military personnel. Iran, with an annual per capita GNP that has increased 600 percent between 1970 and 1978 has one of the most lopsided income distribution ratios in the world.[39]

Kuwait, Qatar, and the United Arab Emirates fall into the authoritarian-technocratic-distributive category. Although they are mini-monarchies whose rulers govern in much the same way as the major kings referred to earlier, they are fundamentally different from the other monarchies. The combination of huge oil revenues and tiny populations permits the leaders of these countries to distribute the wealth downward through the population. And there is much wealth left over. In Qatar, annual oil revenues hover in the area of $2 billion, while budgetary expenditures only approach half that figure. Besides oil, natural gas has been discovered in such quantities that Qatar is ensured of enough energy to satisfy its needs for many years to come. In Abu Dhabi, the leading member of the United Arab Emirates, annual income from oil jumped from less than $1 billion in 1973 to almost $6 billion in 1977. Citizens of Abu Dhabi are provided with everything from free schooling and health care to free housing. The same is true of Kuwait, where citizens enjoy a welfare system unequalled anywhere. These countries are blessed with such natural wealth that the social and economic demands of all citizens are rather easily met. In this situation, the issue of political participation, for the time being at least, is less urgent.

Most Middle Eastern developmental strategies involve some kind of progressive or radical leadership committed to mod-

39 Vahid Nowshirvani, "Iran's Economy: Reflections on Recent Performance," lecture delivered at the University of Texas, Austin, Texas, 10 March 1977. See also the articles by F. Vakil and M. H. Pesaran in *Iran: Past, Present and Future*, ed. Jane W. Jacqz (New York: Aspen Institute for Humanistic Studies, 1976).

ernization and the mobilization of the masses. Often born in a
military coup, this kind of regime represents a new form of
authoritarianism that stresses a very specific form of political
participation. "Because people are mobilized in the implementation of policies formulated by the party elites, rather than in
the making of policies, it is a form of mobilized or structured
participation."[40] Examples of this authoritarian-technocratic-
mobilizational system include Algeria, Egypt, Iraq, Libya,
Syria, and Tunisia. While the popular-participatory systems
tilt in the direction of anarchic instability, these regimes veer
towards repressive control. Here capacity takes precedence
over freedom, although the relatively equitable distribution
of goods and services is a major priority of this kind of rule.
Within this category there is much variation; such countries
as Iraq have moved much further along the road to oppressive control than have such countries as Egypt, Tunisia, and
Algeria. The major difference between the authoritarian-traditional and the authoritarian-mobilizational strategies concerns the question of distribution. Although political style and
tactics in the two strategies are often very similar, there is
greater commitment to both political participation and social
and economic development in the latter case. The traditional
authoritarianism focuses more on economic growth than on
economic development. And rule is by family rather than by
a larger group or class. These, then, are some of the differences
between the shahs and kings on the one hand and the revolutionary command council leaders and military junta members
on the other hand.

The final developmental category is the traditional regime
in the society with a very traditional social structure. This
type of society is severely lacking in both technical skills and
natural resources. The economy is predominantly agricultural;
the educational system remains primitive; even military technology lags significantly behind that in other Middle Eastern
societies. The middle class is either nonexistent or embryonic
in size. In the Middle East, such societies include Afghanistan,
Sudan, and the two Yemens. In these four countries, the

40 Almond and Powell, *Comparative Politics,* p. 381.

greater contemporary emphasis on military rule has not been accompanied by basic change in either the political or the social system. The modernization that initiates and propels developmental change is largely absent.

The developmental struggle is always a grim one. In the Middle East, it has taken on a special urgency because of the accompanying intense and unsettling process of modernization. Gaps, divisions, imbalances, and inequalities are visible everywhere. In one area (Abu Dhabi), the annual per capita GNP approaches $25,000 per year, while in another country (Afghanistan) the figure is little more than $150. Such imbalances are as common within countries as between them. Even in Tunisia, a country with a relatively successful record in developmental terms, the top 20 percent of the population have monopolized 55 percent of the national income, and the lowest 40 percent have shared only 11 percent of the wealth. The same situation has prevailed in Turkey, where over 60 percent of the income has been in the hands of the top 20 percent of the population, and the bottom 20 percent have shared less than 10 percent of the income.[41] The winds of modernization blow unevenly through the area. In the oil-rich states, such as Iran, Saudi Arabia, and the shaykhdoms of the Persian Gulf, they regularly reach gale proportions, while in such places as Afghanistan and the Arab Republic of Yemen they barely whisper through the land.

The challenge of development is complicated by four further factors. First, no Middle Eastern society has yet found that it could relax in its quest for development. There are no plateaus and no end points in this journey. Both monarchs and their military-oriented successors have learned this lesson the hard way. Second, there is no particular political or ideological path that ensures success. As our typology of developmental strategies indicates, there are examples of failure in all categories. The popular-participatory model so much admired in the West was dealt a severe blow when Lebanon came apart at the seams. The three authoritarian models have a history of

[41] These data are drawn from Montek S. Ahluwalia, "Inequality, Poverty and Development," *Journal of Development Economics* 3 (1976):340.

stifling oppression interlaced with continual plotting and coups. Middle Eastern political leaders must write their own prescriptions for development. The third complication concerns the historical and cultural backdrop against which developmental programs must occur. The traditional Islamic system was one of considerable dynamism, social mobility, and personal participation. That such a system is supremely resistant to developmental transformations will be documented in the chapters that follow. Finally, the issue of political development in the Middle East is complicated by interregional and international considerations. The Arab-Israeli conflict has already been mentioned. Both the competition between the United States and the Soviet Union and the deepening international energy problem have also had profound effects upon the developmental issue. With some exceptions, the United States has tended to support the authoritarian-traditional regimes, while the Soviets have more often stood behind the authoritarian-mobilizational regimes. The extent of this assistance can be seen in the case of American military aid to Iran and Saudi Arabia. Between 1971 and 1975, the figures were $9.5 and $5 billion respectively.[42] Such massive infusions of resources cannot but have an impact upon the related issues of modernization and development. In these two countries, such infusions have tended to strengthen the forces of security at the expense of liberty.

In the Islamic Middle East, Turkey and Egypt still must rank among the leaders in political development. Although both countries witnessed many instances of social unrest and political instability from the mid-1970s to late 1970s, they both have middle-class regimes which have been relatively supportive of genuine political participation. Algeria and Tunisia have also done relatively well in the developmental struggle. In Algeria, strong central control is balanced against genuine concern for the masses of people. This concern is reflected in a heavy emphasis on equal opportunity for education as well as in support of the idea that workers and peasants should man-

42 Roger D. Hansen et al., *The U.S. and World Development: Agenda for Action — 1976,* published for the Overseas Development Council (New York: Praeger Publishers, 1976), pp. 186–87.

age their own factories and farms. The Neo-Destour party in Tunisia is one of the few strong political party systems in the region. Both Algeria and Tunisia, however, face serious political problems. In Algeria, the strong central control is becoming less acceptable as economic problems deepen, and in Tunisia the Neo-Destour party is increasingly seen by the growing middle classes as an instrument of political repression.

The other authoritarian-mobilizational regimes (Iraq, Libya, Syria) have been even less successful in political development. Iraq and Syria labor under the severe handicap of deep sectarian, ethnic, and ideological divisions. Although sensitive to the need for popular participation and social equality, the Libyan regime has not yet succeeded in seriously loosening its grip from the center. All three of these countries (especially the Hassan al-Bakr-Saddam Husayn regime in Iraq) share a preoccupation with control that far overshadows any concern for the sociopolitical demands that emanate from the population at large.

The families that rule the mini-monarchies that are the Persian Gulf shaykhdoms have avoided political development consciously and consistently. Because of their extraordinary wealth, however, they have a record of distribution in the social areas of health, education, and housing that is unrivalled anywhere. This distribution has disguised the absence of political participation and has also cushioned popular discontent. Political control remains firmly in the hands of a few members of ruling families, who have shown no inclination to share it. If anything, the trend has been in the opposite direction. The ruler of Kuwait, for example, closed the doors of his National Assembly and suspended the country's constitution in August 1976. This was done in the face of some political opposition that had crystallized in the assembly as a result of the elections in 1975. As one source stated at the time, "the regime has demonstrated its determination to defend the Kuwaiti establishment without the annoyances of constitutional nicety."[43]

43 *Middle-East Intelligence Survey* 4 (November 1–15, 1976) :120.

The most explosive developmental problems in the Islamic Middle East exist in the major monarchies. Here, traditional power and authority relations persist alongside growing middle classes whose members remain locked out of the hallways of power. Even rulers as politically astute and experienced as the Shah of Iran resisted to the very end expansion of political participation and representation. Unlike their tiny counterparts along the Persian Gulf, these monarchies do not have comprehensive social programs that can serve to alleviate tensions arising from the increasing gap between economic modernization and political development. For these countries, the failure to develop politically can only have violent and costly long-term consequences; a short-term preoccupation with security and stability is a sure guarantee of long-term insecurity and instability.

The collapse of Lebanon in 1975 contains many lessons concerning the related issues of modernization and political development. Perhaps the most important of these is that an impressive record of modernization does not indicate that political development is also occurring. Rather, modernization may often hasten the destruction of the political system by persistently widening the modernization-development gap. Impressive growth in Lebanon in per capita GNP and even in the PQLI has had the further effect of lulling both political leaders and political observers into a false sense of complacency. In Lebanon, the deep group and class divisions as well as the leadership vacuum were disguised by the deceptively successful processes of modernization. When Lebanon crumbled, it dealt a final blow to the theory supporting the popular-participatory road to development. Since that time, the pendulum of developmental strategy in Lebanon has swung even further back toward an emphasis on security and control.[44]

All of these case studies indicate the complex delicacy of the related issues of modernization and political development in the Middle East. In a constantly changing situation, there are

[44] The crash of Lebanon was, of course, also hastened by the presence of the Palestinian refugees who were always a direct threat to the delicate consociational equilibrium that prevailed in that country until 1975.

no obvious success stories and no developmental strategies proven to be successful. Many of the fundamental problems that now confront the Middle Eastern peoples are directly related to this situation. These problems will be analyzed in depth in the following chapters.

CHAPTER II

Islam and Politics

THE GREAT REVEALED RELIGIONS all came into being in the Middle East. Its history is rich in religious wars and conquests. The storm center of the area today, Israel, was founded on the right of a religious people to return to ancestral pastures. It is not an exaggeration to say that no understanding of the complex political patterns of the area can be attempted without giving prior attention to its religious characteristics.[1]

The contemporary Middle East is a crazy quilt of religions. Although Islam pervades most of the area, the Muslims them-

---

[1] There is still only a modest literature on the general question of the effect of religion on development. Perhaps the best known study of this is Donald Eugene Smith's *Religion and Political Development* (Boston: Little, Brown and Co., 1970). There is, however, a wealth of material on the changing religious patterns of the Middle East in general, and on Islam in particular. Prime among them is A. J. Arberry, ed., *Religion in the Middle East*, 2 vols. (Cambridge: Cambridge University Press, 1969). H. A. R. Gibb, *Mohammedanism* (London: Oxford University Press, 1949) is still an excellent introduction to Islam. Cambridge University Press has published the *Cambridge History of Islam* in two volumes (1970), edited by P. M. Holt, Ann K. S. Lambton, and Bernard Lewis. Edinburgh University Press has now published eight volumes in its *Islamic Surveys* series. See also Bernard Lewis's collection, *Islam in History: Ideas, Men and Events in the Middle East* (New York: Library Press, 1973). Maurice Gaudefroy-Demombynes, *Muslim Institutions* (London: George Allen and Unwin, 1950) is also useful. For Islamic reform, see Charles C. Adams, *Islam and Modernism in Egypt* (London: Oxford University Press, 1933); and Malcolm H. Kerr, *Islamic Reform: The Political and Legal Theories of Muhammad 'Abduh and Rashīd Ridā* (Berkeley: University of California Press, 1961). For the intricacies of Islam, the *Encyclopedia of Islam*, new ed., 4 vols. to date (London: Luzac and Company, 1960–) is indispensable.

selves differ in culture and orthodoxy. Furthermore, religious minorities are to be found in most Muslim countries. The Druze, a mystic heretical sect of Islam, inhabit the mountains of southern Lebanon and Syria, and live in Israel as well. In the north of Syria are the Alawites, who maintain a mixture of Christian, Muslim, and pagan beliefs. In 1973, the Alawites were formally recognized as part of the Shi'i community in Lebanon. (President Hafez al-Assad is an Alawite.) Also in Lebanon are various Christian groups, notably the Maronites and the Greek Orthodox.[2] Remnants of another minority, the Armenian Christians, are to be found in many parts of the

2 In spite of the flux that it is in, the Lebanese political system deserves some comment here. There are enormous religious differences among the Lebanese, with Druze, Sunni and Shi'i Muslims, and a variety of Christian sects (notably the Maronites) represented. Thus, the Lebanese were forced in the past to cooperate politically in spite of their religious differences and mutual distrust. The solution, which worked for some years, was to divide the entire government and public employment along sectarian lines. Among other prescriptions, the president of the republic was always to be a Christian and the prime minister a Sunni Muslim. Lebanon was often lauded for the successful way in which it had resolved a difficult problem, but recent years have revealed many chinks in the political armor. Where religious differences are deep, and where they are institutionalized politically, it is hardly surprising that religious leaders become poltical leaders as well. The religious label for each Lebanese (a part of his identity card) implies specific roles and opportunities, and, in the recent civil war, dangers as well. It is hardly possible in Lebanon to become a *national,* rather than a sectarian or regional, leader, and such leaders as there are can hardly create or support national policies.

In the mid-1970s, Lebanon was rocked by a tragic civil war. The causes are still somewhat uncertain. In one sense, it was a conflict between the Palestinians and other Lebanese factions and later between the Palestinians and the Syrians. But the main dimension still seemed to be the broad split between Christians and Muslims (although the Muslims themselves were also fragmented). The war gave the opportunity for pent-up emotions, fears, and frustrations to be assuaged by violence against what was perceived to be the "enemy"—that is, other Lebanese of a different religious complexion. There was also a paucity of responsible sectarian leadership. The result was literally the destruction of Lebanon, with many thousands killed, untold damage to towns and cities, and the opening of religious wounds that might well take generations to heal. One can only say, then, that religious leadership (or the lack of it) in Lebanon has led to unfortunate political consequences. The future is hardly promising. Two recent books of interest are John Bullock, *Death of a Country: The Civil War in Lebanon* (London: Weidenfeld and Nicolson, 1977) and Halim Barakat, *Lebanon in Strife* (Austin: University of Texas Press, 1977).

Middle East. The few Assyrian Christians that are left live in Iraq, Iran, and eastern Syria. In Egypt is another Christian group, the Copts, numbering about 10 percent of the population. In southern Sudan, the people are racially and religiously different from the Sudanese of the north, who are Arabs and Muslims. In Iran, there are the Zoroastrians and the Bahais (originally Babists), although neither group is very significant in numbers. The Israelis are, of course, largely Jews. But these Jews are by no means all identical; they range from the extreme orthodox to the agnostic. Indeed, the Israelis are compelled to consider as Jews, for the purpose of the Law of Return, many who are only nominally religious but who might suffer persecution in other countries for their "Jewishness." This brief list hardly exhausts the many religious groups that can be found in the Middle East. We shall later discuss the great split of Muslims into Shi'i and Sunni sects.

Most Middle Easterners are Muslim. Islam, however, is to be found outside the Middle East. There are large numbers of Muslims in Soviet Central Asia, and in India, Pakistan, and Indonesia; and Islam is also rapidly gaining adherents and influence in Black Africa. Altogether Islam's members throughout the world now number more than 600 million.

ISLAM

It is the Middle Eastern Muslims that concern us here. What does it mean to be a Muslim in the Middle East? How does being a Muslim there affect one's political life and the political life of one's community? And very particularly in this transitional age, how does the presence of the Islamic spirit influence the directions in which political change will occur? Is there a plasticity to Islam that has accommodated considerable modifying change over the centuries, while remaining resistant to ultimate transformations?

Islam, which literally means the surrender of man to God (Allah), is one of the great religions of the world. The messages that became the essence of Islam were revealed to Muhammad beginning in 610. To become a Muslim takes but a simple affirmation of faith, repeating the *shahada*: there is no god but The God and Muhammad is the messenger of The

God. The creed of Islam is simple, and although there is a voluminous, sophisticated literature on various aspects of Islam, belief in the basic shahada is the main characteristic of the mass of Muslims.

Muhammad brought his message to the Arabs of Mecca, the "idolators," whose confused animistic and totemistic religious practices were repugnant to him. He also hoped that Christian and Jew would be attracted to his message — after all he believed that it was their God, as well as his, from whom the message came.

The message, if we strictly count only what the Muslims term the revelations, was the Quran.[3] It was probably not wholly recorded until after Muhammad's death; its language, the sacred language, was Arabic. Muslims have always believed in the completeness of the Quran; it is not to be supplemented by recurrent messages. The Quran contains the principles of eternal truth from which modern science or any other kind of knowledge (however much it may change in detail) must be derived. Among the Quran's truths is a prescription for regulating the political and social affairs of man. Islam makes no distinction between the state and the realm of believers; in theory at least, there is nothing to render unto Caesar. There is nowhere in Islamic history, as there is in that of Christendom, any recourse to a doctrine of "two swords," or any proliferation of a political theory of the rights of a secular ruler against those of God.[4]

Conservatism forced the Arabs of Muhammad's time to resist his blandishments; it was only after he and his followers had demonstrated a certain *baraka* ("heavenly blessing" or "grace") in war and caravan raiding that great numbers of followers rallied to his cause. But however fervently his adherents embraced the message of the Quran, they needed more direct and personal counsel for the regulation of their daily lives. Much of this is to be found in the Hadith, or the Traditions, of the Prophet's life. What would Muhammad have said, or done, in such and such a situation? Although every

---

[3] W. Montgomery Watt, *Bell's Introduction to the Qur'ān* (Edinburgh: Edinburgh University Press, 1970) is particularly useful here.

[4] See Muhammad Asad, *The Principles of State and Government in Islam* (Berkeley: University of California Press, 1961).

Muslim concedes that Muhammad was only a man, nevertheless they believe that his life was exemplary. Indeed it fur-
nishes a guide for all good Muslims to follow.

On one crucial question, however, Muhammad offered no
guidelines. Who would assume the role of the leader of the
Muslim community upon the Prophet's death? The first caliph — a title originally signifying successor to the messenger
— was Abu Bakr, Muhammad's father-in-law. He and the next
three caliphs were chosen by the leading members of the Muslim community in Medina. The last of this group, Ali, the
Prophet's son-in-law, was defeated in battle by Mu'awiya, one
of the generals who disputed Ali's claim to the caliphate.
Mu'awiya founded the Umayyad dynasty of caliphs by insist-
ing that his son, Yazid, be accepted as his successor.

The early caliphs were wielders of power. Gradually they
changed their role from the lesser one of acting as successor
to Muhammad's spiritual leadership to that of being God's
viceroy on earth, a viceroy that increasingly became a mun-
dane monarch of immense power and authority. Ultimately,
however, the strength of the caliphs waned, and, retaining
only the symbolism of their position, they surrendered their
power to ambitious generals and strongmen.

This development, which occurred over a period of several
hundred years, resulted from the imposition of political neces-
sities on a religious community. Muhammad himself was a
superb politician, knowing when to persuade and when to
coerce. In the process of establishing a new religion, he created a military machine and a semblance of political organization for an area extending far beyond Mecca and Medina. He
outmaneuvered rivals and forced recalcitrant tribes to cooperate and accept his leadership. After his death, Islam spread
rapidly into North Africa, Byzantium, and Persia. The maintenance and support of conquering armies, the control of their
leaders,[5] the supervision of the division of spoils, and the ad-

[5] These included such successful and powerful military commanders as
Khalid Ibn al-Walid, the conqueror of Iraq and Syria; Sa'd Ibn Abi-
Waqqas, the conqueror of Persia; and Amr Ibn al-As, the conqueror of
Egypt — all in the seventh century. See Philip K. Hitti, *History of the
Arabs*, 7th ed. (London: Macmillan and Co., 1961) ; and Sir John Bagot

judication of disputes among followers and newly assimilated peoples — all of these required political leadership of a high order and the necessary administrative apparatus to give it substance. Without the powerful figures that some of the early caliphs became, the large Arab Muslim empire that once existed could not have been created. With the firm establishment of a hereditary caliphate,[6] prestige and authority could be maintained despite the gradual deterioration of the power of the caliph. Power was assumed by those who could hold it. Often some subordinate of the caliph with exceptional abilities and command of military force wielded great political influence.[7]

Muslims believe in one god, Allah, to the exclusion of all others. In so professing their faith, they acknowledge the special historical role that Muhammad played as the messenger of God. As a religion, Islam is relatively uncomplicated. Other than the profession of faith, there is little that a Muslim is obligated to do. He ought to make a contribution (*zakat*) to the poor; he should at some time in his life make a pilgrimage to Mecca; he should ritually submit himself to prayer five times a day; during one month (Ramadan) of his lunar year, he must fast during the daylight hours. But it must be noted that there is really no distinction between religious and secular acts and obligations. The true Muslim state operates under the *sharia*, that is, Muslim law as derived from the Quran.

Glubb, *The Great Arab Conquests* (London: Hodder and Stoughton, 1963).

[6] As Hitti points out, hereditary succession did not mean that sons always succeeded. Speaking of the Abbasids, he says, "of the first twenty-four caliphs, whose reign covered almost two centuries and a half (750–991), only six were immediately succeeded by a son." (*History,* p. 318.) But what the hereditary principle did mean was that succession would occur within the family of the caliph. In the few modern Muslim monarchies that remain, such as Saudi Arabia, the official crown princes have more often been brothers than sons of the ruling monarchs.

[7] By the middle of the ninth century, the Abbasid dynasty was in rapid decline. Typical of the state to which the dynasty now fell was the rule of the eunuch soldier Mu'nis al-Muzaffar, who deposed the caliph al-Muqtadir in 932. In 945, the general Ahmad Ibn-Buwayh established a dynasty of sultans that lasted for a century, independent of the caliphs, whom the sultans created or destroyed at will. See Hitti, *History,* pp. 469–71.

Thus, the practicing Muslim finds himself immersed in rules and practices, not as obligations of his religion per se, but rather as obligations of a legal system that is the only conceivable one in Islam.

The political and social life of Muhammad's time did not necessitate an elaborate system of law. The early Islamic law reinforced some of the customary law of the Arabs of pre-Islamic times, but it also contained much that was new. It dealt largely with family matters and with the simpler forms of interpersonal relations. It spelled out the detailed circumstances of marriage and divorce; regulated the legitimation and custody of children;[8] and, most important, specified in

---

[8] The question of legitimation was a particularly thorny one. "Hanafi [along with Shafi'i, Hanbali and Maliki, these constitute the schools of orthodox jurisprudence] law presumes that a maximum period of two years may elapse between the conception of a child and its birth, while the other schools recognize even longer periods; four years is the term of Shafi'i and Hanbali law, while there is considerable Maliki authority for a term of seven years. Such rules were not entirely due to the ignorance of the mediaeval jurists on matters of embryology, although belief in the phenomenon of 'the sleeping foetus' may well have contributed to their acceptance. It goes without saying that the jurists were well aware of the normal period of gestation, which formed the basis of many legal rules, . . . It was, however, the particular effects of illegitimacy which probably induced the jurists to adopt an attitude of excessive caution. There was the desire to avoid attributing the status of illegitimacy to children born to widowed or divorced women after the normal period of gestation had elapsed since the termination of their marriage; for the illegitimate child had no claims whatsoever, particularly as regards maintenance, upon its father. Again, for the Malikis at any rate, the birth of a child out of wedlock and outside the recognised periods of gestation after the termination of a marriage was *prima facie* evidence of fornication, which might entail the *hadd* penalty of lapidation, on the part of the mother; and the jurists had consistently demonstrated an unwillingness that these severe *hadd* penalties should be applied except where there was proof positive of guilt. In short, humanitarian principles seem to have influenced the jurists to accept the possibility of protracted periods of gestation. As the question was bound up with the criminal law, their general attitude was that legitimacy should always be presumed unless circumstances made its non-existence certain beyond any shadow of doubt" (N. J. Coulson, *A History of Islamic Law*, Islamic Surveys 2, [Edinburgh: Edinburgh University Press, 1964], pp. 174–75) . But as Coulson continues, "Such considerations . . . had largely lost their force in modern Egypt, where fornication was no longer a criminal offence and where provision had been made for the support of illegitimate children by their father" (Ibid., p. 175) . The abuses are obvious: divorced women, for example, could argue that they were pregnant and secure support from their former husbands for a

great detail the rules of inheritance. Penalties for a number of criminal delicts were also specified, but even the criminal law "did not exist in the technical sense of a comprehensive scheme of offences against the public order."[9] Even homicide, although "regulated in meticulous detail . . . was treated as a private and not as a public offence. For the rest the doctrine (of the criminal law) was largely confined to the exposition of six specific offences — illicit sexual relations, slanderous allegations of unchastity, theft, wine-drinking, armed robbery, and apostasy — in which the notion of man's obligations towards God predominated and which, because God himself had 'defined' the punishments therefore, were known as the *hadd* . . . offences."[10]

The sharia has always been subject to interpretation. When an entire body of legal scholars can agree on a certain interpretation, this consensus is called *ijma*. When the individual scholar (*mujtahid*) makes such an interpretation, it is termed *ijtihad*. And even today in Muslim countries an individual called a mufti will issue legal opinions, or *fatwas*, on the pressing questions of the day.[11] Such are the processes, although sometimes tortuous and slow, through which change is introduced.

Islam, like any great religion, has suffered heresies and splits. The main group of Muslims is called Sunni. A much smaller group, the Shi'ites, is largely found in Iraq, Iran, Pakistan, India, and Yemen. Theoretically, the Shi'ites are

---

considerable period after the termination of the marriage; or quite obviously illegitimate children, in the modern sense, could legally secure inheritance rights from men not their fathers. See Ibid., pp. 175–77.

This quotation and example are presented in such detail because they illustrate well the ability of Muslims to adjust to changing times without rejecting the literal word of their religion. The pattern is evident: the first *hadd* penalties were accepted in order to correct what were thought to be abuses in the pre-Islamic period; then a reaction to the severity of these penalties produced an interpretation that in most cases practically nullified them; and in modern times, the abuses of the earlier humanitarian interpretation produced a new interpretation, yet without return to the original *hadd* penalties and without specific alteration of the Quranic message.

[9] Coulson, *A History*, p. 124.

[10] Ibid.

[11] Birth control is one such problem. In general, religious authorities have supported family planning.

those who exalt Ali, the fourth caliph, and argue that the imamate (religious leadership) of the Muslim community should descend through the family of Ali. More practically today Shi'ism is the blend of Islam with Persian culture. (The founder of the Safavid dynasty, Shah Isma'il, made it the state religion in the early sixteenth century.) It is by no means completely homogeneous. Well known today are the Isma'ilis (headed by the Agha Khan) and the Ahmadis (largely in Pakistan). The Black Muslims in the United States also are Shi'ites.[12]

More difficult to classify are the sufis, the Islamic mystics, Sufism is not a sect, but rather the product of the apparent human need for a religion with more mysticism and color than are to be found in the normally austere practice of Islam. Philosophically, sufism is monistic; organizationally, it is divided into a number of orders. In addition to the regular obligations of the Muslim, sufis undertake still more, often a variety of spiritual invocations. The most famous sufi was al-Ghazali (twelfth century), who was also one of the great Islamic philosophers. The sufis themselves have generally eschewed political leadership, but they have widely influenced those who have exercised power. Hasan al-Banna, founder in 1929 of the puritanical Muslim Brotherhood, was strongly influenced by the sufis in his youth.[13] Most importantly, sufism often serves as a retreat for the oppressed. It offers an escape from the world and one that can be shared vicariously with large numbers of ordinary people who have no other way of enduring the difficulties and agonies of lower-class life.

THE CONTEMPORARY ROLE OF RELIGION

The twentieth century has been one of great stress for all religions. Perhaps man, in the abstract, is scarcely less religious than he was earlier, but the forms of his worship have altered. If he is not more basically tolerant of the idiosyncrasies of

---

[12] See Seyyed Hossein Nasr, "Ithna 'Ashari Shi'ism and Iranian Islam," in Arberry, *Religion in the Middle East*, vol. 2, *Islam*, pp. 96–118.

[13] See Martin Lings, "Sufism," in Arberry, *Religion in the Middle East*, vol. 2, pp. 253–69. An important work in English on the sufis is A. H. Zarrinkoob, "Persian Sufism in its Historical Perspective," *Iranian Studies* 3 (1970) :139–220.

others, he has found it necessary to come to terms with beliefs and practices foreign to his own. The rapid growth of communication and the dissemination of knowledge have forced a reexamination of much of tradition, including religion. Middle Eastern countries have, in varying degrees, become enamored of modernization. This process of modernization inevitably affects traditional religious practices and beliefs.

In attempting to assess the impact of outside challenges on Islam, it is important to understand that Islam has no formal organization. Since the abolition of the caliphate in Turkey in 1924, there has been no central symbolic figure of leadership. A Muslim's obligations are to God and not to any church or to any individual who purports to speak for God. There are no priests or ministers as such. Some men claim, however, to be particularly learned in the intricacies of Islam. They may occupy certain political positions (mufti, qadi) or they may have different titles (shaykhs, mujtahids, mullahs). Collectively they are known as the *ulema,* and what organization Islam has resides in this body. Entrance to the group is sometimes by co-optation and sometimes by simple acceptance by others of a newcomer's right to speak with authority about religion. The individuals in the ulema are usually learned in such traditional subjects as philosophy, theology, rhetoric, law, and literature.

The ulema have, as much as any others, represented the forces of tradition in the otherwise rapidly changing Middle Eastern world. Relatively few members of the ulema have sought to accommodate the insistent secularization of the age. Most have tried to brake the changes that have occurred. They have often objected to the emancipation of women and to the liberalization of the marriage and divorce laws. They have not noticeably encouraged the growth of science. They have greatly influenced the creation of literature and art, and in recent years the production and screening of motion pictures and television performances. They have demanded observance of the old practices: the daily ritual prayers, the pilgrimage, the fasting during Ramadan, and the dietary laws. They have generally struggled for the maintenance of an "Islamic state," an "Islamic constitution," and an "Islamic law."

Nevertheless, their influence is waning. They have, of

course, hung on most successfully in the backwaters of the
Middle East — Oman, Yemen, and Afghanistan — but even in
these places their power and control are slipping.[14] Nowhere,
perhaps, has their contemporary failure been more vividly
displayed than in the attempts to establish Pakistan as an
Islamic state free of other determinants.[15] But though the
ulema have not held the forces of change in permanent check,
it would be foolish to argue that they will in the future lose
all of their influence. For many Muslims there are no doubts;
their lives are led as closely as possible in harmony with the
Quranic precepts. For many others there are doubts tempered
with feelings of guilt; they surrender to the pressures of the
times, but they remain susceptible to religious nostalgia.
There is also a small group that has cut all ties with the past
and embraced the new secular age as fervently as possible.

One of the most appealing characteristics of the Muslim
clerics is the fact that they have often effectively served as the
protectors of the struggling masses. Although they have
sometimes been portrayed as venal, selfish, and ignorant, they
have perhaps more often been sincere, honest, and intelligent.
It has been the mullah in the countryside, for example, who
has traditionally shielded the villager from oppressive and

14 For example, in contemporary Afghanistan one can find (1978) an
incredible acceptance of modernism in Kabul, the capital, where the government pursues a deliberate policy pushing social and economic change;
in the countryside it is another matter.

15 When India became independent in 1947, Pakistan broke away as the
core of the predominantly Muslim areas of India. The events of late 1971
indicate that the essential question of Pakistan's political viability had
not been solved. Its *raison d'être* was its religion, so it was not surprising
that great enthusiasm was generated over the prospect of putting together a modern Islamic state. Leonard Binder describes and discusses the
tribulations of this enterprise in his *Religion and Politics in Pakistan*
(Berkeley: University of California Press, 1961). His conclusions, among
others, were that the ulema, though divided, were not unyielding in the
face of modernization; that fundamentalism, in Pakistan at least, "remains the most fruitful source of Islamic intellectual innovation" (Ibid.,
p. 379); that the political forces in Pakistan (1956) had few solid links
with religious forces (with the possible exception of the ulema themselves) and still fewer with the people; and that the "original enthusiasm
of the people of Pakistan for an Islamic state has been largely dissipated"
(Ibid., p. 379). See also chapter 5, "Pakistan: Islamic State," in W. C.
Smith, *Islam in Modern History* (Princeton, N.J.: Princeton University
Press, 1957).

rapacious governmental agents. The mullah has been the one who has advised the peasant during times of travail, and who has provided a modicum of education for the children of the masses. Throughout the history of Islam, the clerics have performed an invaluable social-welfare function. Even today in the Middle East, the practicing Muslim will turn to the cleric for protection and support against secular forces considered corrupt and oppressive. He finds it difficult to believe that individuals who have consistently extorted should suddenly become the standard-bearers of reform. Thus, when the mullah seeks to resist modernizing programs, he will do so more effectively because of the strong bonds of trust that he has often developed with the people themselves. This is one reason why some scholars strongly argue that reform must develop through traditional channels if it is to be at all effective.

Those who rule have much stake in the extent and direction of political change. Their commitment to religion is therefore important. Equally important is the degree to which the populace demands religious observance (and the resulting extent of the influence held by religious leaders). This is well exemplified by modern Israel. Although it was founded as a haven for a religious minority, its leadership has been decidedly secular, and much of the middle class remains alienated from religious orthodoxy. Yet it is impossible to describe the politics of Israel, or its daily life, without considerable reference to the role of its religious functionaries and their organizations. The operation of taxis on the Sabbath, the serving of nonkosher food on the steamship line, even the delineation of what is a Jew[16] — many things like these have forced compromises from a government that needs parliamentary support from the relatively small, but politically potent, religious parties.

In the Muslim countries, to varying degrees of course, there

[16] The question of who is a Jew has been a practical problem of great complexity for the Israelis. The Israeli Supreme Court finally decided in the Shalit case that the Shalit children were indeed Jews, based on the cultural milieu of their upbringing, in spite of the fact that their mother was not Jewish. Rabbinical law normally demands that the mother be Jewish. Extreme pressure was exerted to reverse this judgment. For analysis see Naomi Shepherd, "What Makes a Jew?" *New Statesman*, 13 February 1970, pp. 215–16.

remain the pervasive demands of the religious community. A Nasser finds it necessary to make the pilgrimage or to keep photographs of his wife out of the press (although his successor, Anwar Sadat, has not found it necessary to be so conservative). The rector of al-Azhar, the great religious university in Cairo, declaims on the length of women's skirts. A mufti issues a fatwa on the acceptability of birth control. In every Middle Eastern country, political and social change must accommodate itself to the lingering religious consciousness of the country's inhabitants and to the vested interests of its cleric class.

RELIGIOUS REFORM

Islam has been altered through time and has adjusted itself to changing conditions. This has been true not only in the modern period but throughout its history.

The Muslim world was in decline by the time of the Crusades, and although there was glory in the Fatimids (Egypt), the Safavids (Iran), the Moghuls (India), and the Ottomans (Turkey) during later periods, it was in every case a glory that had been achieved in traditional terms. Strong leaders — Salah al-Din, Shah Abbas I, Akbar, Suleyman — by military prowess, shrewd alliances, and political acumen, as well as good fortune, managed to build impressive dynasties. Such dynasties might have survived if all of the leaders had been of the caliber of these. In the case of the Ottomans at least, survival was accompanied by other changes. Competent administrative processes were created, and mechanisms for handling the diverse problems of empire came into being.[17] Yet almost all of this was done within a traditional framework. No challenge to any of these empires from within or without occurred in any but these traditional terms.[18] It was only with

---

[17] Some of this can be found in H. A. R. Gibb and Harold Bowen, *Islamic Society and the West:* vol. 1, *Islamic Society in the Eighteenth Century*, pts. 1, 2 (London: Oxford University Press, 1950, 1957).

[18] This is not precisely true with respect to Akbar (and his successors) and the Moghuls in India. The Moghuls were Muslim rulers of heterogeneous peoples of differing religious beliefs (notably Hindus); many of their practices and innovations could hardly be said to have been tradi-

Napoleon's conquest of Egypt in 1798 that tradition in the Middle East, including religious tradition, was severely challenged.

As is so often the case, it was military defeat that dramatized the need to change some aspects of the traditional system. The immense and successful challenge of the West — young, brash, and unbelieving — forced, for the Muslim world, a painful introspection that has now lasted nearly two centuries. The direct challenge to Islam itself began in the nineteenth century, although Islam is undergoing the most traumatic changes now, in the last quarter of the twentieth century.

Religious reform in the nineteenth century began with the attempt to answer the simple question: How is it that power, skills, and material comforts have come to those who reject Islam, the right path to the life of man in God? (Such questions were posed even in the columns of popular newspapers, and readers would reply with their own suggestions.) The alternative answers were not many: (1) the right path was in fact wrong; (2) the proper life of man is not to be defined in terms of power and material comforts; and (3) somehow man has misinterpreted and misunderstood God's word. The third attitude was the most palatable to many of the deeply religious shaykhs of the nineteenth century.

It was this view that characterized the position of Jamal al-Din al-Afghani, the most prominent of the reformers of that period:[19]

---

tional. Akbar himself had religious beliefs that transcended Islam and were certainly heretical by all ordinary standards. See S. M. Ikram, *Muslim Civilization in India* (New York: Columbia University Press, 1964).

[19] See Adams, *Islam and Modernism* for a brief but laudatory appraisal of "this remarkable man." Later scholars, notably Elie Kedourie (in his *Afghani and 'Abduh* [New York: Humanities Press, 1966]) and Nikki R. Keddie, have seriously questioned both his motives and his piety. Kedourie suggests that al-Afghani was in fact somewhat of a charlatan: a Freemason (p. 20), a sexual "lady-killer" (p. 9), a troublemaker, a lover of "boastfulness and self-glorification" (p. 47), and a subverter of Islam (p. 45). "[O]ne of Afghani's aims . . . was the subversion of the Islamic religion, and the method adopted to this end was the practice of a false but showy devotion" (p. 45). Even if true, all this does not negate the fact that in his lifetime and after, al-Afghani was enormously influential in the movement for Islamic reform. See also Nikki R. Keddie, *An Islamic Response to*

The chief aim of Jamal al-Din in all his untiring efforts and
ceaseless agitation, was the accomplishment of the unification
of all Muslim peoples under one Islamic government, over
which the one Supreme Caliph should bear undisputed rule, as
in the glorious days of Islam before its power had been dissipated in endless dissensions and divisions, and the Muslim
lands had lapsed into ignorance and helplessness, to become the
prey of western aggression. The present decadent condition of
Muslim countries weighed heavily upon him. He believed that
if these countries were once freed from the incubus of foreign
domination or interference, and Islam itself reformed and
adapted to the demands of present-day conditions, the Muslim
peoples would be able to work out for themselves a new and
glorious order of affairs, without dependence on, or imitation
of, European nations. To him, the religion of Islam was, in all
essentials, a world religion and thoroughly capable, by reason
of its inner spiritual force, of adaptation to the changing conditions of every age.[20]

Al-Afghani's view was clear enough: Islam is not wrong.
It is the perfect prescription for the attainment of happiness
for man in God. This means the achievement of material prosperity; it certainly means the victory of Muslims over unbe-
lievers in whatever conflicts are generated. But reality was not
like this. Therefore, the only possible explanation was that
man, in spite of proper guidance, had turned aside and gone
astray. His loss of power was his punishment for leaving the
sunna, or "true path."

It was obvious that many Muslims were not living in accordance with the Quran. Political leaders were often lax.
Their personal lives were frequently caricatures of the good
Muslim life. They often led their peoples into activities, conflicts, and acts that had never been countenanced in the Quran
or by the Prophet. The solution to this was to admonish peo-

---

*Imperialism: Political and Religious Writings of Sayyid Jamal ad-Din
"al-Afghani"* (Berkeley and Los Angeles: University of California Press,
1968) .

[20] Adams, *Islam and Modernism,* p. 13. As phrased, this resembles
Hasan al-Banna's program. There is indeed a philosophic connection from
al-Afghani to Abduh to Rashid Rida to al-Banna. Rashid Rida was the
biographer of Abduh, the editor of *Al-Manar,* and a distinguished Islamic
publicist.

ple to live better lives, and when necessary to use whatever political resources were required to achieve behavior more in keeping with Muslim belief. Al-Afghani did not hesitate to suggest extreme measures. For recalcitrant rulers his remedy might even be the assassin's touch. (Nasir al-Din Shah of Iran was felled by one of al-Afghani's followers in 1896.)[21]

It was also apparent that man was not alive to what the Quran really meant. He subjected himself too readily to traditional formulas without contemplating their essential meaning. It was al-Afghani's follower, Muhammad Abduh, who was perhaps most famous for this point of view. He blamed most of all the religious leader who merely and blindly repeated old views. A leading shaykh from al-Azhar, a judge, and finally mufti of Egypt — and throughout his adult life an indefatigable agitator and writer — Abduh was the leading religious reformer of modern Egyptian history. His fatwas, while mufti, were famed for their liberality. "Two of these fatwas are best known: one declaring it lawful for Muslims to eat the flesh of animals slain by Jews and Christians; the other declaring it likewise lawful for Muslims to deposit their money in the Postal Savings Banks where it would draw interest."[22] More typical, but equally famous, were his views on polygamy. Because the Quran does not endorse, although it permits, the luxury of as many as four wives to a husband, and because it specifically enjoins husbands to treat their wives equally, Abduh chose to interpret the Quranic statements as an indirect, but nonetheless clear, prohibition of polygamy. His grounds: that it is clearly impossible for a man to treat his wives equally. Abduh was struck with the fact that the powerful nations of his day did not permit overt polygamy.

In India, Muhammad Iqbal, who wrote magnificent poetry in Urdu, attempted to find in his *Six Lectures on the Reconstruction of Religious Thought in Islam*[23] the basis for all of

---

21 "Jamal once said . . . : 'No reforms can be hoped for till six or seven heads are cut off'" (Adams, *Islam and Modernism*, p. 14). Adams also points out that Jamal's followers in Egypt had discussed at considerable length the prospects of assassinating Isma'il Pasha.

22 Ibid., p. 80.

23 London: Oxford University Press, 1934.

modern science. For example, he argued that the Quranic verse that speaks of the light (*nur*) of the world was equivalent to Einstein's assumption that the speed of light was constant (invariant) under all transformations.

It is not fair to ridicule these attempts. They were made by men who combined a religious faith with a knowledge of the modern world. If the attempt, at an earlier date, was worthy of a Thomas Aquinas, it was an equally worthy enterprise for a modern Muslim philosopher. But twentieth-century time, buffeted about by incredible transformations, is not equivalent to the time of the thirteenth-century *Summa Theologica*. An Abduh or an Iqbal can contribute to the ferment of thought and can lay the groundwork for later behavioral changes, but he cannot alone carry the burden of reform. This task belongs to the political leader.

Because Islam is so entwined with everyday life, any kind of social reform must produce religious reform as well. Most of the well-known Middle Eastern reformers of the twentieth century have been primarily social reformers, and most of these would have denied any intention to alter Islam. In fact, however, they have altered it profoundly. We cannot exhaustively examine their efforts. (The legal and constitutional reformers of the nineteenth century — such as Midhat Pasha of Turkey,[24] — would have to be included here.) But something must be said of the efforts of such individuals as Kemal Atatürk (Turkey), Reza Shah (Iran), Gamal Abdel Nasser (Egypt), Abdul Karim Kassem (Iraq), and Habib Bourguiba (Tunisia). These individuals are similar largely in that they produced religious change in very practical ways.

Kemal Atatürk[25] is the most famous of the twentieth-century Middle Eastern social reformers. Finding power in the Turkey of the post–First World War period, Atatürk rid it of its enemies, reestablished viable government, and set about implementing a major program of social and political reform. He was virtually unique among reformers in admitting his atheism, and he struck at religious institutions in many

---

[24] See Robert Devereux, *The First Ottoman Constitutional Period* (Baltimore: Johns Hopkins Press, 1963).
[25] See Chapter V below.

ways.[26] The last caliph in Islam, Abdülmecid, was deposed in 1924, perhaps because Atatürk felt that the sources of political reaction were primarily religious in nature. In 1925, the fez, a rather ersatz religious symbol, was banned in public, along with other religious garb. The monasteries and retreats were taken over and religious orders were abolished in the same year. Of that act, Kemal had this to say:

> To seek help from the dead is a disgrace to a civilized community. . . . What can be the objects of the existing brotherhoods (*tarikat*) other than to secure the well-being, in worldly and moral life, of those who follow them? I flatly refuse to believe that today, in the luminous presence of science, knowledge, and civilization in all its aspects, there exist, in the civilized community of Turkey, men so primitive as to seek their material and moral well-being from the guidance of one or another *şeyh* [shaykh]. Gentlemen, you and the whole nation must know, and know well, that the Republic of Turkey cannot be the land of *şeyhs,* dervishes, disciples, and lay brothers. The straightest, truest Way (*tarikat*) is the way of civilization. To be a man, it is enough to do what civilization requires. The heads of the brotherhoods will understand this truth I have uttered in all its clarity, and will of their own accord at once close their convents, and accept the fact that their disciples have at last come of age.[27]

In 1926, a form of the Swiss civil code was adopted and the sharia abolished; in the process, "polygamy, repudiation — all the ancient bars to the freedom and dignity of women — were abolished. In their place came civil marriage and divorce, with equal rights for both parties. Most shocking of all, to Muslim opinion, the marriage of a Muslim woman to a non-Muslim man became legally possible, and all adults were given the legal right to change their religion at will."[28] In 1927, the

[26] It is only fair to say that a number of Turkish specialists deny Atatürk's atheism. See N. Berkes, *The Development of Secularism in Turkey* (Montreal: McGill University Press, 1964) .

[27] Quoted from Bernard Lewis, *The Emergence of Modern Turkey*, 2d ed. (London: Oxford University Press, 1968) , pp. 410–11.

[28] Ibid., p. 273. See Chapter 21, "Law," in Arberry, *Religion in the Middle East*, vol. 2, for an up-to-date discussion of the problem of mixed

Arabic alphabet was superseded by a Latinized one. This is of importance because Arabic is the language of the Quran. Even the call to prayer in the mosque was now to be in Turkish, not Arabic.

Of course, not all people were enthusiastic about these changes, and in the countryside many resisted them. In any event, not all of this frantic attack on the Islamic institution survived Atatürk's death in 1938; in later years the ill-fated Democratic party and its successor party, the Justice party, found a responsive chord in the rural areas through their promises to treat religion more favorably.[29] Yet the role of religion in Turkey will never again be quite the same.

As important as Atatürk's direct attack on religion was his political-nationalist revolution of "Turkey for the Turks." Religion stood in the way of his modernizing Turkey economically and politically; the country would have to adjust to the new exigencies. At the same time, Atatürk was so successful in freeing Turkey from the disabilities of the First World War and in giving it dignity and stability that many Turks were generally willing to accept the antireligious tone of many of his acts. One remaining legacy: While the Pakistani constitution proudly proclaims an Islamic state, in Turkey the post-

---

marriages in Muslim countries. A fairly typical practice in Egypt is that the non-Muslim male goes through a sham declaration of conversion to Islam.

29 "During the Democratic Party's management of affairs, a marked return to Islamic practices became obvious. The study of Muslim religion became practically obligatory in primary and secondary schools, which grew in number parallel with the building of new mosques. According to the Directorate of Religious Affairs, in the ten years from 1950, 5,000 mosques were built in Turkey, fifty of them in Ankara, as well as almost equally numerous schools. In the same period schools for *imam* and *khatib* had grown from seven to nineteen, and in these the instruction had been sensibly modernized, so that ignorant *imams* might be replaced by better educated ones. The secularizers resolutely opposed this, preferring an ignorant *imam* to one capable of exerting some intellectual influence over the people. They blamed the government for countenancing reaction, and the government knew it; but they could not afford to lose the popular vote, all in favour of religion. Atatürk had forced his views on the people. Now it was the turn of the people to bring force to bear on their governors" (F. M. Pareja, in Arberry, *Religion in the Middle East*, vol. 2, p. 469) .

Kemalist constitutions have maintained a rigidly secular character.[30]

In the 1920s, the example of Atatürk was emulated less enthusiastically, as well as less successfully, by Reza Shah Pahlavi, and also by Amanullah Shah in Afghanistan.[31] Neither had the political or personal resources of Kemal. Reza Shah was much more interested in introducing economic improvements than in social and political reforms. Amanullah Shah was even more of a dilettante in reform — he was much impressed, during several trips to Europe in the 1920s, with the trappings of Western affluence — and he was always careful to insist upon his devotion to Islamic principles. But such insistence did not save him from overthrow in 1929.[32]

In later years, men rose to political leadership because of their commitment to such policies as military modernization and militant nationalism. Certainly, men like Habib Bourguiba or Ahmad Ben Bella had not come to power because of any attachment to religious orthodoxy. Though it may be necessary to refrain from overt actions against religion, most of these contemporary political leaders have initiated or supported decisions that have seriously undermined the traditional religion.

One of the issues that contemporary political leaders have had to confront is the position of women in society. In Egypt and other progressive Islamic countries, divorces are now easier for a woman to obtain. Although the inequity still favors the male, his privileges are more difficult to come by. Despite considerable opposition, Bourguiba in Tunisia for a time offi-

[30] See the interesting article by Richard H. Pfaff, "Disengagement from Traditionalism in Turkey and Iran," *Western Political Quarterly* 16 (March 1963) :79–98.

[31] For the reforms in Iran, see Amin Banani, *The Modernization of Iran, 1921–1941* (Stanford: Stanford University Press, 1961) . For an account of those in Afghanistan, see Vartan Gregorian, *The Emergence of Modern Afghanistan* (Stanford: Stanford University Press, 1969) .

[32] One of the items of modernization for Amanullah was the construction of new palaces in accordance with European architecture. One of the authors (Leiden) remembers wandering in 1953 through one of these unfinished and unused palaces in Kabul. Zahir Shah had never felt secure enough to use the finest building in his capital. A few years later they were finally put to use, as government offices.

cially discouraged the fasting during Ramadan (typically, activities in Muslim countries come to a standstill for this month, when fasting is obligatory during the daylight hours) by opening restaurants during the day and closing them at night, and by treating the fasting period as just another month.[33] The bedrock of Muslim law, the congeries of regulations on inheritance, underwent alteration in Iraq during Kassem's tenure. *Waqf* ("endowments") reform has been initiated almost everywhere except in the most traditional of Islamic states; of Egypt, Gabriel Baer has said, "Waqf reform has been perhaps the most successful part of the Egyptian land reform."[34] This reform resembles the confiscation of church property and lands in the West, and has seriously affected the funding of traditional religious activities. And it was a former minister of waqfs, Dr. Muhammad Husayn al-Zahabi, who was murdered by religious extremists in Egypt in the summer of 1977.

It is sometimes argued that reform proceeds too rapidly. Y. Linant de Bellefonds has said:

> The legislator must proceed, even towards . . . a modest objective, with caution. He must not advance too far ahead of the social evolution of his country, otherwise he runs the risk of being obliged to retrace his steps and to return, crestfallen, to the system which he had pressed to abolish. Witness the case of Libya. The Libyan law of Judicial Organization of 20 September 1954 abolished there the jurisdiction of personal status and the civil courts became competent in all matters and with regard to all litigants, whatever might be their religion. The reform was premature. The people (especially the Muslim litigant) soon missed the simplicity of the qādi's court, to which they had been accustomed and which seemed to them superior to the complexities of civil justice. In order, therefore, not to offend public opinion, the new law of Judicial Organization of 18 December 1958 re-established the duality of jurisdictions in

---

[33] In late 1971, Bourguiba was ailing; perhaps because of this, he abandoned much of his fight against Ramadan. By 1978, he had lost considerable control over events in Tunisia.

[34] *Studies in the Social History of Modern Egypt* (Chicago: University of Chicago Press, 1969) , p. 92.

all matters concerning personal status. The Libyan reform had
lasted for exactly four years.[35]

It has been argued, on the contrary, that because of the
resilient nature of Islam, rapid and radical alterations are
necessary in order to insure the retention of any change whatsoever. Rather than an accumulating adsorption of change in
the Islamic context, it is perhaps essential that genuine absorption be required. This can be effected only by massive and
sharp transformations.

The twentieth century is a secular age. The very location of
the Middle East, the resources (notably oil) that it possesses, as
well as the resources it requires — all of these and other factors
push the area into increased contacts with a world religiously
alien. It seems very probable that Islam will undergo severe
readjustments because of these contacts and pressures. Interestingly enough, the Israeli Jews face a somewhat similar
readjustment. One thesis with respect to the future of Judaism
in Israel is expounded by Georges Friedmann in his *Fin du
Peuple Juif?*[36] in which he argues that, to the degree that
Israel becomes a viable political and cultural entity in the
Middle East, to that degree will the traditional Judaism that
sustained the Jews throughout the centuries be abandoned.
A similar thesis could be constructed for the broader world of
Islam.

RELIGIOUS REACTION

Not all response to modern pressures has produced a desire
for reform. Some Muslims argue that indeed man has gone
astray by not following the prescriptions of God. What is
needed is not new interpretations of old principles, but more
vigorous adherence to what has already been revealed to be
the true path. This view can be termed religious reaction.

The history of Islam has contained an element of reaction
virtually from its inception. As early as 657, in the struggle
between Ali and Mu'awiyah, a group called the Kharijites

---

35 Arberry, *Religion in the Middle East,* vol. 2, pp. 457–58.
36 Paris: Editions Gallimard, 1965.

deserted Ali on the grounds that, in agreeing to arbitrate his differences with Mu'awiyah over his claim to the caliphate, he was not following the Quran literally. The remnants of this movement were still in existence by the time of the Crusades. In the thirteenth and fourteenth centuries, the most conservative voice was that of Ahmad Ibn Taymiyyah. Philip Hitti says of him that he "bowed to no authority other than the Koran . . . and lifted his voice high against innovation, saint worship, vows and pilgrimage to shrines."[37] He apparently in the eighteenth century inspired Muhammad Ibn Abd al-Wahhab, who was determined to cleanse the "corrupt" Islam of his day, "to purge it and restore it to its primitive strictness."[38] What came from all of this was the Wahhabi movement, largely centered in the Arabian peninsula, and which has survived to contemporary times.

By far the most prominent and interesting of the Islamic puritanical movements has been the Muslim Brotherhood. It was founded in Ismailia, Egypt, in 1927 by a schoolteacher named Hasan al-Banna. Al-Banna had incredible organizational talents and mesmeric appeal. He gradually put together what was in fact a highly popular and aggressive political movement. Al-Banna himself always denied that his movement was anything but one of dedicated Muslims who wanted to return to the life of a purer, earlier period. But in the 1930s and 1940s in Egypt — which was affected by the world depression and later by the Second World War, a British occupation, a corrupt government, and a rising Zionism in neighboring Palestine — an atmosphere developed in which almost any popular movement became political. The Muslim Brotherhood attempted to force the government to mend its ways, and ultimately the secret cadres of the movement resorted to violent techniques — including assassination — to gain their ends. From the mid-1940s to the late 1940s, they assassinated two prime ministers of Egypt, Ahmad Mahir Pasha and Nuqrashi Pasha. It was the latter event, in December 1948, that prompted the government to resort to assassina-

---

37 *History*, p. 689.
38 Ibid., p. 740.

tion in return, and in February 1949 Hasan al-Banna was gunned down in the streets.[39]

After al-Banna's death, the Brotherhood was rent by discord. In 1952 the revolution came, but the Muslim Brothers were not able to gain from this event. To Nasser and the young officers who made up his junta, competition from the Brotherhood could not be allowed. A Brother attempted to shoot President Nasser in 1954; since then, the Brotherhood has been outlawed in Egypt. Its appeal also splashed beyond Egyptian frontiers into Syria, Iraq, and Saudi Arabia. In Egypt itself, it remains a secret organization that everyone knows about and that many support. A weekly journal is published by the Brotherhood and is widely distributed.

Another force today in Egypt is the *Takfir Wal Hijira* ("repentence from sin and retreat"). Led by Ahmed Mustapha Shukri, the members of this group believe in a return to the pure life of the past and the rejection of much that is modern. They consider themselves particularly the enemies of President Sadat and have mounted a terrorist campaign to gain attention and perhaps force the government into concessions. By murdering in July 1977 the former waqf minister, Dr. Zahabi, they pushed the Egyptian government to vigorous retaliation. Hundreds were arrested; about fifty were tried by military court and five were sentenced to death in November. This group is typical of religious extremism in Egypt, which has almost always been accompanied by terrorism.

In other Muslim countries, there are a variety of organizations resembling the Muslim Brotherhood. Usually they are insignificant. More important is the *Fidayan-i Islam* in Iran. In the late 1940s and early 1950s, this religious teaching organization wielded considerable coercive influence in Iran. Elaborately organized in the form of an inner cell of fifty to sixty

---

39 See Murray C. Havens, Carl Leiden, and Karl M. Schmitt, *The Politics of Assassination* (Englewood Cliffs, N.J.: Prentice-Hall, 1970), Chapter 10, for an account of the assassination of al-Banna. The best book on the Muslim Brotherhood is Richard P. Mitchell, *The Society of the Muslim Brothers* (London: Oxford University Press, 1969). See also Christina Phelps Harris, *Nationalism and Revolution in Egypt* (The Hague: Mouton and Co., 1964); and Ishak Musa Husaini, *The Moslem Brethren* (Beirut: Khayat's College Book Cooperative, 1956).

members surrounded by two concentric circles of membership totaling approximately one thousand dedicated individuals, the Fidayan-i Islam was directly implicated in the assassination of important Iranian political figures, including Prime Minister Razmara in 1951. In Syria, religious murders (often of Alawites by Muslims) have continued into the late 1970s. And in Israel, too, there are minor pockets of reactionary Judaism. It is, of course, not necessarily religion itself that is reactionary. Rather, some of its adherents make it so by their desire to return to some earlier day.

What are the reasons for this kind of reaction? A surprising number of young, middle-class individuals have been drawn to the ranks of the Muslim Brotherhood. It was not, and probably is not today, simply a repository of religious fanatics. There are, of course, those individuals who are drawn to a movement by expediency, just as there are those who assuage nostalgic guilt by supporting a religious posture that they find increasingly uncomfortable. There are also individuals who are genuinely bewildered, and who no doubt wonder whether the secular age that they have entered is truly right. These persons have often become alienated from a system that they see as corrupt, unjust, and venal. And there are the fanatics. But the large numbers who have supported some of these movements belie the assertion that all the members can be characterized as fanatics. The feelings of insecurity, the trauma of discovering a self in the political and social innovations of the times, an embryonic suspicion at least of the world outside of Islam (the *Dar al-Harb*) — all of these perhaps explain the seeming need of many people of all descriptions to lose themselves in religious reaction.

ISLAM AND MODERNIZATION

Modernization, which involves man's increasing control over his environment, does not mean the same thing to all of those who consider themselves to be modernizers. For many, it indicates little more than the gaudy possession of air-conditioned hotels, jetports, casinos, and cinemas. To others, it means the physical and frequently counterproductive existence of sophisticated military systems, or even such things as dams and macadamized highways. But one thing does characterize the modernizing nation. There is deep dissatisfaction with the existing political, social, and economic systems. The standard of living is too low. Educational skills are too few. Frustrations are too many. To the leaders in modernization, what they lack is seemingly possessed by others. The process of modernization generally becomes one of emulating as many of the outward features of these other peoples as possible. Ideologically, it may seem necessary to couch these desires in such indigenous terms as Turkish nationalism or Arab socialism.

How does Islam in its contemporary setting affect this drive for modernization? Equally important is the question of how Islam is affected by modernization. Perhaps the term *modernization* can itself provide insight into these questions. This is not the first time in history that societies have undergone confrontation with other "advanced" societies and have learned to accommodate to them.[40] Every such confrontation was, in a sense, a clash or contact with modernization. Examples abound: the Romans were modernized by the Greeks (as were the Macedonians by their southern and eastern neighbors), the Gauls and Britons by the Romans, and the New World by the French, English, and Spanish. Islam was, of course, originally quite Arab — although it is evident that Muhammad wove many strands of Christian and Jewish doctrine into his revelations — but even by the time of the second caliph, Umar, it had had major contacts with the Egyptians (who could not then be termed Arab), the Byzantines, and the Persians. In religious terms, these contacts were with Christians of varying hue, with Zorastrians, and with pockets of Jews. But in a broader cultural sense, these contacts were between the relatively simple and primitive Arab society and the vastly more

---

[40] In 1969, C. D. Darlington, the geneticist, published *The Evolution of Man and Society* (New York: Simon and Schuster, 1969), in which he treated particularly the alterations in society and culture, with emphasis on the breeding factor. Chapter 15 is devoted to Islam. Of the Muslim Arabian Arabs, he says that they "have failed to transform themselves and have for the most part survived the revolutions of 1300 years as little changed as any people on earth" (p. 327). But he says of the Persians that the "subtle intelligence of the defeated Persians overwhelmed the political strength of their Arab conquerors and gave a new twist to their artistic invention and also their religious enthusiasm" (p. 346).

complex and sophisticated societies of the periphery. Although basic acceptance of Islam followed Arab conquests, the religion, as well as the cultural behavior, of its original followers were gradually adjusted to views and attitudes held by those who had been conquered.

Islamic culture then, as it had emerged by the time of the Abbasids (749–1258), was already an amalgam of other cultures. This is to suggest that Islam at least has had a tradition of confrontation with other cultures and a tradition of accommodation to them. This was true in North Africa and Spain; it was equally true in both the conquest of the Byzantine possessions and the subsequent fraternization with its empire for several centuries. During the Crusades, the Christian princes (of, for example, Antioch, Jerusalem, and Tyre) resembled the Muslim amirs who opposed them. Persia became Muslim but absorbed its conquerors; later the Mongols (many of whom were Christians) and Turks (representing lesser cultures in their periods of history) passed on still further contributions to the Islamic culture.

Darlington considers the peasants and artisans the most conservative influence in historical Islam: "Thus beneath the sparkling changes on the surface of Islam lay the solid stable world of the peasant and the craftsman, partly excluded from the privileges of Muslims. They were both crystallized by their inbreeding. Both were utterly conservative; they created nothing new but they lost nothing old. They preserved everything so that we see them today working their fields or their anvils as they worked them a thousand years ago."[41] Actually, all societies are an amalgam of the traditional and the modern. Few societies can live and prosper when one heavily overbalances the other. In general (although the truth of this varies from region to region), Islam has demonstrated a vital blend of these ingredients in its history.

It is interesting that in Black Africa the greater proportion of conversions are to Islam, not to Christianity.[42] The Christian missionary is usually less accommodating than the Mus-

[41] Ibid., p. 344.

[42] See James Kritzeck and William H. Lewis, eds., *Islam in Africa* (New York: Van Nostrand-Reinhold Co., 1969).

lim, and less willing to accept traditional features of a society alien to him. It is also true that in the history of the holy places in Jerusalem, the most generous and tolerant of the rulers with respect to the followers of other religions were the Muslims; the least tolerant were the Christians.

Islam has been incredibly resilient to the pressures of an outside, and sometimes hostile, world. This has been particularly true of Shi'ism. In Sunnism, the body of law is theoretically complete and unchangeable. Shi'ism, on the other hand, teaches that the law is always alive and changing. Through the chain of imams that stretches to this very day, Shi'i Islam is continuously able to interpret and account for the new and the different. This is precisely the key role of the mujtahids, "who can practice ijtihad or exercise their opinion in questions of Law. They are living interpreters of the Law who interpret it in the absence of the Imam and in his name."[43] One learned mujtahid explains this ability of Shi'ism to adapt dynamically to new circumstances by writing: "What deserves attention is the unique process by which the institution of ijtihad can adapt, scientifically, the basic principles of Islam to everyday problems of Life. Since it always can apply the principles of Islam to the everyday problems of life of the people, the scholastic group (mujtahids) believes that there is no contradiction between modernity of life and religious inclination in the country."[44] In Shi'i communities, the mujtahids have the immensely significant role of controlling and channeling change. In Shi'i Iran, for example, the success of programs of social change initiated by the secular authorities depends to a large degree upon the position taken by the mujtahids.[45]

[43] Nasr, *Ideals and Realities*, pp. 104–5.

[44] Mehdi Haeri, "Islam and the State in Iran," mimeographed paper, n.p., p. 7.

[45] For three excellent sources that accurately present the complex role of Shi'ism and the mujtahids in society and politics, see Hamid Algar, *Religion and State in Iran 1785–1906* (Berkeley and Los Angeles: University of California Press, 1969) ; Leonard Binder, "The Proofs of Islam: Religion and Politics in Iran," in *Arabic and Islamic Studies in Honor of Hamilton A. R. Gibb*, ed. George Makdisi (Cambridge: Harvard University Press, 1965) , pp. 118–40; and Charles F. Gallagher, *Contemporary*

Islam has in the past always managed to respond to the challenges of change in a wide variety of ways. Certainly it will respond to the contemporary processes of modernization, although it is difficult to ascertain exactly what form this response will take. The ulema will increasingly make pronouncements that will liberalize the role of women, support land reform programs, encourage economic reorganization, facilitate the growth of a new literature, and make it possible for Muslims to participate in the broad stream of world culture. The religious leaders will do this, however, in a manner that will make modernization palatable to Islamic doctrine. At times, they will be forced to follow the lead of politically perceptive leaders who have their own reasons for mobilizing popular support for their programs of modernization. The shape that modernization takes in the Middle East will, to a large degree, be the result of "creative tensions which have so often crackled between the religious and the political establishments."[46]

Modernization will, in fact, progress to the degree that mass support for it can be generated; this in turn is a function of the spread of communications. Modernization will proceed as money for its objects is raised and priorities for its effectuation are sorted out. Support for modernization is often, but not always, self-generating; once the material benefits of modernization become evident, rationalization will follow. The problem becomes one of finding a government strong enough to catalyze its beginnings, and one imaginative enough to select wisely among competing priorities. If Islam is not overtly denounced — indeed some effort may well be spent to placate its functionaries and laud its virtues — there may be small reaction from a citizenry eager to find a way to reconcile tradition with the glitter of something new. It is easier for this to happen in the city than in the village, and among individ-

---

Islam: The Plateau of Particularism (American Universities Field Staff: Reports Service, Southeast Asia Series, vol. 15, no. 2, 1966). For a comprehensive, sympathetic study of Shiʻism, see ʻAllāmah Sayyid Muḥammad Ḥusayn Ṭabāṭabāʼī, *Shiʻite Islam,* translated from the Persian by Seyyed Hossein Nasr (Albany: State University of New York Press, 1975).

46 Gallagher, *Contemporary Islam,* p. 2.

uals prosperous enough to share the bounties of a world culture. But eventually it will spread throughout the area.

Islam is not alone in facing modernization. Christianity is likewise encountering it. The Roman Catholic church, for example, faces enormous issues emanating from a changing society in a world culture. The beginnings of concessions on celibacy, birth control, and divorce represent the degree to which this church has already gone to pacify its critics and mollify its friends. There is no reason to believe that Islam will prove any less malleable. Although one could not say that modernization is aided by Islam in any real way, Islam will have to adjust to modernization.

The political process in the Middle East differs in a number of ways from that in the West. It is less often open, and the formal channels of political influence tend to be fewer in number and less effective. Though associational politics are rarer, those of the clique are more commonplace. All this affects the role that religion plays with respect to politics.

Islamic religious leaders have rarely been very well organized. To be sure, they have shared this weakness in most states of the Middle East with professional men, workers, and others whose strength in the West is a function of their organization at work. But Islam has never had a hierarchy, and seldom have its functionaries been able to forestall public policy except through the influence of individual leadership.[47] It has been difficult for Muslim leaders qua Muslims to play a political role. Even when they have had the desire to do so, they have often lacked the technical resources to do so. Often there is no party system, and when there is, it is rigidly controlled. In Israel, for example, religious leaders have sometimes organized their own party formations and have, as a consequence, been able to exert enormous political leverage. In most Muslim societies, on the other hand, such opportunities are less obvious. Political parties in the Islamic world tend to be con-

[47] Certainly, a good example of the power of traditional religious leadership was the boycott of the foreign tobacco concession in Iran in the late nineteenth century. The full story is told in Nikki R. Keddie, *Religion and Rebellion in Iran, the Tobacco Protest of 1891–1892* (London: Frank Cass and Co., 1966).

stellations of personal groupings. Although the groups themselves may exert considerable influence, the parties exist
largely as facades. Whatever power religious leaders exert is
wielded through these personal groups and not through more
formal party organizations.

The religious leader is compelled to fall back upon traditional and relatively ineffective means of disseminating his
views and influencing opinion. These are the Friday sermon,
informal discussions within the confines of the mosque, and
religious writings and pronouncements. On occasion, these informal contacts may be sufficient to generate political activity
on the part of followers.[48] But compared with the secular
leader — who has available to him such facilities as radio, television, newspapers, billboards, and motion pictures — the religious leader has few means of influencing opinion. Although
the religious may indeed use these same facilities, they do so
at the sufferance of the secular authorities. It is interesting
that those religious movements that have held political
strength (the Muslim Brotherhood, for example) have had to
emulate the secular system in organizational style, fund rais-
ing, and opinion formation. For all its denunciation of modernity, the Muslim Brotherhood equipped itself with the lat-
est-model printing presses and other gadgetry.

Even where moderately open party systems have not prevented their entry, overt religious parties have not been
greatly successful. In Israel, there is nothing to prevent the

[48] The following example, with respect to the Persian land reform, is
drawn from Ann K. S. Lambton, *The Persian Land Reform 1962–1966*
(Oxford: Clarendon Press, 1969). It illustrates the continuing strength of
the religious leader in a modernizing society. "On 23 February 1960
Ayatullah Burujirdi, the leading religious dignitary of the day, wrote to
Sayyid Ja'far Bihbahani, one of the deputies of the National Consultative
Assembly, stating that for some time there had been rumors that the size
of landed estates was to be limited, and that he had informed the prime
minister personally, and the Shah in writing, that such a step would be
contrary to the laws of Islam" (p. 56). Burujirdi developed considerable
support, naturally from many landlords, and although the bill was passed
at that time, it was, in the words of Ann Lambton, "window dressing"; its
implementation had been seriously undercut by religious opposition. Note
briefly in contrast how futile Catholic excommunication of Communists
in Eastern Europe in the late 1940s was in affecting political policy of the
regimes there.

growth of the religious party itself; indeed, the nature of the electoral law encourages the formation of splinter parties. Although religious parties have influence beyond their numbers because party coalitions in the Knesset invariably need their support, they have had no broad-scale appeal among the masses.

There does not seem to be a way for "Islam," without an organized hierarchy, and without great fortune in political opportunity, to carry on effective political activity except through sporadic, and usually face-to-face, attempts to influence. It is important to be clear here. Islamic influence and control are strongest when maintaining the status quo in a backward community — in a Yemen or an Oman — where Islam does not have to compete with a political authority possessing facilities disproportionate to its own. In an industrializing nation, the gap between political and religious authority in facilities for dissemination of opinions becomes progressively greater. In time it is possible to imagine a reconstituted religious authority competing on more equal terms, but this can come about only after the first fever of modernization has passed.

JUDAISM IN THE MIDDLE EAST

The ancestral home of the Jews was in Palestine (Canaan), from which they were generally expelled by the Romans in the second century.[49] The result was the Diaspora, in which Jews were dispersed over most of the Western world. There was to be no real return until the twentieth century.

The term *Sephardim* was given to those who originally lived in Spain and Portugal, and *Ashkenazim* to those whose roots were in Central and Eastern Europe. More recently, the former has come to mean simply the Oriental Jew and the latter the European Jew. There was, of course, a dispersal of Jews

---

[49] "A distinction should be made between two terms — Exile, which means a compulsory banishment, and Diaspora, which signifies a voluntary scattering. Both have been part of Jewish existence from earliest history. Exile became Diaspora when the Jews adjusted themselves to their new environment." Abba Eban, *My People: The Story of the Jews* (New York: Random House, 1968), p. 108.

that antedates Rome and certainly preceded the Muslim conquests of the seventh and later centuries. After the rise of
Islam, the Jewish communities within the Arabian peninsula
proper gradually faded, with the exception of the community
in Yemen.

Throughout North Africa, however, and in the peripheral
Arab territories (Iraq, Syria, Palestine), as well as in Turkey,
Iran, and Afghanistan, there were sizeable Jewish communities
that had flourished for centuries. Flourishing in many cases
meant merely surviving. Nevertheless, both before and after
the rise of Islam, many Jews engaged in professions and occupations that were discouraged for Christians and/or Muslims
(for example, moneylending and goldsmithing). Generally,
the Jews were not discriminated against, although from time
to time they were forced to wear distinctive clothing. The
principle was established by Samuel in the third century "that,
where it does not conflict with Judaism's religious demands,
the civil law of the country in which Jews are living must be
considered religiously binding for the Jew."[50] In any case, the
Jewish minority rarely gave its hosts any trouble.

Those Jewish communities in French North Africa suffered
some disabilities with the departure of the French in the early
1960s. This was particularly true in Algeria, but Morocco and
Tunisia, as moderate states on the Arab-Israeli dispute, were
much more congenial to the survival of a Jewish minority.
Jews continue to live in Turkey,[51] Iran, and Afghanistan. The
once prosperous community in Egypt — numbering 75,000 as

50 Jakob J. Petuchowski, "Judaism Today," in Arberry, *Religion in the
Middle East*, vol. 1, p. 5.
51 The Jews did not play any great role in the Ottoman Empire. They
suffered some disabilities but were not generally persecuted. By the time
of the Young Turks, however, one Jew, Çavid (Djavid) Bey had risen to
the rank of finance minister. (But Bernard Lewis says, "Çavid, who did
play a role of great importance, was a *dönme* [a Judeo-Islamic syncretist
sect founded in the seventeenth century] and not a real Jew; he seems in
any case to have been the only member of his community to reach front
rank" [*The Emergence of Modern Turkey*, p. 212]). Between 1942 and
1944 the Turkish government instituted a capital levy with no published
or set rates that was discriminatorily applied to "non-Turks," particularly
the Greeks, Armenians, and Jews. Lewis refers to it as the "misbegotten
offspring of German racialism on Ottoman fanaticism" (Ibid., p. 300; see
also pp. 297–302).

recently as 1950[52] — for a time all but disappeared. It may perhaps regain some of its vitality with the Egyptian-Israeli rapprochement. Jews in Syria and Iraq suffered considerable harassment, and most left for Israel. In Yemen, a community of Jews existed probably from the time of the destruction of the first Temple.[53] With a few exceptions, this entire community removed to Israel between 1948 and 1962. At the end of the Second World War, perhaps a million Jews lived in the Middle East other than in Palestine; today probably less than 20 percent remain.[54]

Consequently, among the Middle Eastern states, Judaism is of importance today only in Israel. However, we must briefly ask two questions. How resilient has Judaism been over the centuries? To what degree does it aid or impede modernization in Israel?

We can state in general that a religious minority, particularly when it suffers persecution, tends toward the conservation of its traditional principles. Reform in such a situation becomes compromise with those who seek to destroy the oppressed religion. Although Judaism had undergone many alterations prior to 1948, these alterations largely occurred during those times when, and in those places where, the Jewish community had become large enough to acquire confidence and free enough to indulge in reform. This meant, for example, Germany (reform here was associated with such names as Abraham Geiger, Samuel Holdheim, Zacharias Frankel, and Samson Hirsch) and the United States (Isaac Wise, Solomon Schechter, and Mordecai M. Kaplan) in the nineteenth century.[55]

As Jakob J. Petuchowski has said, "German Judaism provided the ideologies and the religious reforms which enabled the Western Jew, qua Jew, to enter the world of modernity. Russian Judaism maintained the reservoir of traditional Jew-

---

[52] H. Z. Hirschberg, "The Oriental Jewish Communities," in Arberry, *Religion in the Middle East,* vol. 1, p. 215.

[53] See S. D. Goitein, "The Jews of Yemen," in Arberry, *Religion in the Middle East,* vol. 1, pp. 226–35.

[54] Estimate based on H. Z. Hirschberg, "The Oriental Jewish Communities," p. 223.

[55] Jakob J. Petuchowski, "Judaism Today," passim.

ish existence. But it was in America that the Judaisms of West and East were given an unhindered opportunity to test their mettle and their ability to adapt themselves to unprecedented circumstances."[56] The Yemeni Jews can be said to illustrate the relatively unchanging nature of a very small minority living without encouragement from or much contact with the outside world. They supported little reform.[57]

Judaism has displayed a resilience, conservative in adversity, but reformist under favorable circumstances. The existence of Israel has, of course, given Jews a majority status for the first time in many centuries. Jews can now live, at least in Israel, without constant contact with the sources of anti-Semitism. This has led an observer, Georges Friedmann, to suggest in his *Fin du Peuple Juif?* that Judaism under such unfamiliar conditions may suffer all sorts of alterations, including perhaps its own destruction.

Israel had indeed faced two very practical problems: (1) political survival in the midst of a hostile Arab community; and (2) the creation of a suitable environment for the preservation and nourishment of a number of diverse cultural strains of Judaism. Whatever religious homogeneity is achieved will reflect these two forces. Idiosyncratic religion will have to give way to the practical exigencies of cultural and political survival. This problem is even more acute for the Jews than it is for the Muslims.

Although some Israeli Jews are so extreme as to deny the legitimacy of Israel itself, and although successive Israeli governments have had to live with the political pressures emanating from their need for parliamentary support from the small, religious parties, there seems little doubt that Judaism in Israel is undergoing considerable change. The nature of Israel has forced technological modernization upon it, regardless of what otherwise might have happened. The same process has produced great changes in the role of women and the cultural standards of the past. Prime Minister Golda Meir is not the only Israeli woman to have occupied what in the Middle East is a man's position. The very diversity of the Israeli

---

[56] Ibid., p. 37.
[57] See S. D. Goitein, "The Jews of Yemen."

population, containing every degree of cultural backwardness and sophistication, has given it all the characteristics of a melting pot. Judaism is the one thing most Israelis have in common, but it is a Judaism that is itself changing. In the broad sense, the Judaism of Israel cannot be considered a serious impediment to modernizing tendencies. Israel is, of course, unique in that it was formed solely as a religious haven for one particular people. The normal concepts of religious toleration and freedom must be reinterpreted within this context.

OTHER MIDDLE EASTERN RELIGIOUS FORCES

Religions other than Islam and Judaism (and the latter only in Israel) are of relatively little consequence in the contemporary Middle East. Nowhere are the other religious groups a majority, not even the Christians in Lebanon. And only in Lebanon do Christians play a major role in politics.

In the Middle East, Christian communities have had to adopt the characteristics of minorities. They have become unbending and unresponsive. Everywhere without authority, and with survival their main concern, Middle Eastern Christians have not been overly eager to adapt. Nevertheless, secularism has swept into these communities. Christianity is hardly an obstacle to modernization, but this is because it has no power with which to obstruct. Surely these characteristics apply to the Copts in Egypt, who number approximately four million in a total population of 40 million. Even the Muslims recognize that the Copts are pure Egyptians and that there cannot be any thought of expelling them. But the Revolution in 1952 did nothing to favor them; they had greater opportunities under the old regime. They are discriminated against in all sorts of small and subtle ways. They are virtually powerless, and most of their energies are spent in trying to survive in an environment generally unsympathetic to them.[58]

---

[58] In 1977, the Coptic community in Egypt (and overseas) was thrown into a frenzy by publicized draft legislation that called for the death penalty for apostasy from Islam. With the current resurgence of religious extremism in Egypt, such concern could be well founded. In this instance, President Sadat gave strong reassurances to the Copts and had the offending legislation altered. It is of interest that President Sadat, in his

The same is true of Bahaism and Zoroastrianism in Iran.
The former still remains strongly aggressive in expansion.
Zoroastrianism is but a relic of its former glory and clings
precariously to its diminished population.

Everywhere religion has some impact upon the political
process. In general, modernizing societies, such as those in the
Middle East, are characterized by strong patterns of religious
influence. As societies change — and in particular, as their
political processes change — their religious patterns also
change. Nothing is stable. Although it is difficult to predict
the dimensions of all these interacting changes, it is necessary
in any analysis of political behavior to understand the religious context.

---

trials with his foreign ministry — losing two foreign ministers in a year —
has utilized the services of Professor Butros Ghali as acting foreign minister. Butros Ghali is a Copt.

CHAPTER III

The Genes of Politics:
Groups, Classes, and Families

IN THE MIDDLE EAST, individuals express their social and political demands through membership in various groups. These collectivities range from family units to class aggregations, from recreational groupings to religious affiliations, from personal cliques to political associations.[1] Middle Eastern societies contain a kaleidoscopic array of overlapping and interlocking groups in constant flux. Individuals maintain membership in a large number of groups. In so doing, they build webs of personal connections that constitute the basic sinews of the social system.

Group formations dominate the vertical dimension of stratification as family, friendship, ethnic, religious, professional, recreational, and political groups and cliques exist in a state of continual interaction. The social and political systems resemble mosaics composed of a "limitless crisscross of groups."[2] Yet this web of fluctuating groups is not a seamless one. Dif-

[1] For purposes of our analysis, a *group* is defined as a collectivity of individuals who interact in pursuance of a common interest or goal. This definition is broad enough to include aggregations exhibiting a wide variety of organizational styles, yet narrow enough to exclude collectivities of individuals who neither interact nor share similar goals.

[2] This is Arthur F. Bentley's phrase. See Bentley, *The Process of Government* (Cambridge: Harvard University Press, Belknap Press, 1967), p. 204.

fering levels of power, wealth, and prestige indicate a system of stratification the lines of which cut horizontally across other group configurations. In this sense, family, tribal, and religious groups, for example, are embedded within a structure of inter-related classes.

The key political dimensions of power and authority are shaped in the Middle East largely by the prevailing group and class structure. Political demands and policies are filtered through a complex prism of group formations, which leaves its own imprint upon the political process. Although a changing political system tends to alter the social structure, political changes are often the result of a shifting social structure. The politics of development and modernization are profoundly influenced by the patterns and processes that mark group and class relationships.

In all societies, social structure strongly influences the political process. The patterns of group interaction, however, vary considerably from one area of the world to another. Distinctive characteristics mark the styles of group and class interaction in Islamic cultures and Middle Eastern societies. Some of these patterns are congruent with patterns in other societies; some of them are not. The Middle Eastern patterns are the subject of our analysis.

GROUP STRUCTURE: VERTICAL STRATIFICATION

In the East persons were more trusted than institutions.
T. E. Lawrence, Seven Pillars of Wisdom

The Middle Easterner belongs to a number of groups that vary greatly in their membership, goals, and modes of organization. These groups also differ considerably in their capacity to further the interests of their membership. On the basis of organizational style, groups in the Middle East can be divided into two major categories, formal and informal.[3]

Formal groups are corporate collectivities that are officially

[3] The terms *formal* and *informal* risk exposing us to the criticism of ethnocentricity. From the viewpoint of many non-Westerners, even informal groups have form and can therefore be considered formal. We use the term *informal,* however, to refer to an unofficial, fluid, personalistic, and relatively covert type of group structure.

organized and visibly operating. Membership is always clearly defined and the members have specific and sharply differentiated roles. In our group taxonomy, formal groups include both associational and institutional structures.[4] Associational groups are highly organized structures that are formed for the articulation of a specific interest. Examples include trade unions, business organizations, civic clubs, and ethnic, religious, professional, and political associations. Institutional groups exist primarily to perform a certain function, but also act to present and pursue their own interests. Although officially organized, like associational groups, they generally operate somewhat more loosely. Institutional groups are usually governmental bodies and include legislatures, bureaucracies, armies, and political parties. Formal groups always maintain a corporate apparatus that includes officials and functionaries, each of whom has a clearly defined responsibility.

Informal groups are noncorporate, unofficially organized collectivities that articulate their interests in a relatively diffuse manner. This category includes such nonassociational groups as kinship, status, and regional groups, as well as anomic aggregations that tend to form spontaneously, such as crowds involved in riots and demonstrations. Most often, however, informal groups are cliques, factions, or coteries. They are highly personalistic in character and take shape on the basis of constantly fluctuating ties and relations among individuals. The personalistic and amorphous nature of informal groups enables them to maintain a degree of fluidity and flexibility that is absent in the more rigid formal types of groups.

---

[4] Associational and institutional interest groups are part of an important typology of groups developed by Gabriel Almond in his comparative study of political systems. For the original presentation of this schema, see Gabriel A. Almond and James S. Coleman, eds., *The Politics of the Developing Areas* (Princeton, N.J.: Princeton University Press, 1960), pp. 33–38; Gabriel A. Almond and G. Bingham Powell, Jr., *Comparative Politics: A Developmental Approach* (Boston: Little, Brown and Co., 1966), pp. 74–78; and Gabriel A. Almond and G. Bingham Powell, Jr., *Comparative Politics: System, Process, and Policy*, 2d ed. (Boston: Little, Brown and Co., 1978), pp. 169–76. The 1978 study places a noticeably stronger emphasis upon nonassociational, informal groups.

Patterns of Group Interaction. Political associations that have been able to take effective action have been conspicuously absent in the social history of the Islamic Middle East. Even economic associational groups have been of limited significance, despite the appearance and growth of trade union organizations during this century. Nor does the mere existence of associational groups necessarily indicate that they play an active role in the sociopolitical life of the area. Often they exist only as empty organizational shells while their functions are performed by other structures. This generalization is, of course, more applicable to certain Middle Eastern countries than to others. In Morocco, Algeria, Turkey, and Bahrain, labor unions not only exist, but occasionally have had an appreciable impact upon political processes. In Iran and Iraq, on the other hand, the existence of modest union organization has been more a facade than a force. In still other countries, such as Saudi Arabia and Afghanistan, this particular associational group has yet to make a credible appearance.

Institutional groups hold a more central position in Middle Eastern political history than do associational groups. Although parliaments and political parties are recently established institutional groups, bureaucracies and armies are institutional groups of a more ancient vintage. Thus, while associations are generally twentieth-century phenomena in the Middle East, certain institutional groups have roots that extend back to pre-Islamic days. These groups, however, have tended to be large, sprawling conglomerations such as personal cliques, familial networks, and regional factions. The Middle Eastern military today is indeed often analyzed in terms of various officer cliques, while the bureaucracies are described on the basis of administration rent by factionalism.

Associational and institutional groups that have played a critical role in Western political systems have been considerably less significant in the Middle Eastern context. The dominant group structure in the Islamic world has been the informal group.[5] Group organization hardens around particu-

---

[5] As we will see in Chapter IV, informality is one of the major characteristics of patrimonial social and political systems.

lar individuals and kinship structures. Small, shifting clusters of individuals form cliques that resemble one another only in their personalistic, informal, fragmented mode of organization. Political decisions are made in the context of this kind of group, and who holds power and authority is primarily determined within this same setting. Formal groups exist either as extraneous facades or as general structures within which small, informal groups carry out their important activities. Informal groups penetrate and many times suffuse the more formal aggregations. Decisions attributable to the formal organization may in fact be the product of a parasitical informal group within it. In local Moroccan politics, for example, political parties are perceived by the people "as amalgamations of individuals bound together by a multiplicity of different personal ties rather than by any all-pervasive organizational structure or ideological commitment . . ."[6] In Lebanon, "loyalty to patrons, relatives or nonrelatives, takes precedence over loyalty to labor unions."[7] In national Iranian politics, the *majlis,* or parliament, "masks a fluctuating and fractionating network of personal cliques, and it is here where decisions are made and business is transacted."[8] The army in such countries as Iraq and Syria has been described as a "collection of factions" because its officers are deeply involved in politics.[9] The situation is excellently summarized by Clifford Geertz: "Structure after structure — family, village, clan, class, sect, army, party, elite, state — turns out, when more

[6] Lawrence Rosen, "Rural Political Process and National Political Structure in Morocco," in *Rural Politics and Social Change in the Middle East,* eds. Richard Antoun and Iliya Harik (Bloomington: Indiana University Press, 1972), p. 229. One scholar of Middle Eastern sociology goes so far as to posit the "uselessness" of the concept of political party in the Middle Eastern context. See C. A. O. van Nieuwenhuijze, *Sociology of the Middle East: A Stocktaking and Interpretation* (Leiden: E. J. Brill, 1971), p. 497.

[7] Fuad I. Khuri, "The Changing Class Structure in Lebanon," *Middle East Journal* 23 (Winter 1969):40.

[8] James A. Bill, "The Politics of Legislative Monarchy: The Iranian Majlis," in *Comparative Legislative Systems,* eds. Herbert Hirsch and M. Donald Hancock (New York: The Free Press, 1971), p. 365.

[9] See P. J. Vatikiotis, *Conflict in the Middle East* (London: George Allen and Unwin, 1971), p. 108.

narrowly looked at, to be an *ad hoc* constellation of miniature systems of power, a cloud of unstable micropolitics, which compete, ally, gather strength, and very soon overextended, fragment again."[10]

The growth of effective formal groups in the Middle East has been stunted by a number of interrelated factors. These are the technical, social, economic, and political conditions of organization. The formation of a viable formal-group structure requires a certain kind of organizational skill, a minimal level of trust and cooperation, a considerable pool of funds for equipment and staffing, and a willingness on the part of political elites to tolerate the existence of such groups. In Middle Eastern societies, these conditions of organization are seldom all present at once. Social and political demands, therefore, are formulated and presented in a much different organizational environment. Groups are necessarily more limited in size in order to maximize trust and cooperative endeavor. Group members protect the private and secret nature of their proceedings in order to strengthen their position against both rival groups and the national political regime. Individuals attempt to retain the greatest possible personal freedom, so that they may move in and out of groups depending upon their perception of their own best interests. This in turn promotes considerable fluidity and fragmentation, since group memberships continually change in a manner that defies any rigidity, officiality, or formal routinization.

Besides these negative reasons for the lack of effective formal groups in the Middle East, there are a number of positive explanations. Small, informal groups are able to attain their common goals readily enough to preclude the need for larger groups. Over the centuries in the Islamic world, these small groups have simply proven to be more efficient and effective structures than larger groups. Recent research by economists and political scientists who work with "collective good" theory casts serious doubt on the assumption that it is rational

---

[10] Clifford Geertz, "In Search of North Africa," *New York Review of Books* 16 (22 April 1971) , p. 20, as quoted in Dale F. Eickelman, "Is There an Islamic City? The Making of a Quarter in a Moroccan Town," *International Journal of Middle East Studies* 5 (June 1974) :280.

for individual members of a large group to work to achieve the collective good of that group.[11] Instead, it is argued that the individual who fails to contribute to the large group will still stand to share in the reward once the group's goal is attained. In large groups, it may well be that an individual's effort will make no perceptible difference in the attainment of the group's goal. In this situation, the rational individual will not contribute his efforts. Such is the case in most associational and institutional groups.

In a smaller group, each individual's efforts are more likely to make a difference in attaining the group's goal. And in such a group the individual will be much more susceptible to the pressures of other group members, who can further cooperation through mutual personal persuasion. In Middle Eastern social history, where action groups have been not only small, but highly personalistic, this has been especially true. In the Middle East, there is much doubt about the efficacy of membership in, or attachment to, large or mass institutional groups. Personal ties based upon kinship, friendship, and religious and regional affiliation have been among the best means of insuring effective individual effort.[12]

One further reason for the emphasis on personal ties in the Islamic Middle East has been a belief that nobility and generosity of manner are virtues. Individuals in Islamic culture who believed in these virtues joined various brotherhoods and guilds that incorporated characteristics of both formal and

11 For the basic presentation of this theoretical approach, see Mancur Olson, Jr., *The Logic of Collective Action: Public Goods and the Theory of Groups* (New York: Schocken Books, 1968).

12 Ibn Khaldun's theory of social solidarity (*asabiyya*) proposes that *asabiyya* is critical to successful group activity and ultimately to civilization. *Asabiyya* is the cement of human relations and is based first upon common ancestry and eventually upon common interest and life experience. *Asabiyya* was most easily developed in small, informal, and highly personalistic groups. As Muhsin Mahdi writes: "Solidarity comes into being as a result of common ancestry, but it is usually sustained by external factors: the feeling of relatedness is dictated by the necessity of cooperation and self-defense." (Muhsin Mahdi, *Ibn Khaldūn's Philosophy of History* [London: George Allen and Unwin, 1957], p. 197.) See Ibn Khaldun's own writings about group formation in the Islamic world in *The Muqaddimah: An Introduction to History*, trans. Franz Rosenthal (Princeton, N.J.: Princeton University Press, 1967).

informal organization. These guilds and brotherhoods have been important political aggregations throughout the history of the Islamic world. The Islamic guild, for example, has generally represented the interests of the lower-class and lower-middle-class members of society. It "was a spontaneous development from below, created, not in response to a State need, but to the social requirements of the labouring masses themselves. Save for one brief period, the Islamic guilds have maintained either an open hositility to the State, or an attitude of sullen mistrust, which the public authorities, political and ecclesiastical, have always returned."[13]

The early craft guilds closely resembled Byzantine structures and were organized on the basis of a common craft or skill. With the passage of time, and particularly following the rise of the Qarmatian (Carmathian) movement during the ninth to the twelfth centuries,[14] the guilds became deeply infused with a moral and often mystical spirit. This contributed greatly to organizational cohesion and inspired the members to dedicate themselves to furthering group goals. Although the various guilds and brotherhoods had differing organizational emphases, they generally blended formal and informal characteristics. Although they exhibited such formal accoutrements of organization as elaborate ceremonial activity and a rigid internal hierarchy, they were also intensely personalistic and highly secretive. The term *tariqa* ("brotherhood" or "order") literally means a "way" or "path" and refers to a

[13] Bernard Lewis, "The Islamic Guilds," *Economic History Review* 8 (1937) : 35–36. The research of Gabriel Baer indicates that the craft guilds were both more formally organized and more closely linked to the government than is commonly thought. Baer's arguments, however, are most applicable to guild structures after the eighteenth century. And the brotherhoods were always better examples than the guilds of the type of informal group that existed in opposition to governmental power. The state was better able to infiltrate and control guild structures than brotherhood organizations. For Baer's conclusions concerning Turkish guilds, see "The Administrative, Economic, and Social Functions of Turkish Guilds," *International Journal of Middle East Studies* 1 (January 1970) :28–50.

[14] This was a great liberal movement that swept through the Muslim world, advocating social reform in general and justice and equality in particular. The movement appealed to all classes, sects, and religions but found special acceptance among the artisans, skilled, and semiskilled workers. See L. Massignon, "Karmatians," *The Encyclopaedia of Islam,* 4 vols. (Leiden: E. J. Brill, 1927) , 2:767–72.

mode of conduct, not to a formal association.[15] Thus, in the Middle Eastern context, even structures as corporate as guilds have an element of informality that renders them a highly diversified composite of organizational types. Like the familial group, which we will discuss below, the guild manages to span the formal-informal dichotomy.

Since informal-group activity is herein considered the most dominant form of group politics in the Middle East, the following discussion will emphasize this type of group rather than associational and institutional groups. This does not mean that we choose to ignore the latter, but rather that we will accord them an emphasis somewhat more commensurate with the political influence they wield in the area of our investigation. To state it quite baldly, a Middle Eastern legislature, for example, is much less important as a decision-making apparatus than are the informal groups that penetrate it, control it, and most importantly, survive it.[16]

---

[15] This point is made in Fazlur Rahman, *Islam* (Garden City, N.Y.: Anchor Books, 1968) , pp. 189–90; and in Morroe Berger, *Islam in Egypt Today* (Cambridge: Cambridge University Press, 1970) , p. 67.

[16] In an ill-fated attempt to demonstrate the importance of both legislatures and the need to study them in order to understand the essence of Afro-Asian politics, one scholar recently chose to base his conclusions on Lebanon. Thus, on what must have been the very eve of the civil war, the author writes that ". . . contrary to the prevalent social science characterization of the Lebanese political leadership as a fractured elite that is divided along sectarian lines, the present-day leaders display a large degree of consensus especially with regard to the political, social, and economic fundamentals of the system. The various ministerial statements, the roll calls, the parliamentary discussion and the leaders' public statements reveal a close consensus with regard to the main issues and goals of Lebanese politics." He goes on to write: "There is an air of confidence in the system, that it has the ability to change structurally and procedurally." And the chapter on legislative and political development ends with this sentence: "Through the stability of its political institutions, Lebanon has achieved its socioeconomic goals without violent changes." Abdo I. Baaklini, *Legislative and Political Development: Lebanon, 1842–1972* (Durham, N.C.: Duke University Press, 1976) , pp. 270–72, 280. In the fall of 1977, the Beirut Chamber of Commerce and Industry reported that the nineteen-month civil war had had such a devastating effect on the country that its consequences could throw Lebanon back among the ranks of the underdeveloped nations. Losses in the private sector of the economy amounted to about $1 billion; 6 percent of the work force were killed in the fighting; and 13 percent fled the country. See the *Christian Science Monitor*, 11 October 1977, p. 2.

The Politics of Informal Groups. Informal groups, usually referred to as cliques or factions, are a fundamental unit of political action in many societies. In contrast to northern and Eastern European, North American, and Australian societies, where formal groups play a prominent role, the informal group is dominant in southern European, North African, Middle Eastern, Asian, and Latin American cultures. It is true that wherever human beings are gathered, they will develop informal groups. Thus, in American society there are many obvious manifestations of informal-group politics. But even within the United States, the tendency to organize informal rather than formal groups differs in strength from one area of the country to another. In the South and the Southwest, nonassociational groups are prevalent. This once led an observer to characterize the state of Louisiana as "the westernmost of the Arab states."[17] Generally, however, the American political process places relatively less emphasis upon informal groups and relatively more upon such aggregates as trade unions, legislatures, and political parties. This is not the case in much of the world. Studies of Brazil, India, Burma, Taiwan, Japan, and Italy, for example, impressively show that informal- and nonassociational-group politics are dominant in these societies.[18]

The gradual recognition of the critical role that informal groups play in the less industrialized world has been recently accompanied by preliminary analysis emphasizing this phenomenon by a small number of scholars of contemporary Middle

[17] For reference to this memorable quote, see T. Harry Williams, *Huey Long* (New York: Bantam Books, 1970) , p. 194.

[18] A growing number of political scientists, heavily influenced by the patron-client analysis of anthropologists, now stress the important connection between personalistic group structures and politics in the developing world. These studies contain much that is relevant to the Middle East. See, for example, René Lemarchand and Keith Legg, "Political Clientelism and Development," *Comparative Politics* 4 (January 1972) :148–78; James C. Scott, "Patron-Client Politics and Political Change in Southeast Asia," *American Political Science Review* 66 (March 1972) :81–113; Carl H. Landé, "Networks and Groups in Southeast Asia," *American Political Science Review* 67 (March 1973) :103–27; and Arthur J. Lerman, "National Elite and Local Politician in Taiwan," *American Political Science Review* 71 (December 1977) : 1406–1422. See also Gabriel A. Almond and G. Bingham Powell, Jr., *Comparative Politics: System, Process and Policy,* 2d ed. (Boston: Little, Brown and Co., 1978) , pp. 170–74, 201–5.

Eastern political systems. Amal Vinogradov and John Waterbury, for example, introduce the term *security group* to refer to a factional group that "is the maximal unit in which
there is some predictability in the exercise of power and
authority."[19] Clement H. Moore discusses what he terms *contingent interest groups* that cut across associational interest
groups and serve as "gatekeepers" for North African political
systems. According to Moore, "examples of contingent interest
groups range from sets of Algerian cousins and fellow maqui-
sards or a Moroccan family of notables to professional veto
groups or a handful of individuals out to convince Bourguiba
that Ben Salah's Plan is a menace."[20]

The most crucial units of interest aggregation in the Middle
East remain informal groups. In Iraq this kind of collectivity
is referred to as a *shilla* or *jama'at,* and in Saudi Arabia the
term most often used is *bashka.* The Egyptians also use the
word *shilla* to refer to a group of approximately two to twelve
members who socialize together and who work to help one
another advance politically and economically. A slightly more
diffuse Egyptian informal group is the *dufaa,* or old-boy network. The *dufaa* (literally "pushing out") is often the general structure from which the more tightly knit *shillas* are
formed.[21] In Kuwait, the *diwaniya* is an informal gathering
where males meet to discuss and determine important political
questions.[22] Other words in the Arab world that carry the idea
of cliques and factions, but sometimes indicate a higher level

[19] Amal Vinogradov and John Waterbury, "Situations of Contested Legitimacy in Morocco: An Alternative Framework," *Comparative Studies in
Society and History* 13 (January 1971) : 34.

[20] Clement Henry Moore, *Politics in North Africa: Algeria, Morocco, and
Tunisia* (Boston: Little, Brown and Co., 1970) , pp. 201–2.

[21] Robert Springborg deserves the credit for introducing the dynamics
of informal group politics in Egypt to Western political science. See, for
example, his provocative article "Patterns of Association in the Egyptian
Political Elite," in *Political Elites in the Middle East,* ed. George Lenczowski (Washington, D.C.: American Enterprise Institute, 1975), pp. 83–107.

[22] The political significance of the *diwaniya* in Kuwait is discussed by
Tawfic E. Farah and Faisal Al-Salem in their excellent paper, "Size, Af-
fluence, and Efficacy: Regime Effectiveness in Kuwait," delivered at the
Annual Meeting of the Midwest Political Science Association, Chicago,
Illinois, 20 April 1978.

of formality, include *kutal* and *fi'at*. In Iran, the sociopolitical system is backed by a gigantic network of informal, personalistic cliques referred to as *dawrahs* ("circles"). Afghan group dynamics are dominated by loose factional aggregates referred to as either *dastahs* ("handfuls of individuals") or *girdabs* ("little whirlpools"). One of the most important of the informal groups in Turkey is the personal collectivity based on *hemşeri* ("from the same region") relations. The *hemşerilik* is a group that forms and re-forms as fellow villagers and "hometowners" aggregate to assist one another with social, economic, occupational, and political aims.[23] In Egypt, the same kind of group formation prevails in the *baladiyya,* which is in fact a kind of informal, expanded-family group.[24]

The juxtaposition of informal groups with formal political associations is seen in the case of Bahrain, an archipelago off the coast of Saudi Arabia, just west of the Qatar peninsula. An early modernizer, Bahrain is the oldest petroleum-producing state in the Persian Gulf and had already established a girls' school in 1928. Strikes and labor unrest have occurred in this small shaykhdom ever since the mid-1950s. Ruled absolutely by the al-Khalifa family, this country has nonetheless had notable experience with municipal and national consultative bodies. But the actual politics of Bahrain have taken place within an extensive network of clubs *(nawadi)* and societies *(jam'iyyat)*. Numbering approximately one hundred, these informal groups, "whose memberships include a majority of Bahrain's elite public, have played the essential functions performed by political parties in other political systems."[25] Ostensibly organized for social, professional, and

[23] For an excellent analysis of the critical importance of hemşeri relations in Turkey, see Allen Dubetsky, "Kinship, Primordial Ties, and Factory Organization in Turkey: An Anthropological View," *International Journal of Middle Eastern Studies* 7 (July 1976) :433–51.

[24] See Mona Sedky, "Groups in Alexandria, Egypt," *Social Research* 22 (1955) :441–50.

[25] Emile Nakhleh, *Bahrain: Political Development in a Modernizing Society* (Lexington, Mass.: Lexington Books, 1976), p. 41. Most of the information in this paragraph is drawn from the Nakhleh book. For another excellent analysis of Bahraini politics, see John Duke Anthony, *Arab States of the Lower Gulf* (Washington, D.C.: The Middle East Institute, 1975), pp. 45–73.

recreational purposes, these clubs are often intensely political. The 250-member al-Arabi Club, for example, is composed of educated workers who push for nationalistic and democratic goals. The Alumni Club, on the other hand, is oriented more toward the elite and consists of college-educated intellectuals from both the middle and upper classes. It is the establishment's liberal conscience. These kinds of informal groups in Bahrain coexist both with formal organizations and with the ruling family, whose tentacles reach deep down into the club network. The National Assembly first convened in December 1973 was dissolved twenty months later; the clubs persist.

Informal-group activity in the Middle East has manifested itself in a myriad of ways. Ranging from tiny dyads that plug in and out of one another depending upon mutual needs to enormously complex coalitions based on kinship, these groups have little in common besides their personal, informal nature. Personal homes have served as locations for the meetings of the more exclusive of the groups, while mosques, coffeehouses, teahouses, common rooms, and bazaar shops have served as meeting places for the more inclusive of the groups. Informal groups operating in these kinds of settings constantly relay information through the various societies. It is largely on the basis of this information that personal and political decisions are made. And, it may be added, it is in precisely such groups and such settings that middle-grade army officers sometimes decide to intervene in the political affairs of their countries. Clandestine activities are, of course, universally informal in nature.

One of the important characteristics of informal-group politics is an intense and pervasive spirit of personalism. The fundamental social and political ties tend to be personal in nature.[26] In moving into a wide variety of informal groups, the individual strives to broaden his range of personal contacts in order to gain representation on as many fronts as possible. What determines the Middle Easterner's power and influence "is not the fact that he holds a certain office or even

[26] See Chapter IV for a detailed discussion of personalism in the Middle Eastern variant of patrimonial politics.

that that office affords certain opportunities for personal aggrandizement but the extent and success with which he as an
individual is able to cumulate a wide range of personal ties, to
display to others a number of highly valued personal characteristics, and . . . to merge them into a larger framework
of political importance reaching up to the very highest government levels."[27] In this kind of environment, individuals
develop great skill at personal persuasion as they seek their
political goals. Decision making is determined by personal
push and pull, as is interestingly indicated by the Turkish
expression *torpil* and the Iranian term *parti*. While the personal element tends to be obliterated in formal groups, the
informal group manages to preserve and promote this characteristic.

The personal nature of group politics in the Middle East
is exemplified well by the Lebanese *zu'ama* system (singular:
za'im). In contemporary Lebanon, the za'im is an informal
group leader whose followers support him on the basis of
personal loyalty and personal rewards. The personal power
of the za'im is rooted in local and regional communities, and
is buttressed by the fact that the leader and his followers share
a common religion or sect. Among the important zu'ama families are the Frangiehs (Maronites), the Jumblatts (Druze),
the Shihabs (Sunnites), and the al-As'ads (Shi'ites). Leaders
with names such as these have been present for years in the
national political institutions of Lebanon. The *zu'ama* system
continues to shape the Lebanese political process in a significant way.

At the level of the informal group, the argument that Middle Eastern politics are basically nonideological would seem to
be highly credible. Commitments are more often to individuals than to ideas. The precedence of strong personal ties over
ties to ideology is seen in the striking examples of family units
containing all shades of political and professional commitment. The Marei family in Egypt is a case in point. The father was a well-to-do supporter of the old regime and a
member of the Wafd party. During the period of Nasser's rule,
the family maintained its influence. One brother, Hassan

27 Rosen, "Rural Political Process," p. 216.

Marei, was appointed minister of commerce and industry in Nasser's cabinet in April 1954. Sayyid Marei, another brother, who was a member of parliament for six years during the Farouk era, served as minister of agriculture for an extended period during the Nasser years. He was also an official in the Arab Socialist Union for a time. During these years, the Marei family had the added connection of their more radical cousin Ali Sabry, a former member of the Free Officers, secretary-general of the Arab Socialist Union, and one of Nasser's five premiers. Despite Sabry's removal from power by President Anwar Sadat in May 1971 and his subsequent imprisonment, the Marei brothers have survived well. Sayyid indicated the family's continuing ability to transcend administrations when he was appointed deputy premier and minister of agriculture in Sadat's September 1971 cabinet. Since 1974, he has been speaker of the parliament, and in 1975 his son married President Sadat's daughter. Hassan remains influential in the industrial community, and a third brother has been both a successful businessman and a director of a state holding company.[28]

This pattern of family tenacity and ideological malleability has also prevailed in such countries as Iran, Iraq, Lebanon, and Morocco. Even the leading families of the very conservative shaykhdoms of the Persian Gulf have had members who have espoused radical causes. Shaykh Saqr bin Sultan, who ruled Sharjah between 1951 and 1965, is a notable example. Saqr, a strong Arab nationalist with Nasserist sympathies and a dislike for the British, was deposed in 1965, primarily for these reasons. In 1972, he returned from exile in Cairo and failed in an attempt to regain the throne. He is now under arrest in Abu Dhabi.

An informal group "is like a cluster of bees round a queen bee. If the queen is damaged they quickly find another to cluster around."[29] The exigencies of politics require an indi-

---

[28] This Egyptian case study is drawn primarily from Springborg, "Patterns of Association," p. 94.

[29] This statement was made concerning informal-group poltiics in India. See B. D. Graham, "The Succession of Factional Systems in the Uttar Pradesh Congress Party, 1937–66," in *Local-Level Politics: Social and Cultural Perspectives*, Marc J. Swartz, ed. (Chicago: Aldine, 1968), p. 355.

vidual to shift positions periodically in order to maintain as much manipulative leeway as possible. The informal group itself will often switch goals and alter the idea that brought its membership together. Such changes, of course, always mean that a certain percentage of the membership will be lost, but this is one important by-product of the fluidity of this type of group. Individuals retain the capacity to circulate among a host of collectivities, depending on what they consider to be in their own interests. Coalitions are fragile and alliances fleeting in such social and political systems. Even the strongest social cement, personal ties, can be easily cracked. Yet, the adhesive quality remains, so that the relationship can be reestablished whenever the winds of fortune dictate that it be reestablished. This plasticity of informal-group politics promotes a systemic stability that is not often recognized with regard to the Middle East.

Informal groups in the Middle East are characterized by alternating fission and fusion. "It is always possible to divide them, to prevent powerful coalitions from forming, for their solidarity, of course, is inversely proportional to their breadth. Hence political showdowns rarely occur."[30] Although tension, conflict, and competition infuse this network of "many-stranded coalitions,"[31] the overall group system persists and prevails. The tension promotes balance. "Equilibrium in conflict is not achieved by both or all sides desisting from conflict but rather in both or all sides persisting in conflict. . . . The best defense of a security group lies in keeping up steady pressure against its rivals short of attack."[32] This principle of counterbalancing in group politics is prevalent throughout the Islamic Middle East, although it manifests itself somewhat differently from one society to another. In Iran and Morocco, it helps foster systemic fluidity and flexibility. In Lebanon, on the other hand, it froze into a more rigid pattern, in which

---

[30] Moore, *Politics in North Africa,* p. 202.

[31] This phrase is borrowed from Eric Wolf, *Peasants* (Englewood Cliffs, N.J.: Prentice-Hall, 1966), and is quoted in Khuri, "Changing Class Structure," p. 40.

[32] Vinogradov and Waterbury, "Situations of Contested Legitimacy," p. 35.

groups directly confronted one another. In Lebanon, the more common pattern of many sides balancing against one another gave way to confrontations between two sides. The fragility of this situation became all too clear in April 1975, when the society exploded into bloody civil war.

This network of floating factions could not persist without a sturdier group backing to help anchor it in the social structure. Individuals require a more reliable vehicle than factions and cliques to defend their interests and to achieve their goals. In the Middle East, this mechanism is the kinship group in general and the family in particular.

The Primordial Group Nexus: The Family. Kinship units are a very special kind of informal group. The family, which is the basic unit and building block of groups in the Middle East, retains characteristics that render it more rigid and formal than most factional and nonassociational groups. Although the lines of association that mark personal cliques and political factions appear and disappear with amazing rapidity, true kinship relations are much more difficult to create and destroy. Ties of kinship remain in existence whether or not political actors choose to recognize them. Since family networks are virtually impossible to rupture or break, they provide the element of permanence needed to offset the impermanence of the other informal groups. Family groupings are the linchpins of the system of group interaction in the Middle East. Indeed, lineage patterns are "the invisible skeleton of the community."[33]

The traditional Middle Eastern family unit is an extended family, usually consisting of a man, his wife (or wives), his unmarried sons and daughters, and his married sons and their wives and children. In the contemporary urban Middle East, the institution of the extended family is increasingly giving way to the nuclear family, which includes only the husband, wife, and children. Family groups, whether extended or nuclear, are consciously and carefully shaped. Marriage pat-

[33] This phrase is John Gulick's. See Gulick, *Social Structure and Culture Change in a Lebanese Village* (New York: Wenner-Gren Foundation, 1955), p. 104.

terns are critical, since they determine the direction in which the family group will move. The most distinctive traditional trait of Middle Eastern marriage is the preferred marriage of a man and his father's brother's daughter (*bint 'amm*). This paternal cousin marriage was designed to strengthen important blood ties and to solidify a constantly expanding family unit. An endogamous marriage pattern such as this one has significant political implications. In the Middle East, it enabled family heads to enlist the critical support of their brothers and their brothers' sons. In societies deeply torn by divisions and cleavages, this minimal unit of coalition was a relatively effective action group. Few family clusters could afford the internecine conflict that might otherwise have occured between brothers, nephews, and cousins.[34]

Every individual in the Middle East thus begins with membership in one important informal group, the family. This group seeks to magnify its kinship ties in at least three different ways. First, contacts are strengthened and communication is routinized with as many blood relatives as is practically possible. Second, family contacts are broadened by the incorporation of new individuals through marriage. As we noted above, special emphasis seems to be placed in the Middle East upon the reinforcement of intrafamilial blood lines, rather than upon attempts to bring new blood into the family. (Both strategies, however, have been common in the Middle East.) Third, kinship ties are often fictitiously manufactured in an attempt to enhance the influence of a particular individual or group. The most common examples of fictive kinship are elaborate genealogical arguments that purport to document one's direct descent from the family of the Prophet Muhammad.

For the family group to remain strong, its members must maintain a continually updated knowledge of the intricate kinship structure to which they belong. In the Ottoman system, for example, "every member of the clan kept a genealogical

---

[34] For a fascinating discussion of the marriage patterns of Middle Eastern families, see Raphael Patai, *Golden River to Golden Road: Society, Culture, and Change in the Middle East,* 3d ed. (Philadelphia: University of Pennsylvania Press, 1969) , pp. 135–76.

map in his head to orient him in his relations with others."[35] In Turkey, the situation is one "of everyone having to know very precisely to what extended family, to what kin village, to what lineage, to what clan, to what clan federation and to what principality or khanate he belongs."[36] This awareness of precisely where one stands with regard to other group members contributes greatly to group solidarity, and ultimately to the capacity to attain group objectives. Strands of kinship serve, at the very least, as relatively permanent lines of access among group members. It is in the individual's self-interest to be familiar with as many of these connections as possible.

Like all other group formations in the Middle East, the kinship group (whether family, tribe, or clan) is internally divided and fragmented. Intrafamilial tensions, quarrels, and feuds are common in Islamic cultures. Yet, within the nuclear family, the divisions are not as deep, nor are the tensions as intense, as they are outside the family. More important, the kinship group presents a united front against outside competitors. Fragmented collectivities gain solidarity and cohesion through the pressure exerted by external rival forces. In this system of balancing opposition, the family unit always fares best. This is because the kinship group is the most cohesive and tenacious of the Middle Eastern group formations.

In addition to being both a biological and an economic unit, the family is very much a political aggregation. Family members support one another in their drives to attain important goals and to improve their respective power and authority positions in the particular community or society. "As a unit in terms of authority, it [the family] is the base line for traditional social organization. The traditional authority pattern of the Middle East along with the traditional social structure, pivots around the kinship principle."[37] Besides providing sup-

---

[35] Şerif Mardin, "Historical Determinants of Stratification: Social Class and Class Consciousness in Turkey" (Paper prepared for the Comparative Bureaucracy Seminar, Massachusetts Institute of Technology, Spring 1966), p. 19.

[36] Ibid.

[37] Van Nieuwenhuijze, *Sociology of the Middle East*, p. 388. Patai writes that "the political systems in the Middle East either grew out of the

port for its members attaining political goals, the kinship group is politically relevant in many other ways. It serves, for example, as the staging ground from which individuals can move on to membership in other groups, both formal and informal. The family, in fact, determines much of its members' participation in other collectivities. Such informal groups as personal cliques and political factions have fathers, sons, brothers, nephews, cousins, and in-laws strategically sprinkled throughout them in patterns that tend to benefit the particular family unit. As often as not, a single family is represented in rival political factions, parties, or movements. Thus, although informal group membership cuts across kinship lines, it is also true that the filaments of kinship cut across the boundaries of cliques and factions. A major function of distributing family members among various other groups is the construction and maintenance of channels of communication among these groups — whether they be rivals or allies.

The ligaments of kinship bind the system of groups into a working whole. They run through rival collectivities, thus softening tensions. And, through membership in both formal and informal groups, blood relatives and in-laws help bind these two major organizational types together. Family members in such institutions as bureaucracies and parliaments are in close touch with relatives who are members of cliques and factions. Decisions made in one of the contexts are directly influenced by what occurs in the other.

Morocco has sometimes been referred to as the kingdom of cousins, and Iran is frequently called the country of one thousand families. The intricacies of family relationships explain a great deal about the orientations, formation, and behavior of political elites in the Middle East. The more traditional the society, the more useful kinship analysis will be in understanding it. In all the Middle Eastern countries, however, patterns of kinship and marriage are valuable in understanding the structure of power and authority. Those societies that are

---

lineage structure and retained its characteristics or, if they had no lineage basis, artificially assumed what can be called a lineage camouflage." Patai, *Golden River*, p. 430.

developing politically and modernizing relatively rapidly may have a relatively large number of ruling families, as well as a high rate of familial mobility. A study of such family structures can explain much about national elites and the political processes of the societies under investigation. Selected examples follow.

In the three decades prior to 1958, the Iraqi political elite represented a tight cluster of families. The core of the elite included such families as the al-Saids, the al-Askaris, the Kannas, and the Kamals. The famous Nuri al-Said held the post of prime minister fourteen times and that of minister twenty-nine times! Ja'far al-Askari, who was assassinated in 1936, was prime minister twice and minister eight times. Nuri al-Said and Ja'far al-Askari married each other's sisters. Tahsin al-Askari followed in the footsteps of his assassinated brother, Ja'far, when in 1942 he assumed two ministerial positions. He was the brother-in-law of Ibrahim Kamal, who was himself a cabinet minister twice. Another al-Askari brother, Abd al-Hadi, married his daughter to Khalil Kanna, who held ministerial posts six different times. Two of Khalil Kanna's brothers were members of the Iraqi parliament.[38] In the 1960s and 1970s, family connections became less important and commonplace of origin assumed increasing significance as a source of cohesiveness in the Iraqi political elite. In the early 1970s, for example, several key political and military figures in Iraq were natives of the town of Tikrit.

In Iran even today, national politics are dominated by family considerations, since the political elite that clusters around the ruling Pahlavi family comes from a small number of families. Among the most influential of the elite families in Iran are the following: Pahlavi, Alam, Diba, Qaragozlu, Esfandiari, Ardalan, Bayat, Sami'i, Farmanfarmaian, Akbar, Afkhami, Adl, Amuzegar, Bushehri, Eqbal, Jahanbani, Emami, and Khal'atbari. The ties among key members of these families are easily as close as the ties among families in Iraq once

---

[38] This information is drawn from Nazar T. Al-Hasso's excellent Ph.D. dissertation. See Al-Hasso, "Administrative Politics in the Middle East: The Case of Monarchical Iraq, 1920–1958" (Ph.D. diss., the University of Texas, Austin, Texas, 1976) .

were. Long-time Minister of Culture Mehrdad Pahlbod is the
husband of Princess Shams, a sister of Muhammad Reza Shah.
Former major general Minbashian is the brother of Pahlbod
(formerly Ezzatullah Minbashian). The influential Senator
Bushehri is the father of the husband of powerful Princess
Ashraf, the twin sister of the Shah. Former air force commander Muhammad Khatami was married to the Shah's sister
Fatima. Ardeshir Zahedi, Iranian ambassador to the United
States, was once married to the Shah's daughter Shahnaz. Recent prime ministers Mansur and Hoveyda married sisters
whose mother was herself the daughter of a prime minister
and a member of the very prominent Vusuq family. Hoveyda's
mother was an aristocratic Qajar princess in her own right.
And so it goes. Today, there are forty national elite families
that dominate the economic and political systems in Iran.

Family connections loom even larger in the shaykhdoms of
the Persian Gulf, where the core of the political elite always
consists of members of the ruling family. Other members of
the elite are almost without exception drawn from other
wealthy, aristocratic families. Figure III.1 represents a diagram
of the Abu Dhabi political elite as it existed in the late 1970s.
Eight of the twelve persons listed are of the ruling Al-Nuhay-
yan family. The six individuals named in the second curve of
influence are brothers who are first cousins of Shaykh Zayid.
Called the Khalifa Six after their late father, Shaykh Khalifa,
they are all relatively influential, although the degree of their
influence continually changes at Shaykh Zayid's direction. The
other four individuals are from important families that have
had a long history of close ties with the Al-Nuhayyans. The
most powerful of these four is Ahmad Suwaydi, an especially
close and trusted advisor to Shaykh Zayid. Suwaydi is Abu
Dhabi's first native college graduate and its major foreign
policy maker. The Suwaydi family has very close ties with
the ruling Al-Nuhayyans.

In Bahrain, where political and economic decision making
is dominated by Shaykh Isa bin Salman Al-Khalifa and his
brother Shaykh Khalifa bin Salman Al-Khalifa, the names of
the leading families such as Kanu, Fakru, Shirawi, and
Mu'ayyid, are well known. The following anecdote illustrates

FIGURE III.1 *The Abu Dhabi Political Elite*

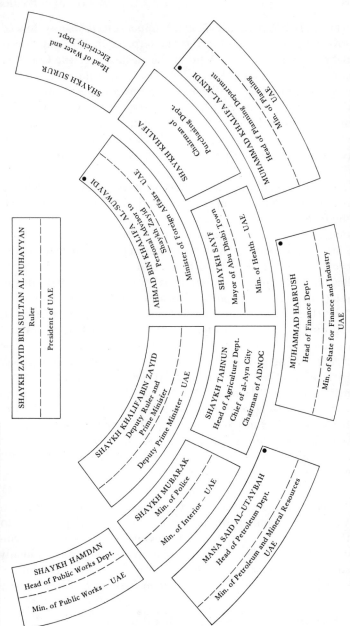

SHAYKH ZAYID BIN SULTAN AL NUHAYYAN
Ruler
— — — — —
President of UAE

SHAYKH SURUR
Head of Water and
Electricity Dept.

MUHAMMAD KHALIFA AL-KINDI
Head of Planning Department.
— — — — —
Min. of Planning — UAE

SHAYKH KHALIFA
Chairman of
Purchasing Dept.

AHMAD BIN KHALIFA AL-SUWAYDI
Personal Advisor to
Shaykh Zayid
— — — — —
Minister of Foreign Affairs — UAE

SHAYKH SAYF
Mayor of Abu Dhabi Town
— — — — —
Min. of Health — UAE

MUHAMMAD HABRUSH
Head of Finance Dept.
— — — — —
Min. of State for Finance and Industry
UAE

SHAYKH KHALIFA BIN ZAYID
Deputy Ruler and
Prime Minister
— — — — —
Deputy Prime Minister — UAE

SHAYKH TAHNUN
Head of Agriculture Dept.
Chief of al-Ayn City
Chairman of ADNOC

SHAYKH MUBARAK
Min. of Police
— — — — —
Min. of Interior — UAE

MANA SAID AL-UTAYBAH
Head of Petroleum Dept.
— — — — —
Min. of Petroleum and Mineral Resources
UAE

SHAYKH HAMDAN
Head of Public Works Dept.
— — — — —
Min. of Public Works — UAE

Designation above broken line refers to position held in Abu Dhabi
below broken line is corresponding United Arab Emirate office held

● These individuals not members of the ruling Al Nuhayyan family

that in Bahrain family is more important than any formal governing body. While in the marketplace in 1973, an elderly Bahraini was told to go vote in the elections for the Constituent Assembly. The old man looked around and asked, "Who owns that building?" "A Kanu," he was told. "And who owns this one?" "A Mu'ayyid," was the response. "And this third one?" "Shaykh Khalifa." The old man then asked, "Will the elections change any of this?"[39] The right family connections remain an important passport to the elite in much of the Middle East.

Social change and modernization have hardly lessened the role of the family group in the political arena. It is true that the form of family organization has changed considerably and that kinship relations now crystallize in new ways. The most evident change of this sort is the transfer from the extended to the nuclear family style of household. This change, however, has not fundamentally altered the important role that kinship relations play in the political process. Fuad Khuri writes that "the change from the extended family sub-culture to that of the nuclear family does not imply the loss of family ties and duties. Family ties and duties, no doubt, continue, but in new forms."[40] The physical living arrangements of the family may be changing, but its sociopolitical demands and supports remain essentially the same.

The following section presents a case study that indicates both the importance of informal politics and the special place that family relationships have in Middle Eastern politics. It should also provoke new insights into the kinds of actors and actresses who play out the political drama.

The Power of Women: A Case Study of Informal Politics. When one examines the informal nature of group politics in the Middle East, a number of previously overlooked and underemphasized dimensions of the political game suddenly come into sharper focus. Persons who were formerly considered peripheral to political decision making take on a more

---

39 This story is presented in Nakhleh, *Bahrain*, p. 129 n.
40 Khuri, "Changing Class Structure," p. 38.

central and critical significance. This is precisely the case in cultures where there is no sharp distinction between the private and the public spheres or where key community and national decisions are made in less visible, informal settings by individuals often considered peripheral to politics. An important case in point is the Middle Eastern woman.

For years, Middle Eastern women have been stereotyped as an oppressed and passive group who have been hidden by veils and whose lives have been dominated by men. Western writers in particular have presented the Muslim woman as someone held captive in the kitchen or harem while her husband frolics personally and protects politically a system of polygamy that rationalizes female servitude. Quotations from the Quran and the relative absence of female actresses on the public political stage have often led outsiders to believe that the woman in Islamic society has been little more than a personal and political cipher.[41] This perspective has been reinforced by Middle Eastern historians and chroniclers who have traditionally downplayed the role of women in their writings. And essayists, both male and female, have distorted the historical position of women in the Middle East as one means of attempting to improve their position today.

In stressing the formal, public, and institutional aspects of political behavior at the expense of the private and informal aspects, Western analysts have overlooked precisely those individuals who dominate the private and informal aspects. In the Middle East, women are important political forces because of their critical position in the webs of informal relationships that make up the private realm. In the crucial world of informal, private groups, they have been more than the homemakers. They have also been "the matchmakers and the peacemakers."[42] As anthropologist Emrys Peters puts it:

> The pivotal points in any field of power in this, a superficially dominant patrilineal, patrilocal and patriarchal society where the male ethos is vulgar in its brash prominence, are the women.

[41] We do not know of any text on Middle Eastern politics that discusses the political role of women in the area.

[42] We are indebted to Gerald J. Obermeyer for this phrase.

What holds men together, what knots the cords of alliances are not men themselves, but the women who depart from their natal household to take up residence elsewhere with a man, and who, in this critical position, communicate one group to another.[43]

This quotation refers to only one of the ways in which Middle Eastern women shape political events at all levels of the societies in which they live.

In both the traditional and the modern Middle East, women have exerted political influence through the wide variety of roles that they have played. Perhaps the most important of these roles have been natal and marital kinship roles. Such natal roles as daughter, sister, cousin, aunt, mother, and grandmother and such marital roles as wife and mother-in-law have been politically strategic throughout Islamic history. The special relationship between mother and son is particularly relevant to our understanding of Middle Eastern political events. As we shall see in the examples discussed below, only the role of wife has been more important in the female repertoire of political roles. One knowledgeable observer writes that "it is hardly surprising that the relationship to the mother is preferred to the paternal one, and that every patriarchal society is condemned to be matriarchal on the edges. On the edges? Not at all! It is a question here of the depths of existence."[44]

[43] Emrys Peters, "Consequences of the Segregation of the Sexes Among the Arabs" (Paper delivered at the Mediterranean Social Science Council Conference, Athens, 1966), p. 15. This important observation has been quoted by such scholars as Cynthia Nelson and Carla Makhlouf, whose works are among the few that stress the political power of women in the Middle East. Anthropologically inclined analysts have been much more sensitive to this power than have political scientists. Two further examples are Elizabeth Warnock Fernea, who has done fieldwork in Iraq, Egypt, and Morocco, and Lois Grant Beck, who has worked in Iran. Cynthia Nelson's field observations come from Egypt, and Carla Makhlouf's from Yemen.

[44] A. Bouhdiba, "The Child and the Mother in Arab-Muslim Society," in *Psychological Dimensions of Near Eastern Studies*, eds. L. Carl Brown and Norman Itzkowitz (Princeton, N.J.: Darwin Press, 1977), p. 133. For another excellent discussion of the power of the mother and mother-in-law in Muslim society, see Fatima Mernissi, *Beyond the Veil: Male-Female Dynamics in a Modern Muslim Society* (New York: Schenkman Publishing Co., 1975), pp. 69–79.

Other roles in which Muslim women have exerted influence in the political arena include such diverse traditional callings as prostitute, concubine, entertainer, servant, religious leader, soothsayer, and advisor. More modern roles, such as career woman and politician-stateswoman, are becoming more important with time. Female revolutionaries and terrorists are also visible and increasingly important.[45]

Among the tools that Middle Eastern women have used to exert influence are such resources as wealth, beauty, intelligence, and information, as well as both psychological and physical coercion. They have often converted the very signs of their oppression into formidable offensive weapons that have enabled them to secure their interests. Excellent examples of such weapons are the harem and the veil, which segregate the sexes. The conventional wisdom is that it is the women who are excluded from the male world, but as one scholar has recently written: "One can venture to assert that it is in fact the men who are excluded from the female world, as much, if not more, than females are excluded from that of man."[46] This researcher goes on to give a number of examples of how much easier it is for women to penetrate men's gatherings than for males to participate in those of women.

A survey of Middle Eastern political history indicates the important contributions that women have made to the political process. From the very foundation of Islam, women have been critical political forces. Indeed, as we will see in Chapter

[45] Among the scholars whose ongoing research on women and politics in the Middle East has been of much assistance to us are Professor Sandra Danforth and Miss Barbara Gates.

[46] Carla Makhlouf, *Changing Veils: Women and Modernisation in North Yemen* (Austin: University of Texas Press, 1979). This study contains fascinating material showing how the veil has traditionally provided Middle Eastern women with a mobile form of security and anonymity, and has even facilitated the expression of aggressiveness. More than religious fervor is involved in the return to the veil in the late 1970s by numerous liberated young women in such Middle Eastern societies as Iran and Egypt. For a fine study of a Muslim culture [Tuareg] where the males are the veiled ones, see Robert F. Murphy, "Social Distance and the Veil," in *Peoples and Cultures of the Middle East*, ed. Louise E. Sweet (Garden City, N.Y.: Natural History Press, 1970), vol. 1, pp. 290–314. On the informal power of women among the Tuareg, see R. V. C. Bodley, *The Soundless Sahara* (London: Robert Hale Limited, 1968), p. 82.

IV, there is little doubt that the Prophet Muhammad could not have succeeded in his mission without the indispensable support of his first wife, Khadija. Other women who helped shape the early social system of Islam were Muhammad's wife A'isha and his daughter Fatima. Fatima's sister-in-law Zaynab was also a powerful force in early Islamic history, as were the wives of the various imams who were the direct descendants of Fatima and her husband Ali.

The political role of women in the famous Umayyad and Abbasid caliphates is little known. In both instances, it was critical. This was especially true during the golden age of the cosmopolitan Abbasid dynasty in the late eighth and early ninth centuries. At a time when Europe was plunged into its Dark Ages and when Charlemagne and his lords "were reportedly dabbling with the art of writing their names,"[47] the powerful Abbasids ruling out of Baghdad were debating philosophic texts and making gigantic intellectual strides in medicine, astronomy, mathematics, and the arts. The glory and grandeur of this period is captured in romantically imaginative terms in *The Thousand Nights and a Night,* and such rulers of the period as Harun al-Rashid (786–809) and his brilliant son the caliph al-Ma'mun (813–833) are among the most renowned of Eastern rulers. Names such as Umm Salama, Khayzuran, and Zubayda, however, are considerably less known, even among scholars of the area. Umm Salama was the wife of Abu al-Abbas, the founder of the dynasty. A wealthy widow who had outlived two influential Umayyid husbands, she married Abu al-Abbas and thus served as a critical link between the two dynasties. A strong personality, she directed her husband's affairs and he "took no decisive measure without Umm Salamah's advice and approval."[48]

Khayzuran was the favorite wife of the third Abbasid caliph, Muhammad al-Mahdi; she was also the mother of the fourth and fifth caliphs, Musa al-Hadi and Harun al-Rashid. A slave girl born in Yemen, she received an excellent education and

---

[47] Philip K. Hitti, *The Near East in History* (Princeton, N.J.: D. Van Nostrand Co., 1961) , p. 244.

[48] Nabia Abbott, *Two Queens of Baghdad* (Chicago: University of Chicago Press, 1946) , p. 11.

caught the eye of the caliph al-Mansur, who brought her to the court, where his son al-Mahdi married her. For thirty years, during the reigns of three caliphs, her political power was enormous. Her agents and secretaries were spread throughout the empire; she intervened directly in the administration of justice; she influenced the rise and fall of the caliph's closest advisors; she financed the construction of public works; and she directed the succession of kings. It was Khayzuran who held the system together and ensured the smooth transition of kings both upon the death of her husband and then again when her eldest son al-Hadi passed away. Khayzuran was an owner of extensive property, and, next to her illustrious son Harun al-Rashid, she was the wealthiest person in the Muslim world of her day. In describing Khayzuran's role during the caliphates of her two sons, one writer succinctly summarizes her position: "The ambitious mother travels in state on the imperial highway of power."[49]

Better known in the annals of Islamic history than Khayzuran is her niece Zubayda, the wife of Harun al-Rashid. One of the greatest builders of public works in Islamic history, Zubayda is remembered particularly for sponsoring the construction of over ten miles of complex aqueducts leading into Mecca. She spent over seventy-five million dinars in digging the Mushshash Spring in that holy city — a spectacular feat in any age. Like Khayzuran, Zubayda was intimately involved in all the important political issues of the time. She had influence over judges, police officials, and military generals, not to mention her husband. The observation that "Zubaidah had (complete) control over Hārūn's mind and did with him as she pleased"[50] is perhaps only a slight exaggeration. In the succession battle between her son Muhammad Amin and al-Ma'mun, she played a critical role in Amin's victory. Zubayda was a major force also in turning Harun against the powerful Persian Barmecids, who had directed the political fortunes of the Abbasid dynasty more than any other family. She indirectly, but very effectively, helped bring about their destruc-

49 Ibid., p. 132.
50 F. Wustenfeld, *Die Chroniken der Stadt Mekka*, vol. 3, p. 15 as quoted in Abbott, *Two Queens*, p. 256.

tion. Although less aggressive than Khayzuran, Zubayda nonetheless left her imprint even more deeply in the sands of Abbasid social and political history.

Moving chronologically onward and geographically south-
ward, we come to the Sulayhid dynasty, which ruled in South
Arabia from 1037 to 1138. This Shi'ite dynasty made its capital in Sanaa and later in the Dhu Jibla of today's Yemen. The
Sulayhi "educated their daughters to the same standards as
their menfolk, instilled in them the same moral and political
principles, and made them their equals in astuteness, ability,
and judgement."[51] The greatest of the Sulayhid queens was
Urwa bint Ahmad al-Sulayhi, who upon her husband al-Mu-
karram's death in 1084 took complete command and ruled for
fifty-three years. A woman of great political acumen, Queen
Urwa ruled the Sulayhid state by judiciously emphasizing
tactics of compromise, personal maneuver, and the wise appointment of assistants and advisors. Urwa's political success
is perhaps largely attributable to the training she received
under the direction of another woman, Queen Asma, the wife
of the founder of the Sulayhid dynasty.

The Ottoman Empire, which boasts a political history that
extended from the thirteenth to the twentieth centuries, is a
much more significant example of an Islamic system in which
women wielded political power. The Ottoman style, however,
is more similar to the Abbasid style of indirect kinship control
than to the Sulayhid style of direct rule by a queen. Although
one can select any particular sultan and discover in association with him a number of women active in the central decision-making process, we will cut into Ottoman history at
perhaps its best-known period of grandeur — the reign of Suleyman I the Magnificent (1520–1566). Suleyman was known
for his legal promulgations and his empire for its architec-
tural creations, naval strength, and military expansion deep
into Europe. Surrounding Suleyman were three women of
particular note, his mother Hafsa Hatun and his wives Hurrem Sultan and Gulbahar Hatun. Their political influence

51 Robert W. Stookey, *Yemen: The Politics of the Yemen Arab Republic* (Boulder, Col.: Westview Press, 1978), p. 67.

was great, especially in controlling the sultan and the grand vazir, the most important administrative official in the Ottoman system. Of these three women, the most powerful was Hurrem Sultan, a former Russian slave girl known in the West as Roxelana. It was she who convinced Suleyman to let her live with him in the seraglio, "where she obtained complete ascendancy over the Sultan and ruled supreme in the harēm until her death in 1558."[52]

Hafsa Hatun and Hurrem Sultan formed an alliance of convenience to expel one grand vazir and to appoint another early in the reign of Suleyman. The new vazir, Ibrahim Pasha, felt indebted to Hafsa Hatun for his position and was careful to do her bidding. Meanwhile, he was independently linked to Suleyman himself, who permitted the vazir to practically run the empire. Ibrahim Pasha in the process became one of the most powerful of the grand vazirs in Ottoman history. An extraordinarily ambitious person politically, Hurrem Sultan saw the vazir as her major competitor and sought to destroy him. When her mother-in-law died in 1534, she moved quickly against the vazir. The now exposed Ibrahim Pasha found an ally in Suleyman's first wife, Gulbahar Hatun, who was anxious that her son Mustafa become the heir apparent. Hurrem Sultan, with her own sons' interests at heart, gathered other supporters (including the French ambassador) and was able to prevail in the struggle. In 1536, Ibrahim Pasha lost not only his job, but also his life.

Hurrem Sultan then succeeded in getting her eldest son Mehmet named as heir to the throne. With his untimely death, however, Gulbahar Hatun, with the assistance of the new vazir, Hadim Suleyman Pasha, finally placed her son Mustafa in the coveted position. But Hurrem Sultan's power was not to be denied and she forced this vazir into exile. And she now saw that someone more reliable got the post. Her own son-in-law Rustem Pasha became vazir. This new alli-

52 N. M. Penzer, *The Harēm* (Philadelphia: J. B. Lippincott, 1937), p. 186. There are many sources that describe this period of Ottoman history. For an excellent recent example, see Stanford Shaw, *History of the Ottoman Empire and Modern Turkey*, vol. 1 (Cambridge: Cambridge University Press, 1976), pp. 87–111.

ance resulted in the execution of Gulbahar Hatun's son Mustafa. When there was a revolt in 1555, partially against this execution, Hurrem Sultan's son Bayizat successfully put it down. When Hurrem Sultan died in 1558, she had pretty well determined that one of her sons would become the next sultan. Her son Selim succeeded Suleyman to the throne in 1566 and ruled for eight years as Sultan Selim II. Selim's wife, Nurbanu Sultan, in fact ruled the empire during his reign, and during the rule of her own son, Sultan Murad III, she shared political power with her daughter-in-law Safriyah Sultan. And so it continued. It is small wonder that the Ottoman empire during the sixteenth and seventeenth centuries has come to be historically known as the Sultanate of Women (*Kadinlar Sultanati*). (For a diagrammatic representation of the women of Suleyman the Magnificent's reign, see Figure III.2.)

Early in this century, women played an important part in the various constitutional and revolutionary movements that swept across the Middle East. An excellent case in point is Halide Edib Adivar, a leading Turkish intellectual, nationalist, and supporter of Mustafa Kemal's movement for independence. Born in 1883, she was educated at the American College for Girls and then began writing and speaking for liberal causes. Her inspired public speeches in support of the nationalist revolution earned her national and even international fame. Her statement that "governments are our enemies, peoples are our friends, and the just revolt of our hearts

FIGURE III.2   *The Women of Suleyman the Magnificent's Reign*

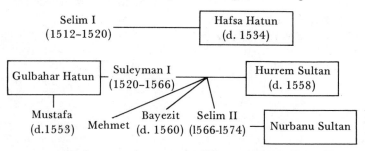

The names of the women in the system appear in boxes.

our strength" became the rallying cry of Turkish national-ists.[53] Halide Edib Adivar actually served in Kemal's army as a corporal, a sergeant, and a sergeant major.

Women also played a critical role in the Iranian constitu-tional movement from 1905 to 1911. They organized them-selves into informal meeting groups (*anjuman*s) and did not hesitate to take to the streets in support of their political ideals. When the newly established parliament (*majlis*) faced extinction in 1911, a large group of women marched on the building:

Three hundred women surrounded the entrance to the *Majlis,* or Parliament, recently formed, and demanded admission. A few only were admitted. They walked in closely veiled, but when they found themselves in the assembly they tore their veils aside, and said that their intention was to kill their husbands, their sons and themselves if the liberty and dignity of Persia were not firmly upheld. They offered their money and jewels, saying: "We are women and cannot fight, but we can give to our coun-try." They had their own places of assembly where they dis-cussed these matters, and they used the Press, and personal influence was largely exerted.[54]

As time has passed, Muslim women have assumed a more direct and dramatic role in Middle Eastern politics. In the Algerian war of independence, women were an important part of the resistance and did everything from hiding fugitives to throwing bombs. National heroine Jamilah Buhrayd, for example, rather than becoming a seamstress, became a revo-lutionary and was eventually shot, imprisoned, and tortured by the French. Young women have been very conspicuous in the Palestine guerrilla movements. Leila Khaled, for example, gained international notoriety when she was captured as part of a four-plane hijacking operation in September 1970. In May

---

[53] Elizabeth Warnock Fernea and Basima Qattan Bezirgan, eds., *Middle Eastern Muslim Women Speak* (Austin: University of Texas Press, 1977), p. 189.

[54] C. Colliver Rice, *Persian Women and their Ways* (London: Seeley, Service and Co., 1923), p. 270. For an even more dramatic description of this event, see W. Morgan Shuster, *The Strangling of Persia* (New York: Century Co., 1912), p. 198.

1972, two young Arab women, former nursing students, participated in the hijacking of a Sabena Boeing 707 to Lod Airport in Israel. There are countless other examples. One observer writes: "Mostly young and often educated in the West — France, England, the United States — the Palestinian girl fedayeen have a better political understanding than their male counterparts. Indeed, they are more the material from which real revolutionaries are made. Proportionate to their numbers they have caused the Israelis more trouble than have their male comrades."[55]

Women were also key participants in the revolutionary struggle in Aden. According to one knowledgeable source, there were 250 hard core women guerrillas involved in the independence movement there. One of them, Nagwa Makkawi, was so famous (or infamous) that when the British captured her, they paraded her through the streets on a tank. She later became the first female ambassador for the People's Democratic Republic of Yemen.[56] In Iran over the last several years, the Shah's regime has been harassed by urban guerrillas, whose dedication to their cause has been complete. An increasing percentage of this opposition has been composed of young women in their late teens and early twenties who carry submachine guns and hand grenades.

This revolutionary role of Muslim women in influencing Middle Eastern politics is only one of many more direct and formal ways that they now exert power. As their legal rights expand and as they gain greater stature in the formal governmental arena, they are conspicuously acquiring political authority. Women's movements are present everywhere in the Middle East, and women are slowly taking their places in the parliamentary, cabinet, and party hierarchies. In so doing, however, they have not relinquished their traditional influence in the informal sphere of power. It is as part of the informal group or family that women continue to operate most effectively.

---

55 John Laffin, *Fedayeen: The Arab-Israeli Dilemma* (New York: Free Press, 1973), p. 138.
56 John Duke Anthony, lecture delivered at the University of Texas, Austin, Texas, 22 July 1977.

In Iran, Empress Farah Diba Pahlavi does not confine herself to social work and charitable causes. Although she heads nearly forty different social work and charitable organizations, she is also involved in political issues. Among other things, she is the Shah's most important link to the people and is perhaps the only person left among his advisors who can take issue with his decisions. Also, Empress Farah is regent and her influence over the crown prince is strong and pervasive. The Shah's twin sister, Ashraf, has long been a feared and powerful force in the country. It was she who helped plan and implement the events in August 1953 that enabled the king to return to the throne after he had been forced to flee the country. In Tunisia, Wassila ben Amar, the wife of President Bourguiba, has long been embroiled in national politics. Her advice and opinions have often shaped the course of events in that country. In November 1977, she visited President Sadat in Cairo to indicate her country's support for his direct approach to peace in the Middle East.

Even Jihan Sadat, the wife of the Egyptian president, has, despite her occasional disclaimers, been an important force in Egyptian society and politics. Amina al-Said, one of Egypt's leading female journalists, has stated that Mrs. Sadat "conceives of herself as a woman, an Egyptian woman first, and the President's wife second."[57] In 1974, she intervened forcefully (although ultimately unsuccessfully) in favor of transforming what she considered Egypt's antiquated family laws. In the shaykhdoms along the Persian Gulf, women have in recent years also been influential politically. In both Abu Dhabi and Dubai, the two leading countries in the United Arab Emirates, the mothers of Shaykh Zayid and Shaykh Rashid converted their royal motherhood directly into political clout. Zayid's mother was the real power broker in Abu Dhabi until her death in the early 1970s. Rashid's mother, Hussah bint al-Murr, "is widely acknowledged as having been the real power in the shaykhdom for most of the first half of this century. Once, during an armed conflict with neighboring

[57] Deborah Mason, "Egypt's First Lady," *Christian Science Monitor,* 18 December 1974, p. 5.

Sharjah, she is said to have charged her husband and sons with indifference and to have led the local forces in defense of Dubay herself."[58] Today, Shaykh Zayid's wife, Shaykha Fatima, is the leading spokesperson for women's liberation in her country. Although a woman of very little formal education, she is an intelligent and important force in her country.

Muslim women in the Middle East have never enjoyed legal equality with men and have suffered discrimination in many areas of existence. Any study of the formal scaffolding of the social and political systems clearly demonstrates their lack of authority. The lack of authority, however, is not the same as the lack of power. Middle Eastern women have never been powerless. Indeed, they have played a pervasive and persistent part in shaping political decisions and determining political events ever since the time when the widow Khadija married and then materially and psychologically supported the young man Muhammad. Only by analyzing politics at the informal level does one begin to understand and appreciate the significance of women to the entire political process.

Our brief survey of Middle Eastern women in politics yields several general observations. First, women throughout Muslim history have had a more profound impact upon political events than is generally thought. Second, this political power has usually been wielded indirectly and informally through men. Natal and marital relationships have often been the most critical ones here. Third, there has been a strong movement over the past several years among Middle Eastern women for legal equality and social and political rights. In the Middle East, women's liberation is a drive not so much to acquire power as to add authority to power. Why must women's political influence be indirect and confined to the informal arena? Fourth, this drive for authority has not, however, displaced the power and position of women in the traditional realm of informal groups. Middle Eastern women after all are quite sensitive to the fact that this is the main decision-making arena. That is why Algerian heroine Jamilah Buhrayd states:

---

[58] Anthony, *Arab States,* pp. 156, 158. We are indebted to Professor Anthony, who has explained the role of women in the Persian Gulf to us in private correspondence.

"It's true we don't find as many women in politics as men, but women have always imposed their views in a quieter way without public fuss."[59]

Although informal groups and networks must be taken into account in any study of Middle Eastern politics, the political process is not played out in a seamless web of interacting groups. The above case studies, for example, indicate that it is only women of the upper class who in fact influence the national polity. The masses of women (like the masses of men) have little if anything to say about major political decisions. By emphasizing only the group dimension, we suggest that group pluralism promotes equality. What is left out of the equation is the issue of horizontal stratification. Slashing across the web of groups are lines of stratification that profoundly affect not only the group dynamics discussed above but also the entire political process of the Middle East. Şerif Mardin cogently summarizes this point when he writes that although membership in a kinship group "raised the expectations of a less prestigious member of the group that he could rise in society, the fact that he belonged to a well-recognized stratum led to frustrations as regards actual capacity to rise in society."[60]

CLASS STRUCTURE: HORIZONTAL STRATIFICATION

It is He who has made us the inheritors of the earth, who has elevated us one above the other by degrees (darajat), in order to help us experience His gifts.

Quran, chapter 6, Verse 156

The late G. E. von Grunebaum once wrote that "the Muslim's personal equality with his fellows in the faith which is guaranteed, so to speak, by his right to a direct relationship with his Lord does in no way preclude elaborate social stratification within the community of Islam."[61] The group network and communalism discussed above cloak a system of hori-

[59] Fernea and Bezirgan, *Middle Eastern Muslim Women Speak,* p. 261.
[60] Mardin, "Historical Determinants," p. 4.
[61] Gustave E. von Grunebaum, *Medieval Islam: A Study in Cultural Orientation,* 2d ed. (Chicago: University of Chicago Press, 1961), p. 170.

zontal stratification in which Middle Eastern societies break down into a fairly small number of interrelated classes. A class structure always involves entities in superior and subordinate positions. The overall hierarchy of classes is founded upon the unequal possession of one of the fundamental values of social and political life. In the sociological literature, class is most often defined according to one of three different emphases: wealth, status, and power. An individual's place in a social class is determined by his or her position with respect to one of these characteristics. Although all three determinants are interrelated in the sense that the possession of one may strongly affect the acquisition of another, the question of which is the basic criterion remains open. In this volume on the Middle East, we define class in terms of power and employment position.[62]

Class and Power in the Middle East. For our purposes, power refers to one's ability to shape and control the behavior of others.[63] This ability may rest as much upon indirect personal maneuvering and verbal persuasion as upon direct threat, coercive demand, or economic inducement. The basis of power may be located in the political, economic, social, educational, religious, or psychological systems. Because Islam is

[62] For two explicit attempts to discuss class analysis as it applies to Middle Eastern society and politics, see Jacques Berque, "L'Idée de Classes dans L'Histoire Contemporaine des Arabes," *Cahiers Internationaux de Sociologie* 38 (1965) : 169–84; and James A. Bill, "Class Analysis and the Dialectics of Modernization in the Middle East," *International Journal of Middle East Studies* 3 (October 1972) : 417–34. The latter article provides the conceptual and theoretical underpinnings for the linkage of class and power. For an analytic overview of the state of our knowledge about stratification and change in the Middle East, see S. N. Eisenstadt, "Convergence and Divergence of Modern and Modernizing Societies: Indications from the Analysis of the Structuring of Social Hierarchies in Middle Eastern Societies," *International Journal of Middle Eastern Studies* 8 (January 1977) :1–27.

[63] This definition of power is slightly broader than those provided by scholars who have chosen to reword Max Weber's original definition. In our view, a power relation can involve more than getting someone to do what he or she would not otherwise do. It can be a reinforcing pattern whereby one individual encourages another to continue behaving in a certain way. Or it may simply be a case of one person causing another to translate a predisposition into action.

a way of life that involves all of these dimensions, power relations in Islamic societies usually involve a subtly integrated complex of factors. One Islamic scholar writes, for example, that "political influence, military power, administrative rank, wealth, birth, and schooling, in every possible combination, strengthened or counteracted one another in assigning a given individual his place in society."[64] Wealth is but one of a number of important variables that determine one's position in the class structure. Material resources have seldom been enough to enable individuals consistently to attain their goals. Personal contacts, social manipulation, saintly ancestry, mystical strength, familial solidarity, higher education, political maneuvering, and an innate sense of timing are all crucial ingredients that help shape class position and movement from one class to another.

Among the more common, if seldom recognized, dimensions of power that have been instrumental in shaping the formation of Middle Eastern class structure are (1) exchange transactions in which one person convinces others to accede to his wishes by rewarding them for so doing; (2) informational exchanges that involve dispensing and withholding information of varying degrees of value; (3) decisional situations in which one person controls the decision-making environment and thus the decisions made therein; (4) debt-inflicting relationships in which one does favors for others with the confident expectation that they will someday be returned; (5) overt deference behavior by which one person gains the trust of another and thus makes the temporarily more powerful person vulnerable; (6) bargaining interactions that occur in environments of doubt, and rest upon such techniques as the bluff and the compromise; (7) kinship patterns in which family members strive to assist one another to improve their relative positions in the class structure; and (8) modes of misrepresentation that distort reality in a manner designed to shift the balance of interpersonal influence.

The exchange transaction is the simplest and most direct means of exerting power; it is a major pattern in all socie-

[64] Von Grunebaum, *Medieval Islam*, p. 212.

ties.[65] It is most often expressed as financial dealings, which range all the way from salary transactions to bribery payments. In the Middle East, a disproportionate percentage of exchange transactions occur in noneconomic terms, since the objects of exchange include personal loyalty, political service, religious approval, and reliable information. Informational exchanges are critical in societies where informality cloaks the exercise of power and where decisions are made within personalistic networks. Indeed, information is a valuable commodity in the Middle East, since it can be used both offensively and defensively. Political elites constantly seek information concerning the actual and potential opposition forces in their societies. Individuals and groups in the middle and lower classes both hoard and barter information in order to improve their own positions in the social structure.

Another dimension of the power syndrome is the phenomenon of "nondecision making," whereby superordinately situated individuals control the behavior of subordinates through the manipulation and control of the environment in which the latter must operate.[66] An example of this phenomenon in the Middle East is the executive control of parliaments and political parties. Decisions tend to be made in the parliaments and parties according to what the deputies believe the will of the ruler or military junta would be. It is not necessary that there be any communication between the leadership and the representatives. Control is thus built into the structure of the system in a less than obvious manner. Learning how to interact in this kind of system is essential to the determination of one's class standing. This pattern was evident when in December 1972 the Egyptian parliament permitted a great deal of critical comment, including attacks against the government. This was done with President Sadat's approval and was used by him as a device to draw public attention to policies and personnel that he wanted changed.

65 For a theoretical exploration of the various facets of exchange transactions, see Peter Blau, *Exchange and Power in Social Life* (New York: John Wiley and Co., 1964).

66 See Peter Bachrach and Morton S. Baratz's classic discussion of the "nondecision-making process" in "Two Faces of Power," *American Political Science Review* 56 (December 1962) : 947–52.

One of the most distinctive facets of power relations in Middle Eastern society is debt infliction. In the Muslim community of North Africa, "every act requires some form of reciprocation as an inherent aspect of its very nature: every act creates an obligation or expresses a right held."[67] Those upon whom debts are inflicted are put into a disadvantageous position of dependence. It is in this sense that Fredrik Barth describes the mechanism as it manifests itself in the Swat Valley in Pakistan. The relationship to political power is unmistakable here, since even "gift-giving and hospitality are potent means of controlling others . . ."[68] As one Lebanese gentleman puts it, gifts are "the lubricants of social interaction."[69]

Deference, which is part of the somewhat extravagant patterns of courtesy and politeness that obtain in the Middle East, can be used effectively to balance highly uneven personal relationships. When properly displayed, deference can loosen the control of the more powerful actor over the less powerful individual. Deferential behavior can stimulate a false sense of security in the superior person in any relationship, thus heightening his or her vulnerability. It was in this spirit that the Ziyarid prince Kai Ka'us Ibn Iskandar wrote his son that "if you are being fattened by someone, you may expect very quickly to be slaughtered by him . . ."[70]

Another context in which power exchange occurs in the Middle East is bargaining, in which the actors in fact agree to disagree. Each side in the encounter uses a wide variety of persuasive techniques in order to further his or her interests. The outcome of the confrontation remains in doubt until the very end of the process, when one side indicates a willingness to accept the terms of the other. An individual who is able to use an effective blend of candor and the bluff, as in bargain-

---

[67] Lawrence Rosen, "Muslim-Jewish Relations in a Moroccan City," *International Journal of Middle East Studies* 3 (October 1972) :438.

[68] Fredrik Barth, *Political Leadership among Swat Pathans* (London: Athlone Press, 1959) , p. 79.

[69] This is reported in Fuad I. Khuri, *From Village to Suburb: Order and Change in Greater Beirut* (Chicago: University of Chicago Press, 1975) , p. 86.

[70] Kai Ka'us Ibn Iskandar, *A Mirror for Princes* (The Qābūs-nāma) , trans. Reuben Levy (London: Cresset Press, 1951) , p. 191.

ing, can greatly enhance his or her position in the social and political hierarchy.

The final two tactics of control and influence have to do with kinship ties and modes of misrepresentation. As we noted earlier, the family is the most cohesive unit in Middle Eastern society. As such, it is least susceptible to radical change and most reliable as a unit of personal and group support.[71] The mobility of one family member affects the potential mobility of the whole family. Entire families often move up in the class structure. They are also downwardly mobile. Because of the centrality of the family in determining one's position in the power structure, individuals constantly seek to attach themselves to rising or already prominent families. This is usually accomplished through marriage, but it is also often done through the invention of fictive kinship ties.[72] This is only one of the forms of misrepresentation designed to help improve one's class position. To exaggerate and falsely embroider reality at propitious times is a technique more frowned upon in the West than in the Middle East, where such behavior often deflects conflict and prevents violent confrontation. It also is a dimension of influence that must be considered when explaining class membership and class conflict.

There is one further consideration in analyzing power relations in the Middle East. Throughout Islamic history, a person's power position has been closely intertwined with his occupational skill. Mode of employment to a large degree determined an individual's capacity to utilize the techniques and to operate effectively in the environment discussed above. An individual was best able to wield power using skills and talents he already possessed. The military, cleric, and bureau-

71 For a rigorously developed and tightly argued demonstration of the relative persistence of family social values in the Middle East, see Robert B. Cunningham, "Dimensions of Family Loyalty in the Middle East," paper prepared for delivery at the Fourth Annual Meeting of the Middle East Studies Association, Columbus, Ohio, 7 November 1970.

72 Fictive kinship is a social pattern that endures in Islamic societies from Morocco to Pakistan. For one case study, see Abdalla S. Bujra, *The Politics of Stratification: A Study of Political Change in a South Arabian Town* (Oxford: Clarendon Press, 1971). Note especially p. 107.

cratic occupations provided their practitioners with unusual opportunities to strengthen and improve their positions in the class structure through informed use of the coercive, religious, and political dimensions of power. The intimate connection between power and employment was a direct result of the development of Islamic social history and the Prophet Muhammad's early strictures concerning the occupational bases of the community of Islam. One of the earliest foundations for stratification was the assignment of the believers "to a more or less definite hierarchy of professions."[73] For purposes of the following empirical analysis of horizontal stratification in the Middle East, we define classes as the largest aggregates of individuals united by similar modes of employment and maintaining similar power positions in society.

The Middle Eastern Class System. Classical Islamic thinkers have presented views of horizontal stratification that range from two-class to eight-class hierarchies. According to the criteria developed above, the traditional Middle Eastern Islamic social structure consisted of seven interrelated classes: the upper (ruling) class, the bureaucratic middle class, the bourgeois middle class, the cleric middle class, the traditional working class, the peasant class, and the nomadic class. This schema includes one upper, three middle, and three lower classes. This designation of upper, middle, and lower refers to the general power categories, while the more specific labels are assigned on the basis of both power and employment. The nomenclature of each class indicates its employment function.

The upper class in the traditional Islamic social structure represented a tiny percentage of the population, usually less than 2 percent. The upper class was a ruling class, since it possessed a monopoly of the instruments of both power and authority in society. This class was composed of the elites that rested at the very apex of the governmental, landholding, religious, tribal, military, and business pyramids of influence. The rulers and the networks of ruling families were at the

73 Von Grunebaum, *Medieval Islam,* p. 177.

core of the upper class. Also included were the military leaders, the large native landlords, the highest-level bureaucrats (for example, vazirs), the leadership of the ulema who supported the system, the tribal chieftains and khans, and the wealthiest merchants and business entrepreneurs. This ruling class exhibited exclusive and inclusive characteristics that tended to balance one another out, ultimately stabilizing membership size. In most cases, a single member of this class had a number of power-laden functions. For example, a member of the ruling family was often at the same time a military leader and a large landlord. The tribal nobility maintained large landholdings and were often among the highest-ranking military officials. In this way, wealth, influence, and coercive power reinforced one another and strengthened one's class position. This helped to narrow upper-class membership. On the other hand, the kinship mechanism tended to expand the size of the upper class while at the same time linking this class to the various middle classes. The extended family ties of a ruler, vazir, or landlord brought new waves of individuals into ruling-class ranks. Indeed, one of the best ways even today to understand ruling classes in Middle Eastern societies is to analyze the structures of leading families.

Ruling classes in the Islamic Middle East are shaped by the lines of kinship along which power flows. Family ties and intermarriage patterns help solidify an inherently fragmented and fissured upper class. The lack of any strong class consciousness, at least among the ruling class, is partially compensated for by a kind of interfamilial and intrafamilial consciousness. Although studies show that family membership in Middle Eastern upper classes is relatively unstable, there are indications that a small number of families remain in upper-class ranks over time. The informality of family structure in many ways mirrors the character of the upper class, which is also relatively fluid. In an impressive study of the upper class ("patriciate") of Muslim Nishapur from the tenth to the twelfth century, Richard Bulliet writes that "the reality of the patriciate consisted in individuals and families who knew each other and recognized each other as being above the ordinary run of people. There was no formal membership in the patriciate."[74] In sum, the upper class in Islamic history has been a complex of leading clerics, generals, vazirs, khans, and merchant kings familially and informally bound together around the person of the ruler and his family. By virtue of its advantageous power position, this ruling class directs the political system of society.

The bureaucratic middle class has been the most powerful of the three traditional middle classes. Its membership is composed of the mass of governmental employees who staff the administrative system. Possessing a minimum of traditional education, these individuals are the scribes, accountants, recorders, and bureaucratic functionaries of the traditional Middle Eastern society. Like the ruling class, this middle class is rather loosely and informally organized. Although in many Islamic societies there were families that came to be known as bureaucratic families, kinship ties are not as important as class indicators here as they are in the upper class.

In our concentric circles of class and power, the bureaucratic middle class most closely rings the ruling class. It is an important intermediary class that translates the directives of the ruling class into action. This administering class appears to be almost an appendage to the upper class because of its many points of contact with the upper class. Owing to this proximity, the bureaucratic middle class has more often served the interests of the ruling class than those of the other middle and the lower classes. While maintaining an important power of its own, this class traditionally saw its interests as bound up with those of the upper class. The proximity to power always held out to the bureaucratic middle class the possibility of movement into upper-class ranks.

Located approximately between the bureaucratic and cleric middle classes is the bourgeois middle class, which is a class of businessmen, merchants, and traders. The symbol and center

[74] Richard W. Bulliet, *The Patricians of Nishapur: A Study in Medieval Islamic Social History* (Cambridge: Harvard University Press, 1972) , p. 86. For an informative discussion of upper-class family networks in the Moroccan city of Salé in the nineteenth and early twentieth centuries, see Kenneth L. Brown, *People of Salé: Tradition and Change in a Moroccan City, 1830–1930* (Manchester: Manchester University Press, 1976) , especially pp. 52–65.

of activity of this class is the bazaar, or *suq*. As an individual, the merchant or trader has little economic power and virtually no political influence. As a class, however, this bourgeoisie has considerable political power. When ruling-class policies have seriously endangered the interests of commerce and the life-styles of the merchant, the bazaar has often become the heart of opposition to the regime in power. It was out of the ranks of the bourgeoisie that Islam itself developed as a community and civilization. And throughout the history of Islam, a number of social and religious movements have sprung up from this class in opposition to the prevailing political order.

There are two reasons why the merchants and tradesmen have been able to give birth to opposition movements. In the first place, the members of this class managed to institutionalize their traditional informal patterns of interaction in a system of guilds and brotherhoods. Secondly, their organizational apparatus had a semblance of ideology, which helped provide a rationalization for their activities. This ideology was composed of various folk and mystic Islamic beliefs. Finally, this kind of organizational and ideological framework linked the business middle class with important elements in both the cleric middle class and the traditional working class. The bazaars were the meeting place for merchant, cleric, and artisan.[75]

The cleric middle class, which is composed of the lower and intermediate ranks of the ulema, is the third traditional middle class. The members of this class enjoy neither the political influence of the bureaucrats nor the wealth of the businessmen. They have, however, possessed important religio-psychological influence over those members of society who have been practicing Muslims. They also have controlled the educational system through their role as teachers and directors of the traditional educational institutions (*maktab*s and *madrasa*s). The constituency of the clerics has been largely concentrated within the lower classes, and because of this, the interests of the cleric middle class have been closely entwined with those below them in the social structure.

[75] For an analysis of the bourgeoisie as a class in Islamic society, see S. D. Goitein, *Studies in Islamic History and Institutions* (Leiden: E. J. Brill, 1966), pp. 217–41.

The three traditional middle classes were closely related to one another in a number of ways. The members of all these classes were the products of the same educational system — a system that was directed by the ulema and that stressed reading, writing, religious law, rhetoric, and the Quran. The educational method used was rote memorization. One result of this was that all traditional middle-class individuals had a similar value system, largely conservative. This meant that these classes rebelled only under very special circumstances. These consisted of either a severe and adverse disruption of business conditions or a series of policies by the ruling class that abrogated and contradicted the tenets of Islam. Usually both these conditions had to come about simultaneously in order for these middle classes to move to active opposition. And even then, the bureaucratic middle class seldom participated.

The bulk of the population of all Middle Eastern societies falls into the three lower classes, consisting of workers, peasants, and nomads. Ideally, Islam commands that the community treat the poor and least powerful with compassion. The giving of alms is one of the acts that all the faithful are expected to consistently practice. In describing the class structure of Islamic communities, Imam Ali, son-in-law of the Prophet, said of the lower classes: "Lowest of all are the afflicted and the poor who are the unfortunate and the suffering. They are always the broken-hearted and the weary."[76] In fact, however, the situation of the lower classes has been little improved by such words of sympathy and ideals of charitable assistance. The harsher realities of class structure are reflected in another scheme of classification presented by the Abbasid courtier Yahya al-Fazl. He divides society into four classes and then writes that "the remainder are filthy refuse, a torrent of scum, base cattle, none of whom thinks of anything but his food and sleep."[77]

Most of the members of the lower class belong to the peasant class. In preponderantly agricultural societies, these are

---

[76] Ali Farman to Malik Ashtar, governor of Egypt, *Sukhanan-i Ali* [The words of Ali], trans. Javad Fazil (Tehran, 1966), p. 242. In Persian.

[77] Ibn al-Faqih, *Kitab al-Buldan*, as quoted in Reuben Levy, *The Social Structure of Islam* (Cambridge: Cambridge University Press, 1957), p. 67.

the individuals who work the land under a variety of arrangements that only alter the degree of their poverty, dependence, disease, and ignorance. The peasant class, located at the very bottom of the social structure, has very little power and is thus exposed to exploitation by all the other classes in society. For the individual peasant, this usually means abuse at the hands of landlord, merchant, and government official. Peasants have also often suffered from manipulation by the clerics and from the raids of tribesmen. The situation of the nomadic lower class is not much better than that of the peasants. The tribal masses have existed in a state of subjection to a hierarchy of khans and have had to struggle to make a living from an often inhospitable land. Because of a modicum of natural freedom and their occasional importance as military forces, the tribesmen have been a cut above the peasant in the social structure.

The traditional working class includes such groups as servants, manual laborers, craftsmen, and artisans. In the Middle East, this class has been as much a rural as an urban phenomenon. Like the members of the other lower classes, these workers have earned their livelihood through the use of their physical skills. Working with their hands, they have been scorned by the middle and upper classes. The members of this class have often joined guilds and brotherhoods, and because of this, they have enjoyed some organizational protection. This has placed the traditional working class in the best power position among the lower classes.

The traditional class structure in the Islamic Middle East is still in place to a large extent in contemporary Middle Eastern society. There have been, however, a number of obvious changes that have largely resulted from the forces of modernization discussed in Chapter I. Land reform programs, coupled with the increasing emphasis upon industrialization, have caused a shifting of the bases of power of the ruling class. Land ownership, which was an important upper-class power credential for centuries, has given way to industrial investment in the form of contracting, banking, export-import trade, and business concessions of all kinds. The traditional middle classes have grown in size relative to the upper and lower classes, with the bourgeois middle class expanding at an especially rapid rate. Nomadic tribes are slowly being forced to settle, and as a result are grudgingly blending into the peasantry. Strong rural-to-urban migration patterns have resulted in the mushrooming growth of shanty towns and the appearance of an unemployed proletariat that continues to expand along the edges of the major cities. This last change is a dramatic one, since it represents the appearance of an important modern addition to the centuries-old class structure. The relatively recent appearance of two new classes is a significant break with the past patterns of horizontal stratification in the area. Both an industrial working class and a professional middle class have emerged as definite formations in the second half of this century. Both classes are the products of the accelerating process of modernization, and their roots trace back to the growth of large industry and the development of modern systems of education in the Afro-Asian world.

Industrialization and urbanization have been the major catalysts for the appearance of the new urban industrial working class. Census data indicate that this class still represents a very small proportion of the population in the various Middle Eastern countries, but that it is growing at a rapid pace. The growing masses of unemployed migrants referred to above are a ready pool of unskilled and semiskilled labor for new industry. This new lower class is more powerful than the traditional lower classes because of its strategic and visible location in the large cities, as well as its growing social awareness. The industrial working class, however, has barely begun to realize its potential as a social and political force. This is not the case with the second and more recent class formation.

The Professional Middle Class. Over the last decade, scholars of Middle Eastern politics have engaged in considerable debate concerning the existence and role of a new middle class. This class, which we here term the professional middle class, has been referred to by Morroe Berger as the "independent middle class," by Manfred Halpern as the "salaried new middle class," by H. A. R. Gibb as the "new administrative-professional class," by Jacques Berque as the "intelligentsia," by James A. Bill as the "professional-bureaucratic intelligentsia," by Ahmad Baha'eddine and Jalal Al-i Ahmad as the "intellectual class," and by Anouar Abdel-Malek as the "new class."[78] Despite slightly differing emphases from one author to another, these observers all agree that a new social class whose power is based on skills obtained through a modern education has appeared in the middle reaches of the traditional social structure. Contrary to what has sometimes been suggested in the literature, a number of scholars native to the Middle East must be included among those who posit the significant appearance of this new middle class.[79]

[78] Morroe Berger, *The Arab World Today* (Garden City, N.Y.: Doubleday and Co., 1962), pp. 271–72; Manfred Halpern, *The Politics of Social Change in the Middle East and North Africa* (Princeton, N.J.: Princeton University Press, 1963), pp. 51–78; Sir Hamilton A. R. Gibb, "Social Reform: Factor X," in Walter Z. Laqueur, *The Middle East in Transition: Studies in Contemporary History* (New York: Frederick A. Praeger, 1958), pp. 3–11; Jacques Berque, "L'Idée de Classes," pp. 174–83; James A. Bill, *The Politics of Iran: Groups, Classes, and Modernization* (Columbus, Ohio: Charles E. Merrill, 1972), pp. 53–72; Ahmad Baha'eddine, *"Al-iqta'iyyun wal-ra'smaliyyun wal-muthaqqafun"* [Feudalists, capitalists, and intellectuals] in *Rose Al-Yussif,* no. 1353 (17 May 1954), as quoted in Anouar Abdel-Malek, *Egypt: Military Society,* trans. Charles Lam Markmann (New York: Vintage Books, 1968), p. 178; Jalal Al-i Ahmad, *Rawshanfikr Chist? Rawshanfikr Kist?"* [What is an Intellectual? Who is an Intellectual?] in *Jahan-i Naw,* no. 4 (1966):15–32; and Abdel-Malek, *Egypt: Military Society,* pp. 167–86. Messrs. Baha'eddine and Al-i Ahmad were leading Egyptian and Iranian intellectuals, respectively.

[79] Scholars of the Middle East are not in complete agreement about the existence of a professional middle class. For a major dissenting view, see Amos Perlmutter, "Egypt and the Myth of the New Middle Class: A Comparative Analysis," *Comparative Studies in Society and History* 10 (October 1967):46–65. The Perlmutter attack was directed against the formulations of Manfred Halpern. See Halpern's reply in "Egypt and the New Middle Class: Reaffirmations and New Explorations," *Comparative Studies in Society and History* 11 (January 1969):97–108. C. A. O. van Nieuwenhuijze is uncomfortably but honestly of two minds on this question and concludes that ". . . it yet is still too early to conclude, beyond doubt, that this is the new middle class, whether with or without capital letters." See van Nieuwenhuijze, *Sociology of the Middle East,* p. 605. At a more empirical level, Leonard Binder seems to both attack and support the concept of a new middle class. In an article on Iran, for example, he prefers to stay away from analysis of the middle class and warns the reader that "the modern middle class is not politically or socially homogenous. There is a modern middle class and a traditional middle class; a commercial middle class, an intellectual middle class; a professional middle class, and a managerial middle class, and a middle class of the minorities and foreigners; there is an urban middle class and a rural middle class."

Many members of the new class seek to advance themselves through their professional skills and talents rather than through the use of wealth and personal connections, two resources that most of them lack in any case. The professional middle class is not a bourgeois middle class, since its members earn their livelihoods less through ownership of property or entrepreneurship in business than through salaries, technical fees, scholarships, and professional activities. This class is composed of white-collar workers engaged in technical, professional, cultural, and administrative occupations. Its membership is drawn largely from such groups as teachers, bureaucrats, professors, students, technocrats, engineers, physicians, writers, artists, journalists, and middle-ranking army officers. Although this is not a class of intellectuals, it may be properly termed an intelligentsia, since it composes the intellectual elite in society. Unlike the educated members of the ruling class, who enjoy the twin privileges of great wealth and political authority, the members of the professional middle class have little other than their education to fall back on. Whereas the members of the traditional middle classes rested their power on the older educational system, dominated by religion, the individuals in the new middle class draw their influence from the modern educational system. And this is what makes them an increasingly indispensable segment of society. Modernization results in constantly accelerated demands for qualified physicians, engineers, technocrats, and teachers. Economic and industrial development guarantees the growth of the new middle class.

In Turkey, Egypt, Libya, and Tunisia, members of the professional middle class have come to hold political power and have begun to implement developmental programs, with vary-

L. Binder, "Iran's Potential as a Regional Power," in *Political Dynamics in the Middle East,* eds. P. Y. Hammond and S. S. Alexander (New York: American Elsevier Publishing Co., 1972), p. 375. In an earlier study of Lebanese politics, however, Binder emphasizes the role of "a modern middle class." See Binder, "Political Change in Lebanon," in Binder, ed., *Politics in Lebanon* (New York: John Wiley and Sons, 1966), pp. 283–327. It is unlikely that the difference in approach is explained by the fact that two different societies are under scrutiny, since vertical stratification assumes an even more important role in Lebanon than it does in Iran.

ing degrees of success. In Iraq, Syria, and Algeria, individuals from the new middle class have taken political control, but have failed to solve the problem of divisions and discord among classes. This failure has severely retarded political development and modernization. In Iran, Morocco, Saudi Arabia, and Jordan, the professional intelligentsia remains largely locked out of the political arena.[80] In Iran and Morocco, where this class is a relatively large one, a number of its members have moved into the political elite as the result of a calculated policy of co-optation on the part of the ruling class. All in all, membership in the professional middle class throughout the Islamic Middle East is rapidly approaching 10 to 12 percent of the population.

The professional middle class is a threat to the traditional sociopolitical system in the Middle East. Many of its members decry the old network of personalism, favoritism, nepotism, and influence wielding that continues in many cases to suffocate their own opportunities to move forward on the basis of technical skills and professional merit. What makes this class such a serious threat to the traditional social structure is not so much that all its members are agents of modernization, but that some of its members demand political development. The latter refuse to relate to the ruling class in terms of subservience and deference. Instead, they demand a share of political authority and promise to uproot the power relations upon which the authority structure rests.

The attitude of the new middle class toward change differs considerably from that of the traditional middle classes. The bourgeois middle class demanded reform only so long as business was suffering and their economic position was endangered. This class could live with any political system and social structure that permitted trade to flourish. The bureaucratic middle class fed off the traditional sociopolitical system and never challenged a power structure that occasionally enabled administrators to move into the upper class. Finally, the class of ulema was a threat to the system only when that system severely and openly contradicted the principles of Islam.

[80] For a discussion of the appearance of the professional middle class in Saudi Arabia, see William A. Rugh, "Emergence of a New Middle Class in Saudi Arabia," *Middle East Journal* 27 (Winter 1973) :7–20.

In contrast, the professional middle class is composed of individuals whose goals include a transformation of power relations and the authority structure. Many of them prefer professionalism to personalism, justice to wealth, intellectual freedom to imposed stability, and effective political participation to political co-optation. Even in Saudi Arabia, when this kind of individual seeks "a role in the economy, he typically places higher value on the prestige or dignity of the job than on its monetary reward."[81] In Lebanon, the new middle class is very weak economically. "But in no sense should this detract from its vital role as carrier of new skills, ideologies, and styles of life. And this is certainly more relevant to its role as an agent of modernization."[82] It was shortly after the Egyptian coup in 1952 that Ahmad Baha'eddine wrote that this new middle class was "the greatest hope we have for progress."[83]

The professional middle class has seldom borne out such hopes, however, as it has not been as much of a force for development as might have been expected. Besides the extraordinary strength of the traditional political system, there are a number of other reasons why the new middle class has failed to implement much deep-seated change. Like every other social unit in the Middle East, this class is torn by internal divisions and tensions. These divisions are along the lines of kinship, ethnicity, religion, occupation, social origins, geography (urban and rural), and university background. All of these in turn affect the individual's orientations toward modernization and political development. It is concerning the latter that the new middle class remains most deeply divided. The influence of those who would uproot the traditional patterns of power and authority tends to be nullified by those who seek to preserve the traditional processes in order to improve their own positions in the system. This group usually supports mod-

81 Ibid., p. 22.

82 Samir Khalaf, "Urbanization and Urbanism in Beirut: Some Preliminary Results" (Paper prepared for delivery at the Twenty-first Annual Near East Conference, Princeton, N.J., 9–10 April 1970) , p. 37. This paper documents the important appearance of a new professional middle class in the Hamra district of Beirut. See also Samir Khalaf and Per Kongstad, *Hamra of Beirut: A Case of Rapid Urbanization* (Leiden: E. J. Brill, 1973) .

83 Baha'eddine, "Feudalists, Capitalists, and Intellectuals," p. 178.

ernization at the expense of political development. These are
the maneuverers in the new middle class who survive by
manipulation without imbuing it with the sincerity and cour-
teous charm that was the hallmark of the older generation. It
is this segment of the professional middle class that is readily
corruptible. In a stirring indictment of this group within the
intelligentsia, one young novelist writes: "Every country east
of the Mediterranean is torn to bits by ever-competing jealous
politicos coming to power by some kind of inheritance. . . .
But I can envisage the day when these countries will be even
worse, torn by degree-holders more self-interested and syco-
phantic than their predecessors, and far, far less charitable. If
you think the sheikh grinds the faces of his tribesmen you
should wait and see the Ph.D. grind the faces of all and sun-
dry, without even a touch of the magnanimity we pride our-
selves on."[84]

The professional middle class remains crippled in its challenge to traditional sociopolitical relations in the Middle East.
The deep fissures throughout the class are intentionally deepened by the ruling class in order to weaken the cohesiveness
of this challenging unit. The upper class encourages and supports those elements in the new class that are most susceptible
to the blandishments of bribery and personal aggrandizement.
Despite all this, however, the professional intelligentsia continues to grow. A few voices within the class continue to
clamor for radical social and political change. And because
the ruling class desperately needs the skills and talents of
these individuals in order to implement their programs of
modernization, the uprooters are slowly improving their
power positions. On the basic issues of power and authority
relations, the ruling class grudgingly gives ground, while working to preserve the ongoing class structure from the challenges presented by the new class. In the short run, the progress of the professional middle class will be unimpressive. In
the long run, this class will remain allied with the forces of
change. Accelerating modernization must eventually disrupt

---

[84] Jabra I. Jabra, *Hunters in a Narrow Street* (London, 1960) , as quoted
in *A Middle East Reader,* ed. Irene L. Gendzier (New York: Pegasus,
1969) , p. 114.

traditional political patterns. In this struggle, the professional middle class is located in the center of the ring.

The Dynamics of Group-Class Interaction. The dynamics of Middle Eastern social structure develop out of an integrated system of both vertical and horizontal stratification. The overall social structure might best be viewed as an intricate web of groups that is partially partitioned by class lines. Group and class structures relate to each other reciprocally, and it is this reciprocity that builds coherence into the sociopolitical system. The multistranded sinews of group relations bind the class structure together by crisscrossing class cleavages. Ethnic, tribal, religious, and military groups, for example, often draw their membership from several different classes. Here class distinctions are somewhat softened by common group affiliation. At the same time, group relations and formations are molded and shaped to a considerable degree by class. Groups are often structured along class lines, and their memberships remain confined within the boundaries of a single class. Family units, for example, tend to belong to a single class. Certainly, class divisions serve to retard individual and group mobility.

Class conflict in the Middle East is a muted phenomenon. There are three major reasons for this, and all of them relate to the impact of vertical stratification. First, the existence of a wide variety of important intraclass groups in the Middle East renders class units relatively diffuse. Fissures within classes are numerous and deep enough to weaken class cohesion and to retard class consciousness. Loyalty to primordial groups such as the family takes precedence over loyalty to class. Second, the plethora of groups with multiclass membership promotes interclass communication and draws together individuals from differing classes on the basis of shared group goals. As we point out above, this helps to integrate the class structure and therefore to mellow class conflict. Third, the group structure provides a system of channels through which individuals can rise and fall in the class hierarchy.[85]

[85] Fuad Khuri stresses a fourth reason for the relative lack of class conflict in the Middle East. In the case of the Lebanese at least, he argues

The pages of Middle Eastern history are dotted with dramatic examples of individual and group mobility. As one writer puts it, in the Middle East "one can be a liar in the morning, a vizir in the evening, and perhaps hanged on the following day."[86] Stretching vertically through the class structure are a number of shifting ladders of group configurations that, although unsteady and unpredictable, nonetheless can be negotiated by enterprising individuals. Many of the rungs of such ladders are difficult to discern because of the informal and concealed nature of their formation. Informal groups are, in general, the most reliable of the groups that span class divisions. Examples of groups that connect the middle and upper classes include military officer cliques, mystic orders, high administrative caucuses, and interfamilial marriage clusters. Let us examine the last example in more depth.

Nuclear families more often tend to be intraclass groups than do extended families, since the latter include a larger number of individuals, each striving to improve his own position in the social system. But once one member of either a nuclear or an extended family is able to improve his class standing, he subsequently acts as a force that helps to propel other family members forward in the power structure. At the very minimum, the individual in the higher class will be able to protect and defend his family's interests.[87] Always, however, when familial membership is spread among classes, it acts as a brake upon class tension and conflict. A more significant aspect of family-group structure in relation to class interaction is the mechanism of interfamilial marriage. In the Middle East, the marriage of two individuals is perhaps better de-

---

that there is a cynicism about ideas and ideology. This nonideological orientation apparently hinders the formation of class consciousness and ultimately stifles class conflict. In view of the recent civil war in Lebanon, Khuri's comments must be questioned. See Khuri, "Changing Class Structure in Lebanon."

86 Vincent Monteil, *Morocco* (New York: Viking Press, 1964), p. 141, as quoted in Rosen, "Rural Political Process," p. 223.

87 This is also true of other units of vertical stratification. In contemporary Iran, the entire Bahai religious group, which is overwhelmingly middle class in composition, is protected by a handful of powerful members of the ruling class who are also Bahais.

scribed as the union of two families. When the marriage partners are of different social classes, entire family clusters develop relatively tight interclass relationships. Indeed, it is
very common and increasingly possible for individuals of
middle-class background to search consciously for a mate who
comes from a powerful upper-class family.

Many members of the middle-class intelligentsia attempt to
improve their power positions by marrying into the ruling
class. Some pursue this strategy in a very calculating manner.
Others are torn between their commitment to merit and
achievement and their desire to gain enough political leverage
to enable them to implement their social and political ideas.
Practically all of them are forced to rely upon familial connections at many junctures in their professional and political
lives.[88] To the more professionally competent and politically
radical among them, this is unpalatable business, and many
are visibly embarrassed by the fact that they either belong to
the ruling class or have married into it. Middle-class professionals thus find themselves in the unenviable position of
denigrating their familial ties while at the same time being
forced to use these ties in order to survive and advance in
society. This kind of pressured compromise is another factor
reducing the effectiveness of their class as a revolutionizing
force. In terms of this discussion, it represents a method
whereby the challenging middle class is bound to the ruling
class. Family clusters cut across class lines and then serve as
bridges for the upwardly mobile members of the kinship
group.

Groups are much more fluid than classes in the Middle East

[88] In Jordan, "the social prestige of the upper class families is seriously
challenged by the increased number of professionals in the middle class
whereby the criteria of social stratification have shifted in the last two
decades from being primarily based on ancestral heritage, on ownership
of land, and on economic wellbeing. Formal education plays a large role
in assigning the strata of individuals. Even so, alliance with notables still
accelerates the advancement of one's social position to a great extent. So
it is not unusual for professionals to hasten to consolidate their position
by the purchase of an estate, or by inter-marrying with the landlord class
and by political and other associations with them." Ishaq Qutub, "The
Rise of the Middle Class," *Middle East Forum* 37 (December 1961) :42–43.

because they have much greater ranges of mobility. A class can improve its position only by rather limited incremental movements. The ruling class will always be the upper class, and so it is down the line. By definition, classes must always remain in a power hierarchy. Individuals and groups, on the other hand, can rise dramatically or fall meteorically within the social structure. The great movement of individuals and groups increases flexibility in a class structure that would otherwise be fragile and much more susceptible to upheaval and radical change.

The social structure described above is a formidable obstacle to the processes of modernization and political development that are under way in the Middle East. The traditional social system refuses to be torn, and the basic power and authority relations that make up this system are extraordinarily difficult to uproot. Since class conflict, often the agent of transformation, is neutralized, change involves chipping away at pieces of the mosaic. This modifying change seldom disturbs the underlying network of power relations that is the basis for the group and class structure of Middle Eastern societies.

The situation analyzed above differs considerably from one Middle Eastern society to another. Some societies, for example, are relatively congenial to modernization and political development. In these societies, the lines of horizontal stratification are only weakly intersected by communal cleavages. As a result, the traditional social structure is more easily torn, because class configurations are more cohesive internally and more bared to conflict externally. In Turkey, Tunisia, and Egypt, for example, the natural lines of class conflict and power confrontation are relatively infrequently intersected by ethnic, religious, and tribal divisions. In such countries as Syria and Iraq, on the other hand, communalism and the many vertical strands of stratification soften class confrontation and invest the traditional system with a stability nourished by a vast interlocking network of competing groups.

Much can be explained about the outbreak of the Lebanese civil war when it is recognized that the lines separating ethnic and religious groups had come to coincide more and more closely with class lines. The groups lost their cross-cutting character and gradually reinforced the explosive class divisions. In other words, the vertical structure of stratification gradually collapsed until it became a reinforcing part of the system of conflicting classes. The Lebanese upper class was dominated by Christian Arabs, while the lower class was overwhelmingly Muslim. Although there was some noticeable overlap, this had become less the case with time. When the explosion came, therefore, it was fueled by both group and class conflict. The presence of the Palestinians, a highly politicized appendage to the Lebanese lower class, only exacerbated the struggle. When group and class lines begin to coincide in the Middle East, the system begins to lose its balanced stability. Violent conflict is often the result, and the consequent changes can either accelerate or retard development. In Chapters IV and V, we will examine those individuals who do most to determine the directions these changes will take.

CHAPTER IV

The Politics of Patrimonial Leadership

AN IMPORTANT COMPONENT of the politics of power and change in the Middle East is the issue of political leadership. Although societies are composed of an interrelated network of groups and classes, there is always one group of individuals who have a disproportionate amount of power and influence on decision making. Sometimes referred to as the political elite, this group of leaders to a large degree shapes the political style and molds the political system of a society. In this chapter, we shall analyze the social characteristics and political methodology of Muslim leadership. In the process, it is also important for us to understand how individuals are recruited into leadership positions.[1]

Middle Eastern political leaders vary considerably from country to country. As the last stronghold of absolute monarchy in the world, the Middle East is the home of four major kingdoms and ten mini-monarchies located along the Persian Gulf. In order of ruling experience, the major monarchs include the following: King Husayn of Jordan, King Hassan of Morocco, Sultan Qabus of Oman, and King Khalid of Saudi Arabia. The other countries are almost all governed by mod-

[1] The growing scholarly interest in Middle Eastern leadership patterns is seen in the publication in 1975 of two separate collections of articles analyzing the political elites of various Middle Eastern countries. See George Lenczowski, ed., *Political Elites in the Middle East* (Washington, D.C.: American Enterprise Institute, 1975) and Frank Tachau, ed., *Political Elites and Political Development in the Middle East* (New York: Schenkman Publishing Co., 1975).

ern authoritarian leaders, most of whom came to power as the result of a military coup or national war of independence. Sandwiched between these two types of authoritarian control are the more representative structures that exist in such countries as Turkey and Israel, and that existed before the current chaos and violence in Lebanon.

Despite all the differences that separate Middle Eastern leaders and elites, there are in the Muslim world a number of deep-seated and persisting similarities in rule. These similarities, which are the subject of this chapter, have existed throughout Islamic history and can be traced to the days of the Prophet Muhammad — himself the model par excellence of political leadership.

The processes of leadership in the Islamic Middle East have been both represented and shaped by the life of Muhammad. Through the establishment of a new world community in the seventh century, the Prophet combined the roles of messenger of God and leader of men. Today, throughout the Islamic world, millions of Muslims continue to pattern their lives after his. It is not surprising, therefore, that twentieth-century Muslim political leaders often have styles and use strategies that are very similar to those instituted by the Prophet Muhammad in Arabia 1,350 years ago.

The very success of Muhammad as a political leader is one of the reasons that he remains a shadowy, distorted, and even frightening figure to many Westerners. In the pantheon of truly great world leaders, the Prophet has been the one most maligned by Western writers, who have for centuries found him an extremely difficult figure to interpret sympathetically. He has been presented in Western literature as a thug, sorcerer, sex fiend, murderer, and epileptic, and even as a defrocked Roman Catholic Cardinal. The ridiculous extreme of this perspective is seen in Guibert de Nogent's statement that Muhammad died "through excessive drunkenness and that his corpse was eaten by pigs on a dung-hill, explaining why the flesh of this animal and wine are prohibited."[2]

Dante's and Voltaire's views on the subject were only slightly

---

[2] Emile Dermenghem, *The Life of Mahomet* (London: George Routledge and Sons, 1930), p. 119.

more enlightened than those of de Nogent, and Diderot stated that Muhammad was "the greatest friend of woman and the greatest enemy of sober reason who ever lived."[3] Even Edward Gibbon and Washington Irving, whose writings about Muhammad were more objective, could not but view him negatively in the end. In concluding *Mahomet and His Successors,* Irving says that Muhammad had "mental hallucinations," which "continued more or less to bewilder him with a species of monomania to the end of his career, and that he died in the delusive belief of his mission as a prophet."[4]

These views of Muhammad undoubtedly result from ignorance and from insecurity because of the threat that his mission carried for the Western world. After all, Islam has been the only major non-Western, non-Christian movement that both posed a genuine political threat and provided an attractive alternative civilization while challenging Christendom on its own soil. Today, our understanding of the genius of Muhammad's leadership as well as of the patterns of rule of the contemporary leaders of Islamic countries remains sketchy and superficial. The fact that partisan Muslim scholars have tended to view Muhammad idealistically, defensively, and uncritically has not helped to improve this situation. In this chapter, we will attempt to avoid both extremes by analyzing Muhammad primarily and objectively as a political leader. By beginning our analysis with the general patterns of rule that Muhammad generated, we hope to be better able to understand the more recent political leaders to be discussed in Chapter V.

MUHAMMAD: THE POLITICS OF A PROPHET

The Prophet Muhammad was born in Mecca in 570. Social and political life was then dominated by the interaction between clans and tribes, and desert nomads were gradually moving into a more settled world of commerce and trade. This was a time of transition marked by continual feuds

[3] Tor Andrae, *Mohammad: The Man and His Faith* (New York: Barnes and Noble, 1936) , p. 175.

[4] Irving, *Mahomet and His Successors,* vol. 1 (New York: G. P. Putnam's Sons, 1893) , p. 391.

among clans and by intense commercial rivalry. The Prophet's personal environment was also unstable; by the time he was six, he had lost both of his parents. Muhammad was raised first by his grandfather and then by his uncle Abu Talib, who was the head of the clan of Hashim. Although little is actually known about his early life, it is safe to assume that he worked in menial positions related mainly to commerce and caravans. During his first twenty-five years, Muhammad gained firsthand experience and knowledge of the business, religion, and politics of the day. We know that he traveled to Syria and was in constant touch with peoples throughout that part of the world.

As an orphan and a member of one of the declining clans of the Quraysh tribe, Muhammad lacked many of the resources and contacts necessary to develop any important influence of his own. The first turning point in his life was, therefore, his marriage to the wealthy and twice-widowed Khadija. For the next two decades, Muhammad lived in the community as a prosperous and influential businessman. During this time, he acquired contacts and influence that were to be of fundamental importance to him in his role as prophet and preacher.

In about 610, Muhammad began receiving revelations, and shortly thereafter he began preaching in Mecca and presenting himself as a prophet. Although there were many Christians and Jews in Arabia at that time, most of the peoples were pagans and worshipped many gods. Muhammad preached the greatness and goodness of one God and emphasized the Judeo-Christian prophetic tradition. Few Meccans, however, chose to follow him. His earliest converts included his wife Khadija, his cousin Ali, his adopted son Zayd Ibn Haritha, and a respected and prominent Meccan, Abu Bakr.

As Muhammad continued his preaching and teaching, opposition to him increasingly grew. The reasons were many. He threatened the established economic and political order of the day, including the handsome income of the Meccans as custodians of the pagan shrines in their city. In a climate of escalating commerce and preoccupation with profit, his teachings emphasized the illusory nature of material wealth while encouraging such virtues as generosity, charity, and compassion. His criticism of the obsession for material gain was especially provoking, since he had made his own fortune in commerce. By striking at the idea of accumulating wealth, the Prophet was delivering a frontal attack on the Meccan lifestyle. Besides presenting an economic challenge, Muhammad posed a serious political threat to the leaders of Mecca. By questioning the economic basis of society and attacking the established order, the Prophet could only weaken the existing system. By attracting followers and building a community of his own, he offered the possibility of an alternative order. It is small wonder that the political leaders and influential persons in Meccan society became his dogged enemies. Muhammad's following was dominated by the young, the poor, and the dispossessed.

Despite this strong opposition, the Prophet was able to build the core of his Muslim movement while in Mecca. He received most of his revelations and gathered his original followers there during a decade of intense missionary activity. There are two basic reasons why this was possible. First, Muhammad was relatively discreet and diplomatic about his activities. His first efforts were directed toward those in whom he had most trust, such as close relatives, fellow clansmen, and intimate friends.[5] At times, important converts were brought into the community through marriage. This was the case with Uthman, a wealthy merchant who married a daughter of Muhammad's. Outside of this intimate circle of family and friends, attention was directed to those individuals who were most prone to conversion because of their peculiar position in society. D. S. Margoliouth writes, for example, that "Abu Bakr probably was aware that women are more amenable to conversion than men, resident foreigners than natives, slaves than freemen, persons in distress than persons in prosperity and

[5] One of the Prophet's very first converts was Abu Bakr, an influential Meccan cloth merchant. He was an extremely valuable ally and possessed a "readiness to follow the fortunes of some one else with complete and blind devotion, never questioning nor looking back; to have believed much was with him a reason for believing more. Mohammad, a shrewd judge of man, perceived this quality and used it." D. S. Margoliouth, *Mohammad and The Rise of Islam*, 3d ed. (New York: G. P. Putnam's Sons, 1905), pp. 83–84.

affluence."[6] A number of slaves were among the first to embrace the teachings of Muhammad. Finally, the meetings and activities of the first Muslims were carried out very quietly and unostentatiously. They took place in informal settings and personal homes, where they would not invite direct confrontation and public condemnation. The most famous site of this kind was the home of al-Arqam, where Muhammad could usually be found during the day and where his followers came and went at their convenience. From the very earliest days of its development, therefore, Islam has been what has been described as a "secret society."[7]

The second explanation for the Prophet's ability to survive in Mecca concerns the clan politics of the time. Each clan had learned that, in the interests of self-preservation, individual clan members had to be protected from all threats emanating from outside the clan. An individual could rely deeply on the support and protection of his fellow clansmen. Muhammad's clan, headed by his uncle Abu Talib, stood by him and provided him with a protective umbrella against his powerful opponents. Unable to penetrate this kind of clan unity, the opposition managed to institute a policy of isolating and boycotting Muhammad's entire clan. But in this system of seventh century politics, even the boycott failed and was abandoned after two years.

The Prophet was able to continue his activities in Mecca as long as his own clan shielded him. However, with the death of Abu Talib in 619, and the accession of Abu Lahab as head of the Hashim clan, Muhammad lost his clan's protective support. In the same year, his wife Khadija died and he was gradually forced out of Mecca. After numerous trials and tribulations, he fled to Medina in 622 in what is known in history as the *hijra* ("Hegira"). He was welcomed in Medina, a city torn by interclan strife and an economic competitor of Mecca. It is generally argued that the Medinans saw in Muhammad a leader who could serve as an effective and objective mediator between the constantly warring factions in their

6 Ibid., p. 97.
7 See ibid., pp. 83–117.

city. At the same time, they felt that the enemy of Mecca would serve them as a friend, and that Meccan hegemony in the area would in this way be weakened.

The significance of the hijra to Islamic political development cannot be overemphasized. It marked the beginning of the end of parochial clan politics and the origination of the *umma,* or "community." Clan divisions were to lose their meaning as clans were absorbed into a new religion and a new way of life. The community now had a "religious base" and could be described as a kind of "supertribe."[8] It was during his residence in Medina that Muhammad came to practice the style of leadership that formed the great Islamic community. During these last ten years of his life, he consolidated his position in Medina, defeated and took control of Mecca, converted numerous Arabian tribes and clans to his cause, and began a campaign of expansion that was to continue and spread long after his death.

Crucial to the success of Muhammad in Medina were his military campaigns, which escalated through time. Initially, they were confined to small *razzias* or "raids," against Meccan commercial caravans. Although these campaigns had very limited success in terms of capture and booty, they served the important purpose of binding together individuals of different clans and backgrounds in a common cause. It was nearly two years before a Meccan caravan was actually captured. Through the constant camaraderie in the relatively safe enterprise of caravan raiding, the followers of Muhammad gradually developed an esprit de corps that enabled them to defeat the Meccans in the critical battles that were to follow. In this regard, it is instructive to note that the extraordinarily significant battle of Badr in 624 developed out of an intended caravan raid. In this battle, the Prophet's forces decisively defeated the Meccans and killed more than a dozen of their most important leaders. One year later, Muhammad's forces brought a large attacking Meccan expedition to a standstill in the battle of Uhud. In this encounter, the Prophet himself played an

8 W. Montgomery Watt, *Muhammad: Prophet and Statesman* (London: Oxford University Press, 1961) , pp. 94–95.

important part in the fighting. Finally, in 627 Muhammad and his community withstood a two-week siege of Medina. This was the last great effort by the Meccans to defeat the new community.

At Medina, the Prophet built solidarity into the community in a variety of ways. Besides the numerous military campaigns directed against a common enemy, there were other catalysts to unity. Those clans in Medina that adamantly opposed Muhammad politically and ideologically were either expelled or destroyed. Preeminent among these opposition groups were the three Jewish clans of Qaynuqa, Nadir, and Qurayza. Scattered cases of political assassination also indicate that Muhammad condoned the use of this kind of force against particularly disruptive and resistant personalities.[9] This kind of civil violence was, however, engaged in only as a last resort. The emphasis was upon conversion and reconciliation. A primary means of accomplishing reconciliation was the web of intermarriage that not only bound the Emigrants (original Muslims from Mecca) closer together, but also helped bind the Emigrants to the Helpers (Medinan Muslims).

The most outstanding example of the Prophet's flair for consolidation by compromise and reconciliation is the Treaty of Hudaybiya, which was negotiated in 628. Muhammad decided to make a pilgrimage to Mecca and was accompanied by some fifteen hundred men. The Meccans, who doubted his intentions and suspected a military invasion, prepared to fight. Muhammad camped at al-Hudaybiya on the outskirts of Mecca and from there entered into negotiations with the Meccans. In the end, an agreement was reached whereby the Prophet and his men were to return to Medina. They had permission to come back in the following year and to carry out their pilgrimage. Another point in the treaty provided for a ten-year nonaggression pact between the Muslims and the Meccans. Despite strong pressures from numerous individuals in his own entourage who considered the expedition

---

[9] An example was the poet Ka'b Ibn al-Ashraf, who continually and bitingly attacked Muhammad and the Muslims. He went so far as to travel from Medina to Mecca, where he attacked the Muslim community in his poetry. He was assassinated in A.D. 624.

a failure, Muhammad returned to Medina. In so doing, he was implementing a brilliant policy of diplomatic tact that insured the peaceful conquest of Mecca two years later. The treaty convinced the Meccans that the Prophet was a reasonable man, that he did not want conflict, and that he did not plan to destroy Mecca. The journey to Hudaybiya was a political move, not a religious pilgrimage.

When the Prophet Muhammad died in 632, he left behind a community of peoples that was to expand and become one of the great civilizations of history. Tribes and clans, cities and empires were drawn together and unified under the ideology of Islam. The political acumen and astute leadership of Muhammad were instrumental in making this possible. These and other qualities of the Prophet have been noted and imitated by Muslims for centuries; Muhammad is the ideal model for all believers. The reasons are not only that he was the Seal of the Prophets, the Mirror of the Almighty, and the Founder of Islam, but also that he was intensely human. Unlike Christ, Muhammad was not considered divine. One leading Islamic scholar writes that the Prophet "married, had a household, was a father and moreover he was ruler and judge and had also to fight many wars in which he had to undergo painful ordeals."[10] In the words of another analyst: "It is a likeable characteristic of Mohammed that he never claimed perfection or infallibility, but always admitted frankly that he was guilty of shortcomings and mistakes like other men."[11] He lived, in short, as a convincing and believable model after whom all Muslims could pattern their lives.

The Course of Compromise. Muhammad was born into a world of interpersonal feuding, factional strife, and tribal conflict. The political system was an atomistic one in which families and clans survived by remaining in a constant state of embattlement against other families and clans. The lines of confrontation that crisscrossed the system were drawn so rigidly that there was little room for flexible policies of retreat and

[10] Seyyed Hossein Nasr, *Ideals and Realities of Islam* (London: George Allen and Unwin, 1966) , p. 69.

[11] Andrae, *Mohammed,* p. 179.

advance. This was an era of the blood feud, punitive reprisal, and the *lex talionis* (law of retaliation). It was into this climate of division and distrust that the Prophet carried the strategy and spirit of compromise. This was, of course, essential if social integration and political unity were to be achieved at all. The need to unite was a fundamental issue in the Middle East then, and it remains a basic issue in the Middle East today. A leader's political success rests to a great extent upon his ability to integrate and unite the divided and fragmented groups that compose society. An indispensable tool to the implementation of this kind of program is a strategy of political flexibility and compromise.

Muhammad's willingness to compromise is particularly noteworthy because of the climate of feuding in which it occurred. One of the most dramatic demonstrations of this talent is, of course, the Treaty of Hudaybiya referred to earlier. This is one demonstration of the manner in which age-old hatreds and animosities were overcome. After twenty years of struggle with the Meccans, the Prophet returned victorious to Mecca in the year 630. "There, at a moment when the very people who had caused untold hardships and trials for the Prophet, were completely subdued by him, instead of thinking of vengeance, which was certainly his due; he forgave them."[12] Although many Islamic scholars tend to explain this forbearance in terms of the great nobility, generosity, and compassion of the Prophet, it can also be analyzed as one in a long series of wise political policies. It is significant, however, that the moral virtue of compassion and the political strategy of compromise were inseparably linked in the career of Muhammad. This again shows the intimate relation between the sociopolitical activity of the Prophet and the ideology of Islam.

Throughout his political career, Muhammad tried to soften confrontation and to gain strength and unity by bargaining. Thus, he and his followers entered numerous marriage pacts with both actual and potential opposition forces. And many tribes joined the Muslim community as a result of the Prophet's long and peaceful march to Tabuk on the Gulf of Aqaba

12 Nasr, *Ideals and Realities,* pp. 71–72.

in 630. When Muhammad dispatched two missions to Yemen, he told the leaders of both missions: "Make it easy and do not make it too difficult. Be the carriers of good tidings, and do not cause disaffection."[13] Resort to violence and warfare occurred only after other avenues to agreement had been closed.

The success of tribal societies in developing a relatively respected and influential place in the world community is almost directly proportional to their ability to overcome internal dissension and to resist external encroachment. The clans or tribes in Middle Eastern history that have formed the basis for national communities or international empires have been precisely those that have been able to overlook past conflicts and to weld themselves into political units seeking common goals. The will and capacity to compromise at critical junctures is an essential element in this process of integration. The Prophet's style of political leadership included this ingredient. It is tempting to say today that Anwar Sadat has a generous portion of this element.

The Character of Charisma. The Prophet Muhammad viewed himself "as a man who had been given a special commission by God."[14] Although he was thoroughly human, he was not an ordinary human. He was the messenger and prophet of God, and his spiritual teachings were bound up in his social and political life. According to German sociologist Max Weber, a charismatic individual is one who "is set apart from ordinary men and treated as endowed with supernatural, superhuman, or at least specifically exceptional powers or qualities."[15] A charismatic leader is one who possesses a special grace and whose followers are irresistibly drawn to him because of this grace. There is a sensed otherworldly quality that engenders in others trust, commitment, and a willingness to follow. In Islam, there is an important concept that is remarkably similar to the idea of charisma. This is the concept

[13] Hasan al-Karmi, "The Prophet Muhammad and the Spirit of Compromise," *Islamic Quarterly* 8 (July and December 1964) :90.

[14] Watt, *Muhammad*, p. 15.

[15] Max Weber, *The Theory of Social and Economic Organization* (New York: Oxford University Press, 1947) , p. 358.

baraka, which is a special blessing of divine origin. "God can implant an emanation of *baraka* in the person of his prophets and saints: Muhammad and his descendants are especially endowed therewith. These sacred personages, in their turn, may communicate the effluvia of their supernatural potential to ordinary men. . . ."[16] In contemporary political analysis, the term *charismatic* has come to be applied so loosely and indiscriminately that it has lost the force of its original meaning. If one stands by the Weberian definition, however, genuinely charismatic leaders have been rather rare in world history. Despite the exclusiveness of this definition, the Prophet Muhammad remains an outstanding case of the charismatic leader and may in fact be the prototype of this rare kind of personality.

All of Muhammad's personal, social, and political activities carried a deep spiritual significance. As a prophet and receptacle of revelation, he held an extraordinary position in the eyes of his followers. The teachings and tenets of Islam became the ideology of his rule, and all aspects of community life were regulated by this ideology. Muhammad's charisma was derived from his role as prophet of God and publicizer of the word of God. As a result, his position as political leader had an extremely solid ideological foundation. Members of the Islamic community, because they were Muslims, considered Muhammad to be the temporal, social, political, and religious leader of society. Muhammad "had been marked out from his early youth, even from his birth, by supernatural signs and qualities."[17] He was a charismatic personality in the full sense of that term.

One of the basic principles of political leadership is that a leader be able to justify his special position by developing a supporting system of ideas and ideals. This kind of ideology may bear little relation to the hard realities of politics and society, but it can play a crucial role in enabling a leader to maintain his rule and to institute effective policies. Muhammad emerges as a model of success in this regard, since the

---

16 G. S. Colin, "Baraka," *The Encyclopedia of Islam,* new ed. (London: Luzac and Co., 1960) , 1:1032.

17 Watt, *Muhammad,* p. 2.

divine and the human, and the spiritual and the material are inextricably entwined in his message. Muslims did not think of questioning his authority in the community. Thus, he stands in great contrast to numerous contemporary Muslim leaders, who assiduously attempt to build supportive ideologies only on the basis of flimsy and fabricated relationships to Islam or to the Prophet himself.

Much of the appeal of Muhammad's ideological message undoubtedly derived from the social and political content of that message. Islam called for equality, compassion, and unity in a world dominated by inequality, self-aggrandizement, and disunity. In its stress upon equality and simplicity, it appealed to the distressed masses. And Muhammad himself lived what he preached. Thus, even Edward Gibbon could write: "The good sense of Mohammed despised the pomp of royalty; the apostle of God submitted to the menial offices of the family; he kindled the fire, swept the floor, milked the ewes, and mended with his own hands his shoes and his woollen garment."[18] In its emphasis upon unity and integration, on the other hand, Islam offered much to the middle and upper strata in society. As the prophet who announced this message and as a leader who lived by it, Muhammad charismatically built the foundation of a civilization.

The Politics of Personalism. Another pattern of politics that enabled the Prophet Muhammad to gain and consolidate a strong leadership position in the nascent Islamic community was the pervasive pattern of personalism. In societies where clans and kinship groups were the key social and political realities of life, personal ties were the basic channels of power and influence. By analyzing and exploiting the intricate web of personal relations that existed in seventh-century Arabia, Muhammad and his associates were better able to form their

18 Gibbon, *Decline and Fall of the Roman Empire*, 3 vols. (New York: The Modern Library, 1932), 3:116. No matter what their ultimate judgment concerning Muhammad might be, well-known Western interpreters of world history are united in their recognition of the simple and spartan life that he led. Besides Gibbon, Toynbee and Durant also comment specifically about this facet of Muhammad's life.

new community. Abu Bakr's expertise as a genealogist, which is emphasized in many sources, is highly significant when viewed in this light. As Muhammad's chief advisor, Abu Bakr continually used his deep knowledge of the complex relations of kinship, as well as of the factions and feuding, that marked the society of the day.

One of the major means of consolidation and integration for the Prophet was the manipulation of this personal web through marriage. For Muhammad, "many of his marriages were political ones which, in the prevalent social structure of Arabia, guaranteed the *consolidation* of the newly founded Muslim community. Multiple marriage, for him, as is true of Islam in general, was not so much enjoyment as responsibility and a means of *integration* of the newly founded society."[19] Muhammad married at least nine times, and one could argue that all of his marriages, even the union with Khadija, were political in nature. W. Montgomery Watt writes that for a "poor orphan" to make his way, "the one possibility was to find a rich woman to marry him, so that he could, as it were, enter into a business partnership with her."[20] It was through marriage that the Prophet hardened the nucleus of his community, while softening the resistance of those outside the community.

The central leadership of the Islamic community was tightly bound together through marriage, since the Prophet developed family ties with those among his closest followers who were later to become the first four caliphs (see Figure IV.1). Muhammad himself married A'isha and Hafsa, who were the daughters of Abu Bakr and Umar, respectively. At the same time, he married three of his own daughters to Uthman and Ali. Ali

19 Nasr, *Ideals and Realities*, p. 70. Italics ours.

20 Watt, *Muhammad*, p. 10. Watt cannot seem to emphasize enough the importance of the political motive in the Prophet's various marriages. In this study alone, he makes the argument in eight separate places. See pp. 10–12, 79, 102–3, 131, 155–57, 195, 206, 233. In another study Watt writes that "all Muhammad's own marriages can be seen to have a tendency to promote friendly relations in the political sphere." See Watt, *Muhammad at Medina* (Oxford: Clarendon Press, 1956), p. 287. Although, like Watt, we have stressed the political dimensions of Muhammad's marriages, we do not mean to deny the human and personal motives that were also obviously involved.

FIGURE IV.1   *Consolidation by Marriage: The Core of the Community*

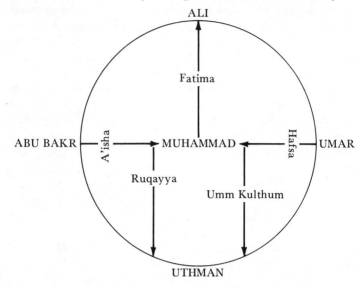

married Fatima, and Uthman first wedded Ruqayya, and then upon her death, renewed this important tie by marrying her sister Umm Kulthum.[21] The concern for holding the community together can also be seen in the tendency for leading Muslims to marry the widows of those members of the community who died or were killed in battle. Four of the Prophet's wives, for example, were widows of prominent early Muslims. Three of these Muslims had been killed in the important conflicts at Badr and Uhud.

The second category of marriages involved those that were contracted with members of potential or actual opposition forces. Many personal ties were developed with tribal groups throughout Arabia by means of this mechanism. Muhammad himself married three women who were the daughters of non-Muslim tribal notables. In each case, the marriage neutralized much political tension. The most important personal ties established through wedlock, however, were those involving

[21] Ali also married a granddaughter of Muhammad's while Umar married both a granddaughter of Muhammad's and a daughter of Ali's.

the opposition in Mecca. By marrying the daughter of the influential Meccan leader Abu Sufyan, and then one year later wedding the sister-in-law of the new head of the Meccan clan of Hashim, al-Abbas, Muhammad managed to establish intimate personal ties that were crucial to his tranquil conquest of Mecca. This two-pronged policy of developing personal relations both to strengthen an ongoing alliance and to absorb opposition forces is reflected in a split that occurred among Muhammad's wives. The wives divided into two factions — those who had come from within the Muslim community itself and those whose original roots had been in the opposition clans in Mecca.[22]

The original Muslim community functioned politically solely on the basis of personalities and personalism. In this sense, it differed very little from the pre-Islamic style of tribal and clan politics. Ruling institutions such as formal administrative organizations were unknown. The Prophet appointed specific individuals to lead military campaigns, diplomatic expeditions, and economic missions, depending upon the exigencies of the moment. As we have seen in the case of the marriage mechanism, this political personalism had real advantages. Not the least of these was the introduction of a degree of social and political flexibility, which is crucial in the construction of a new social and political system.

The Unity of the Community. Through the interrelated patterns of compromise, charisma, and personalism, the Prophet Muhammad was able to build integrative patterns into a system otherwise prone to disintegration. Through a universal message delivered by a charismatic leader, peoples of widely differing background were attracted to a single community. This process of integration and consolidation is the main principle of Muhammad's message, for as Seyyed Hossein Nasr has written, "Unity is the alpha and omega of Islam."[23] Muhammad's charisma was an integrating force that intertwined the spiritual with the material and combined the social, the

---

[22] W. Montgomery Watt, " 'Ā'ishā Bint Abī Bakr," *The Encyclopedia of Islam,* new ed. (London: Luzac and Co., 1960) , 1:308.

[23] Nasr, *Ideals and Realities,* p. 29.

religious, and the political. The leader himself exhibited an
internal unity by combining such virtues as compassion and
strength, and this in turn strengthened his charismatic appeal.[24] The ideology professed by a charismatic personality
was a key ingredient in sealing the fissures and rifts that
characterized the social structure. The more practical political
policies of compromise and personalism as adopted and implemented by Muhammad, then enabled him to confront on
a daily basis the centrifugal social tendencies. The capacity to
compromise dulled old antagonisms and hatreds in a way that
allowed policies of personalism to acquire new meaning. Personal ties could now signal a kind of cooperation and con-
ciliation that more often than not led to conversion and consolidation. These three qualities of compromise, charisma, and
personalism, combined with the obviously important military
dimension, were the key elements in the Prophet Muhammad's
style of leadership.

PATTERNS OF PATRIMONIALISM IN THE MIDDLE EAST

> *My good Pasha, the will of the people emanates from my
> will!*
>
> King Farouk of Egypt[25]

In his important analysis and typology of traditional political systems, Max Weber includes two types that he labels
patriarchal and patrimonial systems.[26] The patriarchal system
is the core of all traditional systems and is generally confined to household kinship groups. In this kind of system,
the authority relation is one that binds master and family.
The head of the household "has no administrative staff and
no machinery to enforce his will. . . . The members of the

---

24 For an interesting discussion of this point, see Frithjof Schuon, *Understanding Islam* (London: George Allen and Unwin, 1963), pp. 87–105.
25 As quoted in P. J. Vatikiotis, *The Egyptian Army in Politics: Pattern
for New Nations?* (Bloomington: Indiana University Press, 1961), p. 39.
26 A third type is the feudal system, which was the dominant traditional
system in Western societies. For the presentation of Weber's analysis of
patriarchal and patrimonial politics, see Weber, *The Theory of Social and
Economic Organization*, pp. 341–58; and Reinhard Bendix, *Max Weber:
An Intellectual Portrait* (Garden City, N.Y.: Doubleday and Co., 1962),
pp. 330–60.

household stand in an entirely personal relation to him. They obey him and he commands them in the belief that his right and their duty are part of an inviolable order that has the sanctity of immemorial tradition. Originally the efficacy of this belief depended on the fear of magical evils that would befall the innovator and the community that condoned a breach of custom."[27] The patrimonial system, on the other hand, is one in which an identifiable administrative structure develops and spreads throughout the particular society or empire. The tasks of government become more specialized, complex, and elaborate. As a result, the ruler's relation with the ruled tends to be filtered through a huge network of bureaucrats. Owing to the introduction of a more complex and differentiated administrative apparatus, the emphasis on the mysterious and the magical becomes somewhat softened.

The literature that has attempted to discuss and utilize this Weberian typology has greatly overemphasized the differences between the patriarchal and patrimonial forms of rule. This has resulted in a misplaced preoccupation with such issues as specialization of roles and differentiation of structures. The key to understanding the traditional processes of leadership is the fundamental human relations that bind ruler and ruled. These were shaped in the patriarchal environment and were hardened and routinized in the patrimonial system. In essence, the patrimonial form of rule represents little more than an extension and expansion of the patriarchal system. The relations that bind ruler and ruled, leader and led, master and servant, and king and subject are fundamentally the same in both Weberian categories. Reinhard Bendix defines patrimonial rule, therefore, as "an extension of the ruler's household in which the relation between the ruler and his officials remains on the basis of paternal authority and filial dependence."[28]

In most Islamic societies, patrimonial patterns of leadership have been dominant. The particular manifestation of patrimonial rule that has marked these societies is referred to by Manfred Halpern as a "relationship of emanation." The poli-

27 Bendix, *Max Weber*, pp. 330–31.
28 Ibid., p. 360.

tics of emanation involves an "encounter in which one treats
the other solely as an extension of one's self. The other accepts
the denial of his own separate identity because of the mysterious and overwhelming power of the source of this emanation
—a yielding which is rewarded with total security."[29] When
the Spanish Ummayad caliph Abd al-Rahman al-Nasir died
at the turn of the tenth century after fifty years of rule, he was
publically eulogized in terms that capture the basic meaning
of rule by emanation: "The souls of the people were absorbed
in his soul; when he died they died also."[30] There is little
doubt that this caliph possessed baraka in abundance. In the
Islamic world, where religion and politics have always been
inseparable, shahs, sultans, and shaykhs have tended to rule
in a paternal, patriarchal, and patrimonial manner. Government has been personal and both civil and military bureaucracies have been little more than extensions of the leader. In the
cases of the Ottoman, Safavid, and Moghul empires, the royal
household developed into a huge administrative octopus, with
the leader as head and the leader's gigantic retinue of personal servants and confidants as tentacles. In patrimonial politics, "bureaucratic recruitment and advances are based on
personal confidence and not on objective qualifications; they
reflect the more or less precarious balance reached by the
prince in his effort to create and maintain a bureaucracy completely dependent upon his power. In each case, the position
of the patrimonial bureaucrat must remain what it orginally
was — an emanation of his relation of purely personal submission to the Lord. . . ."[31]

[29] Halpern, "Four Contrasting Repertories of Human Relations in
Islam," in *Psychological Dimensions of Near Eastern Studies,* ed. L. Carl
Brown and Norman Itzkowitz (Princeton, N.J.: Darwin Press, 1977) , p.
64. In this article, Halpern sensitively explores the significance of the
politics of emanation to the Middle Eastern peoples and political systems.
We have chosen to emphasize his conceptualization of emanation as the
central pattern in patrimonialism.

[30] Lisan al-Din Ibn Khatib [Book of works by leading authors concerning those accepted as kings of Islam] (Rabat: New Press, 1934) , p. 44. In
Arabic.

[31] Magali Sarfatti, *Spanish Bureaucratic-Patrimonialism in America,*
Politics of Modernization Series, no. 1 (Berkeley: University of California
Institute of International Studies, 1966) , p. 8.

In the patrimonial Middle East, the sovereign is located at the center of the political system. Here, he is surrounded by advisors, ministers, military leaders, personal secretaries, and confidants. The one thing that all members of this inner circle share is unquestioned personal loyalty to the leader. This is best indicated by their continual reflection of the will and personality of that leader. Although these individuals may relate submissively and passively to the leader, they do not relate in this way to their own peers and followers. Here, they are caught up in the most intense manipulations and machinations possible.[32] The reason for this, of course, is that a minister who relates passively towards a monarch on one level is the central source of leadership on another level. Therefore, within his own ministry, he may be the emanating influence, and his subordinates (deputy ministers, director generals, etc.) survive by remaining passive before him. Although the vertical relations tend to be one-sided, the horizontal patterns are characterized by balanced rivalry. Those who are relatively equal in power and authority are locked in constant conflict and struggle. This conflict can occur only below the level of the sovereign, since the sovereign has no equals in a patrimonial context. This kind of division and rivalry is constantly being sharpened by the competition among rivals to demonstrate the greatest loyalty and submission to their leader. The leader, in turn, encourages and manipulates this competition. The traditional politics of patrimonial leadership in the Middle East, therefore, tends to consist of chains of vertical emanation and horizontal competition that cut through the sociopolitical fabric (see Figure IV.2).

In the patrimonial style of Middle Eastern leadership, the leader becomes the fount of all important ideas and strategies. Policies and programs emanate from him. New ideas and suggestions that others might have must somehow be submitted to the leader, who may propose them as his own. Historically, the Middle Eastern political landscape is littered with individuals who attempted and failed to project themselves into the

---

[32] The Watergate incident indicates that this situation is not unique to the Middle East.

Figure IV.2 *Patrimonial Leadership*

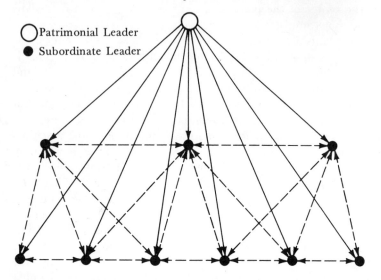

political limelight through their own ideas and ambitions. Often, they were the very closest confidants of the leader himself; by staking claim to their own political ground, they challenged the very relation of emanation and hastened their own inevitable political demises. This is precisely what happened when Abbasid caliph Harun al-Rashid in 803 disposed of his powerful Barmecid friend and advisor Ja'far ibn Yahya and imprisoned the other members of Ja'far's family. Numerous similar examples exist in both Ottoman and Persian history.

We have already mentioned how Suleyman the Magnificent suddenly turned on his intimate friend the vazir Ibrahim Pasha in 1536. The most famous example of a leader turning against an independent-minded subordinate in Persian history occurred in the mid-nineteenth century during the rule of the Qajar dynasty (1779–1925). Nasir al-Din Shah, who ruled Iran for half a century, gave the orders that led to the dismissal and death of his strong-willed and illustrious minister Mirza Taqi Khan Amir Kabir. Mirza Taqi Khan has gone down in Persian history as that country's greatest reformer and most beloved prime minister. Because of this man's brilliance and dramatic administrative programs, the young Shah's light only flickered until Mirza Taqi Khan was disposed of in 1851 — after having served only three years in the post. As we shall see in Chapter V, there are many contemporary examples of this pattern.

The nearer individuals are to the patrimonial leader, the more likely they are to have their ideas accepted and put into practice by the leader. In such a personal system of politics, physical nearness to the leader is an especially significant variable in explaining the distribution of power and influence. It would be wrong to assume that in a patrimonial system those who surround the leader have no influence at all. They always exert a subtle and passive influence, largely by having their ideas absorbed into those of the leader. In such a system, "advisors" never demand, seldom suggest, and only advise when advice is actively sought. They more often applaud than appraise. Although their influence on the leader may be sporadic, their influence on everyone else will usually be very intense. The closer an adviser is to the leader, the more influential he will be both with the ruler and with the people.[33]

Middle Eastern societies have been governed by authoritarian patrimonial systems throughout most of history. Islam fostered patrimonial patterns both through its ideals and in reality. The entire philosophical framework that evolved with Islam stressed relations of emanation. The term *Islam* itself means submission, and Islam demands that all believers perfect their acceptance and reflection of the Almighty. The Prophet Muhammad is the prototype of the leader linked in the chain of emanation, since he is the one who relates the material to the spiritual. Muhammad represents perfect passivity before

33 Because of the continual competition and wielding of influence that occur at all levels of Islamic society, the intricate but effective manner in which subordinates can have their ideas incorporated into those of the ruler, and the constant challenging of particular relations of emanation by those who wish to assert their own power, we cannot characterize Islamic leadership as either "Oriental despotism," to use Wittfogel's terms, or "sultanism," to use Max Weber's term. As we shall see, the informal, bargaining, and balancing nature of Middle Eastern politics contradicts such an emphasis on absolute authority, total power, and hardened hierarchy.

God and perfect activity before man. He was the mirror who reflected the word of God, and "he saw nothing except in God and through God."[34] In his relations with man, however, the Prophet lived a most vigorous social, political, and religious life, since he traded, fought, judged, and ruled. He was "that warrior on horseback who halts before the mountain of Truth, passive towards the Divine Will, active towards the world. . . ."[35] As Muhammad modeled his life after the Divine, millions of Muslims labor to model their lives after his. The Prophet's community in Medina was a patrimony infused with the charisma of a special leader.

The intermeshing of religion and politics in Islam has meant that political leaders have often had the opportunity to present themselves as linked directly to God. This has helped invest them with a mysterious and otherworldly aura that has allowed them to be exalted as models to be imitated and followed by the people. This is one reason why political leaders in Islamic societies have historically attempted to trace their ancestry back to the family of the Prophet. The only innate aristocracy in Islamic civilization consists of those individuals in the community who are related to the family of the Prophet Muhammad.

The personal rivalry that has always been central to patrimonial society has led to numerous schisms and divisions within the Islamic community. What has marked all of these splinter movements, however, has been their tendency to reform themselves by placing extreme emphasis upon leadership by emanation. Part of the reason for this is the need for any political movement playing the role of challenger to legitimate its existence and its claims. This must be done as convincingly and dramatically as possible. All Shi'i societies have exhibited the patrimonial rule by emanation in its most pronounced form.[36] This is seen in the significant figure of the imam, who is the leader par excellence in the Shi'i community.

34 Nasr, *Ideals and Realities,* p. 84.

35 Ibid., p. 9.

36 For an exceptionally fine analysis of the Fatimid caliphate, which emphasizes the theoretical aspects of patrimonial patterns of emanation, see P. J. Vatikiotis, *The Fatimid Theory of State* (Lahore: Orientalia Publishers, 1957).

Ali was the first Imam, and he has been succeeded by other Imams, their number varying with the different sects. The critical point here is that the imam is not selected by the community, but succeeds by virtue of divine appointment, or *nass*. The imam is the vicegerent of God, and the line of imams consists of a divinely fashioned chain of emanation that is unquestioned in the minds of the believers. Whereas the Sunni caliph is an ordinary mortal, the Shi'i imams exist in a state of permanent grace that renders them infallible, impeccable, and immaculate.[37] The imam is the one who rules by the will of God and in the name of God. In the Iranian version of Shi'i Islam, the twelfth and last imam has gone into hiding and is meanwhile represented by the important cleric leaders known as mujtahids. According to strict Shi'i doctrine, as representatives of the Hidden Imam, these mujtahids are the major sources of interpretation for all social, political, and religious affairs. The shahs, however, have traditionally attempted to lock themselves into the legitimizing tradition of the imams. Much of Iranian politics, therefore, revolves about the relationship between mujtahids and shahs as they compete for legitimacy by emanation. The mass uprisings against the Shah in 1978, for example, were organized around the leading mujtahids who criticized the Iranian government for its alleged repressive, corrupt, and anti-constitutional activities.

Muhammad's early community was organized according to patrimonial principles. The Prophet stood at the head of the sociopolitical household, and personal ties and relations knit the entire community together. These relations were made particularly binding by the fact that most of the main leaders and followers were brought into the Prophet's own familial household. The dynamics of Muhammad's leadership that have been briefly sketched above highlight these patterns. Muhammad's charismatic personality and his relation to the Divine enabled individuals such as Abu Bakr to become absorbed in his affairs and to accept his leadership completely. The special charismatic nature of the Prophet's rule by emanation overcame much of the intracommunity dissension and conflict endemic to systems of patrimonial politics. It was when

---

[37] Professor Martin B. Dickson of Princeton University has clarified this particular point for us.

Muhammad died that all of these submerged dissensions broke to the surface and schisms became common.

The patrimonial leaders who succeeded the Prophet found relations of emanation less persuasive and effective. This became more and more the case as dynastic heads became further removed from the days of Muhammad's rule. Islamic history, therefore, is replete with examples of leaders at all levels and in all communities who made dramatic efforts to strengthen the patrimonial patterns by infusing new life into increasingly unbelievable relations of emanation. This was done in two complementary ways: (1) the original charismatic leaders to which the new leaders were attached were accorded supernatural status; and (2) a proclaimed leader attempted to build a special relation between himself and the earlier prototype.

In the first case, the leaders in early Islam are glorified and purified until in some instances they appear to have possessed godly qualities. This has been particularly true in the case of Ali, the fourth caliph and son-in-law of the Prophet. In the second instance, communities develop around individuals who claim to be special representatives or messengers either of these early patrimonial heroes or even of God himself. Saints and holy personages play an important role in Middle Eastern politics and society. One scholar writes, for example, that "the most characteristic social institution of North African religious life is the saint, the holy personage. As Islam does not enjoin celibacy, saints proliferate and form lineages and dynasties."[38] Mahdis, marabouts, and imams have formed political movements of great influence in the Middle East. The Moroccan marabouts were the major force shaping the social and political systems in large areas of North Africa until the end of the nineteenth century.[39] In a patrimonial political system, the

[38] Ernest Gellner, "Sanctity, Puritanism, Secularisation and Nationalism in North Africa: A Case Study," mimeographed (n.p., n.d.), p. 1. See also Gellner's fine study, *Saints of the Atlas* (Chicago: University of Chicago Press, 1969).

[39] Dale Eickelman tells this story well. He defines marabouts as persons "to whom is attributed a special relation toward God which makes them particularly well placed to serve as intermediaries with the supernatural and to communicate God's grace (*baraka*) to their clients." See Eickelman, *Moroccan Islam* (Austin: University of Texas Press, 1976), p. 6.

basic patterns, which often shatter and disintegrate, have traditionally been reknitted through the appearance of a new leader claiming either special supernatural power or a special relation with those who are believed to have had such power.

Patterns of leadership in the Middle East have been highly congruent from institution to institution and from community to community. In the family, school, guild, and government, patrimonialism prevails. Much of the reason for this is the influence of Islam, which penetrates all aspects of a believer's life. In patriarchal or patrimonial societies, the patriarch is the main social and political reality. He is the model, the guide, the innovator, the planner, the mediator, the chastiser, and the protector. The community wraps itself around the leader, who governs through a constantly expanding web of personal relations. Within the family, which is the basic social unit in the Middle East, the father is the unrivaled leader. The situation is best summarized as follows: "The Muslim family has remained patriarchal, and the head of it maintains his authority . . . down to the last day of his life."[40] Traditionally, wives and children have been little more than extensions of the will of the father, whose authority is in his own opinion "natural and divine."[41] One Middle Eastern writer refers to a "blind reverence" that the father receives from his children, who relate to him "as if fearing a mysterious superhuman force."[42] The personal tension that is built into patrimonial systems is dramatically evident in the family, where sibling rivalry takes a particularly intense form. Brother competes against brother, and various shifting alliances are formed as mothers, children, cousins, grandparents, aunts, and uncles are pulled into the continual competition and conflict. The father or leader tends to promote rather than to alleviate this kind of rivalry.

In educational and occupational settings, the roles and styles of leadership are essentially the same as those that mark the

[40] Maurice Gaudefroy-Demombynes, *Muslim Institutions* (London: George Allen and Unwin, 1961) , p. 128.

[41] Cyrus Parham, "Divine Authority of a Persian Father," mimeographed (n.p., n.d.) , p. 1.

[42] Ibid., p. 2.

family and the government. The master-apprentice, teacher-student, and shaykh-*murid* (brotherhood disciple) relations are patterns of superordination and subordination in which the follower's existence is an extension of the leader's being. The teacher-student relation is, in fact, somewhat closer to the father-son relation than to the patterns found in guild and brotherhood organizations. The latter have preserved much more of the otherworldly quality that serves to strengthen the bonds of emanation. This quality has been gradually lost in the educational system as the religious direction of education has given way to secular control. The basic pattern, however, can still be seen in almost any Middle Eastern classroom, where the teacher's person is deferred to and the teacher's word is memorized. In the environment of guilds and brotherhoods, deference becomes devotion, and shaykhs, who are the leaders, command a charismatic control that is generally absent in familial, governmental, and formal educational institutions. In the case of sufi orders or brotherhoods, "all authority and allocation of authority positions in the hierarchy lie within the purview of the Sheikh, and the subordinates derive their statuses from him."[43] Those who are closest to the shaykh's person have the greatest influence in the order. Therefore, the personal secretaries and attendants of the shaykh are extremely important figures in these organizations. They are, of course, entirely devoted to and dependent upon the leader. In describing this kind of relation between a private secretary and the shaykh in a contemporary Egyptian brotherhood, one member explained that the secretary does not even go to sleep "until the Sheikh tells him to."[44]

Patrimonialism has been the dominant pattern of leadership in Middle Eastern politics for centuries. The strength of this pattern has fluctuated greatly, depending upon the leader, dynasty, society, and era. Patrimonialism was most evident in the heyday of the shahs and sultans. The politics of patrimonial leadership as manifested in the Middle East reflects six

[43] Michael Gilsenan, "The Sufi Orders and the Modern World," mimeographed (n.p., 29 September 1967), pp. 7–8.

[44] Ibid., p. 45.

major characteristics: personalism, proximity, informality, balanced conflict, military prowess, and religious rationalization.

Personalism. Patrimonial society rests upon personal relationships. The community or society is essentially an enlarged household, and the personal ties that dominate in the household are the model for the ties in any other patrimonial unit. Middle Eastern societies and political systems grew out of tribal constellations, and the personalism that prevailed in the family and the clan has had a pervasive and protracted influence. The Middle Eastern leader has led by virtue of his personal relations with his followers. Formal organizations and institutions have seldom effectively intervened. Even when institutions such as formal bureaucracies have developed and expanded, the real business of ruling and political decision making has resided in personal networks. These networks tend to hold together groups of people, and it is through these networks that the leader has attempted to establish as wide a range of contacts as possible.

In order to rule in this kind of setting, it is essential that the leader gather and retain as much personal information about others in the network as possible. One famous eleventh-century manual on the conduct of kingship advises the prince, "never omit to inform yourself of the doings of others . . . ,"[45] and tells the king that "it is your duty not to be ignorant of conditions in your realm, of the circumstances of your people or those of your soldiers. More particularly you must be vigilant concerning the doings of your vizier. He should not be able to swallow a drink of water without your knowing it . . . ."[46] In this setting, the art of genealogy and the knowledge of friendship relations are serious political pursuits.

The prevalence of personalism is best seen in the great Islamic dynastic systems, where the rulers built gigantic households around their own persons. A more formal bureaucratic state organization also evolved in these systems in answer to

[45] Kai Ka'us Ibn Iskandar, *A Mirror for Princes* (*The Qabus-nama*), trans. Reuben Levy (London: Cresset Press, 1951), p. 194.
[46] Ibid., p. 235.

the pressure to administer the large political empires. A distinguished Islamic scholar summarizes this situation as follows: "Throughout the whole system of the Eastern Muslim political organization there runs like a red thread the division of all the organs of administration into two main categories, the dargah (palace) and diwan (chancery)."[47] In the Iranian Safavid system, the royal household was referred to as the *khassah* and the state bureaucracy was known as the *divan*. In the Turkish Ottoman system, the division was between the "imperial household" and the "central administration." In traditional Islamic polities, the royal household has been the crucial arena of politics, since it has consistently dominated the state bureaucracy proper. This has occurred not only because of the superior concentration of power within the royal household, but also because the personalities of the palace have infiltrated the state bureaucracy. Hence, the royal household, which is organized around the person of the king, has in turn wrapped around itself the formal bureaucracy, which expands with the growth of the political unit itself.

The actual transition from a completely personal pattern of leadership to one with bureaucratic and institutional appendages occurred mainly during the rule of the Abbasids (749–1258). This represented, in Weber's terms, a movement from a patriarchal to a patrimonial stage. The Abbasid leaders built an elaborate administrative system that included the office of *vazir* ("prime minister") and more than a dozen large organizational boards that were in turn composed of numerous departments.[48] Despite this bureaucracy, personal relations dominated the system, and the court staff remained the critical force. This dependence of the more formal state bureaucracy upon the person of the king is seen in the role of the vazir himself. Although the vazir usually headed the state bureaucracy in these political systems, he did so as the personal servant of the king and as a leading member of the royal household. It was the *person* of the vazir, not the *office* of vazir, that was the important political consideration.

---

[47] V. V. Barthold, *Turkestan Down to the Mongol Invasion*, 2d ed. (London: Oxford University Press, 1928), p. 227.

[48] Vazir is most closely translated as prime minister. It is sometimes transliterated as vizir, vizier, or wazir.

This traditional style of political rule has carried over into contemporary Middle Eastern politics to a surprisingly large degree. Personalism predominates in such societies as Morocco, Jordan, Iran, Saudi Arabia, Yemen, and the shaykhdoms that still have traditional authoritarian leaders. In other Middle Eastern countries, the personal dimension of leadership prevails more at the subnational level, in such institutions as the family, the school, and the guild. In all of these societies, however, patrimonial personalism continues to shape leadership processes, although it is more and more submerged beneath the growing facade of formal institutions and bureaucratic machinery. Contemporary Middle Eastern political monarchs constantly describe their societies as large families and emphasize their own special positions as heads or fathers of these families. It is in this spirit that King Hassan of Morocco speaks about "the innate nature of Our family, characterized by its profound wisdom, its great nobility, and the solid communion which unites Us ultimately to Our people."[49]

Proximity. Patrimonial leadership attaches particular significance to physical proximity. Regardless of occupational designation or formal title, those who live closest to the leader regularly hold major political positions in the traditional Middle Eastern system. Zayd Ibn Haritha, who was a black slave adopted by Muhammad and Khadija and brought into their household, illustrates the power of proximity. Because he was the Prophet's adopted son, and despite his having been a slave, Zayd became one of the leading figures in early Muslim history. Throughout Islamic history, slaves have risen to great influence, and one of the most powerful Islamic political systems was built by a dynasty whose kings were once slaves. These were the Mamluks; the word *mamluk* itself means "owned" or "possessed." They were originally slaves who had served as bodyguards to the Ayyubid dynastic leaders. Proximity to leadership has meant that slaves, cooks, musicians, and stable keepers have often been able to exert great political power in traditional Muslim societies. In the dying days of

[49] John Waterbury, *The Commander of the Faithful: The Moroccan Political Elite — A Study in Segmented Politics* (New York: Columbia University Press, 1970), p. 150.

King Farouk's reign in contemporary Egypt, his barber had such power.

Although proximity is a consideration relevant to any political system, it assumes special importance in those societies where leadership is built on a far-flung network of personal relations. Here, those closest to the *person* of the leader tend always to be the most influential. In patrimonial politics these are often, in the first instance, such family members as brothers, wives, mothers, and uncles. Those who marry into the leader's family and become in-laws also become potential centers of great influence. The special personal ties and ideal position of proximity that relatives of the leader hold often mean that when the pattern of emanation is broken, it is broken within this familial core. If anyone makes direct suggestions to the patrimonial leader, or questions or criticizes him, it is almost always a member of the ruling family. Certainly, it is from this source that new ideas are most likely to be entertained and absorbed. In an extended household administration, or patrimonial system, those in the core household or nuclear family will play major roles in political decision making. Western discussions and condemnations of nepotism, ascription, and favoritism must be reevaluated in light of the general structure of patrimonial politics.

Proximity counts most in systems where decision making is highly centralized, highly personal, and highly informal. In nonpatrimonial systems, decision making tends to be more equally distributed throughout the society. And such systems also have formal and associational channels that carry the influence and ideas of those distant from the centers of political decision making to the leader. In the patrimonial Middle East, the most effective way to submit a request or present a petition is to get as close as possible to the leader. The closer an individual is to the center of the personal web of politics, the more likely he is to share in decision making and to have his interests served. It is for this reason that there is constant and unrelenting pressure towards the center of power in traditional patrimonial politics. The leader is always being pressed in upon by individuals who attempt to be in his presence as often and as long as possible. At the same time, those closest to him, such as his advisers, ministers, and confidants, attempt to resist and control the flow of others to this precious territory. In *A Mirror for Princes,* Muslim vazirs are warned, "wherever the king goes, accompany him; do not leave him alone. . . ."[50]

It is proximity rather than professional merit or occupational position that explains why gardeners, cobblers, barbers, and physicians have moved into positions of great influence in Islamic politics. The patrimonial leader has more often sought the advice and counsel of these individuals than of any others, and at times such service personnel have eventually replaced their masters and become political leaders in their own right. It is not surprising, therefore, that even in the contemporary Middle East, political leaders rely heavily upon their personal attendants for advice and information. The former Shah of Iran, for example, said that he relied upon his valet and gardener when he needed "proper information."[51] Those nearest to the person of the leader serve to filter demands and requests, act as information bearers and receptacles of advice, and stand as influential intermediaries between the leader and his masses of followers. Where power is personal and politics are patrimonial, the issue of proximity is critical. The concept of the "inner circle" is particularly relevant to Middle Eastern politics.

Informality. Personal politics tend to be informal politics in the sense that the most important leaders are often those who are not bound by formal contracts or limited by institutional constraints. Even those leaders who visibly combine power and authority have consistently operated in highly personal settings rather than in well-defined and formal organizations.

In today's bedouin society, the great importance of the informal leadership structure is still seen in the person of the *rajal khayr,* or "good man." In the Ayshaybat tribe in western Egypt, this person is more influential than the *aqila,* in whom resides the contractual authority of the tribe. The aqila is, in other words, the formal leader. The rajal khayr is a cultural

---

[50] Iskandar, *A Mirror for Princes,* p. 214.

[51] E. A. Bayne, *Persian Kingship in Transition* (New York: American Universities Field Staff, 1968), p. 235.

and political broker who has the loyalty and friendship of the people as well as the attention of high regional government officials, who prefer to work through him. As G. J. Obermeyer writes in an excellent case study of bedouin leadership: "The power of the 'āqila is limited by the very structure of the role. The role of the rajal khair, being less institutionalized and structured, is less confined with respect to the kind and amount of influence the role-player might exert."[52]

Political decision making in the Middle East has been marked by behind-the-scenes planning and negotiation. Leaders have seldom occupied themselves with the establishment of formal political institutions such as parliaments and parties. Where such formal institutions have been constructed, they have been rationalizing gestures more than seriously conceived political organizations. Once in existence, formal bodies have had relatively little impact upon a leader's political activities.

Informal patterns of control and authority have been responsible for a great deal of uncertainty in the decision-making environment. Middle Eastern political processes reflect a high level of intrigue and counter-intrigue as leaders at various levels maneuver in secret and semisecret settings. It is partially because of this emphasis on secrecy and organizational informality that rumors have always been an important political phenomenon in the Middle East. Secrecy and uncertainty breed speculation, and the ability to uncover decisions and deals is an important political resource.

The propensity for informal organization that has marked Middle Eastern social life is most evident in the numerous secret and informal groups. These include secret orders and societies, religious brotherhoods, underground minority organizations, political cliques and *anjumans,* informal coffeehouse groups, sufi meetings, ritualistic religious gatherings, regular meetings of extended families, royal social circles and *khalvats,* and bureaucratic and parliamentary factions.[53] This style of

---

52 Obermeyer, "Leadership and Transition in Bedouin Society: A Case Study," in *The Desert and the Sown,* ed. Cynthia Nelson (Berkeley: University of California Institute of International Studies, 1973) , p. 164.

53 *Anjumans* are usually translated as "societies." *Khalvat* was a term used in Iran to refer to a regular social gathering of the Shah and his closest male advisors.

social organization has been a critical factor in the development of patrimonial patterns of leadership. This has been discussed more fully in the previous chapter.

Middle Eastern leaders have tended to operate as the centers of webs of personal relationships in which the lines of power and authority are indistinct and constantly changing. Spheres of political authority overlap. Hence, there is always doubt concerning who is closest to the leader and who influenced what decision. With the possible exception of the national political leader, there is even question about *who* the leader really is. Often, the most influential political actors remain in the background, where they are members of the family, the harem, or friendship circles. In Middle Eastern politics, an informal personal organization has tended to rest behind the formal institutional organization. The resulting confusion has been compounded by the presence of the identifiable leader at the center of both organizations and the presence of certain advisors and confidants in both.

This environment of informality has carried several political advantages for the patrimonial leader. It has provided him with an unusually flexible system, since lines of authority and responsibility tend to be fluid and blurred. In such a system, it is difficult for opposition forces to concentrate because targets are neither stable nor well defined. At the same time, the leader enjoys a broad capacity to intervene in governmental affairs and to move subordinates around with ease. Since there are no clearly defined responsibilities, and since hard and fast assignments are nonexistent, the patrimonial leader can interpret spheres of authority in almost any way he chooses. Those individuals who are most apt to challenge the leader find themselves severely crippled in this informal environment. They lack institutional foundations and formal legal supports that they can cling to, and therefore find themselves highly dependent upon the personal whim and will of the leader. Informal politics tend to conceal the merit of aspiring statesmen, and as a result these statesmen are seldom able to build the popularity necessary for the crystallization of opposition to the leader. Finally, informality builds distrust between and among those who are relatively influential in the system. Individuals report confidentially and personally to the leader, and this often involves statements about the activities and ambitions of other political figures. Such an informal and semisecret pattern of politics enables the leader to engender a great deal of division and distrust among his subordinates. This division has been institutionalized as overlapping lines of authority by which officials exert control in one another's area of expertise.

In patrimonial leadership, visibility and formality have been subordinated to personalism and covert organization. This characteristic has provided Middle Eastern leaders with a maximum amount of maneuverability and a minimum degree of accountability. Even in the contemporary Middle East of complex and sophisticated organization charts, the business of politics is negotiated outside of and in spite of these instruments. Political blueprints such as constitutions and fundamental laws heavily mask the actual patterns and processes by which political leaders make decisions and protect their interests.

Balanced Conflict. The patrimonial leader in the Middle East has ruled on the foundation of pervasive division and personal rivalry. In the Middle Eastern context, the dictum "divide and rule" takes on special meaning. Cutting through all levels in the Islamic system is a built-in rivalry that marks interpersonal, intergroup, and interclass relations. The leader who seeks to divide and rule, therefore, has an ideal social system within which to operate. Rivalry is institutionalized in the system, and the traditional ruler had only to encourage processes that were already at work. This is why unity is the most sought-after and least achieved goal in Islamic history.

Personal rivalry has so permeated the Middle Eastern social structure that it manifests itself in institutions all the way from the family to the national bureaucracy. In Egyptian village society, for example, intense sibling rivalry is considered essential to a child's growth. Parents continually sharpen and intensify rivalry among their children. This is done in numerous dramatic ways, including labeling the children with names that invite conflict. In one Egyptian family, for example, the elder brother was called "the stupid one," while the younger brother was nicknamed "the clever one."[54] In a study of Lebanese village life, it was found that less than half of the children sampled could name three persons they considered friends. The reasons for this reported scarcity of friendship relations were explained in terms of grudges, feuds, and rivalries.[55] The oft-quoted Arab proverb "I against my brother, my brother and I against my cousin, my cousin and I against the stranger" describes this general pattern very well.

At the national political level, the same pattern is evident in the way that leaders and rulers play their advisors and subordinates off against one another. The contemporary rulers of Morocco, Iran, and Saudi Arabia have become especially adept in this skill and largely owe their continued existence as powerful monarchs to it. By splintering the potential opposition forces and at the same time standing above them as supreme arbiter, several Middle Eastern monarchs have managed to maintain firm control in the political arena. Any concentration of skill, energy, or power is immediately shattered through leadership tactics of division and redivision. In the traditional Abbasid, Ottoman, Safavid, and Moghul administrative systems, the most important and influential political functions were constantly divided and redistributed among larger and larger numbers of officials. When a political figure became particularly influential, his title and function were given to a second and rival administrator, and influence was thus divided and shared. Tension was thereby instilled into the particular political sphere, and the personal power of the individual in control of this sphere was substantially lessened, if not halved.

The politics of rivalry and conflict not only served to buttress leadership positions but also reinforced systemic stability. The tension was balanced in such a way that overwhelming concentrations of power seldom developed outside the sphere of the national political ruler. Manfred Halpern analyzes the

[54] Hammed Ammar, *Growing Up in an Egyptian Village* (New York: Octagon Books, 1966) , p. 110.

[55] Judith R. Williams, *The Youth of Haouch El Harimi: A Lebanese Village,* Harvard Middle East Monograph Series, vol. 20 (Cambridge: Harvard University Press, 1968) , pp. 91–92.

Islamic system in terms of its "ability to convert tensions into balances" and its capacity to bind society together "through conflict no less than through collaboration."[56] In contemporary Morocco, "all seek to maintain in the midst of the group that tension which is life, that variety that is solidarity."[57] The Moroccan monarch operates a system in which "no group may be permitted to become too strong, and to counter hegemonic tendencies life is breathed into rival groups."[58] In Iran, the Shah has created a stable balance of tension in which ministers, courtiers, security agents, military leaders, industrialists, and clerics are systematically divided against one another at all levels. The last three kings of Saudi Arabia have promoted the distrust and animosity that mark the relationships between many of their half-brothers, while at another level the national guard stands in direct rivalry with the regular army. The Nassers, Bourguibas, al-Bakrs, Qaddafis, and al-Assads have also promoted rivalry. In the Middle East, political leaders have traditionally expended much of their energies in manipulating personal networks of stabilizing tensions. A premium has been placed upon a leader's ability to sense the location of threatening power concentrations and then to splinter those concentrations either by heightening existing divisions or by fostering new personal rivalries.

Military Prowess. Max Weber writes that "with the development of a purely personal administrative staff, *especially a military force* under the control of the chief, traditional authority tends to develop into 'patrimonialism.' "[59] The key to patrimonial politics is the existence of a military force that is at the personal disposal of the leader. Within the Islamic world, this consideration has been a central one. Here, among the most highly respected qualities of leadership are personal bravery and physical courage. Islamic scholars present "com-

56 Manfred Halpern, *The Politics of Social Change in the Middle East and North Africa* (Princeton, N.J.: Princeton University Press, 1963), pp. 10, 18.

57 Jacques Berque, *Structures Sociales du Haut-Atlas* (Paris, 1955), p. 449, as quoted in Waterbury, *The Commander of the Faithful,* p. 61.

58 Waterbury, *The Commander of the Faithful,* p. 148.

59 Weber, *The Theory of Social and Economic Organization,* p. 347. Italics ours.

bativeness" as one of the three great characteristics of the Prophet Muhammad.[60] The famous Islamic leaders are known and remembered for their bravery in battle and their victory in military campaigns. The warrior hero is a deeply admired figure in Middle Eastern history. Leaders who have been able to conduct themselves well on the field of battle have always had an extreme advantage in the arena of domestic politics.[61]

This emphasis on physical courage and military prowess is to be expected in a culture that developed out of a tribal context, and in which tribes continue to play a prominent social and political role. Throughout the Middle East today groups still exist that follow the Shi'i path or worship Ali primarily because of his personal courage and valor, which are summed up in his titles Lion of God and Sword of Islam.[62] Much of Ali's appeal as a political leader and religious imam resides in this characteristic commonly credited to him.

This emphasis upon personal courage and valor runs deeply through Middle Eastern society. Bravery is so highly esteemed that it carries favorable moral connotations. The Arabic word *shaja'a,* which is also commonly used in Persian, implies a personal bravery that is especially infused with virtue and uprightness. It implies a kind of chivalrous courage. Throughout Middle Eastern history, the personally brave and physically courageous have had about them an aura of knightliness. Combativeness and chivalry could not be separated. Local champions such as *pahlavans* not only had tremendous physical strength but also were exceptionally kind, generous, and noble. Islamic guilds and brotherhoods traditionally supported and promoted ideals of physical and moral courage. Military valor and success, therefore, have invested Islamic leaders with additional strength and appeal in the eyes of their followers.

Military force was a major factor in the rise to and mainte-

[60] See, for example, Nasr, *Ideals and Realities,* p. 73; and Schuon, *Understanding Islam,* p. 88.

[61] The reverse is also true, since failure in combat is as much a moral as a physical blow to Islamic leaders and societies. The impact of the Arab-Israeli conflict, for example, must be interpreted in this light.

[62] One of the authors (Bill) had the opportunity to live for a short time with the Qashqa'i tribesmen in southern Iran in 1967. The Islamic leader most admired and respected by these tribesmen is Ali, who is worshipped because of his virtues of personal courage and bravery.

nance of power for Middle Eastern political leaders. "The struggles for succession were mostly settled by civil war and by coup d'etat, with the outcome generally as closely related to the structure of the military command as to the prevailing political environment."[63] And a leader who has had several successful foreign military campaigns to his credit has been more effective in preserving his domestic rule. The deep patterns of division and discord described above persistently threaten to shatter the system and to destroy the ruler in the process. One scholar stresses the fact that "a patrimonial system is characterized by constant tension between centripetal and centrifugal forces."[64] The patrimonial leader's key instrument in encouraging and buttressing the centripetal forces is his military organization. While promoting tension and discord in particular areas throughout the system, the patrimonial leader must at the same time guard against having balances become imbalances and rivals unite in a common front against him. It is only his military that can enable him to salvage his position and his life in such circumstances.

Despite its importance, the military organization is subject to the same patterns and pressures that characterize other institutions in patrimonial settings. The leader or ruler attempts to control the military as an emanation of his own will and personality and usually assumes the title commander in chief or commander of the faithful. The military forces are his "personal instrument."[65] The centrality of the leader in military matters can be seen diagrammatically in the Middle Eastern "battle order" described by Ibn Khaldun.[66] Surrounded by his closest confidants, the ruler stands at the center of his forces. The latter consist of four armies, situated at the front and rear and on the right and left flanks of the leader.

Throughout the history of the Middle East, the characteristics of personalism, proximity, informality, and balanced

---

[63] J. C. Hurewitz, *Middle East Politics: The Military Dimension* (New York: Frederick A. Praeger, 1969) , p. 20.

[64] Robert H. Jackson, "Social Structure and Political Change in Ethiopia and Liberia," *Comparative Political Studies* 3 (April 1960) :38.

[65] Bendix, *Max Weber*, p. 344.

[66] Ibn Khaldun, *The Muqaddimah*, trans. Franz Rosenthal (Princeton, N.J.: Princeton University Press, 1967) , p. 225.

rivalry also infiltrated the military organization. Only the most trusted relatives and confidants were appointed military leaders. Those closest to the ruler, such as bodyguards and armed retainers, were recruited among slaves, orphans, and prisoners, and as a result maintained no entangling alliances or loyalties outside of their relation to the leader. It was essential that they be completely subsumed in the shadow of the ruler, to whom they owed everything. To insure this kind of absolute loyalty and submission, the mechanism of balanced rivalry is seen in perhaps its most critical manifestation in the arena of the armed forces. Different military leaders and different military bodies have existed in constant tension with one another and have served as watchdogs of one another. Sometimes these intramilitary divisions reflected tribal cleavages; sometimes entirely new tribes were created both to strengthen loyalty and to serve as armed checks against other military units.

The modern Middle East has its authentic military heroes. For the Turks, Atatürk was the great hero of the First World War. Abdul Aziz Ibn Saud was the illustrious warrior king in Saudi Arabia; his son Saud was renowned for his physical courage in battle. King Husayn of Jordan has demonstrated that same courage on numerous occasions. Both Gamal Abdel Nasser and General Naguib, the titular leader of the 1952 Egyptian coup, had distinguished records in the fighting in Palestine. Where opportunities for valor have been few, the modern patrimonial leader has not lacked courage. King Hassan of Morocco and Muhammad Reza Shah of Iran have faced assassins' bullets with fortitude; they would have, of course, preferred the accolades that accompany successful battle.

There is bound to be a close connection between military upheaval and the turnover of political leaders. The proliferation of military coups that continues to mark Middle Eastern politics represents the failure of leaders and rulers to establish viable patrimonial patterns with respect to the military. The challenge to leadership has come not so much from the society at large as from within the military itself. When leadership rests so heavily upon the military reed, then it must be prepared to fall whenever that reed breaks.

Religious Rationalization. Islam provided the patrimonial leader with an ideology that buttressed and strengthened the political patterns by which he ruled. Chains of emanation are more firmly fashioned when they lead to the Almighty, and Islamic leaders have traditionally endeavored to demonstrate their own linkages with God and his Prophet Muhammad. Although actual theocratic leadership died with the Prophet in 632, Islamic leaders ever since have sought to be theocratic leaders. As time passed, this tendency became more and more pronounced, while theocratic leadership became less and less credible. The political meaning of the word *caliph* was gradually transformed from "deputy of the emissary of God" to "God's representative on earth."[67] The Islamic political leaders, who had at one time been considered the Prophet's deputies, later became known as God's deputies. Even the concept of *sultan,* which developed a connotation of secular as opposed to religious authority, soon made the linkage with the Divine. This occurred when the actual sultan began referring to himself as the Shadow of God.[68] The concept of *imam* has been the best example of leadership related directly to the Divine, for unlike the caliph and the sultan, the imam has always been considered the infallible vicegerent of God. Despite the various titles and personalities involved, however, the Middle Eastern style of patrimonial leadership has usually meant the conscious establishment of some form of linkage between the leader and the Divine.

This pattern has provided political leaders with a rationalization and justification for their positions. It has been argued that "stiff religious cement" has been the strength of the patrimonial system of rule.[69] In one of the classic studies of politics, Gaetano Mosca analyzes the traditional strength of the Turkish nation in the following terms: "The Turkish peasants in Rumelia and Anatolia believed sincerely and deeply in Islam, in the Prophet, in the sultan as the Prophet's vicar, and the

[67] V. V. Barthold, "Caliph and Sultan," *The Islamic Quarterly* 7 (July and December 1963), pp. 124–25.

[68] Ibid., p. 130.

[69] Gaetano Mosca, *The Ruling Class,* trans, Hannah D. Kahn (New York: McGraw-Hill Book Co., 1939), p. 345.

beliefs for which they were asked to make the utmost sacrifices were the beliefs that ordinarily filled their lives and made up their moral and intellectual worlds."[70] In a smoothly functioning system of leadership by emanation, to challenge the leader often meant nothing less than to challenge the rule of God. It is for this reason that political rebellion took the form of religious schisms and that the challenging political figures stressed their own special relation to the Almighty.

The Politics of Patrimonial Recruitment: General Observations. Contrary to what is often thought, the ranks of Middle Eastern political leadership are relatively permeable. Within certain patrimonial limits, vertical mobility is possible, and outsiders are often able to penetrate elite circles. In such systems, the personalistic networks of leadership can be penetrated, especially on the basis of family, kinship, and friendship relations. As Almond and Powell point out: "Perhaps the oldest and most traditional means of access to political elites is personal connection. By personal connection channels we mean the use of family, school, local, and social ties as instruments for contacting political elites."[71] In the Middle East, the determination of who is to move in or out of the elite is often still determined by these factors.

Built into and stretching throughout these webs of personal connections are three broader channels of mobility. These are the military, bureaucratic, and religious channels, and it is through them that most individuals have made their entrance into the political elite. Although the personalistic-patrimonial factors discussed above decidedly influence who moves through these channels, the very existence of the channels has helped to institutionalize mobility.

The Middle Eastern patrimonial system of leadership remains largely intact today. There are, however, a number of strong new recruitment considerations that increasingly influence leadership composition. The most important of them

[70] Ibid., p. 108.
[71] Gabriel A. Almond and G. Bingham Powell, Jr., *Comparative Politics: System, Process, and Policy,* 2d ed. (Boston: Little, Brown and Co., 1978), p. 178.

are professional skill, talent, and merit. Political elites have been driven, because of the forces of modernization, to recruit individuals who have technical and professional competence. Ministries of health are increasingly headed by medical doctors and health administrators; national petroleum companies are directed by better and better qualified petroleum engineers, geologists, and economists; national educational systems are guided by Middle Eastern specialists in the field of education. A look through the curriculum vitae of the representatives of various countries in the Organization of Petroleum Exporting Countries (OPEC) is one good way of documenting this trend. Even in the most traditional of patrimonial systems, such as Saudia Arabia, Iran, and Abu Dhabi, the educated technocrats have moved into decision-making positions. In the late 1970s, for example, the Saudi cabinet had more American-trained Ph.D.'s than did the United States cabinet. A prime minister of Iran, Jamshid Amuzegar, received his M.A. in sanitary engineering and his Ph.D. in hydraulics from Cornell University. In Abu Dhabi, where professionally trained talent is admittedly scarce, Shaykh Zayid and his royal advisors imported a bright and dedicated French-educated Algerian, Mahmoud Hamra-Krouha, to build and direct the Abu Dhabi National Oil Company (ADNOC). The members of the professional middle class, to use the terminology introduced in Chapter III, are inexorably moving into the ranks of political leadership in the Middle East.

Despite the changes in some of the qualifications necessary for entry into the elites, there are impressive indications that patrimonialism prevails. First, recruitment processes are personally and firmly controlled from the center of the system. This is as true in the authoritarian-mobilizational systems of Algeria and Iraq as it is in such authoritarian-traditional systems as those of Jordan and Morocco. In all of these systems, the considerations of political loyalty, personal connections, and complete central control remain at least as important in determining entry into the elite as those of professional expertise, personal merit, and institutional position.

The second sign of patrimonial persistence in the Middle East concerns the directional flow of the recruitment patterns.

In their recent analysis of the politics of recruitment into the elite, Almond and Powell stress that the political party is the most common contemporary channel of recruitment.[72] This has not been the case in Middle Eastern patrimonial politics. Although political parties exist in most of the societies, political leaders are not generally recruited from the parties. Instead, the parties (as well as the legislatures) are headed by individuals who are already national political leaders. The patrimonial head selects the party leadership from among proven confidants, advisors, or ministers. In several Middle Eastern systems, party positions (whether leadership or rank-and-file) more often reflect a move out of than a move into the national political elite. Parties and legislatures many times serve as the political dumping grounds for former members of the elite who have fallen from favor in the patrimonial establishment.

The continued strength of patrimonialism in the Middle East has meant that the personalistic networks that are directed from the center have a profound effect on both the shape of the political system and that system's capacity to confront the problems of modernization and political development. The patrimonial leaders and the political elites that surround them play a disproportionate part in determining the future of their societies. Although their policies at one level may be very similar from society to society, at another level there are striking differences. In some societies, the traditional webs of patrimonialism operate today just as they have for centuries; in other societies, these webs have begun to be torn and are unraveling in differing ways. In Chapter V, we will examine a number of case studies of Middle Eastern patrimonial leaders with special focus upon the differing ways that they have coped with the challenge of change.

[72] Ibid., pp. 123–26.

CHAPTER V

The Politics of Leaders and Change

THE POLICIES WHEREBY Middle Eastern societies have confronted the challenge of change have been determined to a large extent by political leaders. As we have seen in Chapter IV, the political processes of patrimonial systems are shaped around the person of a patrimonial leader, who plays a disproportionate role in the decision-making process. The centrality of the national political leader assures him a critical position in confronting the important related issues of modernization and political development. The leader's tactics and strategies in this regard have far-reaching consequences for the political system and for the peoples of the society concerned.

Throughout Middle Eastern history, leaders have held a wide variety of attitudes toward change. In many cases, the political leadership has been determined to resist any forces of change. In other cases, Middle Eastern leaders have taken a more flexible stance and have attempted to meet the challenge through programs of reform and revision. Their strategy has been to forestall major transformations by promoting continual incremental adjustments. In still other instances, leaders have on occasion pursued revolutionary goals that involve radical social and political change. In all these cases, however, the leader has maintained a special position — he has controlled the instruments of persuasion and coercion that are essential to the implementation of any of these policies.

In this chapter, our analysis will emphasize Middle Eastern political leaders who have in this century chosen to promote various programs of change. Modernization has been a goal shared by all of these leaders. Political development, however, has not been so generally favored. We will analyze three pairs of leaders from three major Middle Eastern countries. These are Mustafa Kemal Atatürk and Ismet Inönü of Turkey, Reza Shah and Muhammad Reza Shah Pahlavi of Iran, and Gamal Abdel Nassar and Anwar Sadat of Egypt. Before discussing these leaders, it is perhaps best to devote a few paragraphs to the more traditional Middle Eastern leader. It is against this backdrop of traditional leadership that the more modern and often more progressive leaders have operated. In all of our case studies, traditional patrimonial styles and tactics have still been very much in evidence.

TWENTIETH-CENTURY TRADITIONAL LEADERS

Twentieth-century Middle Eastern political history has been largely dominated by a number of colorful traditional leaders, who did much to shape the destinies of their nations. In most cases, they resisted change and as a result became its victims. Some were hopelessly corrupt and venal in their personal and political lives; others were models of integrity whose life-styles were simple and ascetic. All failed in one way or another to understand a world of new challenges and new forces. Among the least impressive of these leaders are King Farouk of Egypt, Regent Abd al-Ilah of Iraq, Sultan Mehmet V and Sultan Mehmet VI of Turkey, Shaykh Shakhbut of Abu Dhabi, and Sultan Said bin Taymur of Oman. Traditional leaders of considerably more talent and integrity include King Idris of Libya, Zahir Shah of Afghanistan, King Abdullah of Jordan, King Muhammad V of Morocco, and especially, King Abdul Aziz Ibn Saud of Saudi Arabia.

Sultan Said bin Taymur ruled Oman for thirty-eight years (1932–1970). Although he was educated at a British school in India, the Sultan spent nearly four decades walling himself and his country in against the forces of change. Even after oil was discovered in Oman, he steadfastly refused to expend his resources on development programs. During his rule, no tractors were allowed in the sultanate; the occasional importation of an automobile had to be personally approved by the Sultan himself; religious taxes were collected in the provinces in Maria Theresa dollars as late as the 1960s; houses could be rebuilt only from the material with which they were originally constructed; women were forbidden to accompany their husbands abroad; and Omanis educated abroad were not allowed to return to work in their own country.

Sultan Said was opposed to education, financial expenditure, and modernization in his country. He felt that the British lost India because they had educated the people, and he therefore decided to close the only three primary schools in Oman, just before he was deposed in 1970. He considered the schools to be hotbeds of communism. The Sultan ruled supreme and kept his people in fear and subjection. The channels of access and personal contact that were such an essential part of Islamic patrimonial politics were destroyed by this traditional leader, who promoted only slavery and repression in his system. After 1958, he kept himself in isolation in the coastal city of Salala. His officials, working in an atmosphere "made even more oppressive by his absence, one might describe it as disembodiment, in Salala,"[1] made no decisions. Sultan Said even locked up his son Qabus (the present ruler of Oman) when Qabus returned to Oman in 1966 after receiving a British education at Sandhurst.

British annoyance with and embarrassment by the old Sultan led to his overthrow in July 1970. His demise was inevitable; his long period of reactionary rule had resulted in a guerrilla war that broke out in the province of Dhofar. By 1970, the opposition forces had taken most of Dhofar and were even shelling Sultan Said's palace. He had been consistent in his determined opposition to any kind of change or innovation. Because of British support and his geographic position in what were then the backwaters of the Middle East, he made this policy stick for a surprisingly long time. But in the end he failed. As Ian Skeet presciently wrote before the Sul-

1 Ian Skeet, *Muscat and Oman: The End of an Era* (London: Faber and Faber, 1974) , p. 168. Most of the material in this section has been drawn from Skeet's informed and entertaining book or from Fred Halliday, *Arabia Without Sultans* (New York: Vintage Books, 1974) , pp. 277–315.

tan's fall, his kind of policy "is just plugging the holes in the barbed wire round the country's borders; one day the barbed wire will be rolled aside, and none of the Sultan's restrictions will help him one iota."[2]

If Sultan Said is one of the least successful traditional leaders in the Middle East of this century, King Abdul Aziz Ibn Saud is one of the most successful. Ibn Saud's style of leadership very closely approximated that of the classical model analyzed in Chapter IV. Born in 1880 in Central Arabia, Ibn Saud grew up in an environment of vigorous conflict among clans and political anarchy. In 1901, he was a banished youth whose clan was ruled by its enemies and whose immediate family was in exile in Kuwait. By 1934, he had conquered the territories of Najd, Hasa, Hijaz, and Asir, and had welded them together into one political unit known as the Kingdom of Saudi Arabia. In so doing, he had healed the rifts within his own family, defeated and co-opted the other clans, taken Hasa from the Turks, and conquered Mecca and Hijaz at the expense of the Hashemite King Husayn (the great-grandfather of the present King Husayn of Jordan).

Abdul Aziz Ibn Saud ruled personally, informally, and patriarchally. He ran his kingdom as a gigantic personal household — which it in fact very nearly was. Ibn Saud had an estimated three hundred wives in his lifetime, as well as large numbers of concubines and slave girls. In 1955, it was estimated that there was one prince for every 5,000 persons in Saudi Arabia.[3] Like the Prophet Muhammad, after whom he patterned his life, Ibn Saud used marriage as an important political tool. Through the years, he married into all the leading families in Arabia. His links with the Sudairi family, from which four of his wives came, were especially strong; these wives bore fifteen of his sons. Today, perhaps the most influential political bloc in Saudi Arabia is the Al-Fahd group, which consists of seven full brothers, who are the sons of Ibn

---

[2] Skeet, *Muscat and Oman,* p. 196.

[3] H. St. John Philby, *Sa'udi Arabia* (London: Ernest Benn, 1955), p. 298. The writings of Philby are invaluable sources on the politics of Saudi Arabia; he speaks on the basis of thirty-five years in residence at the Saudi court.

Saud and Hussa bint Ahmad al-Sudairi. The first deputy prime minister and crown prince, Fahd, is the most important of these Sudairi Seven.

In this setting, Ibn Saud balanced rivalries and directed the personal and political fortunes of all of the other main actors in the system. He made it his business to stay informed. "He had a deep knowledge of his people, their friendships and intermarriages, their blood feuds and causes of quarrel, so that he could play the one against the other."[4] He never allowed power to concentrate at any point in the system other than at his own feet. He once stated: "Two things I will not stomach: firstly a rebel (*marij*); and secondly the feigned loyalty of two persons inwardly leagued against me."[5] Ibn Saud was also famous for his accessibility and approachability. Quite unlike Sultan Said, he spent several hours each day listening to the complaints and problems of his people.

Finally, Ibn Saud was a great warrior. The first thirty years of his leadership were a time of constant warfare. It was during this period that he became a legend as he personally developed military strategy, recruited his soldiers, and led them into battle. At the end of these three decades of military struggle and political consolidation, Ibn Saud carried the marks of a dozen wounds, all attesting to the central role he played in the business of physical combat.

Although he founded a country and forged a following of disparate peoples into a nation, he stumbled when confronted with the challenges of modernization and political development. Between the time when oil was discovered at Jebel Dhahran in 1938 and when he died in 1953, Ibn Saud clung desperately to tradition. As a result, he was unable to cope effectively with the new forces and demands that burst upon him and his society. He did not think to concern himself with widening the base of political participation; he watched social and economic gaps widen among his peoples; he could not or would not stem the tide of peculation, corruption, and waste

4 H. C. Armstrong, *Lord of Arabia* (Beirut: Khayyat's, 1944), p. 111.
5 H. St. John Philby, *Arabian Jubilee* (London: Robert Hale, 1954), p. 106.

that washed through his kingdom; he did little to build health and educational facilities. These tasks were only taken up later by his son Faisal (who was King from 1964 through 1975) and the current king, Khalid.

Still, Abdul Aziz Ibn Saud was the greatest traditional leader of this century. He combined wit and physical courage with personal charisma and deep religious beliefs to consolidate a people and build a nation.[6] The political leaders discussed in the following sections tried to move out ahead in their societies and directly confront the forces of modernization. The one who did this earliest and most dramatically was a Turk born only a year before the great Ibn Saud. His name was Atatürk.

ATATÜRK: THE REVOLUTIONARY FATHER OF TURKEY

The modern Turkish state owes its political form and indeed its very existence to one remarkable military and political leader — Atatürk. First called Mustafa, he was given the additional name of Kemal ("perfection") by an instructor in secondary school. After his victory over the Greeks at Sakarya in 1921, the Grand National Assembly at Ankara gave him the title of Ghazi ("victor"). In 1934, the Assembly bestowed on him the surname Atatürk, or Father of the Turks. In this book, we will refer to him both as Kemal and as Atatürk.

Kemal was born in Salonika in Macedonia in 1881. His family was of the very lowest echelons of the middle class. His father, a onetime low-ranking civil servant, was a failure in both the timber business and the salt trade and died when Kemal was only eleven. A direct and often rebellious person, Kemal was thrown out of one school before he settled into a military education that included military prep school in Salonika, a military academy at Monastir, and finally the War College and the Staff College at Constantinople. In 1905, he graduated from the Staff College as a captain in the sultan's army. On his final examination and in his personnel file, the following assessment was reportedly written: "A brilliant stu-

---

[6] For our detailed analysis of the patrimonial politics of Abdul Aziz Ibn Saud, see J. A. Bill and C. Leiden, *The Middle East: Politics and Power* (Boston: Allyn and Bacon, 1974), pp. 125–33.

dent officer, difficult in temperament, precise and technically a perfectionist, politically unstable."[7] Shortly after graduation, Kemal was arrested and imprisoned for plotting against the ruling authorities.

Kemal was born into a world of transition in which ancient social and political institutions were crumbling. The once powerful Ottoman Empire was on its last legs. On all its borders, the empire was besieged by various ethnic minority groups who fought to separate themselves from the system. Meanwhile, liberal ideas from the West were breeding dissatisfaction among the empire's educated and middle-class populations. It is thus not accidental that the Young Turk movement was born and nurtured in the westernmost sector of the empire. Macedonians were conspicuously present among the revolutionaries.

The sultanate in Constantinople was corrupt and venal, and its policies were increasingly unpopular. When pushed, Sultan Abdul Hamid had declared some reforms, only to repeal them when pressures were relaxed. In 1876, he agreed to a constitution providing for the establishment of a consultative assembly; in 1877, he dissolved the assembly; in 1896, a major coup attempt failed. Meanwhile, political opposition had spread everywhere and had become deeply rooted even within the sultan's own armed forces. Kemal was one of the most disenchanted of the young officers who saw their decrepit system crumbling around them. A fierce nationalist, he determined from the beginning that the Turkish nation had to be reformed, strengthened, and regenerated.

After a few months in jail, Kemal was posted to the Fifth Army in Damascus, where he immediately began to establish political opposition societies among his military colleagues on the Syrian front. His Vatan ("Fatherland") Society was soon swallowed up by the Young Turks' Committee of Union and Progress, which on 23 July 1908 forced the sultan to restore

---

[7] Ray Brock, *Ghost on Horseback: The Incredible Atatürk* (Boston: Little, Brown and Co., 1954), p. 21. Although this book tends toward the sensational and owes too much to the fertile imagination of the author, it makes interesting reading and succeeds in capturing the colorfully human nature of Kemal.

the constitution and recall his consultative assembly. Between 1908 and the outbreak of World War I in 1914, Kemal floated on the fringes of the Young Turks in a relationship marked by mutual distrust. Although his military skills were used by Enver Pasha and the other leaders during this time, he was carefully kept out of the corridors of power. "He was a realist, who thought in terms not of gestures but of action, thoughtfully conceived, scientifically planned and systematically executed. Too many of those whom he saw around him, and who were pretending to govern the country, were men of words, of undigested feelings and vague ideas."[8]

Although Kemal personally opposed the Turkish alliance with Germany in World War I, he earned his place in military history for his brilliant defense in 1915 at Gallipoli, where the Turks repelled a major Allied offensive spearheaded by the finest soldiers of the British Empire. Poorly armed and outnumbered, the Turkish troops under Kemal successfully held off the seasoned Australian, New Zealand, and English troops who desperately fought to break through to the Dardanelles and to clear the way to Constantinople. During this nine-month siege and bitter fighting, Kemal proved himself to be not only a brilliant military tactician, but also an inspiration to his soldiers. He moved constantly among his men in the front trenches and miraculously survived a direct hit in his chest when shrapnel shattered the watch in his breast pocket. As he told his outgunned Fifty-Seventh Regiment: "I don't order you to attack, I order you to die. In the time it takes us to die, other troops and commanders can come and take our places."[9] The men of the Fifty-Seventh did die for their leader and for their country. Kemal somehow survived; he had taken the first major step toward becoming the Father of the Turks.

The Allies' victory in 1918 ended the Young Turks' ascen-

8 Lord Kinross, *Atatürk: The Rebirth of a Nation* (London: Weidenfeld and Nicolson, 1964), p. 44. This remains the best biography of Atatürk. For a fine article-length study, see Dankwart A. Rustow's own analysis in his edited volume *Philosophers and Kings: Studies in Leadership* (New York: George Braziller, 1970), pp. 208–47.

9 Kinross, *Atatürk*, p. 76.

dancy and forced their leaders into exile. The British appearance in Constantinople and a subsequent Greek movement
into Smyrna were shocking and unacceptable events for Turkish patriots. Kemal left for Anatolia, where he began an opposition independence movement. In 1919, he organized congresses at Erzerum and Sivas, where delegates drafted and
ratified a national pact legitimizing their movement. Turkey
was in upheaval. During the next four years, Kemal put the
pieces of the country back together. The task was a formidable
one, since in the process he had to organize a political and
military force that would not only hang together but also be
strong enough to defeat the tribes and brigands in Anatolia;
repulse and drive a major invading Greek force from the heart
of Turkey; maneuver the British and Russians out of the area;
and replace the Sultan's government, still claiming legitimacy
in Constantinople, with a new nationalist government, resident in Ankara.

In three and a half years of brutal but brilliant military
campaigns and pressure-packed political infighting, Kemal
somehow accomplished all these goals. In November 1922, he
proclaimed the abolition of the sultanate; in October 1923,
Turkey was declared a republic and Kemal became its first
president; and in March 1924, the caliphate was abolished.
Kemal was president of Turkey until his death in 1938.

During his fifteen years as president, Atatürk did not choose
to rest on his military laurels. Instead, he began a program of
social, cultural, and political modernization that shook the
country to its roots. His program struck at the foundation of
the conservative religious culture of the day and stressed national, secular, and modern goals. In a characteristic style, he
directly and publicly attacked the very symbols of the old
system by outlawing the fez, condemning the veil, and reforming the alphabet. He introduced such changes by personally
initiating them in the very heart of the most conservative areas
of Turkey.

These shattering changes in important symbols were accompanied by major reforms in the fields of administration, education, and law. One of Atatürk's most important contributions was the successful establishment of an independent and

LIFE OF ATATÜRK: MAJOR EVENTS

1881 Born in Salonika
1893 Enters military secondary school in Salonika; given added name Kemal
1899 Enters War College in Constantinople
1905 Graduates from Staff College with rank of captain
1908 Young Turk revolution
1914 Beginning of World War I; Turkey signs secret alliance with Germany; Russia, Britain, and France declare war on Turkey
1915 Kemal distinguishes himself at Gallipoli
1919 Leaves for Anatolia; issues declaration of independence; calls nationalist congresses at Sivas and Erzerum
1921 Defeats the invading Greeks at Battle of Sakarya
1922 Proclaims abolition of the sultanate
1923 Founds the Republican Peoples' Party; becomes president of the Turkish Republic
1924 Abolishes the caliphate
1926 Trials and suppression of opposition at Izmir and Ankara
1934 Takes name of Atatürk; women given the right to vote in parliamentary elections and to become members of parliament
1938 Dies in Istanbul

effective judiciary. These programs were backed by an international policy that was astutely conceived and implemented. This foreign policy was based on a premise stressing the consolidation of national power, not the expansion of national boundaries. It also emphasized the necessity of avoiding international entanglements such as the one that contributed to the disaster of World War I. It was Atatürk who established the policy that enabled Ismet Inönü to keep Turkey out of the Second World War. Despite tremendous pressures, Turkey did not take a formal position until February 1945, when it declared war on the Axis powers.[10]

Atatürk was not a liberal democrat. He was an authoritarian

[10] For Atatürk and his successors as makers of foreign policy, see Metin Tamkoç's excellent book *The Warrior Diplomats* (Salt Lake City: University of Utah Press, 1976).

ruler who exercised power bluntly and forcefully. In his own words, "I don't act for public opinion. I act for the nation and for my own satisfaction."[11] He had climbed the ladder of power by himself and had survived everything from several serious illnesses[12] and difficult military campaigns to political plots and assassination attempts. When he finally reached a position of national political power, he did not hesitate to take severe measures against those whom he considered threats to himself or to his programs. The major example of this occurred when in 1926 Kemal used an abortive plot against his life as a rationale for imprisoning, exiling, or executing those he considered members of a serious political opposition. Among them were several of his oldest comrades and closest friends who had stood behind him in the difficult years in Anatolia. Many of these individuals were liberal thinkers who had begun to resist his personal, arbitrary rule. As Kâzim Karabekir, a trusted military leader whose assistance was crucial to Kemal's success in Anatolia, put it, "I am in favour of the Republic, but I am against personal rule."[13]

Yet there is another side to the story. Kemal was always scrupulously careful to seek legitimation for his actions and to base them upon legal principles emanating from the people or their representatives. Even as a rebel, he insisted on congresses and constitutional pacts that would provide political legitimacy for his movement. He also campaigned hard among the people and created a major and lasting political party, the Republican Peoples' Party. He twice experimented with a two-party system, but gave it up when it proved farcical. Atatürk once admitted that he was a dictator yet went on to point out: "But I have not had pyramids built in my honour

---

11 Kinross, *Atatürk,* p. xvii.

12 Physical ailments plagued Kemal throughout his life. Yet he conquered these problems just as he overcame the social and political problems that confronted him. Besides sustaining a minor battle wound and some broken ribs, he survived two major attacks of malaria, three severe cases of influenza, a debilitating ear infection, and kidney problems that tormented him for twenty-five years. As a young man, he contracted gonorrhea, the effects of which were lasting. He died of cirrhosis of the liver and complications thereof.

13 Kinross, *Atatürk,* p. 382.

like the Pharaohs of Egypt. I did not make people work for my sake, threatening them with whips when I wanted an idea to be accepted by the country. I first called a congress, I debated the situation with the people, I carried out my plans only after taking authority from the people."[14] His may not have always been a government by the people, but it was in many ways a government for the people.[15]

Patterns of Rule. Atatürk was one of the more colorful of the political leaders of this century. He was a man of imposing appearance, with peculiarly striking eyes. "Wide-set beneath the broad brow and the eyebrows that curled upwards like whiskers, they gleamed with a cold steady challenging light, for ever fixing, observing, reflecting, appraising, moreover uncannily capable of swivelling two ways at once so that they seemed to see both upwards and downwards, before and behind."[16]

Kemal's personal life was almost completely uninhibited. He drank and gambled incessantly; and he enjoyed the company and entertainment provided by women and spent a good part of his life in cafes, hotels, brothels, and other similar settings. During the critical early years of his political opposition both to the sultan and to the Young Turks, these personal activities led the establishment forces to underestimate the danger that he posed to them. At the same time, Kemal used these informal gatherings to discuss social and political issues and to gather information that passed through these grapevines. Just as Ismet Inönü was able to convert his physical liability of near-deafness into a political asset, Kemal's personal habits were not complete liabilities to him. A French writer wrote at the time that Turkey was governed by one drunkard, one deaf man, and three hundred deaf-mutes (the assembly

14 Ibid., p. 438.

15 This terminology is Kemal Karpat's as presented in his study *Turkey's Politics: The Transition to Multi-Party Politics* (Princeton, N.J.: Princeton University Press, 1959), pp. 50–51. It is quoted in Metin Heper, "Transformation of Charisma into a Political Paradigm: Atatürkism in Turkey," in *Charisma and Political Idolatry in the Twentieth Century,* ed. Mattei Dogan, forthcoming.

16 Kinross, *Atatürk,* p. 163.

deputies). When he heard this, Kemal responded: "The man is mistaken. Turkey is governed by one drunkard."[17]

Atatürk's political style and strategy in many ways sharply broke with traditional Middle Eastern patterns. Although he would on occasion use the *hocas* (clerics) to legitimize a particular political move, he refused to use Islam as any kind of overarching ideology. Quite to the contrary, he had a strong personal aversion to religion and sought to smash its influence. Much is written about his charismatic personality, and he indeed had many of the extraordinary attributes of a charismatic leader. This can be seen even today in Turkey, where the anniversaries of his death are national mourning days, and where thousands upon thousands of Turkish citizens from all walks of life continue to file past his mausoleum in Ankara. But Atatürk was little impressed by his own charisma. He was often annoyed, for example, when other dignitaries would fawn over him. He once became so irritated when the mayor of a city he was visiting insisted on waiting on him in person at the dinner table that he snapped, "For God's sake, sit down! Are you a waiter, or the mayor of this city?"[18] Atatürk institutionalized and routinized his charisma by building organizations such as the Republican Peoples' Party that would transcend the existence of one man. This is why one leading authority on Turkish politics writes that one might call Atatürk "an organization man thrown into a charismatic situation."[19]

Although Kemal learned to play off his subordinates one against the other and on occasion to maneuver clandestinely and personalistically, he was essentially very direct. In the context of Turkish politics of the day, this directness often seemed crude, brutal, and even stupid. As his major biographer writes: "He detested the shifts and evasions of the oblique approach to Oriental politics, the circumlocutions and imprecisions of its thought and speech. He liked to speak his mind directly, to call spades spades. His outspokenness indeed not only infuri-

17 Ibid., p. 261.
18 Ibid., p. 368.
19 Rustow, *Philosophers and Kings*, p. 212. For a recent, thoughtful analysis of Atatürk as a charismatic leader, see Heper, "Transformation of Charisma."

ated his enemies but, on occasion, embarrassed his friends."[20] Nor did Kemal really play favorites with friends and relatives. One of the major reasons he divorced his wife Latife was that she continually interfered in matters of national politics. Finally, Atatürk was not in the least interested in amassing a fortune for himself and his family. Although he lived comfortably, he was by no means financially corrupt. His life-style was in fact quite modest.

Atatürk was above all a realist. He understood power and people and had an unusual ability to bridge the gap between ideal and reality. He used idealists and dreamers, but he never trusted them. He considered them much more dangerous than the small-time politicians who lacked vision. Atatürk himself was both a visionary and a hard, experienced political realist.

Champion of Change or Camouflaged Conservative? A number of excellent social and political analyses of the Atatürk period make rather compelling arguments that Kemal's programs and policies were in essence conservative and nonrevolutionary. Although this school admits that dramatic changes were initiated in the cultural and religious systems of Turkey, the question at issue is that of social structure. Atatürk's programs and policies were initiated without basically altering the traditional class structure. Special care was taken to avoid upsetting the local landlords and aristocracy that controlled power throughout the country. Those at the bottom of the power structure witnessed very little change in their standard of living. If anything, the peasants' standard of living became worse during Kemalist rule. Land reform, for example, was almost completely ignored during Kemal's lifetime. In his important analysis of this question, Arnold Leder supports the following statement with cogent reasoning and convincing evidence.

> From its earliest days in the Turkish War of Independence when it sought the cooperation of the local notables in the countryside, the Kemalist movement became a collaborative movement. The nationalist struggle led by the Kemalists was

20 Kinross, *Atatürk,* p. 45.

fought against foreign enemies and not against a particular social class. The Kemalists did not undertake radical change in
Turkey's social structure. In fact, they established a tacit alliance with the traditional elites in the countryside. This alliance
was reflected in Kemalist political organization where local
notables dominated the lower levels of the Republican Peoples'
party. The Kemalists made no effort to broaden the party's
popular base and to enlist the support of the peasants. Similarly,
Kemalist ideology emphasized not the drastic restratification of
society but rather harmony, national solidarity, and the prosperity of all segments of society.[21]

Another recent study by a leading Turkish political scientist
concludes in this regard that "the Atatürk Revolution exploited the basic bifurcation between the educated elite and
the uneducated masses, rather than deploring it or immediately attacking it."[22]

This failure to transform the national class structure has
been one factor in the political problems that have plagued
Turkey since Atatürk's death. Indeed, the creation of the
Democratic party in 1946 and its stunning victory over the
Republican Peoples' Party in the general election of 1950 may
have been major symptoms of the depth of the social and political problems inherited from the days of Atatürk. Since
Atatürk's time, there has been a slowly broadening diffusion
of power into the Turkish countryside, although the real inclusion of the provincial lower classes within the national decision-making structure remains to be seen.[23]

These questions concerning the depth of Atatürk's reforms
are legitimate ones. His revolution did not transform the social, political, or economic conditions of the masses of Turkish

[21] Leder, "Collaboration Politics and the Turkish Revolution" (Paper
delivered at the 1976 Annual Meeting of the Middle East Studies Association, Los Angeles, California, 11–13 November 1976) , p. 29.

[22] Ergun Özbudun, *Social Change and Political Participation in Turkey*
(Princeton, N.J.: Princeton University Press, 1976) , p. 43. The writings of
Frederick W. Frey also impressively document this position.

[23] See Frank Tachau, "Turkish Provincial Party Politics," in *Social
Change and Politics in Turkey*, Kemal H. Karpat et al. (Leiden: E. J.
Brill, 1973) , pp. 282–314; and Karpat's own article "Political Development
in Turkey, 1950–1970," *Middle Eastern Studies* 8 (October 1972) :349–75.

peasants. Still, this failure should not be allowed to obscure the immensity of the social and political changes that Atatürk did implement successfully. At bottom, his revolution was a middle-class movement that destroyed a number of traditional symbols and built a new political system. In this sense, it was more radical than the American Revolution and in some respects paralleled the French Revolution, also a middle-class affair. In the context of the time, and without the benefit of scholarly hindsight, it must stand as a revolution of modernization and a movement of substantial political development.

Politically, a 600-year-old national ruling institution and its attendant ruling class were destroyed and replaced by a middle-class elite that introduced new political ideas and institutions, including a political party of genuine consequence. These were structural transformations of lasting impact, which set the stage for subsequent political development, such as the birth of a political opposition (the Democratic party) that was permitted to win in elections. In this rare political event, in which an authoritarian regime voluntarily relinquished power, it was Atatürk's old lieutenant, the dedicated Kemalist Ismet Inönü, who made the decision to permit the opposition to win.[24]

In the section above, we have seen how Atatürk broke many of the traditional interpersonal patterns that had dominated patrimonial rule in the Ottoman Islamic culture. These and the broader political changes discussed above were successfully implemented despite the serious opposition of at least four

24 Inönü's decision was based on a number of personal, political, and ideological factors. First, he hoped at the time to demonstrate to the West the democratic nature of his regime. See Dankwart A. Rustow, "The Development of Parties in Turkey," in *Political Parties and Political Development,* ed. J. La Palombara and M. Weiner (Princeton, N.J.: Princeton University Press, 1966), p. 122. Second, Inönü felt that the establishment of an opposition political party would help lower the level of discontent in the country. See Leslie L. Roos, Jr., and Noraloo P. Roos, *Managers of Modernization* (Cambridge: Harvard University Press, 1971), p. 40. Third, Inönü and his advisors believed that the Republican Peoples' Party was strong enough in the Turkish countryside to guarantee victory in any election. See Kemal Karpat, "Society, Economics, and Politics in Contemporary Turkey," *World Politics* 17 (October 1964):58. These points are drawn together by Arnold Leder in his article "Party Competition in Rural Turkey: Agent of Change or Defender of Traditional Rule?" *Middle Eastern Studies,* forthcoming.

groups. Of these groups, two were obvious forces of the *ancien regime* — the sultanate's political establishment and the omnipresent religious hierarchy. The two others, however, were groups of former liberal allies who were ironically more conservative than Kemal. These were the Young Turks on the one hand and the group of his earliest supporters and comrades on the other hand. In the case of the former, ". . . theirs was essentially a conservative revolution . . . Imperialists in essence, blind to the new nationalist forces now at work in the modern world, the Young Turks aspired merely to conserve, if in a more liberal form, the Ottoman Empire of their forebears."[25] At the same time, old comrades such as Husayn Rauf, Ali Fuad, and Kâzim Karabekir were more liberal idealists and preferred democracy over revolutionary change. "Kemal was embarking on a social revolution. Rauf and his friends, at this stage, preferred social evolution."[26] Despite this encircling and committed opposition, Atatürk rammed through as much radical political change as was perhaps humanly possible.

A comparison of Atatürk and his longtime friend and trusted lieutenant Ismet Inönü also helps demonstrate the nature of Atatürk's revolution. Inönü had served Kemal loyally and was the one lieutenant who survived his leader's personality and inner-circle purges.[27] The two men complemented

---

[25] Kinross, *Atatürk,* p. 30.

[26] Ibid., p. 392. These associates were generally of well-to-do upper-class and upper-middle-class background and were therefore more closely tied to the old system than Kemal, who was obviously their social inferior. In 1924, this group resigned from the Republican Peoples' Party and formed their own organization, called the Progressive Republican Party. Kemal used a Kurdish rebellion as the major excuse for disbanding the Progressive Party. For an analysis of the character of Atatürk's political elite, see Joseph S. Szyliowicz's study of leadership in modern Turkey in Frank Tachau, ed., *Political Elites and Political Development in the Middle East* (New York: Schenkman Publishing Co., 1975), pp. 23–68. Another good source is Frederick Frey's article in *Political Elites in the Middle East,* ed. George Lenczowski (Washington: American Enterprise Institute, 1975), pp. 41–82.

[27] Toward the end, personal tensions that had been building up for many years between Atatürk and Inönü began to break into the open. Kinross reports one such exchange that took place in 1937. The pressured and normally unflappable Inönü lost his temper and blurted to Atatürk,

each other perfectly. Atatürk was direct, forceful, and mercurial, while Inönü was conservative, retiring, and unspectacular. When Atatürk died in 1938, Inönü was the natural choice to replace him as president. For the next thirty-five years, he played a prominent role in directing Turkish political destiny. Inönü's most famous political decision was his call in 1945 for the formation of an opposition party (referred to above). This remarkable move transformed Turkey into a multiparty state and was an example of Inönü's great commitment to liberalization. In taking this action, Inönü not only broadened participatory politics in Turkey but also carved out a place for himself, independent of Atatürk, in the Turkish political hall of fame.

Although many observers interpret Inönü's programs as moving far beyond the policies of Atatürk in the field of political development, there is another position that needs to be presented. The argument has been made that in promoting liberalization and introducing pluralist politics into Turkey, Inönü in fact hampered the system's capacity for development. By stepping aside and opening the arena to all comers, he introduced a period of tense and competitive factional politics that have ever since slowed the Turkish drive to develop. From the days of Menderes's prime ministry, beginning in 1950, to the debilitating political struggles in 1977 and 1978 between Suleyman Demirel of the Justice Party and Bülent Ecevit of the Republican Peoples' Party, the weakening of the political process in Turkey has been evident. The severity of the crisis is seen in the instances of direct military intervention (1960, 1971), as well as in the outbreaks of ugly violence and terrorism involving forces both of the far left and the far right — incidents that have been on the increase over the last decade. Raging economic problems in the late 1970s were further evidence that Turkey's drive to modernize and develop has been stalled.

This position is supported strongly in an excellent and pro-

"How much longer is this country going to be governed from a drunkard's table?" To this Atatürk coldly responded, "You seem to forget that it was a drunkard who appointed you to your post." Ibid., p. 486.

vocative study by a young Turkish social scientist and diplo-
mat, who wrote that with Inönü's "democratization of political life, the principle of revolutionism was effectively shelved.
. . . The capacity of Turkish leaders to introduce orderly
change from above, a capacity that was in evidence during
Atatürk's time, was lost for the sake and as a result of democracy. Atatürk had started a revolution; Inönü arrested it."[28]

There is certainly truth in both sides of this debate, which
focuses directly upon the developmental dialectic discussed in
Chapter I. Authoritarianism at the center endangers participation in the periphery (Atatürk's case). But also, liberalization
tends to create fragmentation, which in turn weakens capacity
for development (Inönü's case). The parallel processes of
modernization and political development must be continuing
ones. Atatürk started a revolution. It was up to his successors
to continue it, widen it, and deepen it.

In the end, Atatürk was a modernizing authoritarian leader
who succeeded in initiating a sporadic program of political
development. A nationalist hero with charismatic appeal and
with organizational skills complemented by a sense of hard-
headed political realism, he won a war of independence, established a republic, gained personal governing power, and pulled
his newly created nation-state well into the twentieth century.

MUHAMMAD REZA SHAH PAHLAVI:
THE TRADITIONALISM
OF A MODERNIZING MONARCH

In June of 1934, President Kemal Atatürk welcomed an important neighboring head of state to Turkey for a three-week
official state visit. The visitor was Reza Shah, the founder of
the Pahlavi dynasty of Iran. Like Atatürk, Reza Shah was a

[28] Osman Faruk Logoglu, "Ismet Inönü and the Political Modernization
of Turkey, 1945–1965," Ph.D. diss. (Princeton University, 1970), p. 255.
With regard to Atatürk's strategy of change, Logoglu writes: "There has
been no rigorous exposition of the meaning of the well-established proposition that Atatürk tried to convert only the elite or the intelligentsia and
did not really try to reach the peasant masses. The meaning of the corol-
lary proposition that Atatürk had the insight to realize he could not
change the masses without first transforming the elite needs to be restated
as well." See pp. 255–56.

man of imposing presence. Standing well over six feet in height, he had the flashing eyes of an eagle and a personality that scorched friend and foe alike. The two leaders had much in common. Both were military men and avid nationalists who consolidated their nations and built strong central political control over their peoples. Both leaders also sought to modernize and reform their countries. Reza Shah, who was three years older than Atatürk, was greatly impressed by the latter's reform programs as well as by the level of modernity he witnessed in Turkey. Partly as a result of this visit, he lashed out at such symbols of tradition as the ulema, while at the same time sporadically modernizing the economic, educational, and military systems in his country. Yet Reza Shah's programs of reform never approached the depth or breadth of those instituted by his contemporary in Turkey.[29]

After participating in the military coup of 1921, Reza Khan crowned himself Shah of Iran in 1926. In so doing, he chose to continue patrimonial monarchy — a system of leadership that Atatürk had vigorously dismantled in Turkey. This style of rule persists in Iran today, where Reza Shah's eldest son directs a dramatic program of modernization from a position of entrenched patrimonialism.

Although an impressive nation builder and leader who rose to power from a lowly and illiterate background, Reza Shah in the end only shuffled the old power relations in Iran. The major political change was the existence of a new royal family at the center of the system. By the time he abdicated in 1941, Reza Shah had acquired in his own name the largest landholdings in Iran and was drawing an annual income of well over $3 million a year.[30] Although he maintained parliamentary forms and procedures, he completely controlled the political process. His rule was absolute and oppressive; he disposed of whomever he considered to be a threat to himself or to his son.

It was within this repressive political climate that Reza

---

29 The classic comparison of Atatürk and Reza Shah as modernizers is Richard H. Pfaff, "Disengagement from Traditionalism in Turkey and Iran," *Western Political Quarterly* 16 (March 1963) :79–98.

30 Great Britain, Public Record Office, F. O. 371/18992, from Mallet (Tehran), 28 November 1935.

Shah built a railway, founded a modern educational system, developed a national army, and supported such strong symbolic measures as the unveiling of women and the condemnation of the clerics. The old social structure and the traditional patrimonialism were strongly protected, however, by the new ruling Pahlavi family. One Persian source describes the patrimonial role of Reza Shah as follows: "The Shah expected that all government employees consider themselves completely subservient to his desires and that they not show any personality of their own. . . . Those favored by the Shah did their best to carry out his desires while at the same time trying to insure that these efforts did not become too well known and thus draw fame upon themselves."[31] The British *Report on Leading Personalities in Persia* in 1937 summarizes the personality and leadership of Reza Shah as follows:

> He is an entirely self-educated man with a natural dignity. He has a strong character, and has a great deal of ability and energy. Full of ambition, he has set out to extricate Persia from disintegration and from the morass of inefficiency into which it had fallen, and to raise it to a position of real independence.
>
> . . .
>
> He is insecure, in the sense that he regards prevarication and duplicity as fair weapons; he is thoroughly suspicious of anybody whom he suspects of being cleverer than himself, and he does not hesitate to put into retirement any army commander who has shown himself too successful in the field. . . .
>
> Reza Shah is avaricious and greedy of wealth, and all means whereby he can acquire money and lands are good to him. . . .[32]

The Reza Shah's eldest son has written that "all over the world, the father helps shape the character of the son. In my case, my father influenced me more by far than has anyone else."[33]

Muhammad Reza Shah Pahlavi was born on 26 October 1919. At the age of thirte, he began his studies at Le Rosey

---

31 *Sharq-i Tarik* [The Dark East] (Tehran: Taban Press, 1942), pp. 69–71. In Persian.

32 Great Britain, Public Record Office, F. O. 371/20837, Seymour to Eden, "Report on Leading Personalities in Persia, 1937," 12 April 1937.

33 Mohammad Reza Shah Pahlavi, *Mission For My Country* (New York: McGraw-Hill, 1961), p. 45.

School in Rolle, Switzerland. He returned to Iran four years later, and between 1936 and 1941 he received a military and political education that was directed primarily by his father. With the Allied invasion of Iran in 1941 and his father's humiliating abdication, Muhammad Reza became Shah of Iran. The next dozen years were very painful and insecure for the young Shah, as is well symbolized by the attempt on his life in 1949, which, face-to-face with an armed assassin, the Shah survived by "shadow-dancing and feinting."[34]

The Shah managed to dodge and weave his way through the 1940s, during which he was the target of challenges emanating from many different directions. On the left, the Communist-oriented Tudeh Party threatened to capture the entire political system, while on the right, both knowledgeable statesmen and conservative clerics sought to control the Shah and to take power themselves. Foreign interference was intense, and the young king found himself sandwiched between nationalist fervor and imperialist power. It was during these early years that the Shah learned the art of political maneuver and perfected the traditional techniques of divide and rule. When such basic rationalizations of rule as charisma and religion are absent, the patrimonial leader is forced to rely entirely upon personal manipulative techniques. This was exactly the situation for the Shah of Iran in the 1940s; besieged and surrounded by opponents and critics, he managed to survive by constantly refining those methods of patrimonial rule that were at his disposal.

In the early 1950s, the Shah and the monarchy of Iran were faced with a challenge of the most serious proportions. A charismatic personality rose within Iran and, rallying the masses behind him, confronted the Shah and threatened to transform social and political patterns. Dr. Muhammad Musaddiq rose to influence primarily on the basis of his attack against foreign influence in Iran and his direct drive to nationalize the Anglo-Iranian Oil Company. Although the apologetic (as opposed to analytic) literature concerning Pahlavi politics has attempted to portray Musaddiq as somehow being in league

34 Ibid., p. 57.

with the British, the British had already, in their diplomatic reports in the 1930s, tagged him as "a demagogue and a windbag."[35]

Musaddiq was known in Iran as an impeccably honest personality who would refuse to accede to foreign interests. The dramatic proof of this was his successful campaign to nationalize the oil company. Musaddiq was prime minister from April 1951 to August 1953. During this time, he became internationally famous as he nationalized the oil company and slowly undermined the power and position of the Shah. He fell from office during the chaotic events of August 1953, which included the Shah's returning to Iran and the throne a few days after a hurried flight out of the country. Street fighting and military activity that month involved the Tudeh forces, pro-Shah elements, Musaddiqists, and Americans who directly intervened on behalf of the King.[36]

Much of Musaddiq's support came from the rising professional middle class, whose members tended to be highly nationalistic and critical of the corruption that pervaded the Iranian socioadministrative system. Musaddiq, who retained behavioral vestiges of the old aristocracy from which he had come, nonetheless entertained middle-class values and was able to gain strength and support across class lines. Although he may have been a poor politician in the Iranian context, Musaddiq was a charismatic leader who challenged the very roots of patrimonialism in Iran by directly threatening the Shah and by disrupting the patterns of corruption that are often nourished in settings of informal personalism and omnipresent rivalry.[37]

The Musaddiq challenge represented an intolerable situation for the Shah, since it directly struck at the very foundation upon which all patrimonial leaders must base their power —

[35] Great Britain, Public Record Office, F. O. 371/20837, Seymour to Eden, 12 April 1937. For the convoluted reasoning that implies Musaddiq's proximity to the British, see Ramesh Sanghvi, *Aryamehr: The Shah of Iran* (New York: Stein and Day, 1968), pp. 142–45, 213.

[36] For a reliable analysis of these controversial and complex events, see Richard W. Cottam, *Nationalism in Iran* (Pittsburgh: University of Pittsburgh Press, 1964), pp. 223–30.

[37] Musaddiq himself was not without patrimonial traits.

their indisputable and central right to rule. The threat from Musaddiq was particularly serious because he donned a patrimonial mantle of his own that was heavily embroidered with charisma.[38] Following the fall of Musaddiq, the Shah began a concerted program to solidify his position as leader of all Iranians. Between 1954 and 1961, he pursued a policy of consolidation through coercion and thus adopted political tactics reminiscent of those used by his father in the 1930s. Besides building up military resources such as the army and the gendarmerie, the Shah organized an extensive secret-police system (SAVAK) in 1957. This complex organization has been a key element in Pahlavi politics ever since.

Beginning in 1963, the style of leadership of the Shah shifted to an emphasis upon the introduction of reform programs. Policies of coercion were balanced with programs of co-optation as the Shah initiated an impressive campaign to foster reform from above. In the mid-1960s, he spoke often about the need for revolutionary programs in Iran. By the end of the 1960s, he was quoting Lenin in his speeches, and more and more of his supporters were referring to opponents of the regime as reactionary, feudal, and right-wing. The Shah outlined the core of the reform program in January 1963, when he announced the six principles of the White Revolution. This Revolution of the Shah and the People, as it is referred to in Persian, has since been expanded and now includes nineteen different points. The most important are the first twelve: (1) land reform, (2) nationalization of forests and pastures, (3) public sale of state-owned factories to finance land reform, (4) profit sharing in industry, (5) reform of electoral law to include women, (6) literacy corps, (7) health corps, (8) reconstruction and development corps, (9) rural Courts of Justice, (10) nationalization of the waterways, (11) national reconstruction, and (12) educational and administrative revolution.[39]

38 E. A. Bayne writes that "the Shah's historic image was dimmed by the burning fire of Mossadegh's charisma." Bayne, *Persian Kingship in Transition* (New York: American Universities Field Staff, 1968), p. 160.

39 The most recent seven points are (13) the sale of stocks of all industrial plants to the public, (14) a national campaign against price

This program has become the creed of the Shah and the Iranian political elite. By 1970, it stood as an important ideology by which the Shah justified his activities and his rule. It is anathema in Iran to criticize the principles of the White Revolution, which are considered by the regime to be part of the wisdom of the Shah himself. This situation has seriously impeded detailed and objective analysis of the implementation of the reforms. Perhaps the greatest attention has been given to the land reform and literacy corps programs, and it is in these two areas that the most widespread changes have been implemented. There can be little doubt that these particular programs have begun to change the face of the Iranian countryside. There has been a shuffling of power in the village context, although this does not imply any basic change in the national power structure or in the very relations that compose that structure. The entire thrust of the White Revolution is in the direction of the peasantry. This is the class that most completely supports the traditional system and the patrimonial leader who is the core of that system.

Despite these reforms and the coercive force that backs them, political opposition, unrest, instability, and violence have all been on the increase in Iran since the mid-1960s. Prime Minister Hassan Ali Mansur was assassinated in 1963, and in April 1965 an attempt was made on the life of the Shah when a Royal Guardsman opened fire on him at point-blank range. In 1970, there was an attempted assassination of Prime Minister Amir Abbas Hoveyda. In 1971, a bold attempt was made to kidnap the United States ambassador to Iran, Douglas MacArthur II. There was also a kidnapping attempt and attack on the son of the Shah's twin sister. A powerful military prosecutor was assassinated after he sentenced thirteen young Iranians to prison and to death. In 1972, the deputy chief of police was assassinated. And in late 1973, a plot to kidnap and as-

---

gouging and inflation, (15) cost-free education for all, (16) the provision of food for the newborn up to the age of two, (17) the expansion of public insurance to include all classes of Iranians, particularly villagers and farmers, (18) the control of land prices to the inflation rate or less, and (19) government officials must declare all private and family earnings.

LIFE OF MUHAMMAD REZA SHAH PAHLAVI:
MAJOR EVENTS

1919 Born in Tehran

1926 Reza Khan crowned Shah of Iran; Muhammad Reza declared Crown Prince

1932 Enters Le Rosey School in Switzerland

1936 Returns to Tehran; enrolls in military academy

1941 Reza Shah abdicates; Muhammad Reza takes oath as Shah of Iran; Tudeh party established in Tehran

1946 Russian army withdraws from Azerbaijan

1950 Shah announces intention to divide lands among peasants

1951 Dr. Muhammad Musaddiq becomes prime minister; nationalization of Anglo-Iranian Oil Company

1953 Fall of Dr. Musaddiq; Shah reassumes power

1957 Establishment of Security Organization (SAVAK)

1959 Shah marries Farah Diba

1960 Birth of Crown Prince Reza

1963 Announces White Revolution; countrywide riots and demonstrations put down with force

1967 Formal coronation of Muhammad Reza Shah and Empress Farah

1971 Celebration of 2,500 years of Iranian monarchy

1975 Establishes one-party system — the National Resurgence party

1978 Masses of Iranian citizens riot and demonstrate against the Shah's rule; Shah institutes government by martial law

1979 Shah goes into exile

sassinate the Shah, the Empress, and the Crown Prince was uncovered in Tehran. During the mid-1970s, urban guerrillas dedicated to the overthrow of the Shah clashed constantly with security forces.

Between 1972 and 1976, the Shah's longtime policy of blending programs of repression with those of reform was abandoned, and a period of stifling police rule was ushered in. People were arrested and harassed arbitrarily and often; censorship became unusually heavy-handed and indiscriminate; and for the first time in the Shah's thirty-year rule, torture was systematically utilized in the prisons. A 1976 study prepared by the International Commission of Jurists reported that "there can be no doubt that torture has been systematically practiced over a number of years against recalcitrant suspects under interrogation by the SAVAK."[40] When questioned about torture, the Shah said: "I am not bloodthirsty. I am working for my country and the coming generations. I can't waste my time on a few young idiots. I don't believe the tortures attributed to the SAVAK are as common as people say, but I can't run everything."[41] Another important political development during this period was the Shah's sudden decision in 1975 to establish a new one-party system. From then on, everyone would be required to join the National Resurgence Party. As the Shah bluntly put it on 2 March 1975:

> A person who does not enter the new political party and does not believe in the three cardinal principles which I referred to will have only two choices. He is either an individual who belongs to an illegal organization, or is related to the outlawed Tudeh Party, or in other words is a traitor. Such an individual belongs in an Iranian prison, or if he desires he can leave the country tomorrow, without even paying exit fees and can go anywhere he likes, because he is not an Iranian, he has no nation, and his activities are illegal and punishable according to the law.[42]

This sharp shift in the direction of repressive rule sacrificed the more subtle and paternal dimensions of patrimonial rule to harsh police control. One result was a marked rise in opposition activity, which took the form of urban violence promoted by growing and dedicated guerrilla groups. Thousands

---

[40] William J. Butler and Georges Levasseur, *Human Rights and the Legal System in Iran* (Geneva: International Commission of Jurists, 1976), p. 22. For various sources discussing the severity of secret police tactics in Iran, see Amnesty International, *Annual Report, 1974–75* (London, 1975); U.S. Congress, House, Committee on International Relations, Subcommittee on International Organizations, *Human Rights in Iran* (Washington, D.C.: Government Printing Office, 1977); Philip Jacobson, "Torture in Iran," *Sunday Times* (London), 19 January 1975, p. 9. See also Reza Barahani's frightening book *The Crowned Cannibals: Writings on Repression in Iran* (New York: Vintage Books, 1977).

[41] Gérard de Villiers, *The Imperial Shah: An Informal Biography* (Boston: Little, Brown and Co., 1976), p. 259.

[42] This translation of the text of the Shah's speech is drawn from *Kayhan International* (Tehran), 3 March 1975, p. 2.

of incidents occurred throughout Iran; new, superbly organized opposition groups even managed to infiltrate the Shah's
highly touted security forces. The tighter the police turned the
screws, the more fanatic the opposition became. Dozens of
young women as well as men joined the guerrillas as a vicious
circle of repression and reaction set in.

Then, at the end of 1976 and in early 1977, and coinciding
partly with the appearance of the Carter administration in
Washington, the Shah began to cut back on the repressive tactics and tried to return to the more flexible Persian patrimonial style. A period of liberalization began and was accompanied by a marked decrease in guerrilla-sponsored violence.
Letters, petitions, and communications of all kinds flooded the
offices of the Shah and his political elite. When a leading Iranian newspaper raised a question in one of its columns concerning "what is wrong in Iran," it received over 40,000 letters. This kind of overwhelming response frightened the regime, and after an exchange of visits between the Shah and
President Carter, the sporadic reversion to heavy-handed police tactics resulted in a wave of violence that shook the country to its roots in 1978. Clustering around the religious establishment, individuals drawn from groups representing all social classes demonstrated violently against the Shah's rule in
the city of Qom in January, in Tabriz in February, and in
Tehran and other cities in March, April, and May. In the
Tabriz incident, the riots assumed the proportions of an insurrection, and the Shah was forced to send in the army, which
was put in the position of having to occupy one of its own
cities.

Then in August and September of 1978, the opposition to
the Shah exploded into mass marches and demonstrations involving hundreds of thousands of dissatisfied citizens. Not since
the constitutional movement of seventy years before had Iran
been swept by such widespread civil discontent. Shaken and
stunned in the face of this upheaval, the Shah desperately tried
to bring the situation under control. In late August, he dismissed Prime Minister Jamshid Amuzegar and several ministers and replaced them with a new cast of old faces, headed by
trusted confidant Ja'far Sharif-Emami. Other more dramatic

changes were made as the Shah began jettisoning long-time friends and advisors including General Nematullah Nassiri, the head of SAVAK, and powerful inner circle member Gen. Abdul Karim Ayadi. The highly publicized National Resurgence Party was dismantled and opposition leaders who had remained silent for decades suddenly came out of seclusion to denounce the Shah and his government.

In the first week of September 1978 hundreds of thousands of Iranians took to the streets of Tehran to demonstrate their dissatisfaction with Pahlavi rule. On September 8, this swelling mass of popular opposition suddenly came to a violent halt. The Shah's troops turned their machine guns into the crowds killing hundreds and wounding thousands of unarmed demonstrators. As the streets of Tehran ran with blood, the Shah ended his experiment with liberalization and declared a six-month period of martial law in Tehran and eleven other Iranian cities. Throughout the last days of 1978 violence and opposition to the Shah continued. The enormity of this opposition was demonstrated in December when, on the two holiest days of the month of Moharram, more than four million Iranians marched peacefully against the Shah.

By early 1979 there was no doubt that the Shah faced a full-scale revolution. The working class joined with the professional and bourgeois middle classes in calling for the Shah's abdication. Meanwhile, the mujtahids led by the charismatic exile Ayatullah Ruhullah Khomayni served as organizing nodes of the mass movement. The Shah's only important support came from a beleaguered military and a diminishing cluster of palace advisors. Ruling behind bayonets, the Shah watched the economy crumble while oil production slowed to a virtual standstill. The educational system closed down completely and the administrative apparatus ground to a halt.

Meanwhile, the Shah, stunned by the extent and intensity of the opposition, hung on desperately by military force. In 1978 his troops were responsible for the deaths of approximately 5,000 Iranians and the wounding of four times as many. As his regime collapsed, the Shah frantically tried to form a new coalition government. On January 16, 1979 Muhammad Reza Shah Pahlavi quickly and quietly left Iran. After 37 years of rule, the once powerful monarch was driven from his country by his own people.

The Shah's dilemma was one that could only lead to the destruction of his dynasty's power. Harsh coercion begets fanatic and violent reaction as confrontation causes the opposition to intensify and then explode. More liberal policies, designed to bribe the challengers through incremental concessions, are always too little, too late. It is politically difficult to permit and, at the same time, to limit freedom of expression. Mass opposition cannot be stifled indefinitely by military force and martial law. The Shah's policies could not survive a revolutionary challenge.

Nineteen seventy-eight marked the end of an era in Iran. Confronted by mass rebellion, the Shah frantically attempted to preserve his rule by traditional methods of coercion and cooptation. These old methods only added fuel to the revolutionary fire. The result was an end to the kind of absolute monarchy practiced by the two Pahlavi shahs since 1926. Although it is still too early to predict the shape of the political system to come in Iran, at this writing one fact seems clear already. In 1979 the most important of the last major absolute monarchies in the Middle East collapsed for good.

Patterns of Rule. Muhammad Reza Shah Pahlavi is a political leader who practices to perfection the techniques and tactics of patrimonialism that have traditionally prevailed in Islamic Iran. As a king who rules by emanation, he is presented as the source of all ideas and the fount of all good. Each of the points in the White Revolution, therefore, is attributed to the Shah, and much has been written about how these ideas suddenly came to his mind.[43]

Individuals compete with one another to have their ideas presented to the Shah, who will, they hope, include them in his personal program for national development. In his most re-

[43] Much of the discussion of Iran was written before the Shah's departure in January, 1979. However, analyses of Iran throughout the book remain valid even though the Shah is occasionally referred to in the present tense as the reigning monarch.

cent book, published in 1978, the Shah patrimonially discusses his role as national mentor, teacher, and creator of revolutionary ideas in the following words: "I accept most willingly this mission for teaching and advice because of the knowledge I command on the most extensive scale of my country's national and international problems and because I am, myself, the architect and founder of the social revolution of which all Iranian developments of the day are the reflection."[44] The strength of this pattern of emanation is also seen in the words of one of the most powerful men in recent Iranian history, former prime minister, minister of court, tribal aristocrat, and lifelong friend and confidant of the Shah, Asadollah Alam: "I cannot say that he is faultless. Everyone, as you say, has faults . . . his fault to my mind is that he is really too great for his people — his ideas are too great for we people to realize it."[45] This kind of subservience, displayed even by the most important officials, is a central ingredient in patrimonial rule by emanation.

A special effort has been made in Iran to portray the Shah to his people as an unquestioned patrimonial leader. Because he had to bargain for survival during the first twelve years of his rule, and because he has lacked charisma, the years following the fall of Musaddiq have been years in which "a sophisticated apparatus would work assiduously to create the supreme patriarchal image, and a secret police would guard it."[46]

The source of emanation must be visible to everyone everywhere. Pictures of the Shah and his immediate family adorn government offices and public places throughout the country. Statues of the Shah stand in the middle of village squares, city parks, and even on the top of mountain peaks. Shrubbery in public gardens is cut in the form of Persian script spelling out the Shah's name. His likeness is woven into Persian carpets, and over seventy-five different sets of Iranian postage stamps carry the royal portrait. Millions of colored lights are lit

44 Mohammad Reza Shah Pahlavi, *Towards the Great Civilization* (Tehran: n.p., 1978).

45 Margaret Laing, *The Shah* (London: Sidgwick and Jackson, 1977), p. 231.

46 Bayne, *Persian Kingship*, p. 167.

throughout the country on the Shah's birthday, and a huge party is held in his presence at Amjadieh Stadium in Tehran.

The Shah has attempted to legitimate his rule in a number of other ways, including emphasizing systems of thought that stress monarchical, religious, and reform considerations. The ideology of reform explained above has been developed to buttress the traditional twin rationalizations of monarchy and religion. The elite constantly argue that Iranians have an inherent need for a monarchical political system. This has manifested itself most recently in the continual national celebrations and festivities that have been organized for almost a decade to commemorate Iran's 2,500 years of monarchy. Nevertheless, it is increasingly difficult to reconcile philospohies of reform with philosophies of monarchy, since "the dialectic of king and modernizing polity has not been fully resolved."[47] High officials in the Military Academy in Tehran have privately expressed the primary need for their study curriculum to rationalize (*ta'bir*) the institution of monarchy in view of the modern world.

The use of religion as a legitimating device has also been difficult for the Shah, who must compete in this regard with the the mujtahids, who are the representatives of the Hidden Imam in society. The Shah does attempt in various ways, however, to reveal his special relation with the divine and the superhuman. He has stated that the peasants often refer to him as the Shadow of God, and he apparently feels that he is guided by some superhuman force that protects him. In his autobiography, the Shah credits his numerous escapes from personal and political disaster to "some unseen hand" and claims that from childhood he has "felt that perhaps there is a supreme being who is guiding me."[48] On more recent occasions, he has said that "my reign has saved the country, and it has done so because God was on my side," and that "God is my only friend."[49] The Shah has also written extensively about dreams and visions in which he has been in touch with such

47 Ibid., p. 97.

48 Pahlavi, *Mission for My Country*, pp. 55, 58.

49 See "An Oriana Fallaci Interview: The Shah of Iran," *The New Republic*, 1 December 1973, p. 17; and de Villiers, *Imperial Shah*, p. 273.

great Islamic figures as Ali and Abbas, who have assisted him in times of travail. He has gone so far as to describe a meeting he had with the Hidden Imam when passing along a Tehran street.[50] In the end, however, the Shah has decided to strengthen the rationalization of his rule by stressing an ideology of reform, since this appears more believable to growing forces within his society as well as to the twentieth-century world at large.

The traditional characteristics of personalism, proximity, informality, and balanced conflict also permeate the rule of Muhammad Reza Shah. His is an "individual approach to kingship,"[51] and he rules at the center of a complex web of personal relations, in which he has contact with as many officials and other persons as possible. In this kind of political setting, the issue of physical proximity assumes reciprocal significance. Individuals hold influences commensurate to their nearness to the patrimonial leader, while the leader feels that it is important to be in personal contact with as many of his subjects as possible. Just as the family patriarch deems it essential to his position as patriarch to maintain personal communication with all of his children, so also does the patrimonial leader consider it important to his position to be in touch with as many members of his society as he can. In Iran, there is tremendous pressure constantly exerted by individuals from all groups and classes to move towards the Shah, who is the locus of power. At the same time, the Shah states that "one of the principal problems of government is to know the right people and in necessary numbers. Either these people must be presented to you — and you need time to become acquainted and to know them — or you must search for them."[52] This particular pattern is reflected in Middle Eastern patrimonialism in the colorful tradition in which kings travel incognito through the streets, alleys, and countryside of their lands, speaking with the people and soliciting their opinions. The Abbasid caliph Harun al-Rashid was famous for this, but contemporary patrimonial leaders profess to do the same thing.

50 Pahlavi, *Mission for My Country,* pp. 54–55.
51 Bayne, *Persian Kingship,* p. 239.
52 Ibid., p. 193.

There are stories of the Shah riding incognito in the hills behind Tehran, where he visits villages to which he later sends
economic assistance. When asked about this, the Shah has admitted that "even now I do this kind of thing, but I never
have wanted to talk about it."[53]

In this highly personal system of patrimonial rule, informality prevails and individuals are balanced against individuals.
The Shah operates through informal meetings, personal
cliques, and trusted groups of friends and family. Rivalry and
tension are omnipresent; the Shah has proven himself a master
at playing key subordinates off against one another. As a result, no one becomes overly powerful and the leader remains far
above any potential challenger. In Iran, the network of balanced rivalry encompasses the royal family, courtiers, personal
adjutants, ministers, military officers, and all economic and
political figures of any important standing. This pattern is reflected most dramatically in the case of twelve different military
and security organizations, all of which stand in rivalry to one
another. This organizational tension is the direct result of the
personal rivalry that marks the relations among the leaders of
these agencies. It is the patrimonial leader who keeps these
lines of tension finely adjusted.[54]

Finally, the Shah of Iran has always sought to maintain a
special and direct control over the military. As Shah and commander in chief, he handpicks the military leaders, primarily
on the basis of their loyalty to him. The downfall of several
important politicians of the past occurred quickly after they
challenged the Shah for control of the military. The Shah
prides himself on his knowledge of military tactics and strategy,
and says that he understands the necessity of military power
because of "my father's examples, *and* because I am a soldier."[55] His special emphasis on the military is seen in the
huge expenditures that are funneled into military and security

53 Ibid., p. 132.
54 For a detailed analysis of these kinds of patterns in Iran, see James A.
Bill, "The Plasticity of Informal Politics: The Case of Iran," *Middle East
Journal* 27 (Spring 1973) :131–51; and idem, "Patterns of Elite Politics in
Iran," in *Political Elites in the Middle East,* ed. G. Lenczowski (Washington, D.C.: American Enterprise Institute, 1975) , pp. 17–40.
55 Bayne, *Persian Kingship,* p. 139.

establishments. By the late 1970s, they absorbed approximately 40 percent of the Iranian budget. Iran, which is now far and away the largest single purchaser of United States military equipment, spent $10.4 billion between 1972 and 1976 on arms produced in the United States. Then, in 1977 alone, the Shah spent another $5.8 billion on United States military goods. These purchases included some of the most sophisticated materiel in the United States inventory, including the F-14 Tom Cat Fighter and the DD 993 Spruance Class destroyer. Since then, the Iranian air force has placed a $4 billion order for 160 F-16 single-engine, multipurpose aircraft, as well as an expensive order for seven planes equipped with airborne warning and control radar systems (AWACS).[56] The Shah of Iran · has summarized his own view of his relation to the military in the peculiarly patrimonial phrase, "I am the army."[57]

Preservation Through Reform. A recent analysis of political leadership is based upon the underlying assumption that "a ruler's first imperative, and his most urgent desire, is to retain his position at the apex of government, for only from there can he affect the future of the polity he seeks to rule."[58] In Iran, the Shah lives according to this priority. He has protected the traditional patterns of patrimonial rule that have proved to be instrumental in maintaining his position as leader of Iran. At the same time, however, he has attempted to preserve these patterns by buttressing them with an ideology of reform and a program of planned change that will place upon his rule a modern imprimatur. It would be a serious mistake to underestimate the importance and the effect of the reforms sponsored by the Shah. It is also a mistake to question the Shah's commitment and dedication to these programs. His

[56] The data contained in this paragraph are partially drawn from U.S., Congress, Senate, Committee on Foreign Relations, Subcommittee on Foreign Assistance, Staff Report, *U.S. Military Sales to Iran* (Washington, D.C.: Government Printing Office, 1976) ; and Daniel Southerland, "Weapons Sales Go On at Busy Rate," *Christian Science Monitor,* 20 January 1978, p. 5.

[57] Bayne, *Persian Kingship,* p. 186.

[58] W. Howard Wriggins, *The Ruler's Imperative* (New York: Columbia University Press, 1969) , p. vii.

own statements and activities clearly reveal that he is well aware of the challenge of modernization, and that he has decided to make a serious effort to confront that challenge.

The Shah's reform program has strategically promoted a breadth of change that protects rather than transforms traditional political patterns. This can be documented on two levels: (1) the direction of reform implementation, and (2) the methodology of reform implementation. With the exception of the twelfth point in the Shah's program, none of the reforms could possibly undercut the patrimonial position of the ruler. Viewed from this perspective, the land reform program serves to weaken exactly those forces that have traditionally been a threat to the patrimonial position. The major threats to the personal position of the Shah have come from the old landed families and from individuals carrying such names as Qavam, Musaddiq, Amini, Bakhtiyar, and Qashqa'i. By replacing a number of these individuals at the national political level with workers and bureaucrats who have no independent power resources of their own, the Shah has been strengthening the politics of emanation.

The professional middle class has been largely left outside the reformation; its members are precisely those who challenge and criticize patrimonial politics. A growing number of these individuals refuse to be drawn into the traditional system, and it is their demands for political development, administrative revolution, freedom of expression, improved education, improved health services, judicial overhaul, and an end to corruption that the patrimonial leader has largely overlooked.[59] This problem is summarized by the Shah himself, who has stated: "I believe that the peasantry are with me but it is not so true with the younger intelligentsia. . . . They are a problem to me."[60]

Beginning in late 1977, the members of the Shah's brain trust (former members of the professional-middle-class opposition themselves) began to discuss these problems publicly

[59] For a study of the Shah's failure to introduce basic change in these crucial areas, see James A. Bill, *The Politics of Iran: Groups, Classes, and Modernization* (Columbus, Ohio: Charles E. Merrill, 1972).

[60] Bayne, *Persian Kingship*, p. 52.

and to admit that political development was lagging at the expense of economic and social modernization. Powerful inner-circle member Hushang Ansari stated that "expecting political liberties is the logical prolongation of developments achieved by the revolution. It is only through these liberties that the will and interests of both the individual and the society as a whole could be safeguarded."[61] The new watchword in Iran became *mosharekat,* or "participation." Influential journalist Amir Taheri wrote in 1977 that Iran is entering a "political decade" and that "the fact remains that the government structure in Iran is still unprepared for meeting the exigencies of the political decade that lies ahead."[62] In a remarkable article that appeared in the *Kayhan International* in January 1978, one of the regime's leading ideologues wrote that "far more political imagination will be required to ensure the continuous consent of the new urban middle class" and that "the nation's political life cannot lag behind its economic and social achievements."[63] The Shah and his elite have an uncanny ability to identify and proclaim the main problem areas — in so doing, however, they often substitute problem identification for problem solving, revolutionary prose for revolutionary action. In the case of the demands of the professional middle class, rhetoric alone will not do.

The actual administration of the reform program has been implemented according to traditional patterns. Personalism, rivalry, insecurity, distrust, and uncoordinated ad hoc decision making have prevailed. Political opportunists have entered the arena and have seriously tainted and impeded the programs. The built-in rivalry that debilitates reform efforts is seen in the important task of land reform. At first, the ministries of agriculture, interior, and economy competed for control of the program. Later, a separate ministry of land reform and rural cooperatives was established, as well as a ministry of agricultural products and consumer goods and a ministry of

61 As quoted in Amir Taheri, "Internal Political Dynamics," in *Iran in the 1980s,* eds. Abbas Amirie and Hamilton A. Twitchell (Tehran: Institute for International Political and Economic Studies. 1978) , p. 72.

62 Ibid., p. 64.

63 *Kayhan International* (Tehran) , 26 January 1978, p. 4.

natural resources. There is also an agricultural bank and an agricultural development fund. All of these organizations are bound together in an interlocking web of competition that prevents any individual or any ministry from becoming too powerful. It also prevents successful land reform from occurring. Both the Shah and the Empress have expressed impatience with the inefficiency and incompetence that have characterized various programs, but this inefficiency is a necessary by-product of the traditional style of patrimonial politics.

The growing gap between modernization on the one hand and political development on the other is seen in Iran's widening urban-rural income distribution gap, the severe lack of skilled and dedicated technicians, and the surprisingly low Physical Quality of Life Index rating discussed in Chapter I. By the late 1970s, the Shah and his deputies were talking ceaselessly about the lack of "infrastructures," the pervasiveness of "bottlenecks," and the sharp increase in "imbalances."[64] They, too, seemed to sense the depth of the problem as they faced the explosive dissatisfaction of the professional middle class and the growing urban violence throughout the country.

Yet, as a seasoned politician with a proven instinct for survival, the Shah of Iran remains a leader dedicated to patrimonialism and reform, in that order. He will undoubtedly introduce as much change as he feels his patrimonial political system can sustain without becoming weaker. This is why he is a patrimonial reformer and neither a social revolutionary nor a political developer. As such, he can at best only buy time against the revolutionary forces loose in his country. And the price becomes higher with the passage of that very time that he has successfully but always and only temporarily been able to purchase.

---

[64] The Persian words for these three expressions are *zirbana, tangna,* and *navasan,* respectively. In Iran, 1976 was the year of the "infrastructure," 1977 the time of "bottlenecks," and 1978 the period of "imbalances." In his 1978 speech presenting his government's annual budget to the majlis (parliament), then Prime Minister Jamshid Amuzegar used all three expressions; at one point he went so far as to refer to "infrastructural bottlenecks."

GAMAL ABDEL NASSER: PATRIMONIALISM
AND TRANSFORMATION

The man is at once feline and massive. His square build
speaks of a peasant ancestry, the long remembrance of stub-
born, fleshy gestures, the recompense of a heavy, miserable diet
over many generations. But this son of the Middle Valley also
carries Arab descent in his blood: a Bedouin strain had pursued
for several centuries in Banī Murr District the synthesis of Ish-
mael and Pharaoh. Perhaps this gives his physique that deliberate alertness, his face that sharp breadth, his eyes that brood-
ing nostalgia behind their hard, almost green, gaze. The Arab
has risen ponderously, one might say, from his long submergence
in the soil of Egypt.[65]

Recent Middle Eastern political history is marked by the
existence of a handful of leaders who have attempted to uproot many of the traditional social and political patterns that
have prevailed in their societies. Besides Kemal Atatürk
discussed above, the other major case in point is Gamal Abdel
Nasser of Egypt. Like Atatürk, Nasser adopted tactics of transformation that left some areas largely untouched while in other
areas fundamental efforts to change were made. The life and
leadership of Gamal Abdel Nasser in particular deserve to be
analyzed in this light, since Nasser introduced many revolutionary programs in a society that contains nearly one-third of
the world's Arab population.

Gamal Abdel Nasser was born on 15 January 1918 in Alexandria. He was raised in the village of Beni Morr in Upper
Egypt, the ancestral home of his family. Nasser's father was a
postal clerk; his mother died when Gamal was eight years old.
Since his father had remarried and was constantly being moved
about in his work, Gamal spent long periods living with various relatives. As a secondary-school student, he developed a
deep social and political consciousness. He harbored an early
concern about the British presence in Egypt; at the same time,
he grew to dislike the debility and dependence that marked
the status of his country.

[65] Jacques Berque, *Cultural Expression in Arab Society Today*, trans.
Robert W. Stookey (Austin: University of Texas Press, 1978), pp. 15–16.

Nasser graduated from secondary school in Cairo in 1936 and afterwards entered the Egyptian Military Academy. Upon graduating from the academy in 1938 with the rank of second lieutenant, he was sent to serve with an infantry company in Upper Egypt. In 1943, Nasser was promoted to the rank of captain and was appointed an instructor at the military academy. In 1948, he distinguished himself in a losing cause in the Palestine campaign. As a patriotic officer, he was disgusted and distressed at the inefficiency and decrepitude of the Egyptian political regime. During the 1940s, moveover, Nasser began to blame imperialism and feudalism for the constantly deteriorating state of his country. He read widely and, as a history instructor, he refined his social and political ideas. It was during this period that he helped form the Free Officers movement and came into contact with the group of fellow officers who were to play the vital role in changing the course of Egyptian history over the next two decades.

On 23 July 1952, the Free Officers movement carried out a coup that overthrew King Farouk and his traditional regime. A Revolutionary Command Council of twelve officers, including Gen. Muhammad Naguib, took control of the government. At first Naguib was the titular political leader, but by the end of 1954 Gamal Abdel Nasser had ousted him and taken control. Nasser remained the internationally famous leader of Egypt until his heart attack and death on 28 September 1970. During these years, both Nasser and Egypt survived numerous vicissitudes, including crises ranging from an assassination attempt to an invasion by the combined forces of three foreign powers. During his eighteen years of leadership in Egypt, Nasser's political activities were divided into three general and overlapping categories: (1) consolidation and maintenance of political power; (2) introduction and continuation of policies of social, economic, and political change within Egypt; and (3) development of an independent foreign policy.

During the first few years of his leadership, Nasser was preoccupied with the task of protecting the ascendant position he had acquired. This meant maintaining the cohesion of the military in general and the Free Officers group in particular, while at the same time repelling opposition forces mobilized by the Communists on the left and the Wafd party and Muslim Brotherhood on the right. Nasser had strongly suppressed the Brotherhood by 1955; in the late 1950s and early 1960s, he moved sharply and successfully against communism within Egypt; and by 1965, he had largely managed to destroy the influence of the wealthy bourgeoisie that had formed the backbone of the Wafd Party. Although these were the most serious organized threats to his power, Nasser's government was faced with political challenges throughout its existence because his revolutionary programs were continually threatening vested interests. As his authoritarianism hardened in order to withstand these kinds of challenges, Nasser came to alienate substantial segments of former supporters within the intelligentsia, who chafed under a cloak of repression that tended to suffocate criticism and innovation from below. Democratization was deliberately sacrificed, since the consolidation and maintenance of power were considered essential to successful modernization. Because Nasser was able to consolidate his forces, he was in turn able to institute change from above. This was in sharp contrast to societies such as Syria and Iraq where military coups have bred only further military coups. Although certain individual freedoms were at times sacrificed, Nasser nonetheless instituted enough fundamental change to lay a new social, economic, and political foundation for Egyptian society.

Gamal Abdel Nasser once stated that he was a revolutionary and not a politician. He wrote: "Every people on earth goes through two revolutions: a political revolution by which it wrests the right to govern itself from the hand of tyranny, or from the army stationed upon its soil against its will; and a social revolution, involving the conflict of classes which settles down when justice is secured for the citizens of the united nation."[66] In analyzing the political history of post-1952 Egypt, Maxime Rodinson concludes that the two main goals of Nasserism were national independence and modernization.[67] Among the important sociopolitical achievements of Nasser's

[66] Gamal Abdel Nasser, *Egypt's Liberation: The Philosophy of the Revolution* (Washington, D.C.: Public Affairs Press, 1955), pp. 39–40.

[67] See Maxime Rodinson, "The Political System," in *Egypt Since the Revolution,* ed. P. J. Vatikiotis (New York: Frederick A. Praeger, 1968), pp. 87–113.

revolution are the agrarian reform program, the transformation and partial leveling of the class structure, the elimination of corruption and nepotism in the personal household of the national political leader, the continuing rise of achievement at the expense of ascription in the administrative system, the expulsion of foreign influence, and the strengthening of the pride and dignity of the Egyptian people. In his attempt to transform the traditional power structure, Nasser came to the conclusion that the process must be a continuing one. Land reform alone could not bring about this transformation, since it was neither deep enough nor fast enough to undercut the power of the entire traditional ruling class. It was in this context that Nasser instituted the extensive nationalization laws of the 1960–1963 period.

The successes and failures of Nasser's domestic programs rested to a great degee upon his ability to guide Egypt through the stormy seas of international politics. It was in this broader arena that the Egyptian president expended most of his political energy, and it was here that he witnessed his greatest triumphs and his greatest defeats. His tenure as leader of Egypt was clouded by deep problems directly associated with the Arab-Israeli confrontation, the American-Soviet cold war, the general drive for Arab unity, and the differing Arab stances concerning the entire issue of social and political change. In 1955, President Nasser attended the Bandung Conference, where he rubbed shoulders with Nehru, Sukarno, and Chou En-lai, and where he was considered a new leader of the Afro-Asian world. He returned home a hero for his role in a conference that condemned "neocolonialism" and supported "nonalignment." A few months later, Nasser accepted a Soviet arms offer and concluded a deal with Czechoslovakia that electrified the Arab world, since it indicated that Egypt was no longer dependent on the West and would pursue a course of positive neutralism.[68] That same year, Nasser refused to align Egypt

---

[68] The arms deal took a great deal of personal and political courage on Nasser's part, since it was signed in the face of deep United States opposition. This was a time when American intelligence forces had helped rearrange political regimes in Iran (1953) and Guatemala (1954). When Egypt's panicky ambassador to the United States urged Nasser not to defy

formist government."[69] It was a "charismatic situation"[70] that helped invest Nasser with extraordinary powers as a political leader.

These early successes were of sufficient magnitude to enable both Nasser and Egypt to ride out later disasters. The most serious of these was the June War of 1967, in which Israel (in an impressive and efficient military campaign) left Egypt battered and demoralized. Nasser, who must bear much of the blame for occasioning the conflict, resigned his position. But only hours later he was called back by the Egyptian people, who seemingly genuinely wanted and demanded his leadership. The existence of Israel haunted Nasser's rule, and he was never able to confront this situation with the same style and success with which he addressed other thorny problems. In the area of intra-Arab politics, the Egyptian president was only slightly more successful. The United Arab Republic, which was a political and economic union with Syria formed in 1958, was dissolved in 1961 when, among other things, the wealthy Syrian bourgeois families feared the impact of Nasser's revolutionary programs. In Algeria, Nasser successfully supported the Algerian rebels, although in Yemen direct Egyptian military support failed to enable the revolutionaries to take control of the country. The latter adventure cost Egypt dearly in terms of domestic resources and international prestige. Despite this, however, President Nasser's revolutionary programs and ideas spread through the Middle East and acted as catalysts for change in the Arab world. If it did not lead to revolution from below, Nasser's example hastened programs of reform from above, since it inspired even the most traditional leaders to try to dissipate discontent by initiating developmental change. The land reform programs in Syria, Iraq, Tunisia, Iran, and Turkey, for example, all followed the Egyptian experiment in agrarian reform begun in 1952.

Patterns of Rule. Gamal Abdel Nasser's leadership broke with many of the patterns of traditional patrimonial rule. Al-

[69] Jean Lacouture, *The Demigods: Charismatic Leadership in the Third World,* trans. Patricia Wolf (New York: Alfred A. Knopf, 1970), p. 110.
[70] Ibid.

though strongly authoritarian, Nasser's techniques did not include the promotion of self-deification. It is true that his image was protected and polished by his governmental and security forces, but he resisted pressures to invest huge resources in the glorification of his person. There were no statues of Nasser, for example, dotting the Egyptian landscape. Nor did his face adorn postage stamps and currency. The Egyptian President consciously sought to transcend the temptation to permit and promote personal exaltation and hero worship. One keen Western observer of Egyptian affairs wrote that "nothing irritates Nasser more than being treated like a modern pharoah."[71]

A truly charismatic personality need not build monuments to himself and myths for his people, since his charisma is due to extraordinary actions. In Nasser's case, the leader also eschewed any special connection with the Divine, whether it be in terms of common ancestry or private visions. Although he never attacked the Islamic clerics in Egypt the way Atatürk did in Turkey, at the same time he did not attempt to build any particularly intimate political relations with them.[72] The fact that Nasser's charisma is traceable neither to manufactured mythology nor to religious connections indicates how divorced his leadership was from the traditional mold. It is precisely this kind of charisma that invested Nasser with the special strength necessary to maintain power and to promote deep change in the face of formidable problems, both internal and external.

The role of the military was crucial to Nasser's leadership. It was through a military coup that he first came to power, and it was through the support of the military that he could maintain power and institute reform. In the absence of a trained and efficient civil bureaucracy, the Egyptian president was able to call upon personnel from within the military organization to implement administrative and economic programs. As in tra-

[71] Ibid., p. 119.

[72] For the finest investigation of Nasser's relationship to Islam, see Josef Muzikar, "Arab Nationalism and Islam," *Archiv Orientalni* 43 (1975):193–323. For analysis of this question in a broader context, see Malcolm Kerr's thought-provoking study "The Political Outlook in the Local Arena," in *The Economics and Politics of the Middle East,* Abraham S. Becker, Bent Hansen, and Malcolm H. Kerr (New York: American Elsevier, 1975), pp. 41–54.

ditional patrimonial systems, the military was an important prop in Nasser's political structure. There is, however, one important quality that separates the Nassers and the Atatürks from the more traditional leaders. The latter continue to present themselves in military guise and garb in order to constantly display their special and intimate relation with the military. They often explicitly state that they are an embodiment of the military. Nasser, on the contrary, retired from the army in 1955 and deliberately refrained from maintaining any military rank or title. Thus, while the kings and shahs are continually putting on medal-encrusted military uniforms, the Nassers and the Atatürks have abandoned theirs. Though the latter may still control the military forces in their societies, they no longer do so in the traditional patrimonial style.

Personalism and informality are two related characteristics of patrimonial rule that persisted in the leadership of Gamal Abdel Nasser.[73] Nasser never succeeded in moving from rule by personalism to political institutionalization, and as a result there was a general lack of political participation and a general surplus of political insecurity in Nasser's Egypt. In the latter days of his presidency, heavy-handed maneuverers, such as presidential advisor Sami Sharaf and interior minister Sharawi Gomaa, were directing an increasingly disreputable intelligence system that reached into all corners of Egyptian society.

There is evidence, however, that Nasser was not insensitive to the need for wider political participation. He tried three times to construct a mass political party in order to insure a measure of popular participation. His last attempt, which was also his most successful, involved the formation of the Arab Socialist Union in 1962. Such structures were largely ineffectual in Egypt, since they existed as rather sterile appendages to Nasser's personal rule, which Nasser felt bound to strengthen

[73] The works of Robert Springborg impressively document Nasser as a patrimonial leader. See especially his "Patterns of Association in the Egyptian Political Elite," in *Political Elites in the Middle East,* Lenczowski pp. 83–107; and "Patrimonialism and Policy Making in Egypt: Nasser and Sadat and the Tenure Policy for Reclaimed Lands," *Middle Eastern Studies,* forthcoming. See also Clement Moore's "Authoritarian Politics in Unincorporated Society: The case of Nasser's Egypt," *Comparative Politics* 6 (January 1974):193–218.

in order to carry on the revolution. Despite the presence of personalism and informality, Nasser was able to break a number of the patterns that follow in the wake of patrimonialism.

The nepotism that stems from personalism and the corruption that often thrives in the net of informal politics were relatively absent in Nasser's style of leadership. Nasser himself was above reproach in this regard, and he led an austere life much in the style of Chou En-lai and Fidel Castro. Throughout the Middle East, Nasser was famous for his personal honesty and integrity. He spoke out constantly against opportunism, corruption, and favoritism. When he died in 1970, he was still living in the modest house that he had purchased as a young officer prior to the 1952 coup. He refused to use his power to further the causes of his family and relatives. Two of his uncles remained fellahin in the village of Beni Morr, and his own daughters were unable to attend Cairo University because their entrance examination scores were not high enough. Mohamed Heikal writes that Nasser "was never interested in women or money or elaborate food. After he had come to power the cynical old politicians tried to corrupt him but they failed miserably. His family life was impeccable."[74] Heikal goes on to point out that although Nasser received millions of pounds in donations, he died with only 610 Egyptian pounds in his personal account. The programmatic manifestations of this new style fostered by Nasser are evident in the Egyptian land reform policy, for, as one expert writes: "The even-handedness with which the distribution was carried out deserves commendation; no suggestion of favoritism in either the taking of land from large owners or the distribution of it to recipients has arisen — a remarkable accomplishment in view of the inherent temptations to corruption."[75]

[74] Mohamed Heikal, *The Cairo Documents* (Garden City, N.Y.: Doubleday and Co., 1973), p. 20. Some of Nasser's leading officials, including what Edward Sheehan calls "the Sharaf-Gomaa cabal," whose members "were nearly all corrupt," were less principled. Edward R. F. Sheehan, "The Real Sadat and the Demythologized Nasser," *New York Times Magazine,* 18 July 1971, pp. 6–7, 33, 35, 38, 42.

[75] Kenneth B. Platt, *Land Reform in the United Arab Republic,* A.I.D. Spring Review of Land Reform, 2d ed., vol. 8 (Washington, D.C.: Agency for International Development, 1970), p. 61.

Although Gamal Abdel Nasser resorted to the traditional tactic of divide and rule, his colleagues and confidants generally operated as a team in leading society. Admittedly, the team was a small and exclusive one. Lenczowski has pointed out that, with only three exceptions, Nasser managed to keep his group of young officers together through more than twelve years of the Revolution.[76] While he undoubtedly made the final decisions, the Egyptian president did consult seriously with his close advisors.

The patterns of patrimonial politics were partially uprooted by President Nasser as he endeavored to revolutionize his society. Although personalism continued to prevail, many of the other traditional traits were destroyed and replaced by new patterns. This represents a fundamental step in moving forward with the social and political dimensions of change.

Transforming Leadership. Egypt is one of the poorest and most densely populated societies in the world. Just before the 1952 military coup, a Rockefeller Foundation team reported that the situation of the peasants in Egypt was worse than that of the peasants in any other country in which they had carried out investigations — and this included China and India. According to this report, on a scale of 106.5 for perfect health, India rated 54 and Egypt 15. In one of the villages surveyed north of Cairo, nearly 100 percent of the population had bilharzia, a debilitating parasitical disease that attacks the kidneys and liver; 89 percent had trachoma; over 20 percent were typhoid or paratyphoid carriers. In a village with a population of 4,172, there was not one healthy person. Most of the villagers had from one to four major diseases.[77]

At the time of the report, the political system was a patrimonial monarchy in which all the negative characteristics of that kind of system were magnified. King Farouk often made

[76] George Lenczowski, "The Objects and Methods of Nasserism," in *Modernization of the Arab World,* ed. J. H. Thompson and R. D. Reischauer (Princeton, N.J.: D. Van Nostrand Co., 1966), p. 207.

[77] For a summary of the findings of the Rockefeller Foundation study from which these figures have been drawn, see Austin L. Moore, *Farewell Farouk* (Chicago: Scholars' Press, 1954), pp. 59–60.

national political decisions on the advice of his infamous "kitchen cabinet," composed of his valet, mechanic, butler, pilot, and doctor, among others. An Italian barber became Farouk's closest adviser, and Farouk named his brother-in-law (an honorary "colonel") minister of war. Nepotism prevailed in a demoralizing environment of political vice and personal corruption. Against this background, the changes wrought under Nasser's leadership were profound. Measured against the demands of the day and the progress of other non-Western societies, such as Israel, Japan, and China, Egyptian social and political change is perhaps less impressive.

Gamal Abdel Nasser was a transforming leader for three basic reasons. He consciously and determinedly sought to insure that his revolution be radical, political, and continuing in nature. In the 1962 Charter he wrote: "The needs of our country were such that it was not enough to patch up the old and decaying building, try to keep it from falling by means of supports and give the exterior a fresh coat of paint. What was needed was a new and strong building resting on firm foundations and towering high in the sky. . . ."[78] By distinguishing between reforming and transforming change in these kinds of terms, Nasser often indicated his sensitivity to the need to support fundamental social and political transformation. Because of this radical philosophy, Nasser "refused to endorse programs which were primarily political palliatives."[79]

Whereas the reforming leader tends to support economic and material development without altering the political system, the transforming leader begins with and emphasizes the political dimension of change. Anouar Abdel-Malek writes that, in Nasser's case, "the principal blow was struck on the sociopolitical level"; Majid Khadduri asserts that "the Revolution's fundamental achievements were essentially political"; and Maxime Rodinson concludes that under Nasser the "political structure"

[78] Nasser, The Charter, as quoted in J. C. Hurewitz, *Middle East Politics: The Military Dimension* (New York: Frederick A. Praeger, 1969), p. 133.

[79] Keith Wheelock, *Nasser's New Egypt* (London: Atlantic Books, 1960), p. 38.

was "completely reshaped."[80] The political change can be seen at two levels. The first level concerns the patterns of relations through which the political leader personally wields power. As is documented above, Nasser transformed these relations at several key points. The second level involves the more general and collective distribution of power, reflected primarily in the class structure. During Nasser's rule, the Egyptian class structure underwent radical change as the influence of the former ruling class, which was composed of both the landed and the industrial aristocracy, was destroyed. The gaps between the various classes were consequently greatly narrowed as a professional middle class composed of technocrats, managers, and professionals took control. It is on this basis that one observer has recently referred to the Egyptian revolution as "the first true revolution in the Middle East."[81]

Nasser carefully referred to the Egyptian revolution as *thawra* ("a persisting and lasting event") rather than as *inqilab* ("an overthrow"), since he recognized the need for the movement to press forward continually.[82] This forward movement was, of course, essential in order to prevent the old power structure from slowly and inexorably seeping back into prominence. The modernizing head of government is especially exposed to this danger, since "the bourgeoisie attempts to minimize its losses by puffing up the leader. It cuts off some of its own flesh and feeds it to the hero to fatten him up, blow him up, lull him to sleep. Soon enough the deified leader will proclaim the revolution fulfilled in him and the class struggle resolved in him."[83] In Nasser's Egypt, the old forces of patrimonialism made gallant efforts to infiltrate back into power, and in the late 1950s, they were backed and provisioned by the wealthy bourgeoisie. Nasser confronted this challenge and destroyed it with his nationalization programs of 1960–1963.

---

[80] For these quotations, see Anouar Abdel-Malek, *Egypt: Military Society*, trans. Charles Lam Markmann (New York: Vintage Books, 1968), p. 157; Majid Khadduri, *Political Trends in the Arab World* (Baltimore: Johns Hopkins Press, 1970), p. 162; and Rodinson, "The Political System," p. 111.

[81] Harry Hopkins, *Egypt: The Crucible* (Boston: Houghton Mifflin Co., 1969), p. 181.

[82] Lacouture, *The Demigods*, p. 94.

[83] Ibid., p. 293.

This effectively tore the web of old families who were the proponents of traditionalism. They had managed to survive the land reform program since their control spanned industry and trade as well as land.

Although he successfully uprooted the traditional power structure in Egypt, Nasser never quite managed to establish a new sociopolitical system. Because of the resilience of the old system and the limited resources at hand, the Egyptian president felt it necessary to maintain an authoritarian technocracy, which alienated the intelligentsia and stifled creativity in the society. He was unable to broaden political participation, and therefore the revolutionary patterns he introduced at the center did not always take root in the countryside. The resources and energies fruitlessly expended in activities against Israel and in Yemen seriously injured his capacity to carry out social change in Egypt. Despite all of this, Nasser survived and, although badly scarred, continued to fight for the transformation of his country. His achievements in this regard, though sporadic, were nonetheless impressive enough to distinguish him sharply from most Middle Eastern leaders, both past and present. By the time he died in September 1970, Gamal Abdel Nasser was personally convinced that, with or without him, the revolution he had begun in Egypt would continue. In 1971, Nasser's longtime friend and colleague, Anwar Sadat, emerged as the new president of Egypt. Sadat has proved to be a remarkable leader whose own style and programs contrast significantly with those of his predecessor.

ANWAR SADAT: THE RETURN OF
TRADITIONAL PATRIMONIALISM

Born in 1918, the same year as Nasser, Anwar Sadat spent much of his youth hating the British and thinking about politics. Like Nasser, he came from the lower echelons of the professional middle class. His father, a hospital clerk, was a great admirer of Atatürk, and a picture of the Turkish hero hung in the Sadat house. Sadat entered the Egyptian Military Academy with Nasser in 1936 and graduated with him in 1938. From this time until the successful coup in 1952, he dedicated himself to secret political opposition. During these years, he plotted constantly against both the British and King Farouk and intrigued his way in and out of prison. At one point, he even sought Nasser's permission to blow up the British Embassy. When released from his second imprisonment in 1948, Sadat eked out an existence as a journalist, truck driver, porter, and used-tire salesman. With his military commission restored, Sadat was the one who announced the news of the successful coup of July 1952 to the Egyptian people.

During the eighteen years of Nasser's acendancy, Anwar Sadat hovered constantly in the shadow of his leader. Although the hotheadedness of his youth occasionally broke to the surface, Sadat did a remarkable job in cloaking his explosive ambition and peasant shrewdness beneath a patient and plodding subservience to Nasser. He refused to join political cliques and power circles, preferring instead to live a life of material pleasure and leisure. Few took him seriously. Meanwhile, he watched and waited, learning all the time. When Nasser died in 1970, Sadat was one of the few members of the original Revolutionary Command Council still around. In 1969, Nasser had shopped around for a new vice-president; he chose Anwar Sadat.

When Sadat succeeded Nasser as president, everyone looked past him to the political heavyweights who would undoubtedly direct Egyptian affairs in the future — menacing figures such as Minister of Presidential Affairs Sami Sharaf, Minister of Interior Sharawi Gomaa, and powerful leftist and Arab Socialist Union figure Ali Sabry. Meanwhile, the patient and poker-faced Sadat went about his business quietly, easily, and disarmingly. He made appearances throughout the country, building popularity as he went along; he silently sprinkled a few loyal spies here and there; and, most important, he came to an agreement with the key army officers. Then, in May 1971, when he had carefully gathered evidence that Sabry and the others had been plotting a coup, Sadat suddenly struck. He forced Ali Sabry to resign on 2 May. Then, ten days later in another lightning move, he fired secret police head Gomaa and happily accepted the resignation of five other ministers, including that of Sami Sharaf. That autumn over ninety persons were tried. Sabry, Sharaf, and Gomaa, among others were jailed.[84] Anwar Sadat has been the unquestioned leader of Egypt ever since.

Although he has been under tremendous domestic and international pressures ever since he became president of Egypt, Sadat has done a magnificent job of maintaining himself in power. One of his most important tactics, and one which he has used throughout his career, has been to deny any interest in political power. In his autobiography, he repeatedly denies that he has ever sought power and that he ever wanted political office. Yet, the reader of this book cannot help observing that Sadat never refused a political post offered him. Nor, deep down, was he ever pleased that he was an outsider to the Revolutionary Command Council. In his own words: "Why did they attack and ridicule me, as though I was an outsider who wanted to usurp their rights or a stranger who sought a different language? I was sad. . . ."[85]

Sadat has thus far been able to make up for his absence of Nasser-like charisma through a brilliant ability to make the right political moves at precisely the right times. While floating somewhere above political factions and ideological positions, he has often darted down to center stage to announce and personally implement dramatic and unprecedented political decisions — decisions that have left the world gasping. The most noteworthy of these moves include the expulsion of the Soviet advisors from Egyptian soil in July 1972, the initiation of the fourth Arab-Israeli war in October 1973, the historic trip to Israel of November 1977, and the announcement of a framework for peace with Israel after two weeks of private meetings at Camp David, Maryland with Israeli Prime Min-

84 Sharawi Gomaa and several less prominent members of the Sabry group were released from prison when President Sadat granted them amnesty in January 1977. Former minister of war Lt. Gen. Muhammad Fawzi had already been pardoned by Sadat in January 1974.

85 Anwar el-Sadat, *In Search of Identity: An Autobiography* (New York: Harper and Row, 1978), p. 122. For examples of Sadat's rather vehement denials that he has ever been interested in power, see pp. 83–84, 90, 126, 136, 138, 150, 196, 204, and 314. This autobiography, although fascinating and important reading, is rather flagrantly self-serving. This is particularly true of Sadat's personal evaluation of Nasser. For a more positive assessment of Nasser's statesmanship, written by a different member of Nasser's entourage, see Heikal's *The Cairo Documents*.

ister Begin and President Carter in September 1978. Whenever domestic political discontent has threatened his government, President Sadat has responded by announcing a major new policy with a flair and flamboyance seldom seen in Middle Eastern political history.

Anwar Sadat's dramatic sense of timing has been developed within the patrimonial political context. He has been a traditional patrimonial leader par excellence. As we have seen, President Nasser retained much of the patrimonial style in his rule, while at the same time instituting revolutionary changes at many points in the Egyptian system. Sadat has by and large been busy repairing these tears in the body politic. The traditional power structure so severely disrupted during the two decades of Nasserist rule is in the process of being reinstated. In this sense, Sadat has begun to roll back Nasser's revolution.

Upon taking the reins of power in Egypt, Anwar Sadat immediately began to liberalize and democratize Egyptian society. Economically, this has meant an opening (*infitah*) of the system to foreign investment and capital. Politically, the liberalization has expressed itself in terms of a cautiously guarded return to more political participation. In the words of one informed scholar of Egyptian politics, Sadat's rule represents an "inclusionist" patrimonialism, while Nasser's style was "exclusionist."[86] Sadat has permitted a wider network of individuals to participate in political decision making, in contrast to Nasser, who relied upon a smaller core of trusted assistants. One result of this is that although Nasser had to involve himself directly in many matters, Sadat can afford to adopt a more Olympian approach to matters that are not only time-consuming but also political briar patches. Nor has the Egyptian president always been consistent in this matter. "He has invoked democracy and the rule of law, then — without too delicate a regard for either — swept all his suspected rivals off to jail. He has promised real power to the people, and gathered most of the Government into his own hands."[87] Sadat has been interested not in converting Egypt into a liberal

---

[86] See Springborg, "Patrimonialism and Policy Making in Egypt."
[87] Sheehan, "The Real Sadat," p. 42.

democracy but rather in lengthening and strengthening the patrimonial strands in a way that will recapture the traditional power structure of Egypt. The evidence for this tendency is impressive.

In his first book, published in 1957, Anwar Sadat wrote a statement that would serve as a classic lead sentence in any manual on patrimonial rule: "In Egypt, personalities have always been more important than political programs."[88] Sadat himself has acted accordingly by drawing his family and friends into the center of the political system. His brother-in-law Mahmoud Abu Wafia was for a time secretary-general of the most important forum within the Arab Socialist Union. Two of his daughters are married to members of the most important and wealthy aristocratic families in the country — Sayyid Marei and Osman Ahmad Osman. The former (already discussed in Chapter III) is Sadat's Speaker of the People's Assembly, and the latter is a powerful contractor who is perhaps Sadat's closest political confidant.

Sadat is visibly susceptible to the pomp and circumstance so important to traditional patrimonial leaders. Although he does not live the life-style of the Shah of Iran, he is easily more self-indulgent than was Nasser. He has ten presidential homes and wears field marshal uniforms designed by Pierre Cardin. From time to time, he has reportedly had thousands of balloons bearing his photo dropped over Cairo. He is much less concerned about such issues as favoritism, nepotism, and corruption than his predecessor. But the major difference between Nassar's and Sadat's style of rule is the service to which Sadat's patrimonialism is being put. Class lines have become deeper and class divisions have become wider in Egypt since Sadat's ascendancy. This is seen in the political unrest that has broken to the surface in Egypt since 1971.

In 1972 and 1973, student demonstrations rocked Egypt, and in 1974 an insurrection at the military academy in Cairo was put down with force. Riots in Cairo on New Year's Day 1975 and in April of that year at the major textile center at Mahalla al-Kubra were sparked by social protest and class disaffection.

88 Anwar el-Sadat, *Revolt on the Nile* (New York: John Day Co., 1957) , p. 27.

Then, in January 1977, thousands of Egyptians drawn from several social classes demonstrated in violent protest against the government's decision to cut back its subsidies on food costs. The army was called in to suppress the rioters in the worst civil upheaval in Egypt in twenty-five years. These demonstrations (especially those in 1975 and 1977) carried heavy overtones of outright class conflict. In 1975, the cry was "We do not need a Pasha but we need a President," and in 1977, one of the slogans was "Where is our breakfast you dweller of palaces?"[89] In the 1977 incidents the patrimonial leader's wife, Jihan, was herself one of the targets of criticism and was given such labels as "the uncrowned queen" and "tomorrow's Cleopatra."[90]

Anwar Sadat's patrimonial rule in the service of tradition has brought back class animosity in Egypt. His open-door policy has served only to widen the gap between the very rich and the teeming masses of the poor. According to Burrell and Kelidar: "Perhaps the most dangerous aspect of this is that the average Egyptian has been becoming more impoverished at a time when the affluence of a small number of Egyptians has been made ever more apparent. The availability of Western imports — imports widely regarded as nonessential luxuries under Nasser's rule — have heightened the sense of impoverishment and deprivation."[91] The fact that rich Arab oil magnates from the Gulf shaykhdoms vacation in Egyptian resorts and mansions in Alexandria while thousands of Egyptian citizens work as skilled and unskilled laborers in the shaykhdoms is an irony not lost on the Egyptian public.

Since the 1977 riots, President Sadat has used his patrimonial

---

[89] See R. Michael Burrell and Abbas R. Kelidar, *Egypt: The Dilemmas of a Nation, 1970–1977,* The Washington Papers, no. 48 (Beverly Hills: Sage Publications, 1977) , p. 72.

[90] *Events,* 11 March 1977, p. 18.

[91] Burrell and Kelidar, *Egypt,* p. 32. This excellent little book convincingly demonstrates that widening class divisions in Sadat's Egypt have led to great political discontent and discord. For further documentation, see John Waterbury, *The Opening: Luring Foreign Capital,* American Universities Field Staff, Northeast Africa Series, Hanover, N.H.: vol. 20, no. 3, 1975. All of Waterbury's reports on Egypt are superbly done and together present an informed, interpretive account of Egyptian social and political life between 1973 and 1976.

prerogative of control by coercion. Veteran politician Kemal Al Din Husayn was summarily expelled from the National Assembly in the wake of the unrest; a new law sharply circumscribing political opposition was passed after receiving strong support in a referendum in February 1977. Students and other university dwellers were assured that from then on participation in demonstrations and illegal political party membership were punishable by life imprisonment and, in some cases, hard labor as well. Sadat redefined his views on liberalization when he told Egyptian students that "politics have no place in our universities" and that "democracy too can have teeth and fangs."[92] Finally, and perhaps more effectively, the Egyptian president managed to pull his country back together by his brilliantly conceived and courageous trip to Israel. The importance of this unprecedented action was recognized by the Egyptian people, who rallied in hope once again behind their leader.

Anwar Sadat is a more accomplished patrimonial leader than was his predecessor Gamal Abdel Nasser. He has more experience, greater flair, and the added political support of the United States, along with considerable economic assistance from the oil-rich conservative Arab countries. Yet Sadat's personal and patrimonial style is enlisted more than Nasser's was in the defense of the status quo, thereby defying inexorable social forces in Egypt which grow more explosive with time. As we have seen, Nasser himself was not averse to patrimonial tactics. Yet he was dedicated to a continuing program of social change and to the transformation of the class structure of Egypt. He tried to generate and absorb change. As a result he ruled Egypt for nearly two decades, despite accepting full responsibility for political and national catastrophes such as the June War of 1967. It is doubtful that President Sadat, despite his international statesmanship and shrewd domestic patrimonial style, will survive politically as long as Nasser did. If he does, it will be not because he has chosen to foresake his patrimonial style of rule, but rather because he has sought to confront the gathering social challenges with revolutionary

92 Burrell and Kelidar, *Egypt,* pp. 41–42.

programs. Only one person knows how he next intends to greet these challenges. That person is Anwar Sadat.

LEADERS AND CHANGE:
A CONCLUDING PERSPECTIVE

Our case studies of selected Middle Eastern leaders indicate the extraordinary persistence of patrimonial politics in the area. Even revolutionary and charismatic leaders such as Atatürk and Nasser retained characteristics of the patrimonial style. This is one reason why it is supremely difficult to transform national power structures and to introduce political development in Middle Eastern countries. Can one build new political systems using old tools?

Kemal Atatürk and Gamal Abdel Nasser did indeed introduce significant change at various points in their social and political systems. Although it has become common to question the depths of the changes they wrought, there can be little doubt that they were in many ways revolutionaries. But they had unusual advantages. Both gathered great personal and political momentum because of their impeccable credentials as nationalists. They had successfully defied and defeated great European colonialist powers. And both men had an impressive charisma that is seldom seen in the Middle East today.

In succeeding their illustrious predecessors, Ismet Inönü and Anwar Sadat were faced with the need to continue and deepen ongoing programs of revolutionary change. Both men chose initially to liberalize and to expand political participation in their societies. Lacking the charisma of Atatürk and Nasser, they sought to build a broader platform of legitimacy and support. Ironically, in the process of doing so they oversaw the gradual decline of revolutionary programs in their societies. The traditional power groups and classes that had been defeated and dismantled by Atatürk and Nasser regrouped and returned to influence.[93] In the case of Egypt especially, patri-

---

[93] Recent research questions the extent to which Atatürk in fact dismantled all traditional power groups. In particular, he did not seek to uproot local notables or provincial aristocrats in Turkey. Many of them are today competing for national political power. See Leder, "Party Competition in Rural Turkey."

monial politics have seeped back into all the nooks and crannies of the system.

Yet there remains a fundamental difference between the monarchical patrimony of the Shah of Iran and the political systems of Turkey and Egypt. In the latter cases, the leadership in drawn from the professional middle class, whose members have overthrown the traditional family rule of kings and sultans. Even though the members of this class may adopt patrimonial tactics themselves, they can never use patrimonial symbols to legitimate their rule since these symbols are the essence of what they rebelled against. The Inönüs and Sadats are at bottom closer to the Atatürks and Nassers than they are to the shahs and kings. As we have seen in this chapter, the Shah of Iran represents the essence of the traditional patrimonial model. The violent revolutionary potential in his society is much greater than that in those societies where the middle class has already taken control.

The challenges of the day are such that patrimonial modes of rule alone will not enable Middle Eastern leaders to satisfy the demands of new social groups and classes. Although this style of rule is so strong that it will perhaps be always present in the Middle East in one form or another, it must be exercised in the context of a strengthened capacity to generate and absorb transforming change. Traditional patrimonial monarchs (such as the Shah of Iran) who promote limited change provide only a limited answer to the challenge. Modern patrimonial moderates (such as Anwar Sadat) who slow and stifle transforming change are also unable to confront the mounting social and political problems successfully. Even newer and bigger versions of the Atatürks and the Nassers would have a difficult time in the contemporary world of the Middle East. The problems are many, and strong but sensitive leaders are few.

CHAPTER VI

Violence and the Military

THE TRADITION OF VIOLENCE

Are the traditions of violence in the Middle East unusual in any way? Historically, there were many violent encounters among groups: tribal raids, colonizing expeditions, wars. Prowess in battle and success in raiding have been virtues historically in the Middle East, especially among the many nomads of the area. Individual lives have not always been very highly valued by rulers; the beautiful folktale *The Thousand Nights and a Night* is full of examples of this. Even in more recent times, roads were built with the corvée, taxes were collected with the bastinado, and army conscripts were obtained through coercive means. Blood revenge and the concomitant blood feud were well known. Assassination of rulers was not unknown and not unapproved. Rulers themselves, notably the Ottoman sultans, went about neutralizing their ambitious relatives or retainers with draconian severity.

Does this indicate that there was an especially strong tradition of violence in the Middle East? It is essential to compare the Middle East with other areas during the same periods. Selim I was hardly more bloodthirsty than Henry VIII. Salah al-Din was no less generous and chivalrous than his famous adversary Richard *Coeur de Lion* (and was surely more generous than Richard's brother John). The Old Man of the Mountain, the religious leader of the Assassins, was assuredly no worse than Pope Alexander VI and his son Cesare Borgia.

During the period of the Crusades the European Christians were as violent as their Muslim adversaries. If anything, the Middle Easterners were less bloodthirsty, less cruel, less violent. Of wars the world has had many; the Middle East has had no more than its share.

The contemporary patterns of urban violence in the Middle East are somewhat different from those in Western Europe and the United States. Student riots and demonstrations have long been a part of the Middle Eastern culture; in recent years, such riots and demonstrations have become a part of European culture as well. But there is much less individual criminal violence in Cairo or Tehran than in New York or Paris. Even in areas such as Afghanistan where men have traditionally gone armed, there is considerably less violence than might be expected. Although Arabs have fought Israelis as Israelis, they have seldom fought them as Jews; whatever else he was, Hitler was a Western European, living in the twentieth century. The wave of kidnappings and political murders in Europe in the late 1970s (exemplified by the Moro murder in Italy in 1978) shows that few areas are immune to terrorist violence. The evidence simply does not support the contention that the tradition of violence is significantly greater in the Middle East than in other areas.

Terrorism and Anticolonialism. At the end of the First World War, the Middle East remained firmly colonialistic. France and Italy controlled all of North Africa except Egypt, which was still to suffer a British occupation for more than a generation. Palestine (including today's Jordan), Iraq, Kuwait, and Aden were in British hands, as was Cyprus in the Mediterranean. Syria and Lebanon were French. By the 1960s all of this had changed, and the process of throwing off these colonial bonds produced much violence.

The Rif rebellion in Spanish Morocco in 1921 was one of the earliest of the struggles against colonialism.[1] Under the leadership of Muhammad Bin Abdul Krim, it splashed over

[1] See David S. Woolman, *Rebels in the Rif: Abd el Krim and the Rif Rebellion* (Stanford: Stanford University Press, 1968).

into French Morocco, and it was French military might that finally destroyed the Rif force. But this was essentially a war of independence and must be considered under that category.

Much of the anti-French and anti-British activity in Egypt, Palestine, and Syria took place in the 1920s. There was certainly opposition to the British in Iraq, but timely concessions and the presence of King Faisal (until 1933) did much to reduce violent outbreaks there. There was also tribal upheaval in the shaykhdoms east of Aden throughout the twenties and thirties, but this stemmed less from anticolonialism than from general tribal unrest. Although the tribes of the Middle East were an anachronism by the 1920s, their leaders stubbornly resisted central authority and forced settlement. This was true in Iran, Afghanistan, India (the western Muslim provinces), Sudan, and Libya. It was also true in Iraq, Jordan, and Saudi Arabia; along the borders of these countries "frontier forces" were established to deal specifically with tribal raiding parties and other groups of this kind. This is where the famous Peake Pasha and Glubb Pasha began their careers. There is still warlike tribal unrest in the Middle East, but it has very much diminished as the tribes themselves have become less powerful and less independent. But even today in the Israeli Negev there are about 40,000 "nomads" whose settlement is a problem for any Israeli government.

In Egypt, a sullen and unhappy population endured a British occupation throughout the twenties and thirties with only periodic outbreaks of violence. There was, however, serious rioting on a number of occasions.[2] This was directed not only against the British, but also against Egyptian governments and the political institutions of the time. There were also assassinations. However, the real waves of violence occurred after the Second World War. The war had solved little for the Egyptians; accumulated frustrations produced a paroxysm of violence against whatever convenient targets could be found. The most destructive of these outbreaks took place in January 1952, on a day that came to be called Black Saturday. The day

[2] See John Marlowe, *A History of Modern Egypt and Anglo-Egyptian Relations 1800–1956,* 2d ed. (Hamden, Conn.: Archon Books, 1965).

before, British troops in the Suez Canal Zone had attacked (with some provocation, of course) a group of Egyptian policemen, killing about fifty. In response, the Egyptian populace went on a rampage. Led by extremist elements, including the Muslim Brotherhood, mobs set fire to much of modern Cairo, concentrating on the luxury hotels and foreign-owned stores and establishments. Altogether at least a dozen Europeans were killed, and damages to the city ran more than $50 million. Order was restored only late in the day, when the army was finally permitted to intervene.[3] The 1952 Revolution was now only months away.

There is hardly space to chronicle the many episodes of terrorist violence in the Middle East before and after the Second World War. There is, however, one prominent example of terrorist violence that needs to be examined in some detail. It is of course the example of Palestine (Israel).

The Palestine problem that has plagued the Middle East throughout the twentieth century might be said to have had its beginnings in 1897 at the meeting of the First Zionist Congress in Basle, Switzerland.[4] At that meeting, a resolution was passed favoring a national home for the Jews in Palestine. The British gave their imprimatur to this notion in 1917 in the Balfour Declaration, and in effect the Palestine problem was born. The idea of a national home in Palestine was nurtured by continued persecution of Jews in Eastern Europe and finally by genocide during the Hitlerian period, which resulted in large-scale immigration of Jews into Palestine. Not all of the Jews who left Europe went to Palestine, but the influx was great enough in the twenties to alarm the Arab inhabitants. By the end of the Second World War, the number of immigrants was so large that it had become impossible to secure Arab approval for their settlement in Palestine.

[3] See Chapter 12, "The Burning of Cairo," in Jean and Simone Lacouture, *Egypt in Transition* (London: Methuen and Co., 1958).

[4] There is a wealth of literature on Zionism and the Arab-Israeli question. For a full treatment of Zionism, see Ben Halpern, *The Idea of the Jewish State*, 2d ed. (Cambridge: Harvard University Press, 1969). For another perspective, see Fred J. Khouri, *The Arab-Israeli Dilemma*, 2d ed. (Syracuse, N.Y.: Syracuse University Press, 1976). See Chapter VIII below for a full treatment of the Arab-Israeli dispute.

Great Britain held a League of Nations mandate for Palestine and was thus responsible for regulating the entry of Jews into Palestine, for maintaining public order, and for preparing the country for eventual independence. These tasks were ultimately too difficult; in May 1948, the British simply disengaged themselves from the situation. War between the Jews and the Arabs was the result of this disengagement.

It is difficult to pinpoint the moment when Palestinian Arabs first resorted to violence. An important early example of Palestinian violence, however, was the riots in Jaffa in 1936, during which a number of Jews and Arabs were killed. One result of these riots was an organized effort (led by Haj Amin al-Husayni, the Mufti of Jerusalem) to oppose Jewish immigration and the British mandate. This organized opposition led to further unrest, riots, demonstrations, raids, and retaliatory police actions. At first, the Arabs directed their energies against the Jews. Arab mobs attacked Jewish merchants. They also attacked Jewish farming settlements, sometimes injuring fields and sometimes injuring individuals. But inevitably Arab terrorists began to make systematic attacks on the British, who, as the occupying power, were facilitating Jewish settlement in Palestine. Out of necessity, the Jews began to form their own terrorist and defense organizations, first to challenge the Arabs and finally to confront the British. The British also began to fight terror with terror, and thus terrorism in Palestine ultimately became three-pronged. It is well to remember that before (and for a time after) the establishment of Israel in 1948, there was no central authority in the area that all Jews respected. Thus, there were several extremist terrorist groups that many Jews (and later Israelis) abhorred, but that others supported. Best known among these were the so-called Stern Gang and the Irgun Zvai Leumi. The Irgun was well organized; one of its early leaders was Menahem Begin, who was to become prime minister of Israel in 1977. Several spectacular incidents of violence emanated from these extremist terrorist groups. In 1944, Lord Moyne (British minister of state for the Middle East) was assassinated in Cairo; July 1946 saw the bombing of the King David Hotel in Jerusalem (with ninety-one dead). In September 1948, Count Folke Bernadotte, United

anticolonial struggle occurred in Aden and the adjacent territories of the hinterland. Again Great Britain was the colonial power involved. By the sixties, Britain was well launched
on her plan to disengage from the Middle East. She hoped to
leave in Aden the semblance of an independent and friendly
Arab government to which power could be transferred. This
government was to be called the South Arabian Federation
and was to be a conglomerate of minor shaykhdoms. All of
these plans came to naught.

One problem was that there was no viable political system
that could easily be constructed from the hotchpotch of fragmented systems that were to be found in Aden and the adjacent
territories. But just as important, from the early sixties to the
middle sixties, Nasserist influence was ascendant in the Arab
world. In addition, there was civil war in Yemen. Nationalist
organizations quickly came into being in Aden City. Terrorists
began to strike against the British and their client shaykhs
and against each other. (A virtual battle between Arab troops
and British forces was fought in June 1967.) Two nationalist
organizations, the National Liberation Front (NLF) and the
Front for the Liberation of Occupied South Yemen (FLOSY),
vied with each other for power. Both frightened some of the
pro-British shaykhs away from participating in a British-
sponsored government. Assassination and the threat of assassination were used with skill and success. The British were
squeezed out. The NLF proved victorious over FLOSY. When
the British left in late 1967, the NLF organized the government of the People's Republic of Southern Yemen. The goals
of British exodus and the termination of British influence had
been successfully achieved through indiscriminate violence and
terror. Independence did not, however, mean an end to internal terror.

A government that survives a period of terror is hardly likely
to be very generous or understanding of the rights of politically despised minorities. Internal Israeli politics, for example,
especially with respect to the Arab minorities, quickly became
calloused and unresponsive. Terror and violence throughout
the Arab world have produced an atmosphere in which freedom of expression, legitimate opposition, broad political par-

ticipation, and a climate of moderation have often had to give way to more extremist forms of politics.

Wars of Independence. What distinguishes a war of independence from the violent terrorist campaigns that are mounted against a government or a colonial regime? Sometimes the distinction is shadowy. Where insurgents have established a sizeable and regular military force and are able to maintain it in the field for some length of time, there is manifestly an internal war of some sort. But what exists may be so ineffective and so poorly organized that it hardly merits the label of internal war. In fact, a war of independence may have gone through several such preliminary phases.

The conflict that broke out in May 1948 between the Israelis and primarily the armies of Egypt and Jordan was more properly an international than an internal war, since the adversaries involved were distinct international entities. The Israelis naturally look upon it as a war of independence. But it was primarily a war not against other Palestinians (Arabs), but rather against outsiders.

There are, however, several quite legitimate examples of wars of independence in the Middle East. The Rif rebellion against the Spanish and French in Morocco was certainly a war of independence. Muhammad Bin Abdul Krim formed an effective and viable government for a time. It maintained internal order, held sway over considerable territory, and effectively put together a fighting machine that was defeated only with difficulty by the French and the Spanish.[7] Unfortunately,

---

[7] General Manuel Silvestre was defeated and killed in battle (22 July 1921) ; General Navarro was captured (9 August 1921) ; and in 1922 General Damaso Berenguer, high commissioner of Spanish Morocco, resigned under fire. Berenguer was replaced by General Ricardo Burgueti, who lasted less than a year. General Miguel Primo de Rivera, the Spanish dictator after 1923, was forced to a policy of *abandonismo* in the summer of 1924. The famous Marshal Lyautey was dismissed as French commander in 1925 when the Rifians successfully attacked in French Morocco. Marshal Petain journeyed to Morocco to give his support. It was during all this fighting that Colonel Francisco Franco was promoted to brigadier at the age of thirty-three. What a galaxy of Spanish and French generals to have met their match in Muhammad Bin Abdul Krim! See Woolman, *Rebels in the Rif*, passim.

Abdul Krim was never able to secure international recognition of the legitimacy of his regime. With military defeat, his government collapsed and he went into exile.

A more recent example of a Middle Eastern war of independence is the war fought by the Algerians against the French. Indeed, it may be described as a classic case. France had annexed Algeria in the 1830s and over the years had increasingly insisted that Algeria was essentially and irretrievably French. Although perhaps nationalism in the modern sense did not develop until the 1920s, rebellion, demonstrations, and disturbances were common in nineteenth-century Algeria. They were generally local in nature and were not self-consciously nationalistic. But the French were never to know peace, although they poured money and settlers into the country and consciously thought of the area as part of France.

By the end of the Second World War (in which French North Africa was involved), a century of the French presence had not offered native Algerians much in the way of economic opportunity or political participation. But what had been tolerated by the "colonies" in earlier years had now become intolerable. A decade after the Second World War, the collapse of the French colonial empire was well under way. Successive French governments hoped that Algeria could be saved. Although many Algerians were apathetic, terrorist efforts by Algerian leaders and the intransigence of the French (including the use of extreme terrorist tactics by the French themselves) gradually produced an Algerian community that was fairly united against the French. The early moderate Algerian leader Ferhat Abbas was replaced by the more radical Ahmad Ben Bella. Between 1954 and 1960, a major, although unusual, war was fought between the French army and an increasingly effective Algerian army. The French could not win and abandoned their position in 1962. In the course of the conflict there was a coup d'etat in France (and a short-lived army takeover in Algiers). Ben Bella was himself forced out in 1965 in a coup led by Col. Houari Boumedienne.

The struggle against the French had been long and painful. The key to Algerian success, however, had been the half-dozen years beginning in 1954. Starting in November of that year, the National Liberation Army (NLA) gradually increased the territory it controlled throughout the country. By 1956, it controlled small but nevertheless significant areas in eastern Algeria, in the mountains close to Tunisia. By 1957, the NLA had enlarged its scene of operations to cover the entire Algerian coast, and the territories it controlled had correspondingly increased. By November 1958, all of populated Algeria was honeycombed with areas of NLA control and influence.

The French army — already demoralized from more than a century of defeats and embarrassments — could not win strategic victories over its guerrilla opponents, who later organized themselves into sizeable military units. It did win tactical victories, but these were not enough. The French army therefore began a brutal, terrorist campaign against its opponents and those it thought were its opponents. This campaign of counter-terror, carried on haphazardly at best, was no more successful than the army's military campaigns had been. The cost of the struggle was immense for both Algeria and France. But the struggle showed the inability of a modern and well-equipped army to liquidate a war of liberation that had captured the support of the masses.[8]

The Kurdish rebellion in Iraq is interesting in that it was a struggle not against a European colonial power, but rather against a "native" Arab government. The Kurds are not Arabs, although they are Muslims. Their ancestral lands have become divided by the present-day borders of Turkey, Iraq, and Iran. The Kurds are an intractable mountain people who have caused difficulties for every government under which they have lived. Before 1918, Iraq (including Iraqi Kurdistan) was part of the Ottoman Empire. After the war Great Britain secured a mandate to Iraq, but its control was never strong. Certainly, the government in Baghdad held weak authority over outlying areas, including those of the Kurds in the north.

---

[8] See the data in Joan Gillespie, *Algeria: Rebellion and Revolution* (New York: Frederick A. Praeger, 1961), pp. 200–201. This material is reproduced in Kenneth W. Grundy, *Guerrilla Struggle in Africa: An Analysis and Preview* (New York: Grossman Publishers, 1971), pp. 86–87. See also Alistair Horne, *A Savage War of Peace: Algeria 1954–1962* (New York: Viking, 1978).

The Kurdish rebellion can be laid to the door of one man as much as any: Shaykh Mulla Mustafa al-Barzani. Majid Khadduri suggests that the merging of the Kurds with the Arabs into a group with a single national consciousness was impossible because of Shi'i concern about the enhanced position of the Sunnis in any such amalgamation, as well as because of the growth of Arab nationalism in recent years. (The Kurds are neither Shi'ite nor Arab.) At the end of the Second World War, al-Barzani led an attempt to establish an autonomous Kurdistan. With its collapse, he left for the Soviet Union, to return only after the Kassem revolution in 1958. The military government of Iraq at this time was unable to solve its Kurdish problem. Fighting between Kurdish and government forces assumed major proportions, particularly in the first half of the 1960s. During the military campaigning season, government troops made inroads into the Kurdish-controlled territory; with bad weather they retired. Throughout this time, great efforts were made to negotiate some settlement.

Although neither side eschewed negotiation in theory, it is difficult to see what could be negotiated. To the central government, national prestige and security as well as petroleum resources were involved; to the Kurds, nothing less than their independence was at issue, although they demanded such things as Kurdish ministers in Baghdad. But the fact was that no national Iraqi army was strong enough to penetrate the Kurdish territories and destroy their fighting forces. Every year or so the central government (often a new one) would announce the end of fighting and a rapprochement with the Kurds. Just as regularly the fighting would break out once more. The most serious claim that a settlement had been made occurred in 1970. But when, in the late spring of 1972, the Iraq Petroleum Company was nationalized and production of oil in the northern fields fell, the Kurds once more expressed their dissatisfaction. There seems to be little hope today for real Kurdish autonomy. The Kurds are under too many jurisdictions; their territory is landlocked and they have few resources; the world does not care about them. This became clearly evident when Iran abruptly withdrew its support of the Kurdish rebels in 1975. Kurdish ability to withstand Iraqi military incursions was seriously weakened, and once again the central government announced the end of the rebellion. The old warrior, al-Barzani, was forced to flee to Iran and he now lives in exile in Washington, D.C. Meanwhile, both Iraqi and Iranian government forces continue in their attempts to crush the Kurds. Kurdish irredentism survives.

There are other examples of struggles against "native" governments in the Middle East. In 1972, the Sudanese government announced the end of the fighting between southern blacks and northern Arabs that had gone on (with little publicity) for years. Casualties had been heavy. The blacks had been unable to secure their independence, but they had created serious difficulties for the central Sudanese government for a considerable period of time. And the Yemeni civil war in the 1960s was hardly a war of independence, yet it was a bloody and major conflict. In the early 1970s, the Dhofar province in western Oman was the scene of an abortive effort to break up Omani authority and control. The rebels were aided by Southern Yemen and the People's Republic of China; Oman itself accepted the aid of Iranian troops in the struggle in Dhofar.

Conflicts of this kind tend to occur in areas in transition, both because internal political systems are themselves changing and because old colonial relationships are breaking down or atrophying. The Middle East is, of course, not the only area in which conflicts of this nature have occurred, but it is an area in which the conditions encourage these conflicts.

What are these conditions in the Middle East?

1. *A weakened central authority.* Where the central authority is colonial in character, successive efforts to undermine that authority by nationalist forces will ultimately be successful. Should a transfer of power occur, the new regime itself is often weak. A nationalist successor regime is thus often susceptible to coups or renewed conflict.

2. *Transitional systems.* Middle Eastern political systems are everywhere challenged by the forces of change. As we noted in Chapter I, the imbalances, inequalities, and frustrations that

accompany transitional politics often give rise to organized and unorganized violence.

3. *Ideological confrontation.* Although lip service is paid by many to such goals as Arab socialism or Arab nationalism, there is in fact considerable ideological conflict in the Middle East. This conflict tends to support large-scale violent movements, which may be generated by other factors.

4. *The presence of unassimilable minorities.* The Middle East is, of course, not alone in this — witness the South Tyroleans in Italy, the Roman Catholics in Ulster, the French Canadians. But in conjunction with other conditions, this has led and will lead in the future to violent movements against central authorities. These minorities may be described sometimes in religious terms, on other occasions in racial, tribal, or ethnic terms. We have spoken of the blacks of southern Sudan and the Kurds of Iraq. Iran also has Kurds, and Israel has its Arabs. These and other minorities may be the seeds of future difficulties.

5. *A tradition of external interference.* Although their role is diminishing, the French and British are still involved in Middle Eastern affairs. The United States is involved too, as is the Soviet Union. And the Middle Eastern countries themselves are not loath to interfere in one another's affairs. Egypt was noteworthy in this respect under Nasser, and Libya and Iran also have reputations for interference.

THE MIDDLE EASTERN MILITARY

Many forms of violence in the Middle East are directly attributable to the roles that the military institutions of the area seek to play.[9] It is well to distinguish between armed

---

[9] There is a substantial literature on the role of the military in the Middle East. Two general books stand out: Eliezer Be'eri, *Army Officers in Arab Politics and Society* (New York: Frederick A. Praeger, 1969) and J. C. Hurewitz, *Middle East Politics: The Military Dimension* (New York: Frederick A. Praeger, 1969). An earlier book was important: Sidney N. Fisher, ed., *The Military in the Middle East: Problems in Society and Government* (Columbus: Ohio State University Press, 1963). P. J. Vatikiotis has written two books on specific countries: *Politics and the Military in Jordan* (New York: Frederick A. Praeger, 1967), dealing only with the period before 1957; and *The Egyptian Army in Politics* (Bloomington:

forces and police forces in the modern state. The latter are primarily responsible for enforcing the criminal law, for administering a variety of regulations, and for facilitating the proper functioning of certain activities, such as those of the traffic police. The police may also contain a *secret* cadre, such as SAVAK in Iran, which conducts surveillance over the populace, undertakes counterespionage, and carries out whatever extralegal activities seem desirable (official assassinations, for example). Quite obviously, police, both open and covert, may engage in violence and may encourage or retard various legitimate forms of political change. Yet the police in the Middle East never act on their own. They are relatively weak and often are poorly equipped. They are the tools of political henchmen and their own officers are rarely powerful enough to carry out independent policies. They are often corrupt. Certainly they possess little popularity among the population at large. They are vulnerable and often expendable, regardless of the institutional power they sometimes have. In short, they are not armies.

What are the functions of an army in the Middle East? The prime function of any army (or air force or navy) is the external defense of the state. In the Middle East, however, the army has many other functions: to maintain internal control and stability, to serve as a symbol of independence, to perform

---

Indiana University Press, 1961). Also see Amos Perlmutter, *Military and Politics in Israel* (New York: Frederick A. Praeger, 1969); and Leo Hamon, *Le Role Extra-Militaire de L'Armée dans le Tiers Monde* (Paris: Presses Universitaires de France, 1966). An important early article by Majid Khadduri should also be noted: "The Role of the Military in Middle East Politics," *American Political Science Review* 47 (June 1953):511–24. See also Manfred Halpern, "Middle Eastern Armies and the New Middle Class," in *The Role of the Military in Underdeveloped Countries,* ed. John J. Johnson (Princeton, N.J.: Princeton University Press, 1962), pp. 277–316; and James A. Bill, "The Military and Modernization in the Middle East," *Comparative Politics* 2 (October 1969):41–62. A further important source is Malcolm Kerr's penetrating review of the Be'eri and Hurewitz studies in the April 1972 issue of the *International Journal of Middle East Studies,* pp. 229–33. See also Roger Owen's review of V. J. Parry and M. E. Yapp's useful edited collection *War, Technology and Society in the Middle East* (London: Oxford University Press, 1975). The Owen review appears in the July 1977 issue of the *International Journal of Middle East Studies.*

certain modernizing functions, and to uphold the honor of the state. Few Middle Eastern states need armies to defend themselves against external foes. This is either because they have few enemies in the military sense, or because the enemies they do have are so powerful that no army they might assemble could perform its defense mission successfully. No Lebanese army could defend itself against any of its neighbors. Nor could any Iranian army or Afghan army defend itself against the Soviet Union. Manifestly, Israel has needed its army, which so far has been successful in defending Israeli territory. Yet most Middle Eastern states spend more resources on their armed forces than is strictly necessary to maximize the chances for successful defense.

In one sense, these expenditures can be viewed as a payoff to the military for performing other functions and duties. The military, it is assumed, desires late-model jet aircraft, heavy tanks, rapid promotion, and pleasant officers' clubs. But in another sense it is important to many countries to exhibit their status by investing in gaudy and expensive military equipment. If conspicious consumption is important to the individual, conspicious military consumption is vitally important to the typical political system in the developing world.

Military systems, however, do perform other functions that justify their existence. Perhaps the most important of these functions in the Middle East is that of maintaining a regime in power. In this role, the army defends the government from its potential or actual internal foes. Martial law is often instrumental not only in putting down disturbances but in rooting out the opposition and forcing unpopular decisions upon the people. The army has certainly played these roles in societies such as Turkey, Iran, Pakistan, Egypt, Jordan, Iraq, Sudan, Libya, Syria, Algeria, and Morocco. Jordan's King Husayn, for example, has owed his throne repeatedly to the loyalty of the army. Without that army he would not be king. The same might be said for Muhammad Reza Shah Pahlavi of Iran (note the riots and the imposition of martial law in September 1978). Sometimes a supporting army will operate so disastrously (as one did in East Pakistan in March 1971) that the regime it maintains collapses because of its ineptitude.

The Lebanese army was unwilling or unable to control domestic turbulence, which led to civil war in 1958 and again in 1975. And a supporting army sometimes spawns enough dissidence within its own ranks to endanger the regime very directly. The several attempts on King Hassan's life in Morocco originated at the highest command levels of the military forces.

Armed forces — the Egyptian and Iranian armies come particularly to mind — sometimes have played educational and practical roles. Large numbers of recruits, often of village origin, will pass through the army, becoming socialized politically, as well as in other ways, in the process. They may be taught a trade as well as to read and write. In this way an army can serve as a modernizing device. It may also participate in roadbuilding or other construction work. In contemporary Iran, young recruits have served in large numbers as literacy and development corpsmen throughout the countryside.

Middle Eastern armies in many ways resemble armies elsewhere. Some are large, while others are quite small. Some are really professional; others are as unprofessional as it is possible to be. The amount and kind of equipment they have vary widely from country to country. The relation between officers and men, and the methods of recruitment, are other aspects of Middle Eastern armies that have varied.

Of all Middle Eastern armies, that of the Israelis[10] has perhaps achieved the most spectacular victories over foreign foes. It has proved victorious in three wars: in 1948, 1956, and 1967.[11] Although in 1973 the outcome was less favorable for the Israelis, their armed forces nevertheless prevailed. The Israeli army is, of necessity, a citizens army; virtually all Israelis, men and women, have an obligation to serve.[12] It has had, in

[10] By far the best book on the Israeli army is Edward Luttwak and Dan Horowitz's, *The Israeli Army* (New York: Harper and Row, 1975).

[11] There seems to be little doubt that Israel found the so-called War of Attrition with Egypt (1969–1971) frustrating and unrewarding. It led to dependence on the thinly held Bar-Lev Line, which crumpled in the 1973 fighting.

[12] There are a number of exemptions open to women that are not available to men; moreover, women are not expected to assume combat roles.

mobilization particularly, a high élan. Its higher-ranking officers, whether they are as brilliant as they are often claimed to
be, are very capable. The Israeli skill in mobilizing their armed
forces quickly is particularly impressive. Their Arab adversaries are much less efficient in this (but they, of course, do
not have citizens armies). Arab-Israeli struggles, at least through
1967, were essentially struggles of one technological age with
another. The conflict in 1973 showed that both the Syrians
and the Egyptians had mastered to a surprisingly large degree
the problems involved in utilizing sophisticated weapons. They
were unusually successful in the employment of surface-to-air
missiles, and the Israeli air losses were most severe. Israeli
casualties in this war were also higher than Israeli casualties
in any other conflict since 1948. Although the Israelis were
tactically surprised, they did succeed ultimately in penetrating
into Syria beyond the Golan Heights and into Egypt beyond
the Suez Canal. They still possess the superior armed forces,
but the gap between them and their Arab foes is lessening.

The Turkish army, too, is a powerful army, well equipped
and well trained. It is not a citizens army like the Israeli army,
but its base (population and other resources) is much broader
and greater than that of the Israeli army. This army has not
been tested in war recently, unless one counts its occupation
of portions of Cyprus. Its record in the Korean War was excellent; in an earlier day, it had a very fine record in the First
World War and in the ensuing struggle with the Greeks.

On the contemporary scene, it is difficult to envision the
Turks engaged in military hostilities with any of their Arab
neighbors. Their major potential foe is the Soviet Union —
Turkey is a member of the North Atlantic Treaty Organization
(NATO) because of this — but it is difficult to see how the
Turks could defend themselves against the Soviet Union in any
but the most conventional of conflicts. The Turks themselves
view the Greeks as enemies, too. Against such a foe they should
acquit themselves very well. Turkey was until recently the
recipient of massive American military aid and was an American military client. But since the Turkish invasion of Cyprus
on behalf of the Turkish minority their political relations
between the United States and Turkey have deteriorated, with

sharp curtailment of military assistance. This deterioration was, to a large degree, the result of the effective lobbying of large numbers of Greek-Americans. The Turks began to reassess their membership in NATO and their relations with the Soviet Union. By 1978 the United States began a reassessment of its own, making it likely that the military assistance to Turkey would be resumed.

In a sense, Iran is also a military client state of the United States, although its substantial petroleum wealth as well as the proud, independent policy of the Shah make American influence there something less than predictable. Iran's military force is currently among the top half-dozen in the world in terms of equipment and size. Most of its equipment has been purchased from the United States, and a American military mission for training purposes has been a large and well-established fixture of the Iranian scene for some years now. The Shah wants the very latest and most sophisticated of American weapons, usually in large numbers. The continuing need for this equipment is not immediately apparent. The result of the purchase of the equipment is that great military and political ambitions are attributed to the Shah.[13] Despite the incredible buildup of the Iranian forces, they remain basically untested, and whatever the Shah's ambitions, his military forces have not really been used. Some were employed in the Dhofar province in Oman, and there have been minor skirmishes along the Iraqi border. But these incidents offer little evidence for judging the strength and ability of the armed forces. Until now, the main function of these forces has been to maintain the Shah's regime. In the unlikely event of war with Turkey, the Iranian military would be sorely tested; it could hardly contend successfully with the Soviet Union. It seems to be clearly superior to the armed forces of Iraq, yet the outcome of conflict even with Iraq seems uncertain. Against Afghanistan or Pakistan, there seems little doubt of its superiority. Nor for that matter is there any doubt about its superiority over the Saudi armed forces. It is clear that the Shah is

[13] See the best-selling novel by Paul E. Erdman, *The Crash of '79* (New York: Simon and Schuster, 1976), for one fanciful attribution.

anxious to defend his access to the Indian Ocean through the Persian Gulf, and his armed forces seem adequate for this purpose.

The Afghan army is virtually of no consequence against any of its external foes. Most of these potential enemies would find, however, an invasion of Afghanistan by conventional means a difficult task. The terrain and the lack of proper roads would be the main obstacles.

The Pakistani army was tested against the Indians and was found wanting. Although strongly aided for years by the United States, the Pakistani army appears, at present certainly, to be of little threat to its neighbors.

As a category, these armies of the non-Arab Middle East include the strongest as well as some of the weakest in the area. In contrast with Arab armies, these armed forces have been relatively reluctant to interfere in the political arena. In Iran, the army has moved to support the regime; in Turkey, it has moved, apparently reluctantly, to support the "principles of Kemalism." In any event, army rule in Turkey has been muted and unlike army rule in most places.[14] Only in Pakistan has the army interfered broadly in political life for an extended period of time. And in Pakistan, in the wake of the disastrous war with India in 1971, the armed forces were so discredited that they permitted their most vocal critic, Zulfikar Ali Bhutto, to simply take over the government. By 1977, the armed forces had intervened once again, this time to jail Bhutto. The bloody coup in Afghanistan in the spring of 1978 was led by the army.

Armies in the Arab world also differ widely. Those of the very small Arab states — Kuwait, Lebanon, Yemen, Tunisia, and so on — are, of course, of no international consequence, and are perhaps of little consequence altogether. In the 1958 civil war in Lebanon, the army refused to intervene; its commander was subsequently elected president. In the second Lebanese civil war (1975–1977), the army was incapable even of preserving its entity as an independent force and collapsed. In 1948, the finest of the Arab armies was the British-officered

14 See Metin Tamkoç, *The Warrior Diplomats* (Salt Lake City: University of Utah Press, 1976), for an extended discussion of the role of the armed forces in Turkish politics.

Arab Legion of Jordan.[15] This army fought in the first Arab-Israeli war and, within the limits of its supplies and its size, fought very well. It fought again in the 1967 war. The overall result was defeat, but the Israelis were and continue to be very impressed with the fighting qualities of the Jordanian army.[16] In 1970, the Jordanians were strong enough not only to defeat the Palestinian guerrillas in Jordan but to stand off briefly an intervening Syrian force. The Jordanian army is small and poorly supplied, but retains a high degree of professionalism.

Until 1973, the Syrian army was of little military consequence against the Israeli army. Its record in the October War, however, was substantially different. Its soldiers fought not only bravely but with remarkable skill and coordination. Over the years, the Syrian army has spawned many coups; its ranks are severely divided along communal and family lines. The Syrian army reflects the permanent instability of the Syrian political system. Yet since 1970, Gen. Hafez al-Assad, president of Syria and himself an Alawite, has given the Syrians a remarkable degree of stability. The Syrians feel militarily threatened not only by the Israelis but by the Iraqis as well. In spite of these threats, Syria intervened in the recent Lebanese civil war and brought the fighting to a halt, leaving behind an occupation force of some 30,000 men. For the size of its country, the Syrian army is an experienced, well-led, and reasonably well-equipped force.

It is difficult to speak with much assurance of the contemporary Iraqi army. Units have fought on occasion on the Israeli borders, but never with any great success. The Kurdish revolt in Iraq prospered as long as Iran was willing to supply the Kurds with weapons; the Iraqi army achieved no noteworthy

[15] See John B. Glubb, *The Story of the Arab Legion* (London: Hodder and Stoughton, 1948). For another account of the Legion, see Vatikiotis, *Politics and the Military in Jordan*.

[16] Luttwak and Horowitz (*The Israeli Army*, p. 267) have this to say: "[The 6 June Jordanian attack near Jenin in the West Bank] was the most effective counter-attack launched by any Arab army during the war. . . . [and the commander of the Jordanian Fortieth Armored Brigade in this struggle, Shaker Ben Zaid, was] the outstanding soldier on the Arab side. . . ."

supremacy over the Kurds. Yet it seems to be well equipped, and threats from it are taken seriously in the Middle East. It seems highly unlikely that Iraq could pose a major threat to Iran, whatever dangers it may pose for others.

The Saudi armed forces, like all things Saudi, are changing rapidly in the late 1970s. Saudi Arabia is a military client state of the United States. The armed forces are small and are not yet thoroughly professional. Indeed, the regime would be very suspicious of high-ranking professional soldiers who might be tempted into political intervention. The Israelis fear the Saudis less than they do the advanced military equipment that the Saudis receive from the United States; the Israelis contend that in a crisis Saudi aircraft, for example, could be lent or given to other more belligerent Arab states and that, if necessary, Saudi air bases close to the Israeli border could be utilized by enemies of Israel. In 1978, this was the backdrop to congressional debates over the sale of jet fighters (F-15s) to Saudi Arabia. It does not seem that Saudi Arabia poses a direct military threat to any of its major neighbors.

A counterpart in some ways to the Saudi army was the army of King Idris's Libya before the coup of 1969. The coup officers in Libya were young and of relatively low rank. In any event, the Libyan army, even with the material resources it now commands, is not a strong or well-organized force. Libya and Egypt fought a short engagement near Tobruk in the summer of 1977. The Libyans were no match for the Egyptians. It is Libyan money as distributed by Colonel Qaddafi that is feared in the Middle East, not Libya's armed forces.

Tunisia, caught between Libya and Algeria, is hardly likely to engage in military adventures. It's army's role must be defined within that general context. Morocco is more powerful than Tunisia and its regime more aggressive. There have been armed conflicts along its borders with several of its neighbors. And in 1971 and 1972, attempted coups showed that within the armed forces' ranks there was enough dissension to endanger the regime. Yet when the march into old Spanish Sahara was essayed, it was done peacefully and without the display of weapons. Against Algeria, Morocco would be hard pressed to maintain its equilibrium.

It is the Algerian armed forces that seem most likely to be able to dominate western North Africa in the future. The fighting a decade and more ago against the French has left a residue of battle-trained officers. The power base of Algeria is greater than those of its neighbors, and its politics may encourage military adventure. For the present, however, in the midst of rapid economic modernization, the military's role has been a muted one.

The Egyptian army, with all its shortcomings, remains the most interesting of the Middle Eastern armies. It has had the most combat experience of any Middle Eastern army, including the Israeli army, although this has not always been reflected in superior performance. It has now fought in four Palestinian wars (1948, 1956, 1967, 1973) and has also fought a long, debilitating war in Yemen. Originally equipped with miscellaneous weapons acquired from the West, it received its first influx of Soviet arms in 1955; today it still remains dependent on Soviet equipment. It was partially trained in the late 1940s and early 1950s by a number of former German officers who had sought asylum in Egypt. In 1952, the army mounted a coup against the old monarchical regime; one result was the reequipping and reorganizing of the armed forces. After the 1967 war, Soviet advisors concentrated on the retraining of middle-rank field officers and on building up a network of sophisticated surface-to-air missiles. The results of this aid program were enormously evident in the October War in 1973. By the late 1970s, Egypt was attempting to reequip its armed forces with American weapons. The political context of Israeli interests made this extremely hazardous for the Egyptians.

The Egyptian military ought to be able to dominate the area. Egypt has a large, fast-growing population and also sufficient wealth and influence to build armed forces of high quality. Its major enemy is, of course, Israel, but its national interests involve at least Sudan (with its control over the Nile River flow) and possible eastern Libya. The missions of the Egyptian armed forces have generally exceeded their abilities. Before the October War in 1973, the Egyptian military forces were held in low esteem. It was assumed that their ranks were filled by men who were so technologically backward that modern sophisticated weapons could not be used. Many of the officers clearly lacked leadership skills, and the cleavage between these officers and their men was well marked. Altogether these factors produced a military organization that had to be characterized as inept.

Either this analysis was wrong or very substantial changes had occurred between 1967 and 1973 — or so the results of the 1973 fighting seem to indicate. Perhaps a little of both! Indeed, the army might never have been as bad as it was made out to be. The destruction of the airfields and planes by the Israeli air force in the early hours of the June War (1967) made the Egyptian army's mission in Sinai then an impossible one. The fact that, in the very peculiar environment of Sinai, Israeli tactical surprise swiftly won several encounters should not necessarily have meant that the Egyptian army was badly organized or officered at all levels. Perhaps the very highest echelons were incompetent in the past (Field Marshal Amer was the main example of incompetence in 1967; since then, many high-ranking officers have been cashiered, including several in late 1973). Perhaps army morale and the psychology of defeat did undermine the past chances for success. And perhaps the educational skills of soldiers do make a difference. The 1973 fighting, however, did break the myth of Israeli invincibility and demonstrated that the Egyptian army was still an army to be reckoned with.

Sudan is of much less importance than Egypt. It has several enemies. Its black southern population has had contacts with Ethiopia. It is not inconceivable that Sudan could become militarily involved with one of its Black African neighbors. But Egypt, precisely because Sudan sits athwart the Nile, is its major concern. Although relatively warm today, relations between the two have not always been good. The Sudanese army is weak and suffers most of the defects common to other Arab armies.

Before 1955, the major arms suppliers to the Middle Eastern countries were the Western powers. This dependence was radically altered by the Soviet-Egyptian arms agreement of 1955. A year later, the Egyptian army and much of its equipment were destroyed by the Israelis. The Soviet Union replaced the equipment lost and provided increased facilities for the training of Egyptian military personnel. By 1961, East German and Soviet military missions in Egypt had begun to reorganize the military forces there. During the months that followed, substantial Soviet military aid (along, of course, with other kinds of aid) was provided on a continuing basis. This aid included bombers of all types, tanks, MIG-21 supersonic jet interceptors, and SAM-2 ground-to-air missiles.

Much of this equipment was lost in the June War (1967), and once again the Soviet Union made replacement. By 1970, several Soviet squadrons of fighter planes were actually stationed in Egypt. These included the very latest jet fighters. Tanks, heavy howitzers, ground-to-ground missiles, and other miscellaneous equipment, as well as approximately 15,000 Soviet military personnel, were among the largess offered to the Egyptians.

Yet the future of the Soviet military presence in Egypt was compromised in July 1972, when President Sadat ordered all Soviet military personnel to leave Egypt. At the time, there was considerable speculation concerning why the Soviet technicians were summarily expelled. There had been dissatisfaction with the inevitable interference that these technicians and other military advisors generated. President Sadat himself said that the Russians had been too cautious; apparently, they had been unwilling to give the Egyptians certain offensive weapons. The Soviet expulsion pleased the United States, and, in effect, Sadat was appealing to the United States to offer a *quid pro quo* by exerting pressure on Israel to withdraw from the Arab lands seized in 1967. The United States either would not or could not do this. The result was that Sadat returned to the military solution and won surprising political and military rewards. In early 1974, Egypt had an army with restored morale, and with the cooperation of Arab oil-producing states had forced the Israelis to reconsider their occupation of Sinai. Sadat thus achieved an important victory — a victory that later made it possible for him to visit Jerusalem and offer an accommodation to the Israelis, and later still, to negotiate his separate peace at Camp David.

Egypt was not, of course, the only Middle Eastern nation to receive military aid from the Soviet Union, although it was the chief recipient of such aid. Major shipments were made to Syria and Iraq, and lesser amounts were given to Sudan, Libya, Algeria, Yemen, and South Yemen. By Western standards, these were mostly radical and largely unstable regimes, but it is not surprising that the Soviet Union has found it useful to supply them. Soviet aid has not always meant that the regime receiving it has proved very grateful (or has demonstrated this gratitude) in very many visible ways. The case of Egypt (and, by 1978, Iraq as well) should make that apparent.

We can, perhaps, sum up Middle Eastern armies with the following observations:

1. Middle Eastern armies vary widely in terms of size, equipment, training, and élan.

2. Few are well equipped to carry on the primary mission of defending their nation's borders, and even fewer are capable of initiating offensive military action externally.

3. For many, the most basic mission is maintaining a particular regime in power.

4. With certain non-Arab exceptions, Middle Eastern armies are likely to be heavily involved in politics.

5. Middle Eastern armies tend to be relatively small with respect to the population of their states, and their defense budgets are not unusually high as a percentage of gross national product (GNP) .[17] But there are exceptions, obviously Israel and Iran, and to a lesser extreme, Egypt.

7. Middle Eastern armies are seldom homogeneous, but rather are often "continually rent by internal cleavage and conflict."[18] This has been particularly true of the Syrian and Iraqi armies.

---

[17] See Hurewitz, *Middle East Politics: The Military Dimension*. Although the figures in this study are considerably out of date, they illustrate the points made. Another somewhat dated study supports these general hypotheses and indicates that the particular societies in Jordan, Iraq, Israel, and Iran are among the world leaders in both categories. See Bruce M. Russett, "Measures of Military Effort," *American Behavioral Scientist* 7 (February 1964) :26–29.

[18] Bill, "The Military and Modernization in the Middle East," p. 54.

8. The officer class in modernizing armies tends to display characteristics different from those of the officer class in traditional armies. Even more marked are the characteristics of those portions of officers corps that are prone to coups. These modernizing officers are likely to be young and of middle-class origin, often have experience abroad, and usually are extremely nationalistic.[19]

The Coup d'Etat. The coup is by now a well-established part of the Middle Eastern political process.[20] It need not be particularly violent, although the threat of violence is always present. Generally, few lives are lost in the coup itself, but recriminatory trials may eliminate numbers of individuals in the post-coup period.

To examine the Middle East during just the last thirty years, only Morocco, Tunisia, Israel, Saudi Arabia,[21] Lebanon, and Jordan have not undergone coups.[22] The potential for coups in most Middle Eastern countries (including Israel) remains high.

Sometimes a coup leads to revolution: Egypt is an example. But often it does not: Syria offers an instance. Almost always the coup is carried out, although not always inspired, by military officers of field-grade rank. Generally, these officers have been radically oriented, and the coups they have mounted have been put together in the name of innovation and modernization.

Usually such coups produce governments that are weak. The first task of such governments is to consolidate power, and, while doing so, they inevitably neglect the goals that rationalized their coup. Gradually conditions worsen, often leading to a subsequent coup. The chain is broken when the leaders of a particular coup are competent or lucky enough to be able to alter political conditions and legitimate their own supremacy.

19 Ibid., pp. 54–57.

20 See Carl Leiden and Karl M. Schmitt, *The Politics of Violence: Revolution in the Modern World* (Englewood Cliffs, N.J.: Prentice-Hall, 1968), for a theoretical discussion of the coup d'etat and revolution.

21 This depends upon the exact definition of *coup*. In 1964, Prince Faisal was able to legally and legitimately depose his brother Saud as king.

22 In Morocco, Lebanon, and Jordan, attempts at coups have been made.

Coup leaders not surprisingly are interested primarily in short-term political payoffs; long-term solutions to political problems are usually neglected. Let us examine two cases of the Middle Eastern coup d'etat.

In the spring of 1952, the conditions in Egypt were such as to make a coup likely.[23] Much depended upon the response of the British, who continued to occupy the Suez Canal Zone. King Farouk and his government were thoroughly discredited. The regime's claims to Sudan and to Palestine had ended ignominiously. The Egyptian army had been defeated and humiliated and was resentful. The Israeli presence was a running sore. It was difficult, if not impossible, to maintain order in Egypt — Cairo had been ravaged by mobs in January. Eliezer Be'eri has this to say about the prelude to the 1952 coup:

> In the Egypt of 1952 there was revolutionary ferment. The mass outburst of Black Saturday in January, the violent struggle for the evacuation of the British bases and the frequent government crises were clear evidence of this; and the movement of the Free Officers was also one of its expressions. Moreover, the class struggle in town and country was becoming more and more acute. In 1951 there were 49 workers' strikes. In the second half of 1951 there were several uprisings of peasants who demanded ownership of the large estates they were cultivating, and in a number of instances the rebellions were quelled only by bloodshed. The forces which controlled the communications media and public opinion maintained a conspiracy of silence about the struggles of the workers and peasants, and only fragmentary accounts came to the knowledge of the public and to history. But whoever wanted to listen could hear subterranean rumblings in 1952 that announced an approaching volcanic eruption.[24]

A clandestine group of young army officers, led by a lieutenant colonel named Gamal Abdel Nasser, had for some years planned an eventual political intervention if the government did not in some way meet its demands and needs. This group was forced to crystallize its plans in the early summer of 1952,

[23] See Leiden and Schmitt, *The Politics of Violence,* for a detailed discussion of the Egyptian coup of 1952.

[24] Be'eri, *Army Officers,* pp. 102–3.

when it became apparent that the government had learned much about its existence and was about to move against it. At the same time, the internal situation in Egypt had completely deteriorated, and it seemed that almost no effort would be needed to topple the regime.

The coup, in spite of all the coffeehouse planning over the years, was a patchwork maze of last-minute decisions. Nevertheless, everything worked beautifully. The king and his ministers had already left the heat of Cairo for Alexandria by 22 July. Late that night, a small body of troops took over the command headquarters in Cairo and then arrested as many leading politicians and possible oppositionists as could be found in the very early hours of the morning. The British, who had military forces in the Suez Canal Zone, sat on their hands. The king found no support in the army or from the British and went into exile. Egyptians of all classes greeted the coup with enthusiasm. An old and respected general, Muhammad Naguib, accepted the nominal role — he later was tempted to make more of it — as head of the junta (the Revolutionary Command Council). The coup was a success. The junta survived relatively intact to lead Egypt into revolution and into an assortment of international and domestic adventures.

This coup can be characterized as one evolving from a conspiracy of young army officers against a very weakened and discredited old regime. There was no foreign intervention. Enthusiasm for the coup was so widespread and lasted so long that it permitted a genuine revolutionary consolidation of power to occur. The coup's leader, Nasser, was unusual in his political skills and in the inordinate popular appeal that he engendered.[25]

Most other Middle Eastern coups, however, have been far different from the Egyptian case. Those in Syria from 1949 to 1970 were noteworthy for the brevity of the regimes they inaugurated. The difference, though, lies not so much in the actual mechanics of the takeover as in the subsequent history of the succeeding regime. When that regime is unable to com-

[25] See our analysis of Nasser in Chapter V.

mand loyalty or to legitimate its existence, it is hardly likely to be able to move seriously in the direction of modernization and political development. In Syria, General Hafez al-Assad has been in power since 1970; it is the longest period of stability possessed by any modern, independent, Syrian government. The history of Iraq has been similar to that of Syria in this respect; it may be useful to examine it for a moment.

Iraq has had a history of coups. The Bakr Sidqi coup of October 1936 was, for the Arab world at least, the first of a long chain of military coups. "The Iraqi coup of 1936 was the first of its type . . . [and] was typical of many that followed, both in their organization and in the course they took. The way in which the military dictatorship met its end was also typical — it was overthrown by a coup of other military officers."[26] On 10 August 1937, Bakr Sidqi was assassinated in Mosul, and the conspirators themselves mounted a successful revolt. They permitted the existence of a semi-independent government, however, and in December 1938 they were forced to intervene again. When the king died in April 1939, the military officers were successful in demanding that Abd al-Ilah be named regent. In 1941, the army intervened once again, this time to back Rashid Ali in his clash with the British over their presence in Iraq. The Rashid Ali revolt, as it was known, was of course put down by the British, with the aid of Glubb Pasha and the Arab Legion. It eventually ushered in, under the control of Nuri al-Said, a period of reasonable stability in Iraqi politics.[27]

In the summer of 1958, Nuri was prime minister and Abd al-Ilah was still the power behind the young king, Faisal II. Abd al-Ilah was widely hated in the country. The debacle of the Palestine war of 1948 had seriously undermined the position of Nuri and the regent. Nuri had consistently clung to his British friendship in good times and bad, and had incurred considerable distrust from many of his own officers as a result. After all, the Western defense alliance, in which Iraq alone of all the Arab states participated, was called the *Baghdad* Pact: Radio Cairo spoke for many Arabs in denouncing

26 Be'eri, *Army Officers*, p. 19.
27 This is well recounted in Part 1, Chapter 1, of ibid.

the Iraqi government's attachment to what it called Western "imperialism." In the summer of 1958, then, there was much dissatisfaction with Nuri and his government, and much uncertainty over the role that Iraq would play in the Arab world. This was reflected in the feelings of the officer class. Any Arab army, but particularly any Syrian or Iraqi army characterized by family, religious, and political cleavages, would have produced conspiratorial groups. And in Iraq the precedents for army intervention were well known. (Kassem himself had been a minor figure in the Bakr Sidqi group.) Abdul Karim Kassem was involved in conspiracy at least as early as 1956; by 1957, he headed — it is said, merely because he had seniority over his colleagues — a sizeable collection of officers who were determined to strike against the government at the first appropriate opportunity.

That opportunity came in July 1958. The Iraqi government decided to transfer an army brigade to Jordan — it may be recalled that Lebanon was in turmoil at the time — and the brigade chosen was the twentieth (including a battalion commander, Abd al-Salam Arif, later president of Iraq), whose temporary divisional commander was Kassem. The brigade was issued ammunition and ordered to go through Baghdad on 13 July on its way to Jordan.[28]

Instead, Kassem overthrew the regime, murdering in the process the young king Faisal, his uncle and heir, Abd al-Ilah, and Nuri al-Said, the prime minister. After only five years of the Kassem regime, Kassem himself was murdered and his government overthrown, with Arif the successful survivor. Those five years were turbulent ones for Iraq, with army revolts and assassination attempts. Had Kassem's personality been different and his power base wider, and if some of the political problems of the area had been resolved, he might have established a government that had greater permanence. In short, he failed at legitimation and found it impossible to embark on long-range political development. The same generally was true of his immediate successors. It is only in 1968, with the rise of

[28] There are many accounts of these events, but a good one is ibid., pp. 171–78.

General Ahmad Hasan al-Bakr, that an Iraqi regime has been able to move ahead with the business of modernization and political development.[29]

Some coups occur without military intervention. In Sudan, a military dictatorship was established in November 1958 by Lt. Gen. Ibrahim Abbud. Six years were to follow before Abbud was finally ousted, but in the interim there were several attempted coups, continued difficulties in the south, and unending political discord. "What is unique in Abbud's overthrow is the fact that this regime was not destroyed by a military coup but by a popular uprising, and he was compelled to yield his position to civilian authority."[30] Students in Khartoum demonstrated against the regime in October 1964, quickly winning adherents from the mass of citizenry. A more or less general strike occurred. Abbud began dismantling the military structure that he had erected, an act that aroused so much popular enthusiasm that he himself was forced to resign on 15 November.

In this example, it is clear that the army had been unable to solve any of the major problems, particularly the disastrous racial struggle in the south. Those army leaders who had assumed power had also lost much of the support of the army as a whole, and if Abbud's regime had not collapsed of its own weight in late 1964, it would surely have fallen to a military putsch. In any event, in 1969 a successful coup was staged, and Sudan returned to the more normal role of Arab military politics.

The December 1971 war between India and Pakistan, beginning with the insurrection in East Pakistan in March and ending with the creation of Bangladesh, resulted in another military regime's collapsing of its own weight. In the brief life of Pakistan, the army had always been influential, but its most important assumption of responsibility came with the rise of Gen. Muhammad Ayub Khan in 1958. Ayub was a fig-

29 Be'eri (ibid., p. 178) argues that in some ways the Iraqi coup was revolutionary. The masses seemed to be involved politically, and significant institutional alterations did occur (i.e., the monarchy was destroyed and the Iraqi connection with the Baghdad Pact was nullified).

30 Ibid., p. 218.

ure of considerable charm, charisma, and ability, and indeed Pakistan under his control underwent some modernization and a modicum of political development. But East Pakistan, separated from western Pakistan by 1,000 miles of Indian territory, harbored many seeds of resentment against its western partner, and the quarrels with India, particularly with respect to Kashmir, remained unsolved. In 1969, Gen. Agha Yahya Khan, the army commander in chief, replaced Ayub, but he too was unable to advance viable political solutions. Leaning ever more heavily on military force to keep the East Pakistanis in line, he permitted that situation to deteriorate into civil war, and the civil war to lead to war with India. The Indians beat the Pakistanis decisively; the result was that the military was so discredited that an opposition civilian political figure, Zulfikar Ali Bhutto, could, with the acquiescence of the military, virtually name himself president. One of Bhutto's first acts was to retire or otherwise rid himself of large numbers of officers. By 1973, however, Bhutto had begun to rely increasingly on senior officers such as Gen. Tikka Khan for support. By 1977, Bhutto's influence with the military had fallen, along with his control of the domestic political situation. The result was another coup, this time led by army general Zia al-Haq. (One of Zia's first acts was to have Bhutto tried and sentenced to death.) The fact remains that demoralization of the military in the absence of alternative military leadership can result in the rise of a civilian government, but it is rare.

One last quasi-example. When the disastrous June War (1967) struck Egypt, even Nasser offered his resignation. The armed forces were so insecure and bloodied that they could offer no resistance to wholesale sackings of their leading officers. Nasser remained in power, backed up by a newly made army. Many of the old leaders, including Nasser's friend Abd al-Hakim Amer, were swept into disgrace. And even after the October War, Sadat found it convenient (and was able) to shake up the top echelon of the army.

Coups, although common in the Middle East, are not unique to the area. The conditions that give rise to them exist elsewhere as well. The coup is a very specific type of violent action. It is almost completely restricted to military forces, for these forces have a monopoly on the weapons that permit them to enforce their will. Popular agitation can dissolve the legitimacy of a regime and facilitate its dissolution. But the coup, sudden and forceful, is not a thing that masses of people, whether they be professors, students, shopkeepers, or even policemen, can easily (if at all) put together. In the Turkish revolt of 1960, general agitation led to an uprising of the cadets at the military academy, but the essential part of the entire action was the intervention of the army. Because the coup has essentially a military nature, it brings to political power a class of individuals who are not completely representative of the political wellsprings of the masses of people:

1. They tend to be imbued with notions of honor and prestige, and seem easily tempted to venture into foreign embroilments and adventures.

2. They are generally narrowly educated. This is, of course, not true when they are compared to the great masses of people in the Middle East, nor is it strictly true with respect to technology. But a major who is quite competent in supervising the repair of a tank may botch things up as the newly appointed minister of finance, and indeed he often does.

3. They emphasize discipline and order above all else. Although they themselves were disloyal to their military oaths in overthrowing a previous regime, they now demand unquestioned obedience (and sometimes enthusiasm) from the population along any path of modernization they choose to follow.

4. They are very willing to use repressive force to gain their ends domestically and military force to achieve success in international affairs.

One coup, because it fractures the myth of legitimation, encourages future coups, although in fact none may follow immediately. (Thus the 1973 coup in Afghanistan set the stage for the far bloodier one in May 1978.) Since the army can spawn the coup so easily, one continuing task of the junta leaders is to keep their fellow officers, and especially their younger cohorts, under control. Benefits are usually ladled out generously. Officers' clubs with subsidized prices and pleasant facilities are conspicuous. Rapid promotion, generous pay and leaves, fancy uniforms, new military equipment — all of these become necessary to keep the army under control.

But they are not sufficient. Inevitably, new cadres of officers come into being whose members desire power rather than perquisites and are willing to be critical of their superiors and their superiors' decisions. This discontent is exacerbated when the army has been forced into an enterprise that adds little honor or luster to its men — a Yemen military expedition, for example. Indeed, the junta members must draw a narrow line. The army must be humored and honored, yet controlled, but not enough to encourage its men to rebellion. Sometimes a Middle Eastern army is split along so many sectarian and political lines that there is almost no way to eliminate constant conspiracy. No army has illustrated this better than that of Syria, which often has seemed to be in a state of constant revolt. Yet, by 1978, Syrian president (and former air force general) Assad had given the Syrians the longest period of stable government in their modern history.

The Revolution. We must distinguish between the coup and the revolution. By the former we mean nothing more complicated than the sudden overturning of a regime, usually by the army. Such an overturning may result in nothing but superficial personnel changes. Revolution is a lengthier process and involves more permanent and deep-seated changes in the social, political, and economic structures. A revolution may be preceded by one or more coups, and in the course of its development, include still further coups and political rearrangements. It may include elements of counterrevolution.

Revolutionary changes may, of course, occur without coups or even without changes in regimes. This is not probable, however. The Shah of Iran claims to be carrying out a White Revolution in Iran by a combination of such things as literacy programs, land reform programs, and capital investments. King Khalid of Saudi Arabia has also claimed that he is introducing deep-seated changes, and so has King Hassan in Morocco. Kings are in a precarious position in the last quarter of the twentieth century; revolution will inevitably sweep them aside, yet to forestall revolution, they think that they must reform. By instituting piecemeal reforms and modifying programs, such leaders only heighten expectations and sharpen aspirations for more radical change. The failure to institute revolutionary programs of transformation in the end costs them their power and, in some cases, their lives. History teaches us that reforming monarchs have often been the last monarchs.

The entire Middle East shares, to some extent, the elements of revolutionary change. In certain countries we can, however, more properly affix the label "revolution" to the changes that are occurring. Changes here are more deep-seated, less evolutionary, perhaps more destructive, probably more violent. In July 1952, the Egyptian *ancien regime* was toppled by a coup; half a dozen years later there was no doubt that Egypt was in revolution. The old political parties had been outlawed, a land reform scheme inaugurated, the public economic sector enlarged, and, in general, the old bases of political power destroyed.

We can also fairly firmly label revolutionary the cases of Algeria and Turkey (at least in this century). Marginal cases are Syria and Iraq. Although much change has occurred in Tunisia, it is largely evolutionary in character. A case can be made for Iran if revolution is viewed in terms of change instituted from above. Indeed most Middle Eastern countries have undergone some revolutionary change that is often a reflection of the revolutionary environment of the entire Middle Eastern area.

What seem to be the conditions for revolution? Quite a large literature has accumulated on the revolutionary process,[31] but the general question why revolution occurs does not interest us so much here. Rather, we are concerned with the conditions that can transform the military coup into revolutionary action.

In the Middle East, one of the conditions for this transformation has been, after the initial coup, the presence of radically oriented leaders with sufficient resources and popularity to struggle for the long haul rather than for mere momentary perpetuation in power. Mustafa Kemal or Gamal Abdel Nas-

[31] See Leiden and Schmitt, *The Politics of Violence,* for a review of the literature up to 1968. Ted Robert Gurr has offered an elaborate analysis of revolutionary motivation in his *Why Men Rebel* (Princeton, N.J.: Princeton University Press, 1970).

ser are prime examples of such leaders. Time is an essential
ingredient — time to perform and time to transform. Nasser
had at least sixteen years, Kassem less than a half-dozen. Ayub
had a decade; Abbud fumbled six years away. Some Arab military leaders have had only months. Another essential condition is the possession of resources — mainly political resources
— that can permit the diversion of energies from "system maintenance" to "system transformation." How popular are the
coup leaders; how detested were their predecessors? How well
known are they in the armed forces, and what connecting links
do they have with other political, religious, and economic
power centers? Also, of course, how radical are they? They
must have been radical enough to mount a coup, assuming
that they want something more than mere power. Mere power
is always hard to maintain for those who want to transform.
But before revolution can proceed, it must be led by those
who desire revolutionary transformation (or at least can be
led into desiring it by reading the public will).[32]

One revolutionary can catalyze another. The example of an
Atatürk could inspire a Nasser (and even Husni al-Za'im in
Syria quoted Atatürk approvingly in 1949). A Nasser in turn
can galvanize an Arif in Iraq or a Sallal (if not very well) in
Yemen.

Nor should the presence of Israel as a revolutionary catalyst be discounted. In spite of the enmity with which the Arab
Middle East, at least, views it, Israel has been a model for
development for many Middle Eastern governments. Israeli
military successes naturally emphasize the value of the changes
within Israel, but even had this not been the case, any system
as modern as that of Israel would inevitably have had repercussions among its neighbors.[33]

---

[32] For an analysis of the relationship between political violence and
political change, see James A. Bill, "Political Violence and Political
Change: A Conceptual Commentary," in *Violence as Politics: A Series of
Original Essays*, ed. Herbert Hirsch and David C. Perry (New York: Harper
and Row, 1973), pp. 220–31.

[33] For a tightly knit argument demonstrating the various ways in which
Israel has acted as a stimulant to radical and revolutionary change in the
Middle East, see George Lenczowski, "Arab Radicalism: Problems and
Prospects," *Current History* 60 (January 1971):32–37, 52.

Assassination in the Middle East. Considerable research on assassination has been done in recent years,[34] in the wake of the deaths in the United States of such figures as the Kennedy brothers and Martin Luther King. Assassination itself has been part of the political scene throughout all of history.

Is there a climate for assassination in the Middle East? Assassination seems to have some complex relationship with political turbulence. Such turbulence has, of course, characterized the Middle East. Assassination may occur at all levels; in the United States it has largely been restricted to the highest political levels, whereas in the Middle East it has pervaded the entire political spectrum. Table VI.1 lists the assassination attempts on chiefs of state and heads of government in the Middle East over the last sixty years.

Table VI.1 does not include the alleged seventeen unsuccessful attempts on the life of King Husayn of Jordan. In addition, other prominent individuals have been assassinated. These have included Sir Lee Stack, sirdar of the Egyptian army (1924); Lord Moyne, British minister of state in the Middle East (1944); Count Folke Bernadotte, United Nations mediator in Palestine (1948); Ja'far al-Askari, minister of defense in Iraq (1936); Abdullah al-Hajri, president of the Yemeni supreme court and former prime minister (1977); and Kemal Jumblatt, leader of the Druze community and former head of the Progressive Socialist party in Lebanon (1977).

The last half-century in the Middle East has been a transitional one, characterized by continued big-power exploitation, the frenzied growth of nationalism, the expansion and confrontations of ideology, and the consequent uncertain struggles for power. These seem to be conditions in which assassination is nurtured. Potential assassins are produced by the chaotic and anomic transitional period; they are encouraged

34 See Murray C. Havens, Carl Leiden, and Karl M. Schmitt, *The Politics of Assassination* (Englewood Cliffs, N.J.: Prentice-Hall, 1970), for a general discussion of the systemic impact of assassination. See also James F. Kirkham, Sheldon Levy, and William J. Crotty, *Assassination and Political Violence* (Washington, D.C.: Government Printing Office, 1969), particularly Supplement F (pp. 545–52), "Assassination in the Middle East." See also Carl Leiden, "Assassination in the Middle East," *Transaction* 6 (May 1969):20–23.

TABLE VI.1   *Assassination in the Middle East: Attempts on
Chiefs of State and Heads of Governments 1918–1978*

Year	Political figure	Country	Suc-cessful	Unsuc-cessful
1919	Habibullah Khan	Afghanistan	x	
1919	Muhammad Sa'id	Egypt		x
1920	Drubi Pasha	Syria	x	
1924	Zaghlul Pasha	Egypt		x
1930	Isma'il Sidqi Pasha	Egypt		x
1932	Isma'il Sidqi Pasha	Egypt		x
1933	Isma'il Sidqi Pasha	Egypt		x
1933	Nader Shah	Afghanistan	x	
1935	Abdul Aziz Ibn Saud	Saudi Arabia		x
1937	Bakr Sidqi	Iraq	x	
1937	Mustafa Nahhas Pasha	Egypt		x
1945	Mustafa Nahhas Pasha	Egypt		x
1945	Ahmad Mahir Pasha	Egypt	x	
1948	Nuqrashi Pasha	Egypt	x	
1948	Imam Yahya	Yemen	x	
1949	Muhsin al-Barazi	Syria	x	
1949	Husni al-Zaim	Syria	x	
1949	Muhammad Reza Shah Pahlavi	Iran		x
1950	Riad al-Sulh	Lebanon		x
1950	Sami al-Hinnawi	Lebanon	x	
1951	Riad al-Sulh	Jordan	x	
1951	King Abdullah	Jordan	x	
1951	Liaqat Ali Khan	Pakistan	x	
1951	Ali Razmara	Iran	x	
1954	Gamal Abdel Nasser	Egypt		x
1955	Adnan al-Malki	Syria	x	
1958	Abd al-Ilah	Iraq	x	

Note: Country indicates where event took place.

by ideological rationales. They direct their efforts against power-holders with varying degrees of success and impact. "An assassination can have a high impact when (1) the system is highly centralized, (2) the political support of the victim is highly personal, (3) the 'replaceability' of the victim is low, (4) the system is in crisis and/or in a period of rapid political and social change, and (5) if the death of the victim involves the system in confrontation with other powers."[35] Surely it

[35] Kirkham, Levy, and Crotty. *Assassination,* p. 551.

TABLE VI.1   (continued)

Year	Political figure	Country	Successful	Unsuccessful
1958	Nuri al-Said	Iraq	x	
1958	King Faisal II	Iraq	x	
1958	Sami al-Sulh	Lebanon		x
1959	Abdul Karim Kassem	Iraq		x
1962	Imam Muhammad al-Badr	Yemen		x
1964	Ahmad Ben Bella	Algeria		x
1964	Adib al-Shishakli	Brazil (Syrian)	x	
1965	Muhammad Reza Shah Pahlavi	Iran		x
1965	Hasan Ali Mansur	Iran	x	
1967	Levi Eshkol	Israel		x
1968	Muhammad Ayub Khan	Pakistan		x
1971	King Hassan	Morocco		x
1971	Wasfi al-Tall	Egypt	x	
1972	King Hassan	Morocco		x
1973	Shaykh Muhammad Ali Uthman	Yemen Arab Republic	x	
1975	King Faisal	Saudi Arabia	x	
1977	Ibrahim al-Hamdi	Yemen Arab Republic	x	
1978	Mu'ammar Qaddafi	Libya		x
1978	Muhammad Daoud	Afghanistan	x	
1978	Ahmad al-Ghashimi	Yemen Arab Republic	x	
1978	Salim Rubay Ali	People's Democratic Republic of Yemen	x	

would be rare if all these conditions obtained. But they do characterize many Middle Eastern political systems.

The Saudi system is certainly a highly centralized one (i.e., one with a high bureaucratic dependence upon the central authority in the most trivial decision-making situation), but it is also inefficient. (Inefficiency produces practical decentralization.) Political support, in Egypt for Nasser, for example, or in Jordan for Husayn, was indeed a highly personal thing. Often a movement or an organization does not survive the death of its leader. (Certainly the death of Hasan al-Banna in February 1949 had profound repercussions on the fortunes of the Muslim Brotherhood.) Because of the personal quality of this leadership, it is difficult to replace a leader suddenly assassinated — that is, to replace him with someone who can continue unabated the program already in being. Moreover, the Middle East is in political and social change and parts of it are often in crisis. Now and then, outside powers are tempted to intervene with an assassination.

Yet the fact is that these conditions do not inevitably produce assassinations. Somehow, too, when they occur, the system seems to survive. Leaders are replaced, if sometimes poorly. Peoples' memories are short, the shock passes, and the system continues to live. Moreover, the Middle East, for all that the different countries have in common, is not a strictly homogeneous area. Syria in the 1940s and 1950s was replete with assassination, but there have been no important assassinations in Egypt since the Revolution (1952);[36] there were, of course, several attempts against Nasser's life. So far as we know, Saudi Arabia was devoid of assassination until the murder of King Faisal in 1975, yet its neighbor Yemen has had several in recent history.

It is difficult to generalize about the Middle East. As an area, it has had a large number of high-level assassinations; however, it is difficult to assert that, as a phenomenon, assassination is endemic there. In spite of a certain vulnerability to assassination, there is little evidence that assassination has been very effective for its practitioners.[37] An assassination of a public figure in the Middle East is noteworthy for the shock it causes. Rioting often occurs, with varied public displays of official and unofficial grief. The lamentations over, it is surprising how quickly the system adjusts to the loss of a leader.[38]

---

[36] Except for the assassination of the Jordanian prime minister when he was visiting Egypt in 1971. The assassins were almost certainly Palestinian terrorists.

[37] This has been true everywhere in the world. See Havens, Leiden and Schmitt, *Politics of Assassination,* passim.

[38] When Nasser died in September 1970, Egypt was plunged into a paroxysm of grief. Without much enthusiasm, the leadership rallied around Anwar Sadat, one of the original members of the RCC. Yet a year later Sadat was firmly in power. Although Nasser was not forgotten, he was now viewed without tears and was the subject of increasing criticism and

PATTERNS OF VIOLENCE AND COERCION: CONCLUSION

The Middle East has its modicum of violence. Street violence — the riot, the demonstration — is indeed endemic and occurs over trivial provocations. Middle Eastern students have been politically volatile and active for much longer than their Western counterparts. Middle Eastern governments have been more repressive against potentially violent movements than have Western governments. The Arab armies have been politically involved quite often. Most Middle Eastern countries have undergone coups; a few, major and prolonged revolution. Assassinations of public figures have occurred not infrequently.

What does this mean in terms of regime viability and stability, and how does it affect the course of political change in the area? The answer needs to be drafted in several parts: student demonstrations and street riots probably do not influence political change more than they do in most other places in the world, including the more developed areas.[39] Yet, to mention just a few examples in the last decade, such riots and demonstrations have had a definite impact upon the political processes in Sudan, Afghanistan, Egypt, Turkey, Iran, and Jordan — and in Israel, too.

Perhaps assassinations have been more frequent in the Middle East than in other parts of the world. It is difficult to compare world areas in this regard. The very multiplicity of political systems multiplies the targets for assassins. It seems fair to say that, although the systemic effects of assassinations in the Middle East have generally not been great, they have exceeded those in the West. What were the real effects of the deaths in 1951 of King Abdullah of Jordan and Liaqat Ali Khan of Pakistan, for example? There is no way of knowing. But in any event it seems highly unlikely that assassination seriously

---

nostalgic disenchantment. Of course, it is true that Nasser was not assassinated, but died a natural death. Yet he had died without warning, and his death had much the same impact as it would have had had he been assassinated.

[39] The wave of terrorism, kidnappings, and murder flooding western Europe in the late 1970s is surely evidence of this.

affected the ongoing sociopolitical patterns. On the other hand, there is no doubt that such action has occasionally re-oriented change, sometimes speeding it up, and sometimes radicalizing it. Probably at most such action adds just one more element to the turbulent adventure called politics in the Middle East.

The most obviously important element of political violence in the Middle East is the phenomenon of military interven-tion resulting in the coup d'etat. One version of the Egyptian constitution contained the admonition to the army to strike should the nation's honor be threatened; such constitutional authorization seems to be needed rarely by those "young" offi-cers who are impatient for change and see themselves as the vehicle for dramatic improvement of the lot of their country-men.

Colonel Qaddafi of Libya seems in many ways untypical (certainly if contrasted with, say, a Gen. Muhammad Ayub Khan), yet there is much about him that is characteristic of those who make coups. He appears to be impetuous and im-patient. He has quite obviously fed upon ideology and found it palatable. He is eager to remake not only Libya — a task that might be feasible — but the Arab world. Yet, however confident he is of his competence to perform the tasks of political and economic rejuvenation, he is not altogether pre-pared to assume them. (This is generally but not wholly true of coup officers. Some Egyptian officers involved in the 1952 coup proved to be highly competent in civilian bureaucratic matters.) He is puritanical and may mistake the symbols of things for their substance. It is possible that he will survive long enough to learn how to survive even longer (probably he has already done so), although occasionally, when there have been ripples of discord in his cabinet, the world has expected him to be toppled. (In the spring of 1978, he was the target in an assassination attempt that resulted in the death of sev-eral visiting East German officials.)

Whether Qaddafi is typical or not, enormous amounts of national resources (in one country or another) are wasted in the process of permitting young army officers to experiment with their nation's destinies. Quite obviously, political change — although not always political development — is modified, stymied, given tangential thrusts, perhaps on occasion even enhanced by the accidental nature of the junta in power. This kind of change is an expensive, inefficient, haphazard process. Little can be said for it except that sometimes it works. Sometimes army intervention is the only way that a country like Yemen can get into the twentieth century; yet in many ways the Sallal coup in Yemen failed. Whatever Faisal's or Khalid's virtues as a modernizer, would Saudi Arabia have been further along the road to modernization, and especially to political development, under some young Saudi colonel?[40]

Revolution is a unique phenomenon, and thorough revolution is rare in the Middle East. It requires time; a sympathetic, yet patient, population; and radically oriented political leaders who can maintain themselves in power with modest investments of energy, reserving their greatest resources for the revolutionary changes they desire to bring about. These leaders must be properly inspired and must have the vision to see beyond immediate political demands and benefits. Revolution often, although not invariably, occurs in areas where there are no foreign involvements. Whatever else he was, Atatürk in Turkey was an isolationist; he was also the greatest Middle Eastern revolutionary in the twentieth century. With regard to Nasser, it is difficult to claim that his unending confrontations with the Israelis, as well as his adventures in Yemen and elsewhere, were very conducive to revolutionary change at home. Nevertheless, he was a revolutionary, and fundamental changes in the fabric of Egyptian life were wrought under his inspiration.

The Middle East is in a state of ferment. The political process has not yet been tamed, and violence is often a part of its ways of seeking change. One must view all of Middle Eastern politics from this perspective.

[40] In a private interview in 1970, the prime minister of Iran bitterly stated that if all the reforms being implemented in that society were introduced by some colonel, then Iran would be praised the world over. Since Iran is a monarchy, however, observers are unfairly critical. The prime minister's comments indicate that monarchical elites are quite conscious of their eroding positions at a time when larger and larger numbers of people clamor for both modernization and political development. Personal interview with one of the authors (Bill), Tehran, 5 December 1970.

CHAPTER VII

The Imprint of Ideology

THE NEED FOR LEGITIMATION

The process of legitimation is very complex.[1] The need for legitimation of whatever authority has been established in a political system is, however, readily apparent to the most ordinary middle-grade army officer who engineers a coup. Most of the decisions promulgated in any political system are accepted, not because of the application of naked force, but because they seem to be made by legitimate authority and are enveloped in an aura of legitimacy. Governments that have little actual force at their disposal often linger long after their ability to coerce has vanished. Thus, the regime of King Farouk in Egypt was moribund long before it fell in 1952, but it had considerably greater legitimacy than power, and it was, until

---

[1] The modern analysis of the process of legitimation really begins with Max Weber. In any system there are those in authority, whatever the method they have used to secure that authority. The stability of their authority position is facilitated to the degree that they are able to convince those whom they rule that they rule because they ought to rule, should rule, must rule, would be failing in their responsibility if they did not rule, and justly rule. In short, they rule because their position is a legitimate one. Coup leaders rule because they have been successful in seizing power; they seek legitimacy by doffing their uniforms and abandoning their military rank, by submitting their rule to referenda (usually carefully controlled), by seeking the approbation of other centers of legitimate authority (religious leaders, kings, or parliaments), by emphasizing their attachment to traditional or cherished symbols, and, of course, in a myriad of other ways. See "legitimacy" in Julius Gould and William L. Kolb, eds., *A Dictionary of the Social Sciences* (New York: Free Press, 1964). See also Michael C. Hudson, *Arab Politics, The Search for Legitimacy* (New Haven: Yale University Press, 1977).

its demise, a functioning system. A similar statement could be made about the regime of King Idris in Libya (overthrown in 1969), although that regime was less colored by corruption than Farouk's had been.

All political elites attempt to maintain their legitimacy and, if possible, to increase it. Every revolutionary government immediately seeks to establish legitimacy; where it is unsuccessful in doing this, its life is usually short, and some more successful claimant takes its place.

Every government attempts to increase the sense of its legitimacy on the part of its population. There are a variety of methods of doing this, including the steady application of power, the recourse to symbols, and the constant verbal reiteration of the government's position. We are particularly interested in this chapter with this verbal umbrella of political solidification. Often facilitated by a controlled or at least a docile press, the government leaders unleash a barrage of arguments, exhortations, appeals, promises, statements of principles, and so on. Wherever possible, these ideas are related by their proponents to already *accepted* notions or *cherished* ideas or *popular* individuals. Gradually this mishmash of argument may assume some semi-organized and rational form; it is then called ideology. Ideology is the most important manifestation of the legitimizing process. What is the role of ideology in the Middle East, and how is it connected with the processes of modernization and political development?

THE NATURE OF IDEOLOGY

Ideology is a widely used term[2] that connotes those congeries of beliefs and assertions that rationalize behavior patterns.[3]

---

2 The literature on ideology is not voluminous. For interesting commentary on the historical development of the term, see the leading essay in George Lichtheim, *The Concept of Ideology and Other Essays* (New York: Random House, 1967). See also Karl Mannheim, *Ideology and Utopia* (London: Routledge and Kegan Paul, 1936); David Apter, ed., *Ideology and Discontent* (New York: Free Press of Glenco, 1964); Gustav Bergmann, "Ideology," *Ethics* 61 (1951):205–18; and the articles by Edward Shils and Harry M. Johnson in the *International Encyclopedia of the Social Sciences*, new ed. (New York: The Free Press, 1968); Max Mark, *Modern Ideologies* (New York: St. Martin's Press, 1973); and Lewis S. Feuer, *Ideology and the Ideologists* (New York: Harper and Row, 1975).

It seems to be necessary to justify all of one's acts. These rationalizing explanations constitute ideology; the beliefs themselves, of course, need not be true, nor need they be consistent or logical. But these beliefs ought to be persuasive, particularly to the populace. Ideology has always been crucial to politics. It exists in an infinite variety of forms. One puts together a personal ideology as a hotchpotch of what one has heard and read. But one may also accept large chunks of preformed ideology from the sources of propaganda: the government of the day (both its official and unofficial organs), the religious spokesmen, and, in general, the spokesmen for various interest groups.

The absorption of ideology is facilitated by the growth of communications media. Even the call to prayer in the Middle East is today in many places electronic. The raucous radio in the coffee shops; the newer television sets in the big cities; the gaudy collection of newspapers, magazines, and placards; the amplified speech — all of these today permit Middle Eastern governments to communicate more readily to their peoples, to propagandize, to ideologize. The dissemination of ideology is

---

[3] Julius Gould says, "Ideology is a pattern of beliefs and concepts (both factual and normative) which purport to explain complex social phenomena with a view to directing and simplifying socio-political choices facing individuals and groups." Gould and Kolb, *A Dictionary*, p. 315. Chalmers Johnson makes similar points very well when he says: "No revolution ever occurred without ideology. It is one thing for a citizen to think he knows *why* a revolution is needed; it is quite another to know *how* to go about making a revolution and to know *what* to put in place of the institutions that revolutionary violence destroys. Some people have argued that the revolutionary is like Hercules: having cleaned the Augean Stables, he is under no obligation to fill them up again [Nasser believed this at first]. As a matter of fact, he always does so, obliged or not [as indeed Nasser quickly learned]. Revolutionary ideology supplies answers to the questions why, how and what — that is to say, it offers a critique of present conditions, a strategy for the use of political violence in order to change those conditions, and a vision of an improved society. It is of course true that leaders and adherents of revolutionary movements are influenced by a variety of motives, and that for an observer to rely solely on an understanding of their shared ideology in trying to explain their behavior would be folly. The problem obviously is not either to ignore or to fixate on the role of ideology in politics but to conceptualize it properly and to study it as one input into the overall processes of political cognition and motivation." *Autopsy on People's War* (Berkeley: University of California Press, 1973), p. 114.

one of the main forces of legitimation and as such is one of the chief functions of any government, whether it be stable or revolutionary, democratic or autocratic.

Much of the energy of Middle Eastern governments is spent in the dissemination of ideology and in the denunciation of alien ideologies. Because at any one time a fair share of the Middle Eastern political systems are run by military adventurers, Middle Eastern ideologies tend at times to be piecemeal and makeshift. And since the Middle East is in the midst of modernization and change, ideologies there tend to reflect the rapid alteration of values. Finally, due to the turmoil (much coming from the unending Arab-Israeli confrontation) that characterizes so much of the area, Middle Eastern ideologies are often extremist and violent in tone.

Ideology plays an important role in the formation of political culture, the process of political integration, and the development of "public opinion." Dankwart Rustow refers to ideologies as the "foundations of politics" in his brief comparative study of Middle Eastern political systems.[4] He develops, as the main themes of Middle Eastern ideology: nationalism, communism, and the issues of monarchies against republics, traditionalism against persistent change, "monism" against pluralism, and religion against secularism. On the other hand, Robert Springborg suggests in a perceptive article[5] that the old ideologies are dead. He suggests that the "center of gravity of newly emerging isms may be labeled, depending in part on the observer's normative evaluation, as conservatism, liberalism, pragmatism, realism, or, what to some may not have an entirely pejorative connotation, opportunism. That which might fit equally well is the opprobrious title of *wasatiya* (middlism) given to Nasserism by the leftist theorist, Sadek al-Azm. Middlism implies, among other things, falling between the two stools of secularism and religion and, at least in the

---

4 *Middle Eastern Political Systems* (Englewood Cliffs, N.J.: Prentice-Hall, 1971).

5 "On the Rise and Fall of Arab Isms," *Australian Outlook* 31 (1977): 92–109. Of the old ideologies, he says, "Arab nationalism, Arab socialism, Nasserism, and positive neutralism now evoke thoughts of dust covered anthologies on library shelves, whereas less than a decade ago they were provocative Arab battles cries" (p. 92).

case of Nasserism, might more accurately have been termed obscurantism."[6] We shall return to these themes below.

IDEOLOGY IN THE MIDDLE EAST

Even in the most quiescent and stable system, there are sources of new ideology. In the Middle East, the turbulence of continued revolution, the frenetic and emotional struggles with modernity, the impacts of alien resources and demands, and the continuing uncertainty of political settlements all make the area alive with ideological fermentation. But what is the general nature of this ideology?

Middle Eastern ideology reflects both the concerns of the area as a whole and the very particular concerns of its political subdivisions. There are considerable overtones of religion in the ideologies of the Middle East. Surprisingly, since the country had in a sense a religious birth this is less true in Israel than in some of the other countries, but even in Turkey the religious themes are never wholly absent. It is believed that men are better because they are Muslims and that governments are better because their behavior accords with Islamic morality. Islam offers the best path to modernization and its achievements, or, for others, the best return to an earlier, better day. All that men can aspire to can be found in Islam; thus Jamal al-Din al-Afghani found in Sura 42 (line 36) of the Quran the justification for a democratic consultative assembly.[7] Man should want things because they are countenanced by God and should move to action to achieve them. There is a tremendous

[6] Ibid., p. 92. The quotation concludes, "Certainly Nasserism and the present strand of political thought I am trying to identify share the schizophrenic tendency made necessary by a dual society of addressing secular appeals to the secular and religious appeals to the faithful, but then it is only those who are content to be permanently on the sidelines of Arab politics who opt entirely for one or the other. The middlism of Nasserism, however, to the extent that it rested on anything and did not entirely fall between two stools, was based on the success of emotive Arab nationalism and Arab unity, which were in the final analysis both strategies and tactics for confronting imperialists and neo-imperialists and their lackeys in the area."

[7] Majid Khadduri develops this point at length in his *Political Trends in the Arab World: The Role of Ideas and Ideals in Politics* (Baltimore: Johns Hopkins Press, 1970), pp. 28–32. This valuable book deals very directly with the question of ideology.

reservoir of religious will among the peasantry and the urban poor. The newer middle and managerial classes are less overtly religious, but they still couch ideological aspirations in religious terms.

Ideology often carries overtones of what might be termed "identity resolution." The Arabs constantly ask themselves, Who am I? and What is an Arab? Their constant questioning suggests a modern uncertainty concerning identity. Do Arabs really exist? If those so labeled keep conjuring up reassurances for themselves, apparently they do, but what are they? And what connections do they have with Arabs in times past? The answer, of course, is ideological. The Arabs imagine that they are as they would like to be and emphasize historical associations that they find currently comfortable. They are by no means alone in this. The Persians recently celebrated (1971) their twenty-five hundredth anniversary of monarchical rule, although what they really have in common with the ancient Medes and Persians is somewhat uncertain. Some Turks, too, (since Kemal Atatürk's time, at least) have tried to identify themselves with the Qaramanids, the Ottomans, and other distinguished forebears. Most uncertain of all Middle Eastern peoples in this regard, however, have been the Israelis. Their connection with their ancient counterparts in Palestine is tenuous at best, and yet it is the necessary raison d'être for the modern Israeli state. Israel was founded as a haven for Jews; it is scarcely surprising that who and what Jews are continues to be disputed. But this concern for identity goes far beyond normal discussion. Are we really Jews? If so, what makes us Jews? What are our characteristics? How should we act because we are Jews? Israeli ideology is heavily laden with questions such as these.

Middle Eastern ideology is also highly nationalistic. Nationalism is a product of collective resentment and the sharing of discontent. There are few people in the Middle East who cannot concoct some sort of justification for being resentful against others, usually foreigners, for the malaise of the times, for the chronic underdevelopment of the area, and for their legacy of political and social problems. Nationalistic energy is itself a pseudo-resolution of the problems facing a people, for blaming others makes the unsolved difficulties more palatable. It is manifestly easier to share discontent when people share other things — a living space or a language, for example. One might, without doing too much harm to Ibn Khaldun's original concept, refer to nationalism on the village and tribal levels as *asabiyya*, that sense of togetherness of family and clan that solidified a people against its external environment.

The Middle East is notorious for its artificial spatial boundaries, often drawn at the whim of colonial powers. But whatever their origin, these boundaries sometimes enclose a nationalism of their own, a *wataniyya* nationalism — an Egyptian or a Jordanian nationalism. The strength of these nationalisms rises and falls with the viability of programs and leaders. Egyptians (*qua* Egyptian) nationalism reached a peak before Nasser, fell as his popularity among Arabs (*qua* Arabs) increased, and rose with Nasser's death and the installation of Anwar Sadat as president of Egypt. Certainly in the late 1970s, in the wake of Sadat's visit to Jerusalem and his later adventures at Camp David, it is very strong indeed. Jordanian nationalism has often been weak in the face of Arab nationalism and the appeals of various Palestinian guerrilla groups.

The boundaries of a state may also contain minority groups generating nationalisms of their own. The ideological message they broadcast proclaims the injustice of their lack of independence and demands boundaries coterminous with the areas occupied by their populations. The Kurds in Iraq are an excellent example; so at one time were the Armenians in Turkey. The Palestinian Arabs wherever they are to be found are a similar group.[8] But not all minorities produce identifiable

---

[8] The various Palestinian guerrilla movements have produced an enormous amount of ideology, but all agree in their enmity for Israel and about the necessity to pursue revolutionary activities. For example, in a pamphlet distributed in the United States by the Democratic Popular Front for the Liberation of Palestine (communist-oriented), one finds the conclusion that "the weakness of the Palestinian national movement lies in the fact that its leadership has never adopted the ideology of the working class, but rather expressed the hopes and goals of the petit-bourgeoisie" in a pamphlet entitled *DPFLP* (which are the initials of the movement), p. 9. All of these movements publish pamphlets and various short-lived periodicals. There is a good summary of these movements in Hisham Sha-

nationalistic ideology, even when discriminated against. For example, the Christian Copts of Egypt have little nationalism of their own, although they may embrace Arab nationalism less than enthusiastically.

Sometimes a nationalism splashes over boundaries to form a larger movement. The most noteworthy example of this is, of course, Arab nationalism — *qawmiyya*. Its strength and appeal wax and wane with the vitality of such issues as the Israeli "menace," the cooperativeness of the oil cartels, and the pervasiveness of some cold war.

Nationalistic ideology, then, contains a mixture of these elements, but always contains beliefs about the rightness of the cause, the inevitability of its victory, and the catastrophy to those who impede it. Certainly much of what is interesting in current Middle Eastern ideology flows from its nationalist content.

The Middle East is in the midst of social revolution. Revolution is one of the most potent of the producers[9] of ideology. Even the most modest of coup leaders finds it necessary to justify an illegal and treasonable activity in the palatable terms of defending the constitution, attachment to the people, honor, dignity, or morality. Ideology in this case is merely the rationalization for an action that is expected to increase support for the coup. However naive a coup leader may be, he must offer a program for the future and must lubricate it with appropriate propaganda to insure its acceptance.

The first stage in building an ideology is usually nationalistic. Even in his earliest statements (1969), Qaddafi emphasized his rejection of European colonial exploitation of Libya. One immediate result was the destruction of all non-Arabic public signs in such cities as Tripoli and Benghazi, an act of tremendous symbolic impact, but of little if any practical value. Nevertheless, ideologically, this act emphasized the regime's rejection of nonindigenous values. Qaddafi also trumpeted his support for the Palestinian refugees and the Arab

---

rabi, *Palestine Guerrillas: Their Credibility and Effectiveness* (Washington, D.C.: Georgetown University, 1970).

[9] See Carl Leiden and Karl Schmitt, *The Politics of Violence: Revolution in the Modern World* (Englewood Cliffs, N.J.: Prentice-Hall, 1968), for a discussion of revolutionary ideology.

struggle against Israel. This is a safe ideological stance through-out the Arab world, and it usually costs nothing.

Ideological declarations such as Qaddafi's may not reflect any real goal at all, but rather serve to divert attention from other acts. However, assuming that revolutionary leaders do have ideological goals, these must be packaged for public consumption. In the Middle East, a social revolution is in progress. Its ideology proclaims the need for land reform, the enlargement of the public sector, the liberation of women, the introduction of democracy (of necessity, vague in detail), and, in general, the establishment of some form of "Arab" socialism.

How is ideology disseminated in the Middle East, and to whom is it directed? The national leader always sets the tone and articulates the main themes of what might be called the official ideology. What people already believe is, of course, also largely ideological. But the government's ideology prevails in newspapers, on television, and in other easily controlled channels of communication. When the leader speaks, his remarks may be printed and endlessly rebroadcast. These remarks may be elaborated upon by newspaper editors, official spokesmen, and ministers of "national guidance" for years. In the process of its dissemination, the message often becomes internally inconsistent and many of its parts outdated.

In the United States, much ideology emanates from government sources, but there is also much that comes from the United Auto Workers, the American Medical Association, the American Legion, and a host of other groups, each with its own interests. In contrast, in the Middle East, the major source of ideology is the government of the day and its propaganda organs. Smaller organizations are not always permitted to exist, and when they do exist, they are seldom permitted to pursue ideological ends different from those of the government. Usually they ape the government's views, sometimes endorsing views that may, in fact, be inimical to their own interests. Thus, newspaper editors and publishers have been known to applaud the nationalization of their own newspapers.[10] More-

[10] This occurred, for example, when the Egyptian press was nationalized in the early 1960s.

over, in most Middle Eastern countries, if the press is not owned outright, it is rigidly censored and controlled. The same is true of radio and television broadcasting and of the importation of books and periodicals. What governments do not own, they control, although often inefficiently.

Individuals may reject, alter, or simply ignore an official government ideology. They may even be ignorant of it. In some Middle Eastern countries, lip service only is given to some of the ideological disseminations of the government, not only among the educated but among the peasantry as well. This should hardly be surprising.

Middle Eastern ideologies vary greatly. This might be expected in an area where governments themselves often change. But the policies of a relatively stable regime can also change, sometimes rapidly, and such changes must be justified. Nasser, for example, oscillated between warm friendship and enmity for Jordan's King Husayn. Egyptian newspapers dutifully explained and reiterated Nasser's latest views. Current views may change before earlier ones have been fully disseminated among the rank-and-file and, not unnaturally, this sometimes leads to confusion.

In spite of the many contradictory changes that an official ideology may undergo, it usually has a veneer of plausibility. In some respects it is addressed to an .audience that never exists: a collection of perfectly loyal and passive automatons. But rarely do the existing audiences talk back. What they accept, with whatever degree of pretense, is a rationale for the status quo in both domestic and foreign political programs. Superficially, the ideology often makes sense. It often includes the following notions: (1) A true way, perhaps Jordanian or Turkish or Egyptian, exists. (2) Those who have ruled in the past and those who interfere from without have subverted the true way. (3) Those who now rule or who are about to rule represent a return to the true way and will interpret its provisions in modern times. Of necessity, a glossary of exhortations and explanations is offered. The ideology may draw upon long-accepted traditional values; it may be radical in its orientation and makeshift in its manufacture.

Ideology tends to be vague and ambiguous; after all, it must appeal to large numbers of divergent peoples. Middle Eastern ideology is no exception to this. Goals may be phrased as the "better life," "justice for all," "genuine equality," and the "Islamic spirit." Even in Israel, present policies are justified in terms of eventual "true peace."

Let us examine in some detail several types of Middle Eastern ideology: religion, nationalism, "revolutionary socialism," and neutralism.

THE PATINA OF RELIGION

Religion is itself essentially ideological. In the Middle East, other ideologies have always had to adjust to the religious proclivities of the people. An Arab socialism must be grounded in Islamic history and thought (even if expounded by an Arab Christian). The nationalist propaganda of a country such as Syria or Iraq must conform to the Islamic background. Even the Turkish nationalism of Kemal, essentially secularist, was not as negative towards religion as is sometimes thought. And it is instructive that, with the advent of the Turkish Democrats in 1950, government propaganda took a very religious turn that garnered considerable support from peasantry and others alike.

It is interesting that the presence of Islam is sometimes adduced as evidence for the historical lack of success of ideological communism. The argument made is that communism is godless and therefore of no appeal in Muslim countries. The question whether this is true is simpler to ask than to answer. Partly it hinges on the difficulty of measuring the success of an ideological message. Communism has never been the official ideology of any Middle Eastern state, with the possible exception of Southern Yemen. It has not had the advantages in dissemination that other ideologies have had. Its lack of success, then, may be due to a number of factors, of which the lack of religious emphasis is only one. The "successful" ideologies may or may not be successful because of their religious hue. But, if true, the lack of appeal of communism can only underline the latest religious aspects of ideology in the Middle East.

We have already discussed the role of Islam in Chapter II. H. A. R. Gibb has said, "The history of Islam in the nineteenth and twentieth centuries is a history of revival and efforts at readjustment under the double stimulus of challenge from within and pressing dangers from without. Slowly at first, and not without setbacks but with increasing momentum, the Muslim community has gathered itself together and begun to look to its defenses; reawakened and alert, it is searching for the programme with which to advance united into an unknown and unpredictable future."[11] Majid Khadduri, in a chapter entitled "Revival of Islam," quotes Muhammad: "At the turn of each century there will arise in my nation a man who will call for religious revival."[12] In the twentieth century, several individuals in various parts of the Muslim Middle East saw themselves in this role. Islam was decadent; the Muslim lands were overrun and exploited by foreign powers; the old piety was eroding in the face of contacts with the West.

The most interesting of the reformers was Hasan al-Banna of the Muslim Brotherhood (see Chapter I). Here we are interested in al-Banna and the Brotherhood as contributors to ideology. Al-Banna's original messages, of course, were designed to gain followers and to rally them with enthusiasm. The times were bad and decadent, he claimed, but not so bad that dedicated attachment to the Quran, catalyzed by his own guidance, would necessarily fail to save the Islamic world. By the time of his death (1949), he had gained the support of many thousands; by then, however, his own goals had altered. He was now intrigued with his possible role as the political leader of Egypt. His words had changed over the years; the religious motif in Egyptian ideology now emphasized the imminence of the Muslim victory. In the succeeding years, this, of course, has vanished. The Muslim Brotherhood now plays a much less significant role in the Middle East.[13]

Nonetheless, the Brotherhood left a permanent mark on

11 *Mohammedanism* (London: Oxford University Press, 1950), pp. 165–66.

12 *Political Trends,* p. 55.

13 Springborg, "On the Rise and Fall," has this to say: "Too much water has passed over the dam for the Moslem Brothers or similar fundamentalists to attract committed followings of sufficient size and strength to dominate the semi-secular political systems now established in the Fertile Crescent and North Africa or even the polities of the Arabian Peninsula which are now growing away from their religious past (p. 107).

Middle Eastern ideology. The mass nature of the movement, the popularity of its program, and its longevity even in adversity demonstrated to all the popular doctrinal nerve that it had probed. Contemporary Middle Eastern ideology, official or otherwise, reflects this basic attachment to religion and concern with its values. This is manifestly not due to the existence of the Brotherhood alone; in Egypt, the experience of the Brotherhood merely pointed up a basic ideological bent that already existed. So much that is political becomes embedded in the Middle East in religious themes. Every Muslim movement finds a response, and one like the Muslim Brotherhood generates an enthusiasm that is wholly unexpected by a Westerner. Even in nationalism one finds religious overtones; they were certainly not absent in the Turkish nationalist Ziya Gükalp or in the Arab nationalist Sati al-Husri (noted below).

NATIONALISM

Some of the terminology that we will use in discussing Middle Eastern nationalism has already been introduced.[14] Nationalism refers to a particular type of political behavior; as such, it colors the current strains of ideology in the Middle East. What nationalists preach is, of course, ideology. Nationalism also inspires a prodigious amount of ideology.

The core of any nationalistic ideology is what might be termed lococentricity;[15] the insiders have special qualities and values that set them apart from their neighbors, particularly those considered outsiders. Those insiders who share special

[14] There is, of course, a considerable literature on nationalism, some of it specifically on the Middle East. One of the earliest of the latter is Hans Kohn, *Nationalism and Imperialism in the Hither East* (New York: Harcourt, Brace and Co., 1932). See also Walter Z. Laqueur, *Communism and Nationalism in the Middle East,* 3d ed. (London: Routledge and Kegan Paul, 1961); and Kemal H. Karpat, ed., *Political and Social Thought in the Contemporary Middle East* (New York: Frederick A. Praeger, 1968). For Iran, see Richard W. Cottam, *Nationalism in Iran* (Pittsburgh: University of Pittsburgh Press, 1964). See also Part 6, "Radical Arab Nationalism," in *The Political Awakening of the Middle East,* ed. George Lenczowski (Englewood Cliffs, N.J.: Prentice-Hall, 1970).

[15] The portion *loco* refers not only to the Latin *locus* ("place") but also to the well-established American connotation of eccentricity and madness!

qualities have not always been able to solve their problems — an understatement for most of the Middle East — and the reason, in ideological terms, can only be that they have been prevented from doing so by malignant outside forces. But now that they are free or about to be free — one special quality of nationalistic ideology is that the special people are never really free; they are always combatting their enemies — their true skills will come to the fore, and problems, hitherto unsolvable, will rapidly dissipate.

And whatever adjectives differentiate them from their neighbors must reflect an innate value that must be preserved at all costs. Language is an obvious example of such a value. In the nationalistic Turkey of Atatürk, it was thought necessary to junk the Ottoman Turkish, filled with words borrowed from other languages and expressed in the Arabic alphabet, and produce a pure Turkish. Success in this endeavor was not really possible. It was one thing to rid the language of a cumbersome alphabet (the Arabic) — and this the Turks did — but it was quite another to sell nationalistic neologisms in place of old-fashioned loan words. In the Arab world today there is a frantic effort to elevate Arabic into a modern technical language. Great efforts have been made to put together an Arabic technical literature and to emphasize the worth of the language above all others. And the Israelis have insisted on resurrecting the equally unwieldy Hebrew language. Any explanation of this other than that grounded in nationalism is inadequate.

A great thing, too, is made of the long and rich history that each people possesses. The Turks hark back to their golden ages as do the Persians and Afghans. Even the Israelis, modern and tough as they are, spend an inordinate amount of attention on extolling their historical connection with the Biblical lands. Until recently, the Egyptians were in their Arab phase of nationalism, and so they stressed things Arab. Yet their history is far older than that of the Arabs and far richer. Currently, they have returned to an "Egyptian" phase.

Qawmiyya nationalism did not arise until after the First World War, but there was ample evidence of local, or *wataniyya,* nationalism. The case of Egypt is particularly important as well as interesting. By the late 1870s, Egypt was under the weight of foreign financial and political control. In 1881, an officer named Arabi led a military revolt against the Khedive, Tawfiq, for surrendering his government to foreign influence. The Arabi revolt was put down only by British military intervention, which began an occupation of Egypt that was not to end until 1956. Arabi Pasha was not so much an ideologue as he was a man of action, but his abortive act was to spur a popular indignation and resentment that were to last for many years. Egyptian (*wataniyya*) nationalism had become a major force.

The most important of the early Egyptian nationalist ideologues were Mustafa Kamil and Muhammad Farid.[16] Theirs was the first major Egyptian nationalist party (*al-Hizb al-Watani*) and theirs also were the most articulate and popular of the nationalist newspapers, pamphlets, and books that galvanized Egyptian opinion against the British occupation. Kamil was particularly forceful. Had he lived — he died in 1908 at the age of thirty-four — he might well have acquired sufficient strength to achieve some modicum of Egyptian independence.

By the time of the First World War, the various nationalist groups were beginning to experiment with violence. In 1910, the prime minister, Butrus Ghali Pasha, was assassinated by a nationalist because he had supported a proposal to extend the Suez Canal concession. With the end of the war, new nationalist figures and movements arose. Egypt demanded the right to send a delegation to the peace conference in France. The British strongly resisted this demand; the birth of the Wafd ("delegation") party was the result. Its leader was the incredibly popular Sa'd Zaghlul, but his early death also sapped the nationalist movement of the leadership needed for expelling the British. Egypt was a hotbed of nationalism until the advent of Nasser, but it was a *wataniyya* nationalism rather than a broader Arab nationalism that characterized its politics.

In the Middle East prior to the First World War, the Otto-

---

[16] An excellent article on the early Nationalist party in Egypt is Arthur Goldschmidt, Jr., "The Egyptian Nationalist Party: 1892–1919," in *Political and Social Change in Modern Egypt,* ed. P. M. Holt (London: Oxford University Press, 1968), pp. 308–33.

mans were the outsiders. An Armenian national movement against the Ottoman Turks existed for a time. Although the Kurds were troublesome, they had no national movement of any consequence at this time. In Syria, the Arabs (or a few of them anyway) formed secret societies that were ultimately considered the beginnings of Arab nationalism. In Turkey itself, dissatisfaction with the regime resulted in the Young Turk movement (culminating eventually in a coup d'etat), but at first this nationalism was Ottoman and adherents were expected to be recruited from various minority groups.

The most fervent and interesting nationalisms, however, were the product of the First World War. In Afghanistan, the Afghans fought their third war with the British in a century; with it they achieved their independence. But they quickly sank into quiescence, and there was no articulated (or nationalist) ideology for years.[17] In Iran, a coup in 1921 put a newspaperman and a soldier in power; the soldier, Reza Khan (later Reza Shah), survived.[18] There were many minorities in Iran — Kurds, Azerbaijanis, Baktiyaris, Qashqa'is, Baluchis, Arabs, Turkomen, for example — and all were now urged to follow the *Iranian* nationalism. This early nationalism of Reza Shah was intended, insofar as it was created at all, to facilitate the building of a modern nation. In passing it must be said that, given the foreign exploitation of Iranian petroleum re-

17 This is essentially true notwithstanding the issue of Pushtunistan, which troubled Afghan-Pak relations for years. Pushtunistan (the land of the Pushtus) was in any event not congruent with Afghanistan. The movement failed.

18 The journalist was Sayyid Zia al-Din Tabataba'i (1889–1969). In February 1921, Sayyid Zia plotted and engineered the coup that ultimately brought about the downfall of the Qajar dynasty and the rise of the Pahlavis. Before his death, Sayyid Zia told one of the authors (Bill) that he had planned coups twice before, but it was the third attempt in early 1921 that succeeded (personal interview, 31 October 1966, Sa'adatabad, Iran). Following the coup, Sayyid Zia became prime minister and began instituting dramatic reforms. These policies, which included the imprisonment of 500 of the most important persons in Iran and the recognition of the Soviet regime in Russia, led to the fall of the Sayyid's government after only one hundred days of existence. Sayyid Zia was forced into exile abroad, where he remained for over twenty years. In the political infighting that took place following Sayyid Zia's expulsion, Reza Khan emerged victorious.

sources, the periodic aggressive incursions of Soviet policy into Iranian politics, and the overt military occupation of Iran during the Second World War, there were plenty of targets for nationalist ire.

Nationalism and its ideology reached a peak in Iran during the Musaddiq period. Muhammad Musaddiq was a longtime nationalist leader in Iran, who reached the apogee of his success and influence in the nationalization of the Anglo-Iranian Oil Company in 1951 and then finally fell in a contest with the Shah in 1953. "It is no exaggeration," Cottam remarks, "to say that for the first time in Iran's very long history a national leader had appeared who enjoyed the respect, devotion, and loyalty of the vast majority of politically aware Iranians." The Americans viewed Musaddiq as a highly dangerous and irresponsible radical. The Shah viewed him as scarcely less dangerous; his own position was seriously undermined by the popular reform measures advocated by Musaddiq. But Musaddiq (in Cottam's words) was "obsessed with his struggle against foreign imperialism,"[19] and he was not able to put together a viable domestic program. He was overthrown in 1953. Ideologically, he had strong liberal tendencies within the Iranian context and sought to alter the traditional power base that supported the Shah and the current political institutions. In foreign policy, he was adamant that Iran's resources be developed for its needs, purposes, and goals rather than for the benefit of foreign concessionaries (as indeed had been the case for a very long time).

In Turkey, the nationalist movement is inextricably connected with the name of Kemal Atatürk, the founding hero of the modern Turkish nation. Kemal was an authentic military hero of the First World War who rallied the Turks in the period after the war to oust the occupying Greeks and neutralize the French, the British, and the Italians, who sought to exploit a defeated Turkey. He abolished first the sultanate, then the caliphate, and instituted major social and religious reforms; he also abolished polygamy and the use of Arabic script in writing Turkish; in general, he forged a new

---

[19] Cottam, *Nationalism in Iran,* p. 22.

Turkish (not Ottoman) nation. He led Turkey until his death in 1938. Of course, there was a Kemalism, of which nationalism was only a part, and Kemal himself had a hand in formulating its principles. Kemalism purported to be composed of six ingredients: nationalism, populism, secularism, statism, socialism, and revolutionism. The ideological nature of this statement needs no elaboration. It is interesting that in 1960 when the Turkish army intervened and overthrew the government of Adnan Menderes, they did so on the grounds that the principles of Kemalism were in danger.

Moroccan nationalism was given a boost by the struggle of Abdul Krim for independence in the early 1920s. But it was only with the religious (as well as political) leadership of Muhammad V in later years that Moroccan nationalism developed into a formidable movement with an appropriate accompanying ideology. There was little if any Algerian national movement until the end of the Second World War; much the same could be said of Tunisia. Still less was there either nationalism or its ideology in Libya. Libya was underdeveloped and underpopulated. It fought no war of independence. It was a loosely formed confederation under a Senussi monarch, King Idris. The coup of September 1969 was a surprise; much ideology was generated by it. Revolutionary Libya, under the leadership of Qaddafi, has assumed new responsibilities in the Arab world and is developing a nationalist ideology.

From the point of view of nationalist ideology, Syria offers an interesting case. It had been in Syria before the First World War that early patriotic Arab societies had been formed,[20] and Faisal's Arab contingents had been in the vanguard of Allenby's troops as Damascus had been freed from Turkish rule. Indeed, Faisal attempted to establish himself as king of an Arab Syria, but was militarily ousted by France in 1920 — in the battle of Maysalun. France was merely asserting its claims under wartime agreements with the British. Although France remained in Syria and Lebanon for more than twenty years,

[20] For details, see George Antonius, *The Arab Awakening* (Beirut: Khayat's, 1961).

it was beset with tremendous nationalist agitation there. Syrian nationalists had some difficulty in distinguishing between adherence to a strictly Syrian nationalism and that to an Arab one. The most interesting of the Syrian nationalist ideologues was Antun Sa'ada, founder of the Syrian Social Nationalist party.[21] The party was formed in 1932 when the French still controlled Syria; Sa'ada was executed by the Lebanese in 1949. By that time, he had been compelled to widen the horizons of his nationalism to emphasize its Arab qualities. But at first, he was essentially a Syrian nationalist. "The Syrian nation," he said, "represents the unity of the Syrian people with a long historical past stretching back to prehistoric times . . . [and there is a] psychological superiority of the Syrians, which is not the result of unconstrained mixture [of peoples] but of the superb quality of homogeneous mixing, perfectly in harmony with the type of environment. . . ."[22] The ambivalence in Sa'ada's thinking is reflected in what he wrote:

> The aim of the Syrian Social Nationalist Party is to effect a Syrian national social renaissance capable of achieving its ideals and restoring to the Syrian nation its vitality and power. The party also aims to organize a movement that would lead to the complete independence of the Syrian nation, the consolidation of its sovereignty, the creation of a new system to safeguard its interests and raise its standard of life, and the information of an Arab front. . . . Syria is one of the nations of the Arab world and is fitted for the leadership thereof. . . . Syrian nationalism is the only practical method and the basic prerequisite for Syrian regeneration and the consequent participation of Syria in Arab affairs.[23]

Syrian society demanded reformation. Not unnaturally, given his Christian heritage, Sa'ada insisted in his program of reformation upon a separation of church and state, the lessening of the religious role, the abolition of feudalism with a

[21] See Labib Zuwiyya Yamak, *The Syrian Social Nationalist Party: An Ideological Analysis* (Cambridge: Harvard University Press, 1966) .

[22] This English translation is taken from Karpat, *Political and Social Thought,* pp. 95–96.

[23] Ibid., pp. 96–97. Majid Khadduri (*Political Trends,* p. 192) sums up all this very well in eight principles of Syrian national superiority.

concomitant economic reorganization, and the creation of a strong army.[24]

What is apparent is that Antun Sa'ada began his career as a student deeply concerned about the fate of Syria. As his commitment grew and the popularity of his movement became more apparent, his need was to integrate a purely Syrian movement with the Arab nationalist movement, itself in its infancy. His solution was to speak of Greater Syria, which was to encompass substantially more of the Arab world than the Syrian borders did at that time, and then of the naturalness of Arab leadership's being Syrian. Probably Sa'ada's movement would have gone into eclipse in any case, but his death deprived it of effective leadership. Arabs progressively interested themselves more in Arab nationalism than in Syrian, or Egyptian, or Sudanese, nationalism.

Before discussing Arab nationalism, it is well to note one other local nationalism in the Middle East — Zionism. Ideologically, modern Zionism stems from the late-nineteenth-century efforts of such men as Theodor Herzl, who believed that the solution of the "Jewish question" could exist only in the establishment of a "national home" for the Jewish people.[25] Quite early, twentieth-century Zionists decided that their national home was in Palestine. Here, Jews might at last be in a majority and be able to create their own political future. Men like Herzl, and later Weizmann and Ben Gurion, faced the need to persuade Jews to follow their cause and also to persuade the world and its leaders to permit the experiment to occur. Thus, Zionism was the nationalism of a people widely dispersed and lacking a territory. By 1917, Weizmann had persuaded the British to issue the Balfour Declaration,[26] which stated that the British government "viewed with favor" the establishment in Palestine of a national home for the Jews.

It was not until the rise of Hitler and his pogroms against

24 Karpat, *Political and Social Thought,* pp. 87–94.

25 The literature on Zionism is immense. One of the very best of the books is Ben Halpern's, *The Idea of the Jewish State,* 2d ed. (Cambridge: Harvard University Press, 1969).

26 The major work on this declaration is Leonard Stein, *The Balfour Declaration* (London: Vallentine-Mitchell, 1961).

the Jews that immigration of Jews into Palestine in sufficient numbers could make possible the dream of a *politically autonomous* national home. But these large numbers provoked dissatisfaction among Palestinian Arabs and concomitant uncooperativeness among the British. Ultimately, of course, a Jewish population in Palestine proclaimed the independence of their state, Israel, and then defended it in four wars (1948, 1956, 1967, 1973) against the Arabs. Zionism, in its original sense, is, of course, passé today: the national home has been established and its viability achieved. In its place is Israeli nationalism. Its ideology calls attention to an ancient history, reminds the world of injustices to Jews, denounces Arab accusations of imperialism, sounds a continual tocsin of dangers to Israel and world Jewry, and in general proclaims the superiority of Israeli ideas and programs. In short, it is a typical nationalism. But if Sa'ada could dream of Syrian leadership of a united Arab world, there can be no comparable Israeli dream. The Israelis cannot lead other minorities or their Arab neighbors in a supernationalism.

The most interesting contemporary Middle Eastern nationalism is that of the Arabs, not as Egyptians or Saudis or Libyans, but as Arabs. Although this nationalism still appears today to be deep-seated and significant, it is almost entirely a twentieth-century phenomenon and, indeed, is really a product of the post–Second World War period. Before that war, many young Arabs — those, for example, at the American University in Beirut — identified themselves as Muslims when asked what they were. When pressed further, they might reply that they were Iraqi or Lebanese. In Egypt, before the rise of Nasser as an *Arab* leader, most Egyptians thought of themselves as simply Egyptians and felt little attachment to the Arabs *qua* Arabs in Jordan or Tunisia. Thus, although the roots of Arab nationalism undoubtedly go back another twenty years and more, this nationalism was not a powerful and driving force until later.

The catalyst for the rise of Arab nationalism, *qawmiyya Arabiyya,* was undoubtedly the growth of the Zionist movement in Palestine, culminating in the establishment of Israel in 1948. Nationalism requires a target for its spleen, and although the British, the French, and others filled this role for individual Arab states, no one of these powers could serve satisfactorily for all Arabs. But the Jewish penetration of Arab Palestine could and did serve as just such a target. Israeli success in the war of 1948, fought primarily against Jordan and Egypt, made each of these two societies more aware of its Arabness. In the recriminations after the war, the dissensions and divisions among the Arabs seemed to have been the primary cause of the military defeat. The cry for Arab unity — that is, unity against the invader, the Israelis — began to grow in earnest.

Early Arab nationalism lacked a leader — King Abdullah of Jordan, General Nuri of Iraq, Shukri al-Quwatli of Syria, King Farouk of Egypt, King Abdul Aziz Ibn Saud of Saudi Arabia, none of these would do — until the Egyptian revolution in 1952. The titular leader of the coup, Gen. Muhammad Naguib, turned out not to be that leader either. It was not until the rise of the tremendously popular Nasser, whose charisma and success against the British pushed him permanently into a position of prominence and adoration, that Arab nationalism and the drive for Arab unity became the rallying cry of nearly all Arabs.

The uneven drive for Arab unity can be seen in a number of recent attempts at cross-national political integration. Syria and Egypt formed the United Arab Republic in February 1958 (to be dissolved in 1961); a few days later, the Arab Federation (of Jordan and Iraq) was formed (to last until July 1958). The United Arab Republic plus Yemen became for a time the United Arab States. In 1971, Libya, Egypt, and Syria formed the Federation of Arab Republics. In 1973, Libya and Egypt were to "merge." Most of the attempts at integration stemmed largely from the disgrace of defeat at Israeli hands — by 1958, twice — and the realization that only a united Arab front could defeat Israel; all collapsed because the forces of disunity were still paramount in the 1950s and 1960s. The existence of Israel was not in itself sufficient to create a durable and effective unity.

But regardless of the practical inability of the Arabs to unite or to defeat the Israelis, Arab nationalism became the political force of the Arab world and an ideology quickly blossomed to give it élan. No Arab leader was immune to its lure or to the dangers of disregarding it. Let us briefly examine some of this nationalist ideology and note its main themes.[27]

Abd al-Rahman al-Kawakibi was one of the precursors of *Arab* nationalism. Writing at the turn of the century about the Arabs and their qualities, he said, among other things, that the Arabian peninsula was favored by God, that "of all countries it is the most free of racial, religious, or sectarian intermixture . . . [the] most worthy to be a land of free men. . . ." These Arabs, he claimed, "are the most ancient of nations in having a polished civilization, as is shown by the proliferation and the excellence of their wisdom and their literature." The Arabic language, he asserted, "takes greatest care of knowledge." The Arabs have practiced "equality of rights" from the earliest of times and have always believed in the "principle of consultation in public matters." Needless to say, he claimed (in a very modern utterance) that the "Arabs know best, of all people, the principles of Socialist living."[28] Al-Kawakibi wrote in a popular religious newspaper, and his audience was in some ways a peculiar one; moreover, in the same period one could find similar statements in the American press about the Americans. Nevertheless, it is the ideological stuff of nationalism. Arabs are the best, with the best history, the greatest potentialities for all that is itself best. The theme was often repeated in later years, although usually in more sophisticated forms.

Who are the Arabs? Are they merely those who speak Arabic or who identify themselves as such? According to the First Arab Students' Congress in 1938 in Brussels, the Arabs are those "who are Arab in their language, culture, and loyalty." Who else? The Arab homeland is "a sacred heritage." Arabs feel "the necessity of independence and unity"; hence, Arab nationalism.[29] The new Arabs have awakened and press on to

---

[27] For introductory commentary, see Hans E. Tütsch, *Facets of Arab Nationalism* (Detroit, Mich.: Wayne State University Press, 1965) .

[28] Quotations from Sylvia G. Haim, ed., *Arab Nationalism: An Anthology* (Berkeley: University of California Press, 1962) , pp. 78–80.

[29] Quotations, ibid., pp. 100–101.

the glorious future, meanwhile proscribing any lesser fanaticisms than Arab nationalism itself.

"Arab nationalism," said Abdulla al-Ala'ili, "is the consciousness of the Arabs of their complete social existence, a consciousness which is internal and not merely external objective knowledge, so that the image of the Arab community as a spiritual and living complex, is everpresent to their conscience. Every Arab must feel with an instinctive compulsion the strong existing connections and ties, in such a way that the community is transferred for him from the externality of life to the internality of the soul."[30]

An interesting figure in the history of Arab nationalism is Sati al-Husri. Born in 1880, he has long contributed to nationalist ideology, but probably experienced his most influential period with the rise of Nasser. He argues that nationalism is nothing more complicated than the merger of the self with the movement that transcends all selves; that is, in the words of Karpat, "he increasingly advocated the fusion of the individual into the nation, even if this meant sacrificing the individual's freedom."[31] He undertook the rationalization of this fusion, or self-identification, in terms of religious mysticism. He has been popular and influential in the modern Arab world as the fortunes of its struggle for unity have waned.

It is surprising — or is it? — how many propagandists of Arab nationalism, even Christian Arabs, find it useful to extol the distinctive virtues of Islam. Islam is something the Arabs really claim for themselves, however many other peoples may be Muslim as well; after all, Muhammad, whatever else he was, was an Arab.

Those who are Arab nationalists often suggest that foreign powers are to blame for all that is bad and unfortunate in the Arab world. Charles Malik, a distinguished Lebanese scholar, was not above saying: "The Western world is responsible for

---

[30] Quotation, ibid., p. 120.

[31] Karpat, *Political and Social Thought*, p. 55. Karpat includes a selection from al-Husri's writings, as does Sylvia G. Haim in her *Arab Nationalism*. For an excellent study of the life and thought of al-Husri, see William L. Cleveland, *The Making of an Arab Nationalist* (Princeton, N.J.: Princeton University Press, 1971).

the situation in the Near East on every level of that situation."[32] He goes on to accuse the West of a lack of unity, responsibility, sincerity, understanding, and love.[33] Although this accusation is probably not untrue with respect to the West's attitude toward the Middle East, it does not explain, as the nationalist insists it does, all of the defects of the area.

Yet the Arab nationalist also argues that whatever the problems, Arab nationalism will solve them. Moral fervor and attachment to the eternal ideals of the Arab nation will somehow lessen the contemporary agony of political crisis and economic stagnation. This is the way of all nationalism.

To whom are these ideological pleas addressed? To some degree, to audiences that do not exist. In no political community is there a sharp division between the makers of ideology, whose attachment to the details of their ideology is questionable, and the absorbers of ideology, the masses of people waiting for a message and the opportunity to demonstrate in its favor. Ideology is produced by the interactions of persons, of elites and masses, of intellectuals and nonintellectuals. It is the hypostatization of emotional ideals, the natural idealistic exaggeration of beliefs. No one quite believes his own ideology! But it is useful to him, perhaps in his search for identity, to lose himself in the immensity of a faith that he does not quite believe. The matter is far too complicated to go into fully here, but the faithlike qualities of ideology are well known; the psychology of its true believers is yet to be fully investigated. Moreover, exaggeration as a polemical device is often effective. Men will applaud and follow those who do not equivocate, even where equivocation would be rational. Political leaders, the wielders of ideology, must generally go where applause leads them. Elite and masses, then, invariably find themselves together out on the ideological limb.

An important point remains to be made:

As Richard Pfaff astutely observed . . . the ultimate function of Arab nationalism would not be to unite the Arab states, but to serve as an ideological bridge in the nation building process

[32] Quotation, Karpat, *Political and Social Thought,* p. 220.
[33] Ibid., pp. 221–22.

between independence and the rise of state-based nationalisms. Seemingly it has performed that function and is now receding as Egyptian, Syrian, Iraqi, and other Arab nationalisms continue to capture the political imaginations of ever larger numbers of citizens. This change in identification from the Arab *ummah* (total Arab community) to individual Arab states has as its most important consequence the increasing imperviousness of the citizens of the various Arab states to appeals from beyond the borders. Nasserism is a waning pan-Arab force not only because its founder died, but also because it increasingly is foundering on the rocks of Syrian, Iraqi, and other nationalisms. In turn, the political elites of these countries now need worry less about their popular support being undercut by charismatic foreigners; hence it can be expected that the defensiveness formerly so manifest in the Syrian, Iraqi and other Arab elites will gradually give way to self-confidence based on the successful completion of the state and nation building processes.[34]

Even in collapse, if the persuasive Pfaff-Springborg thesis is to be believed, Arab nationalism has facilitated the local development of *wataniyya*. Should the Arab-Israeli dispute diminish in force, this development would emerge even more strongly.

Arab Socialism. This volume, if it has a theme, points up the vast political change occurring in the contemporary Middle East. Some of this change, such as that resulting from many of the successive coups in Syria and Iraq, is superficial, but much of it is increasingly deep-seated and substantial. Social revolutions of one sort or another have occurred in Egypt and Turkey, and in Iran the Shah has introduced his White Revolution. Moreover, in most of the rest of the Middle East, revolution in the form of violent exchanges of personnel and policy has been a common occurrence.

Twentieth-century social revolution is largely *socialistic;* little wonder that socialism has had a profound ideological impact upon the Middle East. But everywhere in the world,

[34] Springborg, "On the Rise and Fall," p. 101. Springborg refers to Pfaff's observations in "The Function of Arab Nationalism," *Comparative Politics* 2 (1970) :158–59.

socialism has acquired an adjective: Russian socialism, Chinese socialism, African socialism, Arab socialism.[35] In the Middle East and Black Africa at least, the reason for this appears to be the need to find ideological roots in the past.

It would seem to many that Arab socialism was the personal creation of President Nasser in Egypt, but this is mistaken. The genius of Nasser was that he was generally attuned to what was in the air, and his greatest successes were the articulation of already half-formed and popular doctrines.[36] Yet there is no doubt that he contributed to the popularity of Arab socialism and spread its name and features far more widely among the Arabs than would otherwise have been possible.

The Arabic word for "socialism" is *ishtirakiyya*.[37] Socialist doctrine was disseminated and socialist movements existed in the Middle East prior to the Second World War.[38] Socialist and communist movements were in early stages of maturation in Palestine by 1919, Egypt by 1920, Syria and Lebanon by 1930, Iraq by 1932, and Jordan by 1935.[39] But the links between Arab Socialism and these early traditional socialist movements are not strong.

Arab socialism has its roots in (1) the educational experi-

[35] An invaluable source has been *Arab Socialism: A Documentary Survey*, by Sami A. Hanna and George H. Gardner (Leiden: E. J. Brill, 1969).

[36] Hanna and Gardner (ibid., p. 23) quote Fayez Sayegh most appropriately in this regard: "In whatever direction [Nasser] has pursued his policies — be it agrarian reform or socialism, Arab unity or neutralism — he has merely put into effect what many other Arabs before him had longed for. Corresponding to every element of 'Nasserism' there had been prior Arab ideas, longings, dreams. But dreams they had remained, for the most part until Nasser succeeded in transforming them into tangible reality. . . . This is especially true of socialism as an essential element of the revolutionary Arab Nationalism which prevails in the Arab world today." (Original citation: "The Theoretical Structure of Nasser's Socialism," *St. Antony's Papers*, pp. 9–10.)

[37] This Arabic term actually means something more than socialism. Literally, it means "to share," "to become a partner with others." And it carries moral overtones.

[38] Rather indispensable for the early period is Laqueur, *Communism and Nationalism*. See also Sepehr Zabih, *The Communist Movement in Iran* (Berkeley: University of California Press, 1966); and George S. Harris, *The Origins of Communism in Turkey* (Stanford: The Hoover Institution on War, Revolution and Peace, 1967).

[39] Laqueur, *Communism and Nationalism*, passim.

ences of the Arab intellectuals in the 1920s and 1930s and their imbibing of traditional socialist doctrine; (2) the ideological creations of such movements as the Ba'th, and such writers as Michel Aflaq and Salama Musa; (3) Nasser's early experiences at Bandung (1955) and with such figures as Tito, Nehru, Chou En-lai, and Nkrumah; and (4) the need for reform and the natural tendency to reject traditional political and economic values. In any event, socialism was in the wind throughout the developing world, and it was hardly surprising that Nasser would give it his ideological blessing. At the same time, the traditional organizations were often outlawed and pushed underground, as in Egypt where all party opposition was prohibited. And, years later, in 1971, Anwar Sadat, as Egypt's president, continued to argue that Egyptians did not want class struggle; rather, he said, they wanted unity.

Nasser said: "Democracy is political liberty; socialism is social liberty; the two cannot be separated. They are the two wings of true freedom, without which, or without either of which, freedom cannot soar up to the horizons of the anticipated tomorrow."[40] Socialism is, according to Nasser, the pursuit of sufficiency, justice, and freedom.[41] Sufficiency is nothing more complicated than acquiring enough of the world's goods to give substance to life. As Sayegh says, "Only the vigorous, methodical pursuit of sufficiency, . . . can make possible the establishment of social justice and meaningful equality of opportunity."[42] Not only Egypt, but the entire Arab world, was underdeveloped, notwithstanding the huge petroleum deposits in some of the Arab states. And even where petroleum was extracted, few Arab states (at least until the 1970s) had derived either a very fair share of its value or much benefit from the use of royalties from its sale. In Egypt, Nasser struck first at the Suez Canal Company in 1956, whose revenues had been but little shared with Egypt. The acquisition of the canal and the use of its revenues to help build the High Dam at Aswan

[40] Actually in *The Charter for National Action*, Chapter 5 (1961). Quotation noted in Fayez Sayegh, reprinted in Hanna and Gardner, *Arab Socialism*, p. 108.

[41] Hanna and Gardner, ibid., p. 108.

[42] Quoted in ibid., p. 109.

did help build sufficiency. But nationalization and sequestration of properties proceeded in other areas of Egypt and ultimately in other parts of the Arab world. These corrected not insufficiency, but maldistribution. This is surely evident in the much vaunted land reform in Egypt (and later in Iran). Land reform in itself solves no problems in sufficiency; indeed the gross agricultural product may be lower because of the breakup of natural agricultural producing units.[43] But this, too, had become a part of socialism.

By justice, Nasser meant "freedom from exploitation and the enjoyment of an equal opportunity to develop one's abilities and to receive a fair share of the national wealth";[44] this philosophy is attractive, especially to those who will never have that fair share. But one should not criticize blindly. What does justice mean but the attempt to reach for ideals such as these? To Nasser they were an inescapable part of Arab socialism.

Freedom, to Nasser, meant "participation in the shaping of the nation's destiny."[45] Again an ideal? Perhaps, but not quite. Although the Fabian Socialists in England had many years before conceived, as their socialist goal, the enfranchisement of more people and the creation of a more representative parliament, Nasser's views on *participation* were perhaps somewhat more parochial. Participation eventually meant symbolic participation; it meant participating in mass rallies and demonstrations (and often meant being trucked into the big cities for this purpose); it meant holding membership in whatever national political organizations were formed (i.e., the Arab Socialist Union); it meant voting enthusiastically for the policies of the regime. Even Nasser's successor, Anwar Sadat, finds it necessary to build illusory majorities, such as the 98 percent support claimed for the *new* constitution in the fall of 1971 or later the referendum of support in 1978.

Arab socialism in Egypt has at least been the rubric under which much social and economic reform has been planned.

43 For a general discussion of land reform, see Doreen Warriner, *Land Reform in Principle and Practice* (Oxford: Clarendon Press, 1969). See also idem, *Land Reform and Development in the Middle East* (London: Oxford University Press, 1962); and Gabriel S. Saab, *The Egyptian Agrarian Reform, 1952–1962* (London: Oxford University Press, 1967).

44 Hanna and Gardner, *Arab Socialism,* p. 108.

45 Ibid., p. 108.

The position of women has improved — Iraq and Egypt were the first Arab states to have female cabinet ministers — limitations on incomes have been instituted, and workers have been given membership on governing boards of industry. Controlled rents, attempts at controlled prices, the introduction of agricultural cooperatives, the beginnings of health services in remote villages — all of these and many more reforms have been introduced under the aegis of socialism.

But, however many genuine steps toward reform were undertaken, ideology remained the vanguard. All problems were to be solved by the combination of Arab socialism and Arab nationalism; at times, the ideological line between these two grew vague. And the emphasis was always Arab; it was not merely socialism that was being adopted but a very special variant — Arab socialism.

The limitations of space prevent us from discussing this movement to the degree that it deserves. But before leaving the subject of Arab socialism, a word must be added about the Syrian party, the Arab Ba'th.[46] The Ba'th is a remarkable party, one of the few genuine indigenous parties in the Middle East. It was founded by Michel Aflaq and Salal al-Din al-Bitar in 1943. In later years, Aflaq became a leading theoretician of Arab socialism, although it was always labeled Ba'th socialism. To Aflaq, Arab socialism is a product of Arab, not European, history,[47] and it is "an alternative method of attack on the problems of modern society, a middle way between capitalism and communism."[48] Ba'thist ideology is nationalistic and is "a means by which Arab glory can be regained."[49] At the same time, Aflaq argues that socialism can come to all Arabs only when their dreams for unity have been realized.

[46] In English, sometimes called the Arab Ba'th Socialist party, sometimes the Arab Resurrection Socialist party. Its constitution, discussed in the text, can be found in Haim, *Arab Nationalism,* pp. 233–41 (translated from the French). This translation is reproduced in Kamel S. Abu Jaber, *The Arab Ba'th Socialist Party: History, Ideology, and Organization* (Syracuse, N.Y.: Syracuse University Press, 1966), pp. 167–74. In Hanna and Gardner, *Arab Socialism,* pp. 305–12, is to be found another version, translated by Leonard Binder and originally published in *The Middle East Journal* 13 (1959):195–200.

[47] Abu Jaber, *The Arab Ba'th,* p. 99.

[48] Ibid., p. 100.

[49] Ibid., p. 101.

As for Marxists, Aflaq explicitly rejects the class struggle and most other doctrinal positions. The Ba'thists believe that their "socialism will come about as a result of the conviction of the majority of the people, that socialism answers the need for a moral and just order in society."[50]

An examination of the Ba'thist Constitution reveals some of the multifarious concerns of its members over the years. The first paragraphs are utter nationalism and reveal, if anything, the desire to move away from all things that were associated with colonial practices. It is only with article 26 that Arab socialism is revealed. Land reform (or redistribution) is called for (article 27); exploitation of labor is denounced (article 28). "Public utilies, enterprises based on great natural resources, large-scale industries, and means of transport are the property of the nation to be administered directly by the State. All (relevant) foreign companies and concessions are to be abolished" (article 29).[51] The owners of small industries are to be regulated, although their property is not necessarily to be confiscated (article 31). Article 32 is important: "The workers will be associated with the administration of [their] factory, and the sum of their wages will be determined by the state in proportion, also to be determined by the state, to the value of their work."[52] Anyone can own buildings, but not anyone can rent them to others (article 33); not surprisingly in a Muslim community, inheritance rights are protected (article 34). No one can lend at interest any longer (except, it is implied, state banks) (article 35).[53] In the section labeled Social Policy, the party establishes its claims in maintaining the sanctity of the family and in encouraging the propagation of children; it intends to raise the standards of public health, and other aspects of the welfare state. It also supports the maintenance of the freedoms of speech and the press (within limits!), and the development of education.

The Ba'th was the vanguard of socialism in the Arab world before the rise of Nasser, and its constitution is the manifesto

---

50 Ibid., p. 105.

51 Binder's translation, Hanna and Gardner, *Arab Socialism*, p. 309.

52 Ibid., p. 309. This is certainly unlike the socialism of the West.

53 By 1978, the Saudis had established an interest-free bank that would share in the profits made from the money lent.

of the socialist revolution there. (But one should compare the Egyptian National Charter [1962], the Statute of the Arab Socialist Union of Egypt [1961], and the Egyptian Constitution [1964] with the Ba'thist Constitution and other modern Arab constitutions.) [54] It might be added that today both Iraq and Syria claim to have Ba'thist governments (although Aflaq is loyal to Iraq) ; not unnaturally, given current Arab politics, these two Ba'thist regimes are often at loggerheads.

It is difficult to overstate the importance of socialism (of which Arab socialism is but one variety) in the ideological coloration of the Middle East. Much is done in its name; much more is promised as its inevitable results. But several important points stand out. Most Middle Eastern socialism is pragmatic rather than doctrinal. It is usually connected with nationalism. Its origins are always given in local terms, and its character is inevitably derived from local history and customs.

COMMUNISM

Communism in some ways has not really been a major ideological force in the Middle East. There are no major states in the area that label themselves Marxist as Cuba does, for example.[55] Currently there are no major Communist parties anywhere in the area; Communist leadership is not particularly noteworthy. Even in Egypt, where the Soviet presence was the most noticeable, the Communists themselves were harassed and often imprisoned.

There has been continuing discussion of the possible reasons for the poor acceptance of communist ideology in the Middle East, at least of that emanating from the Soviet Union.[56] There are those who believe that communism, because it is atheistic, could never be compatible with Islam; there are also those who believe that this is largely irrelevant to the ques-

---

[54] The Egyptian documents are in Hanna and Gardner, *Arab Socialism*.

[55] Perhaps one should except Southern Yemen, whose rulers proclaim their Marxism. And in Dhofar (Oman) , Chinese-supported rebels fought for some time the forces of Sultan Qabus.

[56] Manfred Halpern sums up the various arguments quite well in his *The Politics of Social Change in the Middle East and North Africa* (Princeton, N.J.: Princeton University Press, 1963), passim (and particularly pp. 156–62) .

tion of its acceptance. Halpern pointed out (in 1963) that "to the degree that tradition survives, the Middle East is unready to receive modern ideas, including communism."[57] This is really more persuasive than the "Islamic bulwark" hypothesis, even if it needs to be qualified. Land reform, neutralism, Arab socialism, and many other things accepted in the Middle East are also "modern," but the difference is that they have been espoused by popular indigenous leaders. There seems to be no compelling reason to assume that communism, ideologically, will never appeal to Middle Easterners or eventually become important in the Middle East. Human beings, despite their cultural differences, are much the same after all and seem equally susceptible to the ideological viruses they encounter.

It is important to note that although there is no strong current communist movement in the Middle East, there have been three occasions since the Second World War when the communists have come within an eyelash of real control. These were in Syria in the late 1950s, in Iran in the early 1950s, and in Iraq during Kassem's regime. Although in the last case one can argue that the communists were as much exploited by Kassem as they were able to exploit in return, it is foolish to minimize the possible results of their success. And it was precisely on these three occasions that covert American intervention was mooted.

Do these instances underline the strength of communist ideological appeal? Only partly. In the Middle East, as elsewhere, a communist movement may evolve out of all proportion to its popular appeal, because of the organizational and political skills of its leaders. But almost any ideology that promises change has some appeal in the Middle East. A communist ideology promises, among other things, a better life through rapid development. The Soviet model is only one of the various communist models of development that has appeal. In Egypt, the Yugoslav model was particularly attractive; today the Chinese model is making inroads in the ideological thinking of many Middle Easterners. Whether or not any particular model is followed by the political elite of any particular

57 Ibid., p. 159.

country, there is no doubt that all communist models point to rapid change, and that is precisely what is so appealing about communism in the Middle East.

Nevertheless, Springborg is not convinced of the viability of the communist alternative:

> . . . improbable is the secular leftist alternative, for while the clock cannot be turned back, neither can it be turned ahead. Given the presence of dual economies, religiously committed peasant bases, patrimonial political systems, and fragmented, unincorporated social systems, communist or socialist vanguards are facing insurmountable tasks. Like the religious fanatics on the right, the Marxists on the left do pose a threat to incumbent political elites in that they could overthrow regimes, but it seems inconceivable that they could then go on to remake society to conform to their religious or socialist model. Like their semisecular predecessors, Moslem Brothers or Marxists, if they were to seize the reins of power, would only retain them by relying on patrimonial bureaucratic authority and by tailoring their political appeals to the preferences and prejudices of the various constituent parts of their citizenry, some of which would be secular, some religious, and some at points in between. Presumably it would be the elite that would change in either composition or outlook, not the society.[58]

Communist ideology indeed appeals most to the educated middle classes. There is some appeal to the industrial working class, but not that much, despite the fact that the communist message has been directed more specifically to the workers than to others. To the rural peasantry, the appeal is less discernible. What has hurt the communist appeal most has been its contradictions with another ideology, that of nationalism. The situation is an interesting one. Here are two clashing ideologies. The strength of one has hurt the success of the other. The Soviets have always been injured in the Middle East because of their Moscow-oriented campaigns. Communist cadres have been wiped out in Iraq, Iran, and Syria, and the Soviets have only stood by and watched. In Egypt, in spite of open friendship with the Soviet Union and enormous Soviet

[58] Springborg, "On the Rise and Fall," p. 107.

aid, Nasser and his successor, Sadat, have strongly suppressed the communist movement. This has invoked only weak protests from Moscow. In Israel, communists have had a difficult ideological time adjusting the exigencies of domestic Israeli politics to the international stance of their mentors.

Halpern has argued that communism has failed as an ideology in the Middle East.[59] In a very direct sense, this may be true, but communism has nonetheless had a tremendous impact in that it has forced many traditional elites to modernize out of self-defense. These elites have perceived the proximity of viable Soviet and other communist models, have daily listened to the mesmeric propaganda from Soviet radio stations, and have not failed to note the restlessness of their own populations. This restlessness is present largely in the middle classes and certainly not among the rural poor. But it has spurred these elites to save what they can, while they can, in effect to create their "white revolutions."

NEUTRALISM

One result of the competition between the United States and the Soviet Union for Middle Eastern minds and political assets was the emergence of "neutralism." The end of the Second World War had given impetus to the departure of the Western colonial powers, although their final exit in any real sense took more than another decade to accomplish. Feverish attempts to recommit the Middle East in military and other political alignments against the forces of international communism generally met with rebuff (witness the fate of the Baghdad Pact). Perhaps this rebuff partly stemmed from the known disadvantages of French or British tutelage and a natural ignorance of the "non-saltwater" colonialism of the Soviet Union on the part of Middle Eastern leaders. Yet certainly another reason for it was the appealing features of a Soviet or Yugoslav model for rapid political development. By the time of Soviet arms assistance to Egypt (1955), the die had already

[59] See Halpern's chapter "Middle East and North Africa" in *Communism and Revolution: The Strategic Uses of Political Violence,* ed. Cyril E. Black and Thomas P. Thornton (Princeton, N.J.: Princeton University Press, 1964).

been cast; many Middle Eastern states were simply unwilling to lose the advantages of aloofness in the ideological quarrel between the Soviet Union and the United States by taking sides. They had natural allies: India, Indonesia, some of the new states of Asia, the emergent states in Africa, and, of course, Yugoslavia (for its own peculiar reasons). Thus, the creation of neutralism.

Neutralism is not neutrality, as a policy vis-à-vis other parts of the world. It is a full-blown ideology, which envelops other issues and ideas, and poses solutions to many problems. To the Arabs of Nasser's day, the trinity of nationalism, neutralism, and socialism was the panacea of the future. In 1964, Fayez A. Sayegh edited a rather remarkable little book, *The Dynamics of Neutralism in the Arab World*,[60] which in something less than 300 pages offered a number of views by leading Arab writers of what neutralism was, what it meant to Arabs, and what its effects might be on the political process.

Sayegh argues that neutralism rests on two premises: (1) there is much more to "contemporary international life" than the cold war; and (2) there are many other independent but grave problems in other parts of the world. He classifies neutralism in various ways and comes up with such terms as traditional neutralism, dogmatic neutralism, ideological neutralism, nationalist-pragmatic neutralism, passive neutralism, negative neutralism, and — of most interest to us — *positive neutralism* and *messianic neutralism*.[61]

He states that both positive and messianic neutralism characterize Egypt. The guiding principle of positive neutralism, he argues, is the "assertion and exercise of the right to maintain relations with other countries — regardless of their cold war positions . . . — provided that such relations do not entail direct or indirect entanglement in the cold-war associations of those countries." He characterizes the posture of positive neutralism as "ignoring the cold-war affiliations of other countries; bypassing or circumventing cold-war barriers; transcending or leapfrogging cold-war fences."

60 (San Francisco: Chandler Publishing Co., 1964).
61 Ibid., pp. 6–7, 10–11.

The principle of messianic neutralism is the "contribution to the relaxation of cold-war tensions and the resolution of cold-war problems; and endeavoring to create a bloc free [sic!], pluralistic, multinational world instead of the dualistic, bi-polarized world which the cold-war parties seek to perpetuate"; its posture is "confrontation of the cold war, and curative grappling with its antagonisms."[62]

These quotations have been given to indicate that in the language alone — of course, in the words of a sympathetic ana-lyist rather than in those of a Nasser — neutralism is ideologi-cal and is one of the most interesting of the contemporary ideologies of the Middle East.

George J. Tomeh (recently Syrian delegate in the United Nations), in trying to describe Syrian understanding of neu-tralism, once again underlines its ideological character. "Posi-tive neutralism," he said, "in its early form was an affirmation of the dignity of the Arab individual, in the face of long cen-turies of foreign rule, and his inalienable right to freedom." He goes on, "The policy of positive neutralism is not a mere reaction against colonialism, but something much more than that. It is a manifestation of the urgent vital needs, *e.g.,* peace in Arab society, . . ." This, he points out, does not mean isolation. "Neither does it ignore the extreme sensitivity of this historical region, the Arab world, or its involvement with the interests of the great powers, which have brought the whole world more than once to the brink of war."[63] In short, it rep-resents a great struggle by the Arabs for peace.

Ideologically, neutralism has moved into the shade since Nasser's death, and fewer Arab (or other) writers continue to articulate its principles. It is unnecessary to add that with re-gard to *policy,* in contrast to ideology, neutralism may con-tinue to characterize Arab governments in ways indistinguish-able from those of the past.

SUMMARY

The world and man have always been ideological; there has always been a need to rationalize an existence, a program, a

[62] Quotations, ibid., p. 11.
[63] Quotations, ibid., pp. 140–41.

goal. But the late-twentieth-century world is one of intense communicative activity. Disparate views are circulated rapidly and find crannies and crevices in human minds in which to lodge, perhaps to multiply, certainly to affect political life. The Middle East is no exception.

Before the Second World War, a text in comparative government (say, of the Middle East, although in fact none had been written at that time) could have been written about constitutions, legal frameworks, institutional structures and patterns, parliamentary rules, and conventions, with no mention of the political forces that give life to a system. It is no longer possible to do this.

It is impossible to understand the Middle East today without trying to comprehend the hold that religion has on its people (the hold that finally forced Bourguiba in the fall of 1971 to abandon his efforts to control Ramadan), the pervasive and corrosive influence of nationalism, the attempts at modernization through attachment to socialism, the attempts to be uncommitted in the cold war. These are, of course, ideological, and the Middle East can only be properly understood through an attempt to understand the bases of its ideologies.

And, in the last quarter of this century, as Asia, Africa, and now Europe seem awash in the seas of terrorism, it is important to reexamine the ideological dimensions of dissent and to reevaluate the traditional notions of political legitimacy. Perhaps in the Middle East it is imperative to do so.

CHAPTER VIII

The Arab-Israeli Connection

A COMMON MISCONCEPTION among Americans is the belief that Israel and its immediate neighbors constitute virtually the entire Middle East. Consequently, it is thought that Israeli problems (as well as Israeli-Arab problems) make up the major challenges for the area. But if the Zionist movement and an Israel had never existed there would still be a Middle East with a myriad of difficulties and tensions. It is foolish to think that had Israel succumbed in the 1948 fighting upon its establishment as a state, or in the October 1973 war a quarter of a century later, there would be no lingering problems for the Arabs or the non-Arabs who live in the Middle East.[1]

It is only fair to say that similar observations are true for the Israelis themselves. If their Arab opponents were suddenly to become friendly neighbors and the life of the garrison state to become a thing of the past, some very serious internal problems, problems perhaps even of survival, would remain. Indeed, is Israel a viable economic and political mass in the ab-

---

[1] There is an immense literature on the Arab-Israeli dispute. We mention only a very few of the latest materials. Howard M. Sachar's *A History of Israel From the Rise of Zionism to Our Time* (New York: Alfred A. Knopf, 1976) is detailed and useful for the period up to 1976. William B. Quandt's *Decade of Decisions: American Policy Towards the Arab-Israeli Conflict, 1967–1976* (Berkeley: University of California Press, 1978) is perceptive and informative. Quandt is associated with the National Security Council. Nadav Safran's *Israel: The Embattled Ally* (Cambridge: Harvard University Press, 1978) is also useful.

sence of Arab hostility? (Or to return to the Arabs, is what little unity they possess merely a product of the existence of Israel, which all Arabs can hate?)

In attempting to put this dispute into proper perspective, one should not downplay it completely. It certainly has colored all things Arab for a generation and more, and while it exists, many other problems and irritations are left to fester, not only in the Arab countries themselves but in the Middle East as a whole. It has affected *Muslim* politics (and unity) within and without the area, and it has been a very real factor in the politics of such disparate things as the sale of Iranian oil and the settlement of the Cypriot question. Certainly, it has tended to retard political development not only among the Arab states surrounding Israel but in Israel itself. Within these states the callous disregard of human rights for minorities — Jews and Palestinians in the Arab world, Palestinian Arabs in Israel — has become commonplace. The existence of the Arab-Israeli quarrel over Palestine has probably given the conservative states such as Saudi Arabia another generation of existence, by siphoning off the ideological and radical energies of the Arabs that otherwise might have been directed toward revolution.

The quarrel, of course, has given a new lease on life to terrorism, with ripple effects that are worldwide. It has encouraged the Israelis to commit disproportionate acts of retaliation — the invasion of southern Lebanon in March 1978 is an example. It has emphasized the inevitable arms race; violence and the military have been enshrined, not only in the Arab states but in Israel, too. One obvious consequence of the quarrel is that its immediate protagonists already live in virtual economic bankruptcy. And for Israel in particular, this is in spite of a history of immense American aid and subsidies.

The Arab-Israeli imbroglio is indeed a major problem in the contemporary Middle East, but it is not the only problem. Should it ultimately vanish, as problems sometimes do, the history of the area will go on, generating ambitions and quarrels, producing ideologies and conceptions of utopia. Nevertheless, it is necessary to study it in order to understand its genesis, the things that keep it alive as a problem, and the realistic prospects of accommodation. It is not possible to do this in fine detail here; the issue is too immense. But the outlines of the issue will be constructed and fleshed out as meaningfully as space will permit.[2]

This problem is, of course, a very emotional and strongly felt one in many parts of the Middle East. Many Americans, too, feel deeply concerned — some because they fear for the survival of Israel, others because they sympathize with the Arabs in this lingering quarrel and some because they do not want the United States to be involved. To the degree that one becomes emotionally involved in the quarrel, one also becomes attached to the "truth" about it, and reasoning together becomes a most difficult enterprise. What follows in the paragraphs below is not "truth," but simply a recital of the facts as the authors see them and of those interpretations that seem most likely to be correct.

THE POLITICAL DIMENSIONS

Israel is one of the very few states that can claim a religious raison d'être, but it is unique in that it was founded as a *national home* for those of one religion, in this case the Jews. The movement to create this national home was called Zionism; it has been treated elsewhere in this volume. Zionism came into existence because of the upsurge of anti-Semitism in late-nineteenth-century Europe. But anti-Semitism was not so much a religious movement as it was a racist one. Anti-Semites found their targets not merely in Jews per se, but in people they did not like or whom they feared or envied. They identified these people as Jews and offered as evidence such flimsy things as names, physical appearance, associations, and ancestral religious practices. It would not be necessary to point this out here except that a national home for Jews would in practice have to be a national home for *all those oppressed by anti-Semites as Jews.* As a result, Israel's population has always contained many who are not very attached to Judaism as a re-

---

[2] Events happen so rapidly — witness the period from late November 1977, when Sadat visited Jerusalem, to September 1978 when he journeyed to Camp David to meet with Carter and Begin — that we have not attempted to discuss all the chronological details. We emphasize what we think are the permanent features of the conflict.

ligion; they may be *cultural* Jews (in the same sense that there are cultural Christians and cultural Muslims who may indeed be atheists), but in any event they invariably fall into some anti-Semitic category of discrimination and persecution. In addition, of course, modern Israel contains Muslims, Christians, and others. And in the early summer of 1977, the Begin government admitted a small number of Vietnamese refugees.

The early Zionists agreed that the national home should be in Palestine, the ancient home of the Jews. Surely this is hardly surprising; moreover, it is reasonable on all kinds of levels — to many people other than Jews, it must be added. In November 1917, the British government formally agreed to the idea of a national home for the Jewish people in Palestine. This was in the famous Balfour Declaration.

But there were problems. Palestine was to a degree a vague geographic term. Before the First World War, it was a part of the Ottoman Empire; after that conflict, it was administered as the mandated territories of Palestine and Trans-Jordan. Historically, there had always been some Jews living in Palestine (as they lived in other parts of the Middle East), but they were not large in number. (As late as 1922, they only composed 11 percent of the population of Palestine.) And they did not always have much in common with the early Zionists, who came to the area after the turn of the century. There were also Muslim and Christian Arabs in the area. It is this group of Arabs that is today called the Palestinians. And around the Palestinians there has solidified a major political dimension of the contemporary Arab-Israeli dispute.

It is impossible in a short space to sort out all the factors of the Palestinian question. The Palestine of 1900 was not overpopulated, and the Zionists who arrived roughly at this time had little difficulty in acquiring land, if they were able to accumulate its purchase price. There was little friction between Arabs and Jews. At the end of the First World War, the emir Faisal — later the ruler of Iraq and whose brother Abdullah became the ruler of Trans-Jordan — and the Zionist leader Chaim Weizmann, signed an agreement of collaboration for the settlement of Palestine. Few then envisaged the intense hostility of later years. Even the 1920s were relatively quiet.

Zionists continued to come to Palestine, mostly from Eastern Europe, but they did not come and stay in large numbers. It is only in the 1930s that the beginnings of a tidal wave of immigrants were to be discerned; the rise of Nazi Germany, and later, after the war, the exodus of refugees from ravaged Europe, gave impetus to a rapidly growing Jewish population in Palestine.

It was in the 1930s that the first major tensions among the Palestinian communities became apparent. Violence in one form or another became commonplace. The Jews organized their own defense mechanisms, out of necessity, and there were ugly intercommunal clashes and riots. It was tragic and also inevitable. Palestinian Jews were eager to help Jewish refugees from Europe, whose very lives might depend upon their success in getting to Palestine. Palestinian Arabs, on the other hand, began to recognize the dangers to their communities of the increasing influx of foreigners who would compete with them for living space, jobs, and political control.

There was a great deal of ugliness in this situation, and both sides were guilty of excesses. Terrorism accompanied the political disputes, and lives were lost and property was destroyed. By the end of the Second World War, Great Britain found itself unable any longer to bear the heavy responsibilities of empire; these responsibilities were especially heavy in Palestine, where the British had not succeeded in establishing rapport with any of the communities. In May 1948, the British withdrew and left the Jews and Arabs to fight it out among themselves. We shall discuss the military aspects of this in later paragraphs; here it should be noted that any fighting puts strains on the civilian population. In Palestine, Arab villages and Jewish kibbutzim were both targets of armed squads, and many of them became in different ways victims of the violence that swept the country. Because the Jews (now the Israelis) won, they were able to reestablish their own communities. For the other Palestinians, the conseqeunces of the fighting were more complicated. Some remained in Israel, some were already in Jordanian-controlled (the West Bank) or Egyptian-controlled (Gaza) territory, others became refugees in one or another of the surrounding Arab territories by being driven from their homes or by fleeing to some sanctuary. Israel was established as a state, and many Palestinians who had lived in Israeli territory were now homeless.

These refugees were not particularly well treated over the years by their Arab hosts. They were political pawns, and life for many of them and for their descendants was harsh. And, it must be added, the oil riches that were increasingly discovered in the Arab world were seldom employed in helping them. Those left behind in Israeli territory could also hardly avoid the status of second-class citizenship.[3]

The Palestinian issue was clear in 1948. Over the years it has changed slightly in detail, but it still remains clear. In essence, the Arabs say of the Palestinians that (1) they were driven from their homes; (2) they should have the right to return; (3) they should be compensated for the loss of their property; and (4) no final settlement of the Arab-Israeli dispute can be had until their "rights" are recognized. (In the late 1970s, these rights increasingly have been understood by Arabs to mean the establishment of a Palestinian state — or "entity" — in some form.) Israelis, on the other hand, argue that (1) the original Palestinian refugees left voluntarily and in effect abandoned their homes and property; (2) it would be politically impossible for Israel to take them back and economically impossible to pay the inflated Arab claims for property lost (an additional argument is that *Jewish* refugees from the Arab countries also numbered many thousands and also abandoned property for which they were not compensated) ;[4] and (3) the

3 Where are the Palestinians today? As of late 1977, it was estimated that there are close to 4 million altogether. Of these, roughly half are in Israeli-controlled territory (760,000 in the West Bank; 400,000 in Gaza and Northern Sinai; and 530,000 within Israel itself). About 900,000 live in Jordan, and there are perhaps 500,000 in Lebanon, Egypt, and Syria. They are also of significance in other parts of the Arab world, such as Kuwait. In 1976 there were sixty-three refugee camps in Lebanon, Syria, Jordan, and Israeli-occupied territories, with a total of about 640,000 inhabitants (although 1.6 million are actually registered as refugees). These figures were taken from Congressional Quarterly's *The Middle East: U.S. Policy, Israel, Oil and the Arabs,* 3d ed. (Washington, D.C.: Congressional Quarterly, 1977), p. 120.

4 They and their descendants make up perhaps 40 percent of the *Jewish* population of Israel today.

establishment in or contiguous to Israel of an independent Palestinian state, probably bent on the subversion or destruction of Israel, is impossible to contemplate. Indeed, the Charter of the Palestine Liberation Organization (PLO) contains a phrase indicating that the goal of the organization is to destroy Israel. Israeli prime minister Begin used this as a reason, in August 1977, to refuse ever to negotiate with the PLO.

Until 1967, the Palestinians were relatively unorganized; they depended upon the promises of Arab leaders such as Nasser, who were willing to fight their battles for them. This policy was ineffective for the Palestinians and disastrous for Nasser. After 1967, they received enough money and became sufficiently well organized to fight the Israelis themselves. The result was terrorism, in many ways rather successful. Yasir Arafat, as the titular leader of the Palestinians (and one who has officially eschewed terrorism), has achieved enormous world exposure and publicity, and with this has come the half-acceptance of the need for a Palestinian state. Arafat no doubt would be its president.

We will return to this issue in the sections on negotiations and prospects for accommodation, but here we need merely note its seemingly intractable nature. How is it possible to reconcile the different, strongly held views?

Related to the event that produced the Palestinian refugees — the establishment of Israel in 1948 — is, to the Israelis at least, a question of fundamental importance. This is the willingness of the Arabs (principally, of course, Egypt, Syria, and Jordan) to accept the legitimate existence of Israel. We need not be detained here by legal niceties involving recognition, exchanges of ambassadors, and so on. What Israel really wants and must have is some *substantive* acceptance of its right to exist. If Egypt and Syria were to agree that Israel exists with some real measure of legitimacy, some of the need for continued war might go away. This is the *sine qua non* of a final accommodation, and Israel must have its way. But President Sadat went to Jerusalem in November 1977. Surely this constituted recognition of Israel in the most dramatic possible way. Certainly Sadat's statements while in Israel and his subsequent statements (such as those after the Camp David meetings) indicate that Egypt, at least, would be willing to "normalize" relations with Israel. But few of the other Arab states by late-1978 seemed willing to do so.

But there are many roads to Jerusalem, and words, especially in Hebrew and Arabic, can gloss over the emotionally prickly problems of "acceptance." All Arabs today — not just the Egyptians — are closer to acceptance of Israel than they were in the late 1940s. They have lived with the Israelis for thirty years; they have fought four wars with them and have learned to give them a grudging respect. In 1950, Arab newspapers would not use the word Israel, or if they did use it, would enclose it in quotation marks. Israel was "occupied Palestine" and eventually, as Nasser said early on, the "Jews would be thrown in the sea." Responsible Arab leaders do not talk this way any more; certainly Sadat does not. Israel is going to continue to exist for a long time to come. It is the task of the Arabs to get the greatest benefits possible from the Israelis in return for their own recognition of Israel as a state. This issue is also of fundamental political importance.

The Israelis and their Arab neighbors hold similar attitudes about a further issue; each side believes in the aggressiveness and intentions for expansion of the other. The Arabs fear the Israelis just as much as the Israelis fear the Arabs. The Israelis feel surrounded by enemies — enemies whose words, in the past at least, vowed destruction of the Israeli state. The Israelis are constantly concerned with "secure borders," but any tourist who visits the area quickly realizes that no Israeli borders can be very secure. They have fought four wars with the Arabs, at least twice — in 1948 and 1973 — instigated by Arab attacks. In 1967, Nasser let his perceptions and rhetoric tempt him to take such a threatening stand that Israel felt it necessary to make a preemptive strike. The 1956 war, called simply "the Aggression" in Egypt, certainly is an example of Israeli willingness to attack its neighbors. Deep penetration raids by the Israelis over the years have done little to quiet Arab fears. And, if further example is needed, the Israeli invasion in March 1978 of southern Lebanon up to the Litani River merely substantiated long-held Arab fears.

In Israel, the decision to attack in 1956 was probably rooted in the belief that some political objectives could be best achieved by military action (it must be remembered that Israel collaborated with France and Great Britain in the attack on Egypt). The willingness to go to war after 1956 (and particularly in 1967) likely stems from the shortsighted euphoria that produced the notion that Israelis are invincible against Arabs; the 1973 war was to be a stunning surprise (as was the short-lived Lebanese adventure in 1978). The truth of the matter is that there are no real military objectives left for the Israelis, and the use of war for political purposes has revealed its own fragility.

Nonetheless, for the Arabs, who are accustomed to seeing the Israelis "throw their weight around," it is very hard to believe that the Israelis do not have some master plan of conquest that will engulf ever larger portions of their neighbors' territories. Menahem Begin's great inspiration has been Vladimir Jabotinsky,[5] whose published comments, at least, make Arab concerns seem justified. Begin's legitimization of West Bank, Golan, and Sinai settlements offer further, if less significant, justification for Arab fears.

Thus Jordan, Syria, and Egypt have indeed feared the Israelis and continue to distrust them deeply. This fear is real and any settlement of the Arab-Israeli conflict must contain some guarantee that Israel will not in the future attempt to achieve its political ends by resorting to military action. But, similarly, many (possibly most) Israelis deeply distrust their Arab neighbors and worry that some day they will fail to stem the tide against an Arab invasion. These fears were particularly strong during the gloomy period before the June War in 1967. And they explain why Israel has quietly produced nuclear weapons, to be used perhaps in some survival or even preemptive scenario.

The fears of both the Arabs and the Israelis are thus very real, however logically or illogically they may be founded in

[5] Jabotinsky was one of the great figures in Zionist history. But he was also probably its most uncompromising, aggressive, brutal, and ambitious figure. It is significant that David Ben Gurion referred to Jabotinsky as a fascist and called him on occasion "Vladimir Hitler" (noted in Sachar, *History of Israel*, p. 188). Jabotinsky died in 1940.

the minds of those who possess them. This, then, is another major political dimension of the solution to the conflict: some guarantee that will enable each side to feel less compelled to fear the other.

Although virtually everyone uses the term *Arab* to denote the enemy of Israel, it should be clear that essentially only three Arab states are militarily involved in the conflict: Jordan, Syria, and Egypt.[6] (This has not prevented Israeli publicists from counting every Arab state from Morocco to Kuwait as the enemy, about to pounce.) These were the states at war with Israel in 1967; each as a result lost territory to the Israelis. These lost and Israeli-occupied territories are another major political dimension of the solution to the Arab states concerned. No Egyptian government can ever give up permanently the Sinai; no Syrian government can abandon the Golan; the situation with respect to the West Bank and Jordan is somewhat more ambiguous. It is likely that if a Palestinian state is created, part of its territory anyway will be the West Bank; any return of this territory to Jordan will be in the nature of a political supervisory role over the Palestinians. The Begin-Sadat accord at Camp David suggested such a role for Jordan but it is evident that King Husayn could easily lose in any such activity.

But of course Israel does not want to give up these territories. Possessing them permanently, if that were possible, would seemingly make its borders more secure and would provide territory for an expanding Israeli population. A portion of Sinai (along the Suez Canal) has already been returned to Egypt, as a result of the Kissinger "shuttle" diplomacy. But it seems clear that ultimately Israel will have to divest itself of these territories, regardless of how attractive keeping them might seem. Until that happens, Egypt and particularly Syria

[6] We refer to genuine hostilities between states. This view excludes pseudo-war, in which hostilities do not occur, although "declarations" of belligerency may have been made. This also excludes the mere presence of nationals of an Arab country, who may indeed be fighting in some conflict, although their own government may officially be non-belligerent. Thus, in 1973, Jordanians, Iraqis, and Moroccans fought the Israelis but their government did not. Most such actions are of course mainly of symbolic value in any case.

will not be likely to concede to Israel some of the other things that are probably more important. It should be added that the Israeli-Egyptian demarche in September 1978 details the return of Sinai to the Egyptians.

Jerusalem is a special case. Unfortunately it has deep religious meaning to Jews, Christians, and Muslims alike. It is easily forgotten that all three of these religions believe in the same diety; Muhammad indeed conceived of his seventh-century mission as bringing together Christians and Jews as believers in *their* god's later messages (the Quran). In this, of course, he was unsuccessful. Many Jews, Christians, and Muslims see their particular dogmas as ultimate truths, and there is no prospect of reconciliation of their differences. In the meantime, most awkwardly, they all cherish the Old City of Jerusalem. Logically, the Muslims should control it since they *accept* many of the historical Jewish and Christian leaders and beliefs as their own; Jesus is a major prophet in Islam. But whoever controls the Old City, all should be free to enter it, to worship there, and to leave it, without hindrance or harassment. It is easy to construct a reasonable solution of this problem; some sort of joint Jewish-Christian-Muslim control comes instantly to mind, or perhaps some international administration. Among some Muslim Arabs — the Saudis, for example — the status of Jerusalem is a very important issue indeed; and it surely is an issue of some significance to all Muslims, Arab or otherwise, wherever they are to be found. A solution will have to be found for it in the ultimate accommodation, but it is not as politically important as the other issues mentioned above.

There is still another political dimension to a settlement to the conflict. Israel is open to the Mediterranean, but her outlet to the Indian Ocean and beyond is contingent upon two passages being free and open. The Straits of Tiran, off Sharm el-Shaykh, where the Gulf of Aqaba joins the Gulf of Suez to form the Red Sea, is the first major narrows through which Israeli shipping from its port Elath must pass. The second lies off Aden at the southern exit of the Red Sea and is called the Bab el-Mundab. The Egyptians have from time to time blocked the Gulf of Aqaba, and this has led to war with the Israelis.

The Israelis argue that international waterways should be open to all flags. This argument of course also applies to the Suez Canal (under Egyptian control since 1956). Israeli cargoes do indeed transit the canal today, but the Egyptians are adamant about keeping out the Israeli flag. The maintenance of free shipping is essential for Israel, and it is certain that the final settlement will include this concession from the Arabs.

These, then, are the essential political issues. Together they constitute the Arab-Israeli dispute. A reconciliation of viewpoints on these issues would constitute a settlement of the dispute itself. But until there is a final wearied acceptance of one another, perhaps facilitated by American and Russian intervention, an accommodation seems unlikely. What is unlikely, too, is that any particular conference (convened in Geneva or Camp David or elsewhere) will produce a resolution that all parties can endorse, even half-heartedly. Within days of the end of the Camp David meetings (noteworthy by the presence of the United States as one of the negotiators), it was evident that most of the Arab world had rejected the agreements. Yet the fact that these meetings had occurred at all was remarkable. What is clear is that outside the Egyptian-Israeli agreements the rest of the Camp David accord was largely cosmetic propaganda in that the most important issue, the future of the Palestinians, was not addressed seriously or conscientiously.

When we speak of acceptable decisions, we mean decisions that are acceptable to a number of different participants. For the Israelis, acceptable means not something merely agreeable to a Meir, a Rabin, or a Begin, but something that will pass in the Knesset. Since no Israeli government has ever controlled the Knesset without resort to coalition politics, the problems of accommodation are great. What seems politically sound to the Israeli electorate may not be identical with what its government has been able to negotiate.[7] The question of acceptability becomes even more complicated in the Arab world. A Sadat has to be satisfied, but so must his followers and the noisy crowds in the Cairo streets. Religious leaders must

---

[7] The Panama Canal treaties and American politics illustrate that this phenomenon is not unique to Israel.

have their say; the armed forces (including those officers who might someday dream of coups) must be considered. But beyond a Sadat in Egypt or an al-Assad in Syria lie the other Arab states who on the final resolution would want their say. Algeria's Boumedienne, Libya's Qaddafi, Saudi Arabia's King Khalid, and others would have to be reconciled for peace really to return. Additionally, however much President Carter would have liked the PLO to "go away," it remains the only viable voice for the Palestinian cause, and it would have to be satisfied. And of course the United States, the Soviet Union, and some other powers would have to play a role in the settlement and would seek solutions in keeping with their own national interests or at least their own domestic political constraints. Thus, the dispute is not an easy problem for men "reasoning together"; it may be generations before it sinks into the oblivion of history.

THE ARAB-ISRAELI WARS

There have been continual hostilities between some Arabs (often Palestinians) and some Israelis since before 1948. But on four occasions these hostilities have flashed into full-scale war: in 1948, 1956, 1967, and 1973. In spite of the current euphoric state of Israeli-Egyptian relations, there is no compelling reason to expect that another war will not occur sometime within the next several years.

Perhaps these past wars should be thought of as episodes in one longer war — more than battles, of course, but periodic campaigns of brief duration in a bigger war that has yet to end. So much has flowed from these campaigns and so many political issues have been affected by them that it seems necessary to speak of them in some detail. Some preliminary comments are necessary, however.

As mentioned above, the Israelis like to believe that all the Arabs in the world are their adversaries. In fact, their enemy is something less than that. In 1948, Egypt, Lebanon, Syria, Iraq, and Trans-Jordan attacked the new state of Israel. (The Israelis would add, of course, the Palestinians.) Of these, only Egypt and Trans-Jordan were of any significance. In 1956, Israel attacked Egypt alone. In 1967, Israel fought successively

Egypt, Jordan, and Syria. In 1973, Egypt and Syria attacked Israel. Egypt has been an adversary on each occasion and Syria on three occasions. Egypt is the largest and potentially the most powerful state in the region; its 40 million people make it Israel's most dangerous enemy. Syria is much smaller and weaker, although through Russian largess it has had formidable armed forces. Jordan is smaller yet and can no longer be thought to be by itself a major threat to the Israelis.

In these conflicts, Israel won tactical victories over all adversaries except the Jordanians (who had the British-officered Arab Legion) in 1948. The 1948 conflict has also to be regarded as a strategic victory for the Israelis inasmuch as this military action gave meaning to the establishment of Israel as a state and made its survival possible. Strategically, the 1956 conflict is less clear. Two things were accomplished.[8] The Gulf of Aqaba was opened by the capture of Sharm el-Shaykh, and, although the Israelis withdrew, a United Nations force that remained there until 1967 kept the Gulf open to Israeli shipping. The campaign also demonstrated Israeli military superiority over the Egyptians, and it was thought at the time that this lesson driven home to the Egyptians would ensure the continued existence of Israel for many years to come. At most, the 1956 war was only a partial strategic victory for the Israelis. The 1967 campaign was from the Israeli point of view one of the most brilliant tactical victories ever to have occurred, but strategically it almost certainly was a loss, although few recognized it as such at the time. (Gen. Ariel Sharon, Israel's most able tactical general, was convinced that the campaign had won peace for a generation or more — but in fact the time span was but six years.)

The major aspect of this loss was that the Israelis captured territory, a fact that almost certainly meant that there would be future conflict. Moreover, the very dimensions of their victory, amazing in detail, showed upon reflection the inadequacies of the military solution. There was little left for the Israelis to win militarily, but their basic political problems re-

8 Some will say that the campaign seriously discouraged Arab fedayin raids on Israeli territory. This does not, however, seem strategic in nature.

mained. This became even clearer when at the end of the 1973 campaign Israeli forces were across the Canal, on the road to Cairo, and in Syria, some thirty-five miles from Damascus. In spite of the tactical victories with which the 1973 campaign ended, it was a clear strategic loss. Once again, there was no real military solution and Arabs with oil riches had finally reared up in a major display of strength. Finally, too, long-standing American support for Israel was clouded and compromised — certainly not destroyed or even damaged seriously, but nevertheless altered in small but significant ways.[9]

The *military* aspects of any future conflict remain difficult to focus for the Israelis, who remain without objectives that can be convincingly connected with political goals. Again, the invasion of Lebanon of March 1978 serves as an example. No one could doubt the Israeli military ability to drive to the Litani River, but it is difficult to see the military success of this maneuver affecting very favorably negotiations with the Arab states.[10] Moreover, in this campaign the Israelis ran behind their timetable and found resistance stiffer than they expected. Their Palestinian opponents properly viewed their own efforts as something of a victory.

From the very beginning of these various campaigns, the world has witnessed such a disparity in the success of the combatants that considerable attention has been given to the alleged backwardness of Arab military technology and armies. At one time, the Israelis officially made the assumption in military planning that the Arabs would not fight very well, and part of the inevitable mythology that grew up around this conflict was that there was something generically different about Arab soldiers and that one could really dismiss their

[9] By 1978, for example, the United States had agreed to sell jet fighters to Egypt and Saudi Arabia as well as to Israel; President Carter condemned the Israelis for the "settlements" policy and insisted on the need for a Palestinian entity in the West Bank and Gaza. And the Shah of Iran, in supporting American policy, intimated his willingness to embargo the shipment of Iranian oil to Israel in order to make Israel more amenable to reason.

[10] It remains to point out that it is entirely possible that this was precisely the object of the maneuver — that is, to make it more difficult to negotiate with the Arabs, especially the Palestinians.

skills and abilities. They were technologically backward, it was said, and generations would have to pass before one could expect them to stand up successfully against Israeli arms. The culture, social organization, religion, education — all were given as explanatory factors.

It is, of course, an incontestable fact that the Arabs usually have lost militarily in their encounters with the Israelis. No single explanation for this is very convincing, the one of backwardness least of all. Close examination of the campaigns themselves reveals that in most instances the Israelis had *local* superiority in such things as fire power, air cover, mobility, and, in many cases, numbers of men. On the other hand, the Arabs generally have had superior weapons and these sometimes in greater numbers. With the exception of the Arab Legion, which was a highly trained and well-led force in the 1948 conflict, Arab armies have been on the whole typical professional armies. Officers have been chosen for their educational qualifications and family status. Men have normally been recruited by conscription; many have not wanted to serve and have not absorbed with any enthusiasm what lessons the organizational cadres have been able to put together. The Israelis, on the other hand, from the very beginning have produced a truly citizens army; virtually all Israeli men physically able, and many Israeli women, have served long terms on active and reserve status. (It is jokingly said that Israelis are in the army permanently, but on eleven months annual leave.) This has meant that the very best men — those with good educations; industrial, technical, and mechanical skills; and the entire spectrum of other talents — have been available in large numbers for combat.

Every Israeli is aware of how closely connected his own personal survival is with the military success of his unit (this is particularly true in the air force, where every pilot knows that his own efforts may have a result all out of proportion to his place in the armed forces). This can hardly be the case for the vast majority of the Arab soldiers who have opposed the Israelis. Nasser once said that some of his troops in 1948 thought they were fighting in the Sudan; this ignorance was hardly common then, and it must be rare today. Nevertheless, few

Arab soldiers can believe that the survival of their families at home is intimately connected with their victories on the battlefield.

Both the Israelis and their Arab foes have been clients of one or more of the greater powers. The most obvious example is the Soviet support for Egypt and Syria. This support in the case of Egypt even included small numbers of combat troops and technicians, as well as vast quantities of supplies and equipment, and large numbers of advisors. Along with such support in later years have gone Soviet tactical and technical ideas, which may or may not be well suited to the conditions in Sinai or the Golan. Surely it has handicapped the Egyptians to have fought with British ideas in 1948, many German ideas in 1956, and Soviet ones in 1967 and 1973.[11] The Israelis, on the other hand, although they have been very dependent on economic and military (equipment) assistance from the United States (and at one time from France), have been masters of their own military tactics and judgments. This independence accounts in part for their success.

At any rate, the Israelis themselves have grudgingly admitted that the Arabs have become better soldiers.[12] The Jordanians fought to the limit of their equipment in 1967; in 1973, the Egyptian destruction of the Bar-Lev Line was almost perfectly carried out; in the same year, the skillful deployment of SAM missiles in Syria and Egypt made the vital difference in the early Arab successes; and the Syrian troops fought bravely in the waning days of the 1973 war, despite the fact that Israeli aircraft controlled the skies. It seems likely that Arab military capacities will continue to improve in future conflicts.

One important element of the Arab-Israeli campaigns has been the inability of all of the combatants to fight prolonged wars. Modern war consumes vast quantities of munitions, fuel, and materiel, as well as lives. No state among those commonly involved in the fighting can bear this burden for long. In 1973, resupply from abroad became vital for all of the combatant

---

[11] And possibly American ones in 1980 or 1985!

[12] The British and French, too, were involved in the 1956 fighting. Had they not appeared to be (as well as become) adversaries then, it is possible that the Israelis would have had a harder time of it.

countries. Not surprisingly, Israel is particularly vulnerable in a prolonged conflict, since mobilization of its population for war paralyzes much of the remainder of the economy. The costs of war for the small Israeli population are staggering, even with assistance from abroad. Wars tend therefore to be "weekend" or "six-day" affairs. The big exception was, of course, 1948, but even then the fighting took place episodically, with intervening periods for recovery. Other than 1948, 1973 was the longest campaign the Israelis had to endure. Exhaustion characterized both sides at its end. And for Israel, the casualty figures, quite high for the size of its population, were appalling.

Let us now look very briefly at the campaigns themselves.[13]

In 1948, the Israelis really did not have an army. What they hastily threw together was badly equipped. The command structure was rudimentary and suffered from civilian interference. The Jordanian army was well trained, well equipped, well led and very modestly supplied. The Egyptian army was surely at its nadir. The British still occupied parts of Egypt; they had never permitted an Egyptian army of consequence to emerge, and the army that finally did come about possessed a motley collection of cast-off World War II equipment. There was corruption in supply; even the king was implicated. Yet the Egyptian army did not fight all that badly and certainly fought bravely. Other Arab armies resembled the Egyptian and in most cases did not come into much combat with Israeli forces.

This war was fought to a considerable degree in the interior of what is today Israel. It was a struggle for towns, roads and crossroads, and fortified places. The first phase of the fighting lasted about a month, and the Israelis were hard put to survive. The first truce took effect on 11 June 1948 and gave the Israelis the respite they needed. While the Arabs in effect sat on their weapons, the Israelis made organizational changes, acquired new weapons from abroad, and rested. When the truce ended (9 July 1948), they promptly won a number of

13 Indispensable is Edward Luttwak and Dan Horowitz, *The Israeli Army* (New York: Harper and Row, 1975).

important victories. The Arabs were happy to have the second truce (19 July 1948). When this broke in turn (15 October 1948), the Israelis were ready to make the best use of what little time they might have. In half a dozen brief operations stretching into 1949, they straightened out their right flank facing the Egyptians and captured the Negev, cleared the Galilee of enemy troops, and in general expanded their borders to the form they took for the next twenty years.

In this conflict, the Israelis created an army, procured weapons for it, and captured the élan necessary to make it all work. The Arabs, beginning at least with organized armies, did prevent the Israelis from overruning all of Palestine and almost, before the first truce, succeeded in demolishing them altogether. In a very real sense, it was a campaign of truces, with ultimate victory going to the side that made best use of its opportunities to reorganize and refurbish. It should not be necessary to emphasize that the Israelis were fighting, as they well knew, for their very survival. The Palestinians themselves were poorly organized, and, although they participated as combatants in the early days of the war, they were not of significance in determining its final outcome.

The Israeli victory in 1949 was misinterpreted by many Israelis. Many believed that they had proved their right to exist and that they could look forward to a long period of peace. In believing this, they also believed that their Arab neighbors would not attack them again. By contemporary standards, there was not very much outcry from the Arabs. The Palestinians were discouraged, disorganized, and weak. Alone, they presented no danger, and there were few indications that the Arab states would join in an attack on Israel. Consequently, the army was largely disbanded and attention was turned to making the political and economic systems work. Defense budgets in the early days were not large. Two Israeli officers made significant contributions during this period, however. Gen. Yigal Yadin systematically put together the organized army, with its regular and reserve statuses. Important decisions on discipline, weapons, and tactics were made during this time. He retired in 1952; by December 1953, Moshe Dayan, a flamboyant, able, and inspiring chief, who had the backing and friendship of Ben Gurion, had become chief of staff. Although Dayan's judgment on purely military affairs has been somewhat faulty over the years, all attribute to him a fantastic ability to inspire leadership and initiative among his followers. He gave the armed forces a spirit that has never quite left it. He made the army a possibility for young careerists, retiring his officers in their forties for second careers. He emphasized the need for tactical improvisation, for unorthodoxy in combat, and for initiative from below; all these changes were to become spectacularly evident in the 1956 conflict.

But in 1952 an army revolt overthrew King Farouk; his successors, chiefly Lt. Col. Gamal Abdel Nasser, were much more aggressive and nationalistic — and also were unpredictable. Nasser himself, as he consolidated his position in Egypt and tasted the delights of *Arab* leadership, became almost inevitably the bête noir of the Israelis. Moreover, he encouraged the fedayin raiders to enter Israeli territory; Israeli retaliatory raids merely embarrassed Nasser and probably forced him into taking a more bellicose stance than he might otherwise have taken. In August 1956, Nasser nationalized the Suez Canal — the year before, he had begun acquiring Russian weapons — in answer to the Western about-face in refusing economic aid for the purpose of building the Aswan High Dam. The stage was set for the war that came in October.

This war was a collusion between the British, the French, and the Israelis, who together attacked Egypt, each for their own reasons. The Israelis won most of the glory for several reasons. It was opportune, to begin with, to have the French and British as allies. Many Israelis had by 1956 come to believe that their earlier optimism was misplaced, that Nasser was their inevitable enemy, and that war would come of necessity; it might as well come at their choosing, rather than at that of the Egyptians. Still, they were uncertain of many things; one demand they made of the French was for French fighter protection based on Israeli airfields. And so they made the preemptive strike.

The conflict itself was a comedy of errors, if that expression can be used to describe a war. The Egyptians were quickly beaten and driven back to the Suez Canal; their own explanation for this action was that it was a withdrawal to face the British and French. But beaten they were, and badly. Yet the Israelis, too, made all sorts of errors. They attacked along the coastal road and again in the middle of Sinai on the way to the crossroads at Abu Agheila; a paratroop battalion was dropped at the Mitla Pass, ten miles from the Canal. But everything quickly got out of hand. Units lost touch with each other and commanders with headquarters. Headquarters in any event were where Dayan was, and he set about flying and jeeping all over Sinai. The most incredible, foolhardy, and really farcical of his exploits was to accompany the small body of troops that followed the Gulf of Suez down the Sinai peninsula to capture Sharm el-Shaykh; at times, he was completely surrounded by Egyptian troops. There were monumental equipment breakdowns. But there were also brilliant tactical innovation, courage, dash, and ultimate success beyond measure. This was Dayan's war, and he was proud of the spectacular outcome, even if luck and Egyptian ineptitude had been important contributing factors in his victory.

International politics quickly forced the Israelis to disgorge their conquests, and Nasser just as quickly rebounded. But now United Nation's forces were along the border and at Sharm el-Shaykh, and the Gulf of Aqaba was open. The Israeli army had stunned the world; Nasser should have been equally stunned. It is true that the war brought nearly eleven years of "peace," yet it did not alter the basic situation very much. Nasser's greatest years as an Arab leader were yet to come, and Israel, an obstacle to any conceivable Arab unity, was inexorably a target. The Russians refurbished the Egyptians with modern weapons, and there was much external evidence that the Egyptian army was unlike the one that had been defeated in 1956.

But the Israeli army had also changed. One of the major achievements of those who have run the Israeli military establishment has been their willingness to take hard looks at system, organization, and weapons, even in the face of victory. The shortcomings of the 1956 campaign were quickly recognized. Great efforts were made to rework the air force and the armored units; tactical reconsiderations were initiated. A new crop of younger officers took charge: Yitzak Rabin ultimately became chief of staff, Ezer Weizman[14] headed the air force, and Israel Tal the armored corps.

In retrospect, all of Israel's wars seem to have been inevitable; that in 1967 certainly so. And yet at the time it did not seem so inevitable. There is much evidence that Nasser did not want war; indeed, that he considered it impossible to win at that time. The Israelis were depressed at the thought of war in 1967; Levi Eshkol, the prime minister, sought all sorts of ways to avoid the conflict. Yet Nasser foolishly ordered the United Nations out of Egyptian territory; equally foolishly, it left without quarrel. With the Gulf of Aqaba once again closed, the *causus belli* was at hand. And when Moshe Dayan was brought into the government as minister of defense, war became a certainty.

The campaign that ensued was a masterpiece of planning and execution. Although Dayan had been given some of the military credit for the victory, in fact the detailed planning had been done by others — Rabin was primarily responsible as chief of staff. Once the decision had been made to go to war, considerable benefits might devolve upon the side that struck first. Israel did just that with its highly trained air force, striking at 8:45 A.M. (Cairo time)[15] on 5 June. The time was chosen as that at which the Egyptian air defenders would be at their least alert (conventional wisdom still suggested dawn strikes); the result of the campaign was the virtual destruction of the Egyptian air force (nearly 300 planes were destroyed on 5 June alone). The Israelis did this by carrying out a complex and carefully timed series of attacks on airfields, using a relatively modest number of planes. They had reduced turnaround times to about ten minutes and by this maneuver alone were able to multiply the effective size of their fighting force several times. With the air victory went control of the air for ground units in Sinai.

The main Israeli thrusts in Sinai were against the Rafah–El Arish coastal road and the Abu Agheila–Umm Katef crossroads. (The terrain in Sinai is so formidable that most of the

14 In the Begin government, minister of defense.
15 See Luttwak and Horowitz, *The Israeli Army*, p. 228.

battles there are restricted to roads and crossroads.) A smaller thrust would be aimed at Kuntilla to the south, with Naklil in central Sinai the main tactical objective. In the 1956 war, the Israelis had labored under the strategical objective of "confounding" the Egyptian army; in effect, they drove the Egyptians west to the Suez Canal. In 1967, the Israelis' "strategic goal was not to reach the Canal at all but to destroy the Egyptian army in Sinai."[16] Politically, it was dangerous to reach the Canal too soon, if at all. But to destroy the Egyptian army, given the nature of Sinai, was an intricate problem. The solution was brilliant. Air attacks were initiated in the *western* portions of Sinai, and fast columns of tanks and troop carriers were sent *through* the Egyptian lines — sometimes moving in a symbiotic fashion on the same roads and in the same convoys as the Egyptians — in order to *block* the Egyptian retreat. The tactical and strategic results of these actions were enormous. As Luttwak and Horowitz have noted, this "phase of the Israeli offensive led to the utter defeat of an army almost four times as large as Rommel's was on the eve of El Alamein, and in forty-eight hours instead of six months."[17]

By 8 June, the Egyptian army was no longer an organized force, and it had no way of defending the Canal, which fell without effort into the hands of the Israelis. Sharm el-Shaykh and Gaza, too, were theirs. Here was the capture of major territories that a decade later continued to plague the Israelis in their search for a *modus vivendi* with their Arab neighbors.

Had the 1967 conflict ended there, it would have been a magnificent victory for the Israelis. But Israel fought Jordan and Syria as well and defeated them just as decisively as it had defeated Egypt. The Israelis themselves have said that the Jordanian army fought in 1967 better than any of the other Arab armies. In fact, it was foolish for Jordan to have entered the war. The front that it had to defend, once the Israelis passed to the offensive, was too long and too brittle; moreover, the Jordanian army was small and not very well equipped. Had the Egyptians beaten the Israelis in Sinai, of course, the

16 Ibid., p. 256.
17 Ibid., p. 250.

situation would have been different, but the actual course of events found the Jordanian army, fighting well and bravely, simply overwhelmed. Along with the West Bank, the Old City of Jerusalem fell into Israeli hands.

The Syrians were well lodged in the fortified terraces of the Golan Heights, rising about 700 meters from the valley below. The Syrians had often amused themselves by lobbing artillery shells on Israeli settlements in that valley; the Israelis were particularly eager, if possible, to root the Syrians out and somehow neutralize the military threat posed by Syrian possession of the high plateau. Considerable uncertainty, both political and military, characterized the Israelis with respect to this campaign. Some were convinced that the Golan was invincible and could be taken, if at all, only with dreadful casualties. Others were concerned about the political repercussions of a move that perforce could take place (it began on 9 June) only after the Syrians had accepted a United Nations proposal for cease-fire. Space does not permit us to recount details, but this late campaign, in which the Israelis were fighting time as well as the Syrians, proved surprisingly successful; by 2:00 P.M. the following day, Keneitra, the main town in Golan, had been captured, and the Israelis were some forty miles from Damascus. More territory now had been acquired.

Euphoria swept Israel. Within hours they had fought three different Arab armies on three fronts and had defeated them all. They were convinced that they had destroyed the Egyptian army for years to come. Jordan was a truncated fragment of what it had been; Golan had been lost by the Syrians, who were in the very vulnerable position of having the Israelis ensconced in commanding terrain overlooking the heartland of Syria and its capital, Damascus. The Israelis, too, thought that in capturing territory they had acquired trump cards in any final settlement with the Arabs. Surely now the Arabs would listen to reason. There were also some foolish Israelis who looked upon the newly won territories as theirs now by right of conquest and who thought of an expanded Israel that would encompass them all. Whatever his position in the recent Begin government, Dayan was then consistently one of the more realistic of the Israelis. He had not wanted to get to the Suez

Canal in either 1956 or 1967; always he wanted to leave a way out for his Arab foes, politically and psychologically. But it was not to be.

In the slightly more than six years that separated the campaigns of 1967 from those of 1973, few things happened as the Israelis had anticipated that they would. Egypt and Syria were quickly rearmed by the Soviet Union. The Egyptians launched a war of attrition against the Israelis, which, as casualties mounted and costs soared, reminded the Israelis that the occupation of Sinai was not to be a peaceful one. As important as anything, the Palestinians bestirred themselves — with help, of course, from Arab governments — to create a fighting force of their own and to establish a wave of terrorism that reminded the Israelis even more forcefully of the costs of continuing war.

The terrorism of the Palestinians is a complicated matter. Although the PLO as led by Yasir Arafat normally disclaims any terrorist activity, it is a little unreasonable to assume that no encouragement is given to it by the PLO. It is also true that there have been a number of lesser, unaffiliated organizations, such as George Habash's Popular Front for the Liberation of Palestine, whose acts of terrorism can be conveniently overlooked by the larger body. Two additional points must be made, which most persons would be willing to admit only with great reluctance. The first is that terrorism, as a surrogate for war,[18] has earned a certain legitimacy of its own. There are few political groups of any size, when the stakes are great enough, that have not committed terrorist acts. The Israelis themselves have not been exceptions. (In 1977, Menahem Begin, the old leader of the Irgun Zwai Leumi, became the prime minister of Israel. Embarrassed about his terrorist past — including the blowing up of the King David Hotel in Jerusalem in 1944, in which ninety-one lives were lost — the Israeli government argued that he had been a "guerrilla fighter," not a terrorist; this is disingenuous. Again in 1977, the Israelis honored the leader of the old "Stern Gang," which is usually credited with the assassination in 1948 of Count

[18] See Murray C. Havens, Carl Leiden, and Karl M. Schmitt, *Assassination and Terrorism: Their Modern Dimensions* (Manchaca: Sterling Swift Publishing Co., 1975) , Chapter 15, for a discussion of this point.

Folke Bernadotte, the United Nations mediator in Palestine. And, if another example is needed, the bodies of the two youthful assassins of Lord Moyne in Cairo in 1944 were returned to Israel in later years and given posthumous honors. Israel too has terrorism in its past.) The Palestinians, in their various organizations, are merely the latest in a long series of terrorist groups whose history goes back many millenia.

The second point is that Palestinian terrorism has paid off, not, of course, by "liberating" Palestine, but by giving wide publicity to the Palestinian cause and thereby generating some sympathy for it. It is safe to argue that President Carter's earlier endorsement of some "recognition" of the PLO is a product, to a degree at least, of its terrorist acts in the past. In any event, this terrorism (not all directed at the Israelis, it must be added) has added a new dimension to the tensions of the area.

But Israel showed little inclination to return or even to negotiate the return of the territories captured in 1967. Nasser's death in September 1970 seemed to provide an opportunity to work out some settlement with Anwar Sadat, his successor. But nothing was done. When Sadat expelled the Russians from his country in the summer of 1972, there were those who expected the United States to exert a little pressure on Israel. Resolution 242 was unanimously adopted by the United Nations Security Council on 22 November 1967 and called for, among other things, a return of territories.[19] But little happened; in

19 The wording of Resolution 242 is as follows:

Resolution 242

The Security Council, Expressing its continuing concern with the grave situation in the Middle East,

Emphasizing the inadmissibility of the acquisition of territory by war and the need to work for a just and lasting peace in which every state in the area can live in security,

Emphasizing further that all Member States in their acceptance of the Charter of the United Nations have undertaken a commitment to act in accordance with Article 2 of the Charter,

1. Affirms that the fulfillment of Charter principles requires the establishment of just and lasting peace in the Middle East which should include the application of both the following principles:

a) Withdrawal of Israeli armed forces from territories occupied in the recent conflict;

b) Termination of all claims or states of belligerency and respect

fact, little could happen, given the vagaries of the Israeli political system. No Israeli government, at least prior to Begin's, has been strong enough politically to make the kind of concessions necessary for any real settlement. And no Egyptian or Syrian government could contemplate abandoning Sinai or the Golan. Here was the problem with no immediate or obvious solution.

Sadat proclaimed that Sinai would be recovered by force and in 1971 proclaimed that year to be the "year of decision." Little happened and his credibility sank. By the spring of 1973, ru-

---

for and acknowledgement of the sovereignty, territorial integrity and political independence of every State in the area and their right to live in peace within secure and recognized boundaries free from threats or acts of force;

2. Affirms further the necessity:

a) For guaranteeing freedom of navigation through international waterways in the area;

b) For achieving a just settlement of the refugee problem;

c) For guaranteeing the territorial inviolability and political independence of every State in the area, through measures including the establishment of demilitarized zones;

3. Requests the Secretary General to designate a Special Representative to proceed to the Middle East to establish and maintain contacts with the States concerned in order to promote agreement and assist efforts to achieve a peaceful and accepted settlement in accordance with the provisions and principles in this resolution;

4. Requests the Secretary General to report to the Security Council on the progress of the efforts of the Special Representative as soon as possible.

Resolution 338 was adopted on 22 October 1973, at the conclusion of the 1973 fighting. It is as follows:

Resolution 338

The Security Council,

1. Calls upon all parties to the present fighting to cease all firing and terminate all military activity immediately, no later than 12 hours after the moment of the adoption of this decision, in the positions they now occupy;

2. Calls upon the parties concerned to start immediately after the cease-fire the implementation of Security Council Resolution 242 (1967) in all of its parts;

3. Decides that immediately and concurrently with the cease-fire, negotiations start between the parties concerned under appropriate auspices aimed at establishing a just and durable peace in the Middle East.

mors that there was to be war in the fall were commonplace in the area. Israel did not take them seriously; neither did the United States.

The fourth round of campaigns commenced on 6 October 1973. Sadat had finally determined on war to break the log jam. He achieved tactical surprise against the Israelis and strategical surprise as well. And, in going to war, he coordinated his attack with the Syrians and secured the financial and political backing of the Saudis. Although almost everyone expected a quick victory on the part of the Israelis, events did not turn out that way at all. The Egyptians smashed across the Suez Canal and made a shambles of the Bar-Lev Line.[20] An initial artillery barrage, coupled with air attacks and the use of infantrymen with antitank weapons, scored a major initial success. Israeli tanks were destroyed in considerable numbers by Sagger missiles, at least 150 (out of 240) during the first day; SAMs took significant toll of Israeli aircraft. And on the Syrian front, Syrian troops made good headway in the early days, breaking through Israeli defenses and threatening to cut off the entire Golan. Indeed the Golan, for the Israelis, was the more critical front.

But the Arabs were unable to maintain their momentum. The Israelis desperately (they were ready to accept a truce in the early days of the war) reformed their units in Sinai, and in the middle of battle changed their tank tactics completely, abandoning the methods that had served so well in 1967. The Egyptians now overextended themselves and lost heavily in tanks. They had not protected their rear adequately, and a rapidly moving column under General Sharon succeeded in forcing its way across the Suez Canal. The ultimate result was to surround the city of Suez, cut the Cairo road, and isolate the Egyptian Third Army. Given the initial conditions, it was a remarkable tactical victory for the Israelis. On the Golan, the Syrian drive ran out of energy, and the Israelis were able to turn the battle around there as well.

---

[20] See *Selected Readings in Tactics: The 1973 Middle East War*, RB 100–2, vol. 1 (Fort Leavenworth: U.S. Army Command and General Staff College, 1975), for a very thorough discussion of these actions.

The war had lasted three weeks. Both sides were near exhaustion. Many Israelis had wanted to move on to Cairo or at least to destroy the Egyptian army in Sinai before agreeing to a cease-fire. But the Russians threatened to intervene, and the United States, having its own reasons for slowing the Israeli advance, went on a brief alert to impress the Russians with its control of the situation.

The war at its end was, in spite of the final military postures of the combatants, a major strategic victory for the Arabs. This had been no weekend war; it had strained Israeli ability to the utmost. Both the Syrians and Egyptians had obtained their initial objectives. The Bar-Lev Line in Sinai had been broken and Israeli military techniques somewhat discredited. The desperate dependence upon the United States for supply was all too apparent. The myth of the invincibility of the Israelis and the innate inferiority of the Arabs had been shattered. Arab oil power had contributed to this victory, not only by underwriting the war itself, but by threatening the West with an oil drought and actually applying an oil boycott for a time. As long as the oil-rich Arab states are willing to support a continuing round of conflict with Israel, there are only two basic options open to the West: acquiescence in some form with Arab demands, or military takeover of some of the oil fields. Because American policy has slowly veered toward the first of these two options, the Israelis can be said to have lost the 1973 war in a major sense. The United States is the only major supporter in the world of the Israelis;[21] any lessening of this support is a setback of considerable dimensions to the Israelis.

[21] The other country with especially close ties with Israel is South Africa, which is a major arms customer of Israel. South Africa and Israel together operate a large plant that manufactures electronic devices for counterinsurgency and other sensitive equipment denied to South Africa by Western governments. Israeli-South African trade rose 400 percent between 1972 and 1977. For this and other information documenting the growing Israeli-South African nexus, see John K. Cooley, "Studies Indicate South Africa and Israel Increase Cooperation," *Christian Science Monitor,* 15 March 1977, p. 9. For a rare and thought-provoking analysis of the Israeli-South African connection see Edward I. Steinhart, "Shylock and Prospero: Anti-Semitism, Zionism and South African Ideology," *Ufahamu* 4 (Winter 1974) :35–36.

THE NEGOTIATIONS

Since the 1973 war, the Arabs, Israelis, Russians, and Americans — and others as well — have moved about in a slowly evolving drama of settling the problem, as it were. Before discussing this in any detail, it is important to explain what is meant by negotiation and what realistically can be expected from the final process of bargaining.

Too often we think of the Arab-Israeli dispute as being similar to the problem of buying, let us say, a used car. A seller, anxious to move his merchandise, deals face-to-face with a usually equally anxious buyer, who has already "psyched" himself into the belief that he has to have a new car, and soon at that. Small wonder, then, that in most cases a deal is soon consummated, each side giving a little here and there. If selling an automobile were as complicated as settling the Arab-Israeli dispute, there would be no automobile dealers left and potential buyers would long ago have settled for bicycling.

To negotiate normally does not mean the presentation of absolutely rigid positions and a mutual unwillingness to make any concessions. One says that something, price perhaps, is negotiable when one means that give and take is possible, that mutual concessions of one sort or another are conceivable, and that a *quid pro quo* is a proper way of filling in details. But this has not over the years characterized the attitudes of either the Arabs or the Israelis. Both have at one time or another been stupidly intransigent, unwilling to bend at all. When the Israelis were weak, in 1949 and 1950, for example, their Arab neighbors were absolutely unwilling to make any concession to them, even the one of recognizing the legitimacy of Israel's existence. When the Israelis were strong, they were equally unwilling to give up anything to the Arabs. They might have desired peace, as they have constantly reiterated, but not enough to pay a political price for it.

Many problems, even those in our private lives, require a certain amount of travail and anguish before solutions are worked out. How many lives must be lost at a dangerous highway intersection before remedial measures are taken? How many wars must be fought by Israelis and Arabs before both sides will finally see the futility of it all and agree to some solution? As Henry Kissinger has said on a number of occasions, it is very easy to solve the Arab-Israeli dispute if you merely look in from the outside and have no personal stakes. What is difficult is *accepting* any such solution if you are on the inside and do indeed have personal stakes in the settlement. Kissinger's view was that only the Arabs and Israelis could settle their dispute when the time was ripe because the essence of the prolongation of the dispute was the need for both sides to accept an answer. The world outside can provide facilities for negotiation; it can put various kinds of pressures on the antagonists to make *not* accepting a solution more uncomfortable than accepting one. When each side views the prolongation of the dispute as more uncomfortable than accepting a solution to it, then it will no longer be a major problem. In the wake of Camp David in the fall of 1978 it seemed that at least Israel and Egypt were prepared to break the pattern of repeated conflict. But this willingness was not true of the other Arab states. The overall problem — the key to which is the Palestinians and the status of the West Bank — remains. Even should Egypt and Israel conclude a separate peace, it is impossible to rule out future military conflict between the two, although such conflict would seem less likely.

As pointed out earlier, the dispute today is not the dispute of 1949; its dimensions have changed. To emphasize just one point, in 1949 the Arab states still denied the very existence of Israel. This is not true today. What has happened is that nearly thirty years of war have convinced most Arab leaders that whether they like it or not, Israel is here to stay. What was at one time nonnegotiable for the Arabs is now a well-understood concession. But no amount of talking or persuasion in the early 1950s would have convinced the Arabs of this. What was needed was time and apparently some violence.

The Arabs in general are convinced that time is on their side. They like to point to the Crusaders, who established for a brief period the Kingdom of Jerusalem — from 1100 to 1187 — but were ultimately dispossessed by Saladin. Palestine is a palimpsest of occupations, conquests, victories, and defeats. The Israelis are, of course, as conscious of history as are the Arabs, but they naturally give more emphasis to their thirty years of success. But ultimately, many Arabs believe, the Israelis will stumble in a future war. The Arabs can wait for this. They have time and people and, increasingly, money.

It is obvious that any serious negotiations leading to a serious settlement of the dispute, whenever that takes place, must satisfy certain actors in the Middle Eastern drama. An Israeli government will have to live with it, that is, get it through the Knesset and survive subsequent elections. It must be politically palatable to the political participants in Israel. If these participants are unreasonable, then the settlement will be skewed and unstable, or more likely there will be no settlement at all. An Egyptian government, too, must be satisfied. That means that a Sadat, or whoever governs Egypt at the time, must discern personal political advantages in a settlement. The army must make its peace with the settlement. And the ubiquitous Cairo "street," which often demonstrates and sometimes riots, must accept the settlement and consider it a victory. And, of course, the Palestinians must derive something from the settlement. Their numbers alone as well as their ability to sabotage any settlement unacceptable to them make it evident that their demands must be heeded. It is in the nature of political negotiation that what is a nest of compromises to the principals must generally be viewed as victories by the people back home. Small wonder, then, that the task of resolving the dispute between Arabs and Israelis has up to now eluded all politicians . . . and statesmen. It should be reiterated here that Camp David did not produce a settlement; at most it was a prelude to a separate peace between Egypt and Israel. Two members of Begin's cabinet voted against the accord with Sadat and Sadat himself lost two foreign ministers, one after his trip to Jerusalem and one after Camp David.

Until recently, there has been very little negotiation between Arabs and Israelis. After the end of the 1948–1949 fighting, Ralph Bunche, the United Nations mediator, succeeded in getting Israeli, Egyptian, Jordanian, and Syrian representatives to go to the island of Rhodes to sign a number of bilateral disengagement agreements. The Iraqis refused to come. But there was no face-to-face give and take. These agreements certainly did not settle any of the main issues between the antagonists; nor could they. In addition, Jordanian and Israeli negotiations over border rectifications and other matters did take place, but secretly and with the direct participation of King Abdullah. But these negotiations ended with Abdullah's assassination in 1951. It must be added that apparently King Husayn has had pourparlers of sorts with various Israeli leaders over the years, but these have not been publicly acknowledged.

There was no mechanism set up to deal with minor disputes and recurring difficulties, with the exception of a small United Nation detachment in Jerusalem. There was absolutely no way of dealing with the activities of Palestinian guerrillas, since every Arab government could disclaim knowledge of and responsibility for their actions.

In the wake of the 1956 war there were no negotiations. Israel was pressured by the United States to disgorge its conquests, which it did. Egypt was similarly prevailed upon to accept United Nations forces on its territory. But the antagonists did not make any effort even to establish a mechanism for negotiation. The Israelis always insisted at this time that they would negotiate only face-to-face with Arab governments, and with the Palestinians not at all. This was, as the Israelis well knew, unacceptable to the Arabs.

The 1967 conflict produced no discussions by the principals of the general issues separating them. Indeed, the conflict added to the problems, inasmuch as Israel ended the war in possession of vast new territories. The United Nations had, of course, played a role in getting a cease-fire accepted; it also provided a forum for polemics from all sides. But it cannot be said that the United Nations or its secretaries-general have been very successful in promoting even fragmentary settlement of the dispute. This lack of success stems partly from deep Israeli suspicion of the United Nations. The United Nations has also failed in this regard because, in expanding to encompass the new "third world" countries, it has become generally hostile to the Israelis and their interests. (The United Nations resolution adopted in 1975 that Zionism was equivalent to racism is the kind of act that could hardly bolster Israeli trust in the organization.) It must be added here that in spite of the boasts of both the United States and the Soviet Union about their desire for peace in the area, neither has displayed much energy in controlling their client states. Each has supplied vast quantities of arms and economic assistance to its clients; each has given covert and overt political assistance when its clients have needed it. Friendship for the Arabs and their causes was the basis for Soviet entry into the Middle East. Friendship for Israel by the United States is a product more of domestic politics than of anything else. The result has been a singular lack of enthusiasm for getting Arabs and Israelis together.

The year 1967 is really a vitally important benchmark in the history of nonnegotiation. The war produced such a skewed military result — to the Arabs' disadvantage — that it should have been evident to everyone, including the Israelis and their supporters, that it could not become the basis for a stable long-term settlement. Some device for defusing this situation was needed. None was forthcoming. The United Nations, it is true, adopted Resolution 242 that provided for a return of territories captured. Through diplomacy, Israel and her antagonists were eventually persuaded to agree to this document, but the two signatories interpreted the words in contradictory and immiscible ways.[22] In addition to this, 1967 saw the beginnings of an effective and aggressive PLO, a development that caught Israel without any means of response, since it did not and does not recognize the PLO as a legitimate spokesman for Palestinian interests.

The sum total of these events is that Israel and the Arabs, because they were unwilling and unable to negotiate together on the issues dividing them, were forced to rely on the United Nations and on their influence with their patron states, the United States and the Soviet Union. Such mechanisms were faulty and unresponsive.

The 1973 war changed some of this. It did not turn out to be just another Israeli victory. Arab oil power became mobilized, an event that effected a worldwide reexamination of attitudes towards the Arab-Israeli imbroglio. Henry Kissinger, as the secretary of state, not only attempted to influence the outcome of the war but the nature of the negotiations that would fol-

---

22 In the spring of 1978, Foreign Minister Dayan argued that the Israelis no longer view Resolution 242 the way they did originally.

low it. He attempted to become the confidant of all the principals, and he created "shuttle" diplomacy.

There is much controversy over the Kissinger role; not all Americans, or Arabs, or Israelis were convinced of his effectiveness or even of his sincerity. The actual fighting ended with Israeli forces astride the Suez-Cairo road and with an Egyptian army cut off from food and supplies (and unable to extricate itself). Similarly, in Syria, after an unfortunate start, Israeli troops had recaptured the Golan and had moved down the Damascus road. It was Kissinger's view that Israel should not win an overwhelming victory, for this in itself would not do much to ease Israel's main problem, but would in fact be precisely the sort of thing that would spur the Arabs to another round of conflict within a short time. To ensure negotiations that were meaningful, Kissinger felt, the Arabs would have to be left in a position that could be interpreted by *them* as a victory. For the Egyptians, this meant that some military force had to be left on the east side of the Suez Canal, for this could be viewed as land captured. For Syria, retention of Keneitra, the main town in Golan, could be similarly viewed. In each case, Israel had to concede something that could be presented to the Arabs as the prize of conflict. Perhaps this would have happened anyway without Kissinger's intervention. But he was heavily involved, parrying, it might seem, threats by the Russians — American forces were put on alert at one time during the closing days of the fighting — unfriendly opinion in the United States, ungrateful Israelis or Arabs, and threats of an oil boycott from the Saudis. A boycott had in fact been proclaimed, as had a slowdown of production; one of Kissinger's most difficult tasks was to procure Saudi cooperation in the maneuvers that he inspired in Sinai and Golan. Out of it all, stretching ultimately into 1975, came the disengagement agreements, the return of prisoners (of special importance to the Israelis), and the pull-back arrangements that left a few miles of western Sinai in Egyptian hands as well as Keneitra with the Syrians.[23]

---

[23] It is tedious to describe in detail the precise arrangements that resulted on observers in Sinai, a symbolic Egyptian presence at the passes,

Given the outcome of the war and the prevailing political attitudes in the Middle East and in the rest of the world, this was probably the maximum degree of concession that any Israeli government could accept. In other words, the success of these and any other negotiations now had to be measured by the willingness of the Israelis to make concessions. (This will be discussed more fully below.) Kissinger had also succeeded in getting the Geneva Conference established, although many were convinced that this was typical Kissinger "grandstanding." In any event, nothing of any consequence happened in Geneva, and the real bargaining and jockeying have taken place in the Middle East and in Washington and Moscow.

The most dramatic event in all of these negotiations was Sadat's visit to Israel in November 1977. It was bold and unexpected. Although it was greeted with enthusiasm in Israel itself, reaction in the Arab world was mixed at best. Ultimately, Sadat was condemned by such states as Libya, Syria, and Iraq. Domestically, Sadat ran risks, but it turned out that his visit to Israel was highly popular in Egypt. Both Egyptians and Israelis seemed eager for a peace settlement.

Indeed, a considerable number of negotiators traveled back and forth between the two countries. But the negotiations soon stalled over two critical issues. Sadat argued that he was not negotiating solely on behalf of Egypt, but for the Palestinians and other Arabs as well. The Israelis simply did not have any viable position to fall back on with respect to the presence of a Palestinian "state" or "entity" on its borders. Yet it was precisely that presence that Sadat said he had to have in any overall settlement that he could approve. In addition, for reasons that seem unreal at best, the Israelis found it difficult to abandon the notion that they should continue to possess "settlements" within Sinai after it had been returned to the Egyptians.[24]

---

and other concessions by the Israelis. Even these concessions would not have been made without enormous pressures being applied to the Israelis.

[24] Indeed, one can say that the Israelis made no real response to Sadat's initiative. In fact, they did just the opposite. They began *building* settlements rather than dismantling them. This put Sadat in a most precarious

The next dramatic development was the Camp David meeting in September 1978. This had been proceeded by months of haggling and posturing, but by late summer both Israel and Egypt seemed willing to entangle the United States in negotiations. Israel previously had always insisted that such negotiations take place only face-to-face with its adversaries. President Carter, slumping badly in popularity polls, was eager to participate. The result was that Sadat agreed to negotiate a separate peace with the Israelis — and lost his foreign minister by resignation in doing so — but claimed misleadingly that the Israelis had met his conditions on the Palestinians. The Israelis did agree to withdraw from the settlements in Sinai but there is little evidence that they expect the situation in the West Bank or Gaza to change very much. Nevertheless, numerous unduly optimistic pronouncements about the future of these areas were made.

By late 1978 the peace treaty between Egypt and Israel was drafted and close to being approved. The signing of the treaty was expected to take place on December 10, the day Begin and Sadat were to receive their Nobel prizes. However, Sadat did not even go to Oslo and the treaty remained unsigned. The next deadline (December 17), three months after the Camp David announcement, again passed without either Begin or Sadat signing the treaty.

Sadat, not satisfied with the treaty, continued to argue over three issues: (1) the linkage between the signing of the treaty and a timetable for implementation of the Israeli "concessions" to the Palestinians, (2) dispute over the quantity of Egyptian oil to be sold to the Israelis in the future, and (3) Egyptian insistence that its obligations to other Arab states be recognized in this treaty by the Israelis.

These objections were not serious enough to cancel hope that an agreement will eventually be signed. The first issue, concerning linkage, could be viewed as posturing on Sadat's

---

position and invited PLO terrorism and retaliation. The fact that the Begin cabinet itself was bitterly split over this issue (with Sharon, the minister of agriculture, playing the hawk and Weizman, the minister of defense, playing the dove) underlines its significance.

part, in an attempt to appeal to the wider Arab world by showing how hard he was working for Palestinian interests. The second objection is minor as there are an infinite number of ways to resolve this particular problem. The third issue is ambiguous; it is unrealistic to believe that signing a treaty with Israel could wipe out all "obligations" to other Arab states. If it was decided to modify some of these obligations, how would they be identified and defined? The draft treaty overall seems unexceptionable, and chances are that Egypt and Israel will initial it when the time is psychologically right for both.

The significant part of these negotiations, regardless of these last minute maneuvers, is that Egypt by agreeing to negotiate with Israel, has fundamentally changed the Arab perception of Israel. Egypt has made this move unilaterally and has provoked discontent and some bitterness in many Arabs, notably the Palestinians. However, it is certain that some form of Arab-Israeli enmity will continue. Egypt's new role in these ticklish affairs assures new dimensions in the conflict, with repercussions spreading to many parts of the Middle East. In the euphoria over this treaty it should not be overlooked that Egypt had indeed deserted most of her Arab friends by agreeing to deal with Israel and has in the eyes of most Arabs "sold out" the Palestinians. Peace between Egypt and Israel now seems more likely, but general peace for Israel is yet to be achieved.

THE PROSPECTS FOR A GENERAL SETTLEMENT

The safest prediction always is that things will remain the same, that negotiations will continue in company with intransigence, and that little change of substance will soon occur. But it cannot be denied that the Camp David accord is a significant development with respect to the *Egyptian*-Israeli dispute; it does not represent significant change in the *Arab*-Israeli dispute, the key to which is the role and fate of the Palestinians. But before discussing this question further, let us back up and try to understand why it has been so difficult for an Israeli government to negotiate the significant issues in dispute.

It was the government of Golda Meir that had fought the

war of 1973 and had participated in the principal Kissinger negotiations in 1974. This government fell, however, and was replaced by another labor coalition headed by former general Yitzak Rabin. Rabin's government was weak, and Rabin himself as well as others in this government became implicated in various financial scandals. Shimon Peres took over as party leader, but lost in the ensuing election (1977) to Menahem Begin and his Likud bloc. It was a surprising outcome to most political observers, but in the post-election analyses it became evident that what had happened was simply the culmination of an increasing and long-term disenchantment with the labor group and its same old group of tired faces.[25] Israel was in fact searching for genuine alternative leadership at the same time that it was drifting into a more conservative stance — the hard-line stance, as it were.

Regardless of the authenticity of the political credentials with which Begin had entered the Knesset, he proved, in the short term at least, to be a clever politician. He was and always had been an advocate of expansion, toughness, and firmness — and, apparently as a necessary precondition for all of this, a belief that Israel could survive in an increasingly hostile world, if only it were unbending in the degree of its concessions to Arabs and others.

Many viewed the Begin government with dismay and were convinced that there was no way of now achieving an accommodation. Others, more cynically, were convinced that Begin's tough talk was just bargaining and that he was as likely to face facts as a Rabin or a Meir. In any event, the summer and early fall of 1977 brought not only tough talk from the Israeli government but also legal encouragement for the establishment of Israeli settlements in the Sinai, the West Bank, and the Golan, and the extension of "services" to the Arab population in the occupied territories — all evidence of intransigence on the question of the return of territory to the Arabs. Begin also steadfastly refused to recognize the PLO or to admit the right of the Palestinians to be present at any bargaining table.

[25] Post-election polls indicated that those Israelis of Middle Eastern origin were particularly disenchanted with Labor party leadership and turned to the Likud bloc as the only way of effecting real change.

The issues are evident. The attitudes of both Israelis and Arabs are clearly known and understood. Whatever accommodation comes about in the near future may simply be the result of shifts in power. Some background factors that may be important in these possible shifts in power should be mentioned here.

1. The proportion of *Jewish* Israelis in the population at large is probably now slightly declining and in absolute numbers is leveling off. Yet these are of the Israelis the most loyal to the concept of Israel, and it is they who would have to defend it in future conflicts. At the same time, the population of the surrounding Arab world continues to grow.

2. The gap between the military technology in Israel, and that in the Arab world (primarily in Egypt) has probably passed its peak, although of course it is still there. But no longer can one say that it is the struggle of one age with another.

3. Israel is locked into a most unfortunate economy, with enormous inflation and a defense budget that is impossibly large for its population. (This is true to some extent of Egypt as well.) Also seriously lacking in natural resources, Israel is today hostage to Iran in that the Shah as of late 1978 supplied approximately 70 percent of petroleum needs.

4. Although United States support for Israel remains strong, there is not much current evidence that Russian support for the Arabs is lessening. But support for the Arab world from lesser powers — those in Black Africa and Asia, for example — has been building. There is much less world support for the Israelis now than there was in 1967.

5. The United States remains in an energy crisis. Our dependence upon Arab (largely Saudi) oil continues to increase. To the degree that this is so, we are open to Arab political influence. This can be uncomfortable; it is not unreasonable to assume that some Arab oil leverage will be applied to the United States to lessen its historically uncritical support of Israel. The Israelis cannot afford to lose this support.

6. Camp David naturally produced euphoria. But even a formal peace treaty between Egypt and Israel — not yet signed at the time of writing — and an exchange of ambassadors can-

not guarantee that some future Egyptian government will not find the pressures for renewed conflict with the Israelis irresistible. Moreover, Egyptian and Israeli governments come and go; there is no predicting what aberrant and conflicting policy paths they may pursue in the future.

7. The essential factor for peace in this troubled area is the Palestinians. Whatever their numbers (4 million perhaps) they must be consulted and they must be accommodated. At the end of 1978, the bulk of these Palestinians still considered the PLO its legitimate representative. The Israelis have good reasons for not dealing with the PLO but without doing so there can be no peace.

As power shifts in imperceptible ways as well as in major ways, the various actors in this drama will be prompted to make judgments and accommodations that would have been unthinkable in earlier times. Certainly Sadat has done so and Begin as well. In late summer 1977, President Hafez al-Assad of Syria said that he was prepared to sign a peace agreement with Israel, although he would stop short of exchanging ambassadors with it. Only a few years ago, such a statement would not have been possible. But in the same interview Assad said: "There's no third choice; it's either peace or war. I don't mean today or tomorrow. But, eventually, Israel will not be able to continue challenging us. Arabs have a population many times that of Israel; we have many times the area; we have many times the resources; we're going to have many times more technicians. The qualitative gap is closing. The future cannot be in favor of Israel."[26] By late 1978, al-Assad was more intransigent. Certainly the PLO, feeling cheated by Camp David, was likely to follow a hard line in the near future.

Even the possession of nuclear weapons — there seems little doubt that such weapons are in Israeli hands, although untested — will not change this conclusion very much. An accommodation probably seemed important to a Sadat for political survival; an accommodation is important to the Israelis for national survival. But much travail and agony — for Ameri-

26 *New York Times*, 29 August 1977.

cans and Russians as well — may still be necessary before a peace settlement is finally initialed . . . for the whole area, it must be emphasized, and not just for the Egyptians and the Israelis.

CHAPTER IX

The Power of Petroleum

THE GEARS OF the Middle Eastern social and political systems are generously lubricated by a precious resource — petroleum. This resource has become the chief basis for the domestic, regional, and international power currently being used by Middle Eastern political leaders to achieve their increasingly ambitious goals. The world shifted to petroleum during the First World War to fuel its industrial, military, and technological machinery; it then became inevitable that the Middle East would be of central significance in the world power equation. For the first seventy years of this century, the potentials of its resources were never realized. Lacking indigenous technological knowledge, economically feeble, and generally subjected to the control of Western colonial powers, the oil-producing countries lacked the strength and market dominance to determine the fate of their own resources. The key decisions concerning exploration, production, marketing, and pricing were made by large Western oil companies or by their parent political systems in Europe or the United States.

Following the Second World War and coinciding with the strong nationalist and neutralist movements that swept through the developing world, the petroleum-producing countries began to demand greater control over what they considered their own resources. At first, these demands took the form of insistence on higher prices for petroleum and larger royalties. In short, the political leaders of the oil-rich countries fought in the beginning for better bargains. With the formation of the Organization of Petroleum Exporting Countries (OPEC) in 1960, followed by the succession of meetings in Tripoli and Tehran in the early 1970s and the quadrupling of prices during the October 1973 war, the entire process of international decision making about oil was revolutionized. The producing countries, now no longer content merely to drive better bargains, challenged the entire bargaining system and succeeded in wresting decisional control away from the multinational oil organizations. From then on, the producing countries became the repositories of authority concerning the entire industry of hydrocarbon production and exploitation. It is now the oil companies and the consuming countries who have been put on the defensive. In fact, the international oil companies are now by and large marketing agents for OPEC.

This transformation in the interrelationships of international oil politics and economics has had a profound effect upon the domestic political patterns of all Middle Eastern countries — whether they are rich or poor in petroleum reserves. It has also changed significantly the interregional and international political scene. And it has affected in new ways the complex interactions between domestic political processes and international politics. In this chapter, we will explore these changing patterns.

Among the questions that we pose here are the following: How did the dramatic changes in the traditional producer, company, and consumer system in fact come about? What has been the changing political and economic role of the international oil companies? What is the political clout and complexion of OPEC? What have been the politics of the pricing conflict? What are the international political consequences of the newly developed petroleum power? How does this power affect, for example, United States foreign policy, or the volatile Arab-Israeli dispute? What are the domestic political consequences of this oil power? How does this power shape the responses of the various countries to the challenges of modernization and political development discussed throughout this book? Is oil power a conservative or a transforming force? And

finally, what does the future of the petroleum dynamics hold
for the political future of the area?

THE POOL OF PETROLEUM POWER

Many Western observers and leaders of opinion seriously
underestimate the extent of Middle Eastern petroleum wealth.
It is often argued that the contemporary international influence wielded by Middle Eastern governments is a transitory
phenomenon, since with the depletion of their oil reserves,
they will be forced to retreat once again to the backwaters of
world politics. This position is buttressed with emphases upon
the potential discovery of huge petroleum reserves elsewhere
in the world, the inevitable shift to alternate sources of energy,
the capacity of the Western world to conserve energy, and by
underestimating just how much oil there is in place in the
Middle East. This perspective has to some extent been reinforced by Middle Eastern spokesmen themselves, who have for
years pursued a calculated policy of understating their own oil
wealth.

This position (which was a particularly popular one in the
early 1970s) had lost much of its credibility by the end of the
decade. The social, economic, and technological difficulties
involved in the creation of viable alternate energy sources
could no longer be denied. Although Western European countries made some progress in energy conservation, the United
States had failed almost completely in its efforts in this area.
What is more, President Jimmy Carter's almost frantic attempt
to institute an energy policy was not in fact comprehensive
and was stalled by regional political considerations. Japan, a
nation that imports over 90 percent of its petroleum and that
can ill afford to be lackadaisical in instituting an effective new
energy program, has also done surprisingly little in the areas
of alternate energy development, energy conservation, and
national energy planning.[1] Finally, the oil reserves recently

---

[1] One analyst writes: "For a country where the government-company
relationship has been so close and where oil imports are so crucial, the
Japanese have been surprisingly tentative in establishing a realistic program." See Louis Turner, "European and Japanese Energy Policies," *Current History* 74 (March 1978):107. In the late 1970s, the Japanese relied
on Middle Eastern countries for 75 percent of their petroleum supplies.

discovered and put into production in the north slope of Alaska, the North Sea, and Mexico, while providing valuable assistance in absolute terms, are very small indeed when compared to those in the Middle East.[2] Ironically, their very existence has served a negative purpose, since when they came on stream in 1977 and 1978, they helped occasion a temporary oil glut that only reinforced the opinions of those who continue to argue that there is no energy crisis, that oil is plentiful, that conservation is unnecessary, and that prices are grossly inflated.

Table IX.1 provides a detailed record of Middle Eastern proven reserves of petroleum, 1955–1978. According to these calculations, the Middle East has steadily accounted for over 60 percent of the world's petroleum reserves. When the reserves of the Communist world are deleted from the equation, the Middle East's percentage of the world's reserves climbs to approximately 75 percent. Petroleum geologists privately estimate that even these figures underestimate the Middle East's share of this resource. It may in fact be as high as 70 percent of the world's supply and 85 percent of the non-Communist world's supply. A recent study published in the *Scientific American* reports that the rich Middle Eastern reserves "have been found in a region that measures only some 800 by 500 miles. Might such a prolific oil-bearing region be found again? It is not very likely. Many of the remaining possible areas of the world have already been evaluated by seismic testing or exploratory wells and no evidence of a new Middle East has come to light."[3]

The reserves of Saudi Arabia alone are staggering. The figure given in Table IX.1, 150 billion barrels, is a conservative

[2] As Daniel Yergin writes: "Alaskan production in a decade or so will only make up for declining production in the lower 48 states. The North Sea oil fields could reach 5 million to 6 million barrels a day by 1985, but, barring some major new finds, their output will then begin to go down. The only major new oil strike of the 1970's was the one in Mexico, and production there is being held back by political and technical problems." Yergin, "The Real Meaning of the Energy Crunch," *New York Times Magazine*, 4 June 1978, p. 99.

[3] Andrew R. Flower, "World Oil Production," *Scientific American* 238 (March 1978) :44.

TABLE IX.1   *The Middle East: Proven Reserves of Petroleum,*
1955–1978   (millions of barrels)

	Jan. 1, 1955	Jan. 1, 1965	Jan. 1, 1975	Jan. 1, 1978
Abu Dhabi	– – –	7,700	30,000	31,000
Afghanistan	– – –	– – –	85	84
Algeria	5	7,500	7,700	6,600
Bahrain	215	250	336	270
Dubai	– – –	– – –	2,420	1,400
Egypt	92	1,500	3,700	2,450
Iran	15,000	38,000	66,000	62,000
Iraq	14,250	25,000	35,000	34,500
Kuwait	30,000	63,000	72,800	67,000
Libya	– – –	9,000	26,600	25,000
Morocco	15	15	– – –	0.1
Neutral Zone	429	12,500	17,300	6,200
Oman	– – –	500	6,000	5,560
Pakistan	20	25	28.7	280
Qatar	1,500	3,500	6,000	5,600
Saudi Arabia	36,000	60,500	164,500	150,000
Sharjah	– – –	– – –	– – –	25
Syria	– – –	500	1,500	2,150
Tunisia	– – –	.1	1,100	2,670
Turkey	65	700	500	370
Total Middle East	97,591.0	230,190.1	441,569.7	403,159.1
Total world	157,536.0	341,273.0	715,697.1	645,847.7
Middle East percentage of world reserves	62.0	67.5	61.7	62.4

Source: *The Oil and Gas Journal,* 27 December 1954; 28 December 1964;
30 December 1974; and 26 December 1977.

one; other sources put Saudi Arabia's proven reserves closer to
200 billion barrels. An indication of the extent of this wealth
can be seen in the news quietly reported that the Saudis discovered three new fields in 1975 — with proven reserves of 7
billion barrels! The estimated total of recoverable barrels in
the highly publicized North Sea fields is in contrast only 500
million barrels, although proven reserves are estimated to be
as high as 20 billion barrels.[4] Even if one takes the 150 billion
barrel figure, the Saudi Arabians still account for one-fourth

[4] Ibid. See also *The Oil and Gas Journal,* 27 December 1976, p. 104.

of the world's proven reserves. Their reserves are five times those of the United States and twice those of the Soviet Union.

Kuwait, Iraq, and Iran also have substantial petroleum reserves. The three of them together have over 160 billion barrels of proven reserves. But even here the figures are misleading. The published figures consistently indicate that Iraq has approximately only half of the proven reserves of either Kuwait or Iran. Again, geologists say otherwise in private. Iraq is generally considered to be the only other Middle Eastern country whose reserves might in fact rival those of Saudi Arabia. This position was lent considerable credibility early in 1978, when a major discovery of a massive reserve near Nasriya in southeastern Iraq was reported. The area was immediately cordoned off by the Iraqi army, and the extent of the discovery is not known. Even Iran, whose reserves are commonly believed to be rapidly diminishing, has perhaps closer to 75 billion barrels than the 60–65 billion usually reported.

Actual production statistics also impressively document the overriding significance of the Middle East in the world energy picture. Table IX.2 summarizes this situation. Well over 40 percent of the world's oil is now being produced by Middle Eastern countries. Today, six of the top ten oil-producing countries are located in the Middle East. In decreasing magnitude of production, they are Saudi Arabia, Iran, Iraq, Libya, Kuwait, and Abu Dhabi. In 1977, 4,161 wells produced an average of more than 5,000 barrels per day per well. In contrast, over 500,000 producing wells in the United States produced at the average rate of 6 barrels per day per well.[5]

A close look at the production trends indicates a severely changing picture for the United States. By 1976, the United States was importing over 47 percent of its petroleum supplies; in 1977, it was importing more than 50 percent. In 1976, 46 percent of these imports came from Middle Eastern countries. At the same time, 84 percent of United States imports originated from OPEC countries. In 1977, these figures were even

[5] These figures are the calculations of petroleum geologist Samuel P. Ellison, Jr.

TABLE IX.2   *The Middle East: Daily Petroleum Production,*
1955–1978 (thousands of barrels)

	Jan. 1, 1955	Jan. 1, 1965	Jan. 1, 1975	Jan. 1, 1978
Abu Dhabi	– – –	185.0	1,750.0	1,680.0
Afghanistan	– – –	– – –	.2	0.19
Algeria	1.6	552.4	888.8	989.8
Bahrain	30.1	49.0	68.0	51.2
Dubai	– – –	– – –	232.0	320.0
Egypt	37.8	124.7	118.3	449.8
Iran	43.0	1,815.0	6,128.0	5,649.8
Iraq	625.0	1,226.7	1,829.3	2,051.2
Kuwait	942.0	2,120.0	2,600.0	1,700.0
Libya	– – –	858.6	1,700.0	2,049.8
Morocco	2.4	2.9	.9	0.27
Neutral Zone	18.7	374.0	485.4	382.1
Pakistan	5.3	8.4	7.1	9.8
Qatar	97.9	220.8	546.0	349.8
Oman	– – –	– – –	297.0	349.8
Saudi Arabia	952.0	1,695.9	8,400.0	8,949.8
Sharjah	– – –	– – –	50.0	29.8
Syria	– – –	– – –	119.0	200.0
Tunisia	– – –	– – –	85.0	86.8
Turkey	1.1	16.3	65.3	64.9
Total Middle East	2,820.9	9,434.7	25,370.3	25,364.86
Total world	13,544.5	27,993.0	56,772.0	57,834.7
Middle East percentage of world production	20.8	33.7	44.7	43.8

Source: *The Oil and Gas Journal,* 27 December 1954; 28 December 1964; 30 December 1974; and 26 December 1977.

more striking. Today, Saudi Arabia is the largest exporter of petroleum to the United States. In 1970, the United States was importing only a little more than 1.3 million barrels of oil per day; by 1977, this figure had ballooned to over 9.5 million barrels per day. More and more of this oil is coming from the Middle East. The political implications of this situation are obvious. As Henry Kissinger put it in August 1977: "For the first time in our history, a small group of nations controlling a scarce resource could over time be tempted to pressure us into foreign policy decisions not dictated by our national interest."[6]

But the Middle East has more than oil. The area also has one-third of all the proven reserves of natural gas in the world.[7] After the Soviet Union, Iran is now the world's second largest repository of natural gas. Algeria, with over 60 percent of all proven reserves of gas on the African continent, is already exporting quantities of this fuel to the east coast of the United States. As this mineral wealth is converted into cash reserves, the Middle Eastern countries have begun to step up their efforts to explore for other resources. We already know that they possess significant amounts of the world's phosphates, copper, wolfram, chrome, coal, and lignite.

These data indicate that the Middle East has a petroleum base that will guarantee it a privileged and powerful position for many years to come. If it succeeds in its goals of developing its other natural wealth and if its leaders invest its wealth wisely, then the area may continue to be a critical force in the world well into the twenty-first century. The future depends to a large extent upon the political leaders of the various countries. In the end, the revolutionary shift in power to the oil-producing countries has been a political matter. The resources and economic strength had always been there; it took a series of imaginative political moves to fundamentally shift the control of these resources. A brief summary of this complex story follows.

THE MAJOR OIL COMPANIES AND THE TRADITIONAL INTERNATIONAL POWER STRUCTURE

For half a century, the politics and economics of petroleum were largely directed and controlled by a small group of international oil companies. Although the governments of the pro-

[6] As quoted in Congressional Quarterly, *The Middle East: U.S. Policy, Israel, Oil and the Arabs* (Washington, D.C.: Congressional Quarterly, 1977), p. 142. The data presented in this paragraph are drawn from Central Intelligence Agency, National Foreign Assessment Center, *International Energy Biweekly Statistical Review*, 22 March 1978.

[7] This figure is calculated on the basis of data provided in *The Oil and Gas Journal*, 26 December 1977, pp. 98–148.

ducing and consuming countries played a part in the overall process, the major companies were easily the dominant force. Today, they are still powerful and influential. The British were the first to move into the area when they began to produce petroleum commercially in 1908 in Iran. Thus, the Anglo-Persian Oil Company (later the Anglo-Iranian Oil Company and today known as British Petroleum) was the first multinational giant to gain a foothold in the region. With the entrance of Royal Dutch Shell into the area, the Europeans gained a tight early grip on oil exploration and production in the Middle East. Much of the history of international oil politics is explained in terms of the struggle between the British and the Americans as United States companies fought to gain entry into the rich Middle Eastern fields.

Although American oil companies had first wedged their way into the Middle Eastern oil business as minority partners in the Iraq Petroleum Company (IPC) and by bringing in their first well in the area in Bahrain in 1931, it was not until 1933 in Saudi Arabia and 1934 in Kuwait that the American companies entered the scene in a major way. In the case of Kuwait, two legendary characters, Frank Holmes and Archibald H. T. Chisholm, representing Gulf Oil of the United States and the Anglo-Persian Oil Company respectively, out-maneuvered each other into a standstill that resulted in the joint concession between the two companies (Kuwait Oil Company).[8] Saudi Arabia was another story. Here, led by Standard Oil of California (Socal), and subsequently joined by the Texas Company (Texaco) and later by Standard Oil of New Jersey (today's Exxon) and Socony-Vacuum Oil Company (today's Mobil), an all-American group took control over the world's richest oil territory. This operating company in Saudi Arabia is well known as the Arabian-American Oil Company (Aramco).[9] The four Aramco companies plus

[8] For an amusing account of the Holmes-Chisholm rivalry over the Kuwait concession, see Leonard Mosley, *Power Play: Oil in the Middle East* (Baltimore: Penguin Books, 1974), pp. 77–86.

[9] For years, Mobil Oil's share of Aramco production was only 10 percent, while the other three partners each controlled 30 percent. In the late 1970s, Mobil renegotiated its share of Aramco. Today it is 15 percent, while that of the remaining partners has fallen slightly to 28.33 percent each.

Gulf are the five largest American oil companies; along with British Petroleum and Royal Dutch Shell, they comprise the so-called Seven Sisters.[10]

The seven international majors were the controlling forces of world oil trade for years. Until relatively recently, they accounted for over 80 percent of all oil production outside North America and the Soviet bloc. They also controlled over 70 percent of the refining capacity and 50 percent of the tanker fleet in this area. Although other major companies, such as Campagnie Française des Pétroles (CFP) of France and Ente Nazionale Idrocarburi (ENI) of Italy, as well as a dozen other large American companies, have made significant inroads into the territory long monopolized by the big seven, the latter still are far and away the world's leaders among the fully integrated multinational oil corporations.[11]

These companies ruled supreme for so long for several interrelated reasons. First, they were all fully integrated units, i.e.,

---

Throughout the 1970s, Aramco and the Saudi Arabian government discussed the participation of the latter in Aramco's crude oil producing operations. The *Mobil Annual Report 1977* explains well the terms of the Saudi takeover. "Currently, the negotiations contemplate acquisition by the government of substantially all of Aramco's assets and the establishment of future arrangements. Under those proposed arrangements, Aramco will provide a broad range of management and technical services, will conduct an exploration program for the government, and will receive a fee. Also, the U.S. owner companies will have access through Aramco to substantial specified volumes of crude oil at a competitive price under a long-term contract." *Mobil Annual Report 1977*, p. 50.

[10] A very readable and informative book analyzing the history, politics, and personalities of these seven huge companies is Anthony Sampson's *The Seven Sisters: The Great Oil Companies and the World They Made* (New York: Viking Press, 1975).

[11] Partial exceptions today, of course, are the national oil companies of the leading petroleum-exporting countries. A case in point is the National Iranian Oil Company (NIOC), which in 1973 was not even listed among *Fortune* magazine's 300 largest industrial organizations outside the United States. In 1974, it suddenly appeared as number twenty-eight with sales of $4 billion. In 1975, it catapulted into third place with sales of approximately $17 billion; by 1978, NIOC sales had climbed to over $22 billion, which put it in second place behind Royal Dutch Shell among non-United States corporations. When United States corporations are included in the listing, NIOC ranked seventh in 1978. National companies such as NIOC, however, lack the assets, the infrastructures, and the integrated, multinational character of the international majors.

they were intimately involved in the exploration, development, production, transportation, refining, and marketing of the product. This provided them with great expertise in all aspects of the business, while at the same time enabling them to shift resources and emphasis back and forth and thus to protect each link in the chain at all times. Second, their very multinational character gave them a flexibility that enabled them to focus their efforts in whatever part of the world was economically and politically most advantageous at any given time. Third, the majors cooperated with one another in a number of subtle and in some not-so-subtle ways. In the Achnacarry Agreement of 1928, the three largest petroleum companies in the world at the time (Jersey-Standard, Royal Dutch Shell, Anglo-Persian) in effect divided up the world among themselves in order to discourage outside competition. In the 1950s, the companies stood together against Iran and Iraq when these countries fought to nationalize the Anglo-Iranian Oil Company and to severely restrict the concessions granted to the Iraq Petroleum Company. In both these cases, the united front of the oil companies successfully thwarted in different ways the demands of these Middle Eastern nationalists. International oil organization unity is also seen in the joint operating companies or consortia in which various combinations of the majors contractually agree to pursue business together. We have seen some examples of such combinations above.

Another cluster of reasons for major-oil-company hegemony for so long resides in the state of the producing countries themselves. Often ruled by weak traditional patrimonial leaders who owed their position to outside powers (primarily the British), the peoples of these countries were in no position to challenge anybody — much less powerful multinational giants. And also, in the case of the European companies, the governments had a direct and controlling interest in the businesses. As late as 1953, a strong nationalist movement in Iran, led by the charismatic Dr. Musaddiq, was suffocated by the international oil companies, backed by the British and American governments. Although Musaddiq's technocracy was able to produce the oil, the international majors made it impossible to market the product.

Throughout this period, the oil companies determined pricing policy. Until about 1950, they simply paid the governments of the producing countries a set royalty that averaged something less than twenty-five cents per barrel. Following the Second World War, Venezuela and Saudi Arabia led a drive that resulted in taxes amounting to half the net income earned by the companies. This move shifted the emphasis from volume to profits, and throughout the 1950s and 1960s government revenues were based on a posted price.[12] A royalty of 12.5 percent was paid on the posted price. This royalty and the production cost were added together, and this sum was subtracted from the posted price. The result was considered the company's profit, and it was on this profit that an income tax (50 percent until 1970) was paid to the oil-exporting country. These rearrangements of the payment process resulted in significantly higher revenues for the producing countries. Yet the rules of the game and all decisions made therein were still essentially determined by the international oil companies. Then, in February 1959 and in August 1960, the major companies unilaterally reduced the posted prices of Middle Eastern oil by 8 and 5 percent, respectively. These actions marked the beginning of the end of the old system.

THE POLITICS OF OPEC

In September 1960, the governments of Saudi Arabia, Iran, Kuwait, Iraq, and Venezuela met in Baghdad and founded OPEC. The goals of the organization announced at the time were to coordinate the member countries' policies towards the companies, to acquire a voice in future pricing policy, and to do something specific to restore the recent price cuts. The five founding members were later joined by Qatar, Indonesia, Libya, the United Arab Emirates, Algeria, Nigeria, Ecuador, and Gabon. By 1977, these thirteen countries (eight of which are Middle Eastern) accounted for 82 percent of the non-Communist world's reserves; an authoritative Library of Con-

---

12 The *posted price* is best defined as the price established in principle by the companies as a basis for business and royalty payment. It is compared to the *realized price,* which is the price actually paid for the oil as determined by market conditions. The realized price was usually lower than the posted price during this period.

gress study has conservatively predicted that OPEC countries would supply 61, 62, and 64 percent of the non-Communist world's oil demand in 1980, 1985, and 1990, respectively.[13]

The creation and drive of OPEC were an integral part of the wave of nationalistic fervor that swept the world in the 1950s and 1960s. Having only recently broken out of the colonial grasp of several of the greatest Western, industrial powers, the leadership of the developing nations fought to develop their nations' own identities by destroying their nations' dependence upon Western countries and multinational companies. The two men most responsible for the creation of OPEC were Perez Alfonza, Venezuela's minister of mines, and Shaykh Abdullah Tariki, Saudi Arabia's director-general of petroleum affairs. Both men were ardent nationalists with remarkable intelligence and integrity. They represented the forces of change then sweeping through the world.[14] In the words of George Stocking, the dissatisfaction of the producing countries "originated in the humus of distrust and suspicion laid down by the abrasive impact of western technology and a business culture on economically underdeveloped countries wholly dissimilar in their political and social institutions and their history and traditions. Once planted, they thrived under a blanket of hostility kept warm by the clash of a corporate quest for profits with the interests of underdeveloped countries as conceived by their politicians and their people."[15]

Little more than a decade after the creation of OPEC, the oil equation had changed. Table IX.3 provides a summary of the critical events and specific steps involved in the transformation. Led by the authoritarian-mobilizational regimes of Libya and Algeria and supported at critical times by the tra-

[13] See Ragaei El Mallakh, "OPEC: Issues of Supply and Demand," *Current History* 74 (March 1978) :127.

[14] For a fascinating account of Tariki as "a new man" in the Middle Eastern political and economic context, see Stephen Duguid, "A Biographical Approach to the Study of Social Change in the Middle East: Abdullah Tariki as a New Man," *International Journal of Middle East Studies* 1 (July 1970):195–220.

[15] George W. Stocking, *Middle East Oil: A Study in Political and Economic Controversy* (Nashville, Tenn.: Vanderbilt University Press, 1970), p. 350.

TABLE IX.3   *The Petroleum-Producing Countries' Drive to Power*

Chronicle of Events

August 1960	Major oil companies, led by Standard Oil of New Jersey, unilaterally cut posted price of oil.
September 1960	Representatives of Saudi Arabia, Iran, Iraq, Kuwait, and Venezuela meet in Baghdad and form the Organization of Petroleum Exporting Countries (OPEC).
September 1968	First meeting of the Council of the newly established Organization of Arab Petroleum Exporting Countries (OAPEC). Founding members: Saudi Arabia, Kuwait, and Libya.
September 1969	Traditional monarchy of King Idris in Libya overthrown in coup that brings to power a more radical government, headed by Colonel Muammar Qaddafi.
September 1970	Occidental Petroleum reluctantly accepts agreement with Libyan government after eight months of pressure-packed negotiations. Posted prices raised 30 cents a barrel, with further increases of 2 cents a barrel for each of the next five years; tax rate on profits raised from 50 percent to 58 percent in Occidental's case.
December 1970	Twenty-first meeting of OPEC in Caracas, Venezuela. Producing countries resolve to push forward on all fronts, raising posted prices and increasing tax rates.
February 1971	Tehran Agreement. Posted prices raised 33 cents a barrel with further increases of 5 cents a barrel over the next five years; income tax rate stabilized at 55 percent. Agreement to remain in effect through 1975.
April 1971	Tripoli Agreement. Posted prices raised 90 cents a barrel and income tax rate set at 55 percent. Agreement to remain in effect for five years and Libyan claims for retroactive payments settled.
February 1972	King Faisal of Saudi Arabia in a strongly worded statement supports producing-country participation in petroleum company ownership and operations. Shaykh Ahmad Zaki Yamani, Saudi minister of oil, had been urging participation since 1969.
October 1972	Shaykh Yamani announces formal agreement between producing countries and petroleum companies concerning participation. Countries can purchase an initial 25 percent interest in the companies, then further interest until they reach 51 percent ownership.

TABLE IX.3   (continued)

Chronicle of Events

May 1973	Iranian Sales Agreement. Iran formally completes nationalization of all its resources and facilities and works out a twenty-year purchase contract with the consortium, which is assured access to Iranian petroleum. Iran is to receive all of its domestic consumption oil at cost and is assured its economic benefits are as good as those won by the Arabs.
August 1973	Libya begins nationalizing 51 percent of the assets of the oil companies still in operation there. By September, this action, which was first directed against Occidental and other independents, was expanded to include the oil majors. This represents the beginning of the total takeover of oil companies operating on Arab soil.
October 1973	October War between the Arabs and Israelis. Arab states deliberately curtail production and institute petroleum embargo. Major OPEC members unilaterally decide that they, not the companies, will henceforth determine pricing. Posted price increased to $5.11 per barrel.
December 1973	OPEC members raise the posted price to $11.65, thus quadrupling the price since the outbreak of the October War.
March 1974	Arab OPEC membership lifts petroleum embargo against the United States.

ditional political elites in Iran and Saudi Arabia, the producing countries took control of the world oil process away from the companies headquartered and nourished in the West. Revolutionary nationalism was an important ingredient in the policy of the mobilizational countries. In the case of Iran, the new policy stemmed primarily from the desperate need of the Shah for increased resources to enable his regime to maintain its shaky political control. In Saudi Arabia, elements of nationalism and of regime survival were both involved, but it was also the staunch American support for the state of Israel that encouraged the Saudis to develop a tougher stand on oil. And there were other considerations as well — not the least of which was the general desire of weak nation-states to improve their power positions in the international arena.

As Table IX.3 indicates, the revolution in fact occurred between 1970 and 1974. During these years, the OPEC countries gained the power both to control prices and to determine production policy. They also began acquiring full ownership of the facilities and control over the technical operations within their boundaries. There is little doubt now that they are also becoming increasingly active in "downstream activities," including transportation, distribution, and marketing. This sharp shift in power, however, has not rendered the major companies obsolete. They remain indispensable technologically and still dominate the critical areas of distribution and marketing. In countries such as Iran and Saudi Arabia, they enjoy favored access to the product. Nor have they yet been seriously wounded financially. As Rustow and Mugno point out, although the companies' profits on production have declined sharply, "they now handle a far more expensive product, so that even a smaller profit margin is likely to yield larger absolute amounts — and the profitability of their 'downstream' operations . . . is undiminished. The steep increases in OPEC's revenue represent a financial transfer not from the companies but indirectly from the consumers."[16] In the end, however, there is little doubt that the petroleum-exporting countries have gained primary control over their own hydrocarbons and that both the companies and the consumers have lost most of their leverage.

The economic reasons underlying the success of OPEC are numerous. First, oil is an essential commodity for which there is no immediate, economical substitute. Second, during the 1960s, OPEC's share of world oil exports climbed rapidly, giving the organization greater and greater control of the market. Third, by 1970 all of the excess production capacity resided in the OPEC countries, especially those in the Middle East. Fourth, the international appearance of a growing number of independent oil companies contributed significantly to producing-country power. Occidental Petroleum, for example, had 96 percent of its worldwide operations concentrated in

16 Dankwart A. Rustow and John F. Mugno, *OPEC: Success and Prospects* (New York: New York University Press, 1976) , p. 32.

Libya, thus making these operations highly vulnerable to Libyan governmental pressures. Fifth, over the decade of the 1960s, OPEC countries had built substantial amounts of foreign exchange, enabling them to confront more comfortably the oil-importing nations of the West.[17]

Ever since OPEC's formation, scholars, journalists, businessmen, and other observers have been predicting its demise. Specialists in econometric modeling and supply-and-demand economics have continually explained why OPEC must shatter and why oil prices must plummet. At every sign of internal dissension within OPEC councils or of a temporary glut of oil on the world market, these prognosticators have come out with their statements that collapse is imminent.[18]

Theories predicting the demise of OPEC have been based on two major scenarios. First, the marginal cost of oil production in the Middle East is about fifteen cents per barrel. Given the current price of oil — of more than $12.00 per barrel — this marginal cost implies a fantastic rate of return. In a competitive market, the price would inevitably fall to approximately one dollar per barrel. Second, the countries within OPEC that need foreign exchange (e.g., Algeria, Indonesia, Iran, Iraq) will undercut OPEC prices in order to sell more oil. As these increased sales become substantial, Saudi Arabia will have to drop its price as well; the result will be a price war that will destroy OPEC.[19]

Despite all this, OPEC continues to exist; it continues to determine the prices of oil; and its major decisions, announced twice a year, are anxiously awaited in every major capital city in the world. In order to explain the continuing strength of OPEC, it is essential to analyze more than the economic di-

[17] These points are discussed in some detail in Hossein Askari and John Thomas Cummings, *Middle East Economies in the 1970s: A Comparative Approach* (New York: Praeger Publisher, 1976) , Chapter 1.

[18] In December 1976, for example, Irving Trust Company's chief petroleum economist, Arnold E. Safer, predicted the "gradual erosion of the cartel's position over the next few years." See Jim Brumm, "OPEC's Grip Won't Last Too Long, Oil Economist Predicts," *Christian Science Monitor*, 22 December 1976, p. 8.

[19] These scenarios are presented and rebutted in Askari and Cummings, *Middle East Economies*, Chapter 1.

mensions listed above — political considerations are also critical.

Eight years after the formation of OPEC, three Arab countries within it initiated the creation of another related organization, the Organization of Arab Petroleum Exporting Countries (OAPEC). A low-profile group that is more politically conscious than OPEC, OAPEC promotes petroleum planning, joint economic projects, and manpower training among its members. Besides the seven Arab countries who are part of OPEC, OAPEC includes Egypt, Syria, and Bahrain. It was OAPEC (not OPEC) that planned and implemented the October 1973 oil embargo. Its sensitivity to political issues is seen in its published bulletin. In a 1977 issue of this publication, for example, European colonialism and economic exploitation were roundly criticized. According to the OAPEC analyst: "In the Arab world, the process of decolonization has been especially harsh. Needless to say, we have been and still are wiping the blood off our wounds."[20] Although OAPEC political concerns obviously carry over into OPEC deliberations, they rarely influence OPEC decisions. One careful study has impressively documented the fact that "there has not been an 'Arab' position on oil pricing at any time during the period that oil prices have been under OPEC control."[21] As we will see below, there are political and ideological divisions that cut across these two organizations; these run much deeper than those that separate Arab from non-Arab.

There are two major interrelated reasons why the OPEC coalition has hung together so successfully for so long. First, although OPEC is usually characterized as a cartel, there are a number of important ways in which it deviates from the usual definitions of this term. These definitions usually demand that the following be present: (1) coordination among a limited number of sellers; (2) a restriction on the amount

20 George J. Tomeh, "Arab-European Political Relations," *OAPEC News Bulletin* 3 (May 1977):17.

21 Mary Ann Tetreault, "Petroleum Cartel: The Role of The Arab Nations in OPEC Bargaining" (Paper delivered at the Annual Meeting of the Southwestern Political Science Association, Houston, Texas, 12–15 April 1978), p. 24.

of the product sold to the market; (3) a common agreement on pricing; (4) a policy of discouraging or destroying the influence of new producers; and (5) a strict system of detecting and policing the actual behavior of members.

In the sense that there is a degree of coordination among members that has resulted in establishing a world price of oil that is enormously higher than the production costs of that oil, OPEC is a cartel, perhaps even "the greatest cartel in history."[22] But there are important conditions idiosyncratic to this organization. The sellers are not small in number, nor is their behavior especially well coordinated. There is little agreement, for example, on production policy. Although the consensus on pricing has held fairly well, even this minimal condition has not always been present — witness the two-tiered system of pricing that was adopted in December 1976 when the Saudis elected to raise prices by only 5 percent while the Iranians and others held out for a 10 percent price increase. Another deviation is the obvious presence of important producing countries outside of OPEC, such as Mexico, Norway, and Canada. Also, there is no effective system of detecting breaches of policy within OPEC. In making this point, one analyst points out that OPEC "has far more shipping points than members, and many more customers and receiving points. Its sources of information are scattered across the globe."[23] Finally, the question of politics is embedded deeply within the very foundation of the organization. "Politics, not economics, dominates the organization's decision making. In fact, no thorough economic analysis has undergirded any of OPEC's daring moves."[24] In the case of OPEC, the sellers are govern-

---

[22] D. K. Osborne, "Prospects for the OPEC Cartel," *Business Review*, Federal Reserve Bank of Dallas (January 1977), p. 1.

[23] Ibid., p. 3.

[24] Louis Kraar, "OPEC is Starting to Feel the Pressure," *Fortune* 91 (May 1975):189. In discussing the goals of OPEC, the Saudi Minister of Petroleum and Natural Resources, Shaykh Zaki Yamani, has stated that "the highest price is not and never has been our goal. In fact, higher prices may not always be in our interest . . ." *Middle East Economic Survey*, 17 October 1975, as quoted in Askari and Cummings, *Middle East Economies*, p. 37.

ments, i.e., political regimes that are subject to all manner and form of policy pressure.[25]

It is small wonder that observers are astounded by the continued existence and success of OPEC. In the very broad meaning of the term *cartel,* it qualifies. But OPEC fails to meet nearly every specific requirement of that type of organization. Its cohesiveness is suspect; there is an obvious looseness and a freewheeling spirit that are antithetical to tightly knit and disciplined coalition unity. This looseness is constantly encouraged by social and political considerations that seep into the decision-making process. How then has OPEC been able to survive so well and to make its decisions stick in the face of an often hostile world?

It is our contention that it is precisely these noncartel-like characteristics that account for OPEC's impressive record both of longevity of existence and of decisional effectiveness. What some might term looseness of organization, we see as a vital flexibility encouraged by a coalition composed of members who differ greatly in geographical, historical, ideological, developmental, and political makeup. Within the organization, coalition alignments constantly change according to the policy issue under discussion. This promotes a fluidity and spirit of compromise among the members, who know that today's opponent may be tomorrow's ally. This is seen most dramatically in the case of divergencies between ideology and politics.[26]

Although not readily visible even to close observers of OPEC politics, the fundamental Middle Eastern division within the coalition is the one between the authoritarian-traditional members on the one hand and the authoritarian-mobilizational regimes on the other. The former consist of Saudi Ara-

25 Some of these points have been made by Zuhayr Mikdashi, among others. See, for example, his *The Community of Oil Exporting Countries: A Study in Government Cooperation* (Ithaca, N.Y.: Cornell University Press, 1972).

26 We are indebted to Lawrence Schulz, who makes this important point within a different theoretical framework in a provocative paper. See Schulz, "OPEC — Deceased Theories Survived by the Patient: A Study of Organizational Response to Interdependence" (Paper delivered at the National Endowment for the Humanities Summer Seminar on Middle Eastern Political Systems, The University of Texas, Austin, Texas, July 1977).

bia, Iran, Kuwait, and Abu Dhabi, while the latter include Libya, Algeria, and Iraq. Despite the colorful forensics and public debate that have sometimes taken place between members on each side of this cleavage, the former group has generally been a more moderate voice on policy and pricing. A close examination of twelve public confrontations between Middle Eastern OPEC members that took place during the period 1973–1977 documents the existence of this basic cleavage.[27] In seven of the twelve cases, the opposing camps divided exactly along these political lines. In four other instances, the member out of position was Iran — a non-Arab country and the traditional system that most desperately needs the increased revenues for its economic and military development programs, upon which the regime has based its survival.[28] In all four cases, there was much made of Saudi-Iranian rivalry, despite the fact that both countries are conservative monarchies with much more in common with each other as trusted American allies than with the more radical mobilizational regimes.[29] In the December 1976 struggle over whether to raise prices by 10 percent (as Iran advocated) or by 5 percent (as Saudi Arabia advocated), the rhetoric did become rather heated. The fact that Saudi oil minister Shaykh Zaki Yamani had some months earlier apparently called the Shah "highly unstable mentally" was brought into the discussions.[30] A 19 December 1976 editorial in a leading Iranian newspaper did its share to enliven the debate; the column was entitled "Yamani Proves Himself to be a Stooge of Capitalist Circles."[31]

Yet, a year later, in December 1977, both Saudi Arabia and Iran cooperated in a major decision to freeze oil prices throughout 1978. This occurred despite the sharply declining value of the dollar during the early months of 1978 as well as

[27] These data are drawn from Tetreault, "Petroleum Cartel," pp. 25–26.
[28] In a July 1974 disagreement over freezing oil prices, Kuwait sided publicly with Iran in taking the more aggressive position.
[29] American officials, journalists, and novelists constantly draw scenarios of the Middle East in which the central political reality seems to be Saudi-Iranian hatred and conflict. Paul Erdman's imaginative *The Crash of '79* (New York: Simon and Schuster, 1976) in which the Shah of Iran obliterates Saudi Arabia with nuclear bombs, is only one case in point.
[30] *Middle East Intelligence Survey* 4 (1–15 October 1976), p. 103.
[31] *Kayhan International* (Tehran), 19 December 1976, p. 4.

the Shah's great need at home for increased resources to enable him to cope with the full-scale antiregime violence that erupted in the major cities of Iran at the time. In the May 1978 meeting of the OPEC oil ministers, the Saudis and Iranians refused even to discuss the possibility of replacing the battered dollar as the oil pricing unit, although the two countries together had already lost several billion dollars because of the dollar's weakness. The Shah's decision undoubtedly stemmed from a bargain he struck with President Carter during their discussions in Washington and Tehran in November 1977 and January 1978. The Shah was assured of the Carter administration's support for his regime as well as continued deliveries of the latest and most sophisticated military equipment in return for his support on the issue of oil prices. The major considerations here were political in nature. Nor was this the first time that Iran had collaborated with Saudi Arabia against the more demanding positions espoused by Libya and Iraq. In May 1973, Iran and Saudi Arabia had stood off a number of radical demands for more participation by countries in oil company operations.

Even though we choose to include Iran among the more moderate voices in OPEC, there can be no doubt that Iran has on occasion been a hawk on the question of pricing. It is precisely this kind of ambivalence that helps invest OPEC with staying power. In the last several years, Iran has allied itself with Saudi Arabia and Abu Dhabi against Algeria, Libya, and Iraq (May 1973), with Kuwait against Saudi Arabia (June 1974), with Iraq and Libya against Saudi Arabia (December 1976), and with Saudi Arabia, Kuwait, and the United Arab Emirates against Iraq and Libya (December 1977). On the other side of the division, Algeria has been the country that does the formal floating back and forth. Iraq, which is always publicly aligned against the Saudis, has been the one country in the more radical camp most apt to cut prices. Iraq in fact refused to honor the 1973 oil embargo. Such crisscrossing of positions and fluidity of movement have served to rather effectively conceal the basic cleavage discussed above. At the same time, this process has helped prevent this fundamental division from destroying OPEC.

In the end, the greater reserves and higher production rates of the traditional bloc give its members the upper hand in OPEC decision making. When Saudi Arabia, Iran, and Kuwait have agreed to support or defeat a particular policy, the mobilizational regimes have been relatively helpless. The radical drive of Algeria and Libya provided the impetus for transforming the system of oil politics. In a sense, they provided the original engine for change. But since then, the speed and direction of the train has been determined by the more cautious and conservative members of the OPEC coalition. In the West, the latter are therefore considered more responsible.

This finely tuned system could easily come apart if domestic political scenes change. Just as OPEC decisions can influence the domestic stability that is based upon the outcome of policies designed to cope with modernization and political development, so too can domestic political events shape the future of OPEC. It is at this point, among others, that domestic and international politics intersect. A revolutionary takeover in either Saudi Arabia or Iran could tip the delicate balance in OPEC heavily in the direction of those who favor a firmer stance on production and pricing. But even this is not certain. Much depends on the sensitivity of the United States to the demands already generated by such forces of the future. And, the American position with respect to issues such as the Arab-Israeli conflict will, if anything, have a greater impact on OPEC decisions in the future than it did in the past. Until now, the politics of OPEC have indicated a great capacity for flexible adjustment. Whether or not this will be enough to accommodate the challenges born of the political modifications and transformations that the future promises in the area is a question we leave to the reader to answer.

THE POLITICAL CONSEQUENCES OF PETROLEUM POWER

The petroleum-exporting countries of the Middle East have gained an enormous amount of international leverage as a result of their newly acquired control over their own resources, which was quickly translated into vastly expanded revenues. Domestically, the explosion of wealth meant that political leaders suddenly found themselves with new opportunities — opportunities to pursue new policies and programs. Table

IX.4 presents in graphic form the magnitude of the wealth that has flowed into the coffers of the oil-producing countries since 1974. In 1970, the revenue paid into the Middle Eastern oil-producing countries approached $6 billion; in 1976, the figure was nearly $96 billion. The revenues of Saudia Arabia alone in 1976 were five times those received by all Middle Eastern countries in 1970. The figures are staggering. Their political implications are just as significant.

The International Impact. The first clear indication of this new international political role occurred during the October 1973 war when the Arab oil-exporting countries implemented the now famous oil embargo. Although every major Arab oil-exporting country (except Algeria) had terminated production shortly after the 1967 war began, this first embargo was short-lived. There was plenty of oil elsewhere in the world, and

TABLE IX.4   *Middle East Petroleum Revenues, 1960–1976*
                 (millions of dollars)

	1960	1965	1970	1974	1976
Saudi Arabia	355	655	1,200	22,600	33,500
Iran	285	522	1,136	17,500	22,000
Kuwait	465	671	895	7,000	8,500
Libya	– –	371	1,295	6,000	7,500
Iraq	266	375	521	5,700	8,500
Abu Dhabi	– –	33	233	5,500a	7,000b
Algeria	– –	– –	325	3,700	4,500
Qatar	34	69	122	1,600	2,000
Others	9	16	150	1,800c	2,000c
Total	936	2,712	5,877	71,400	95,500

a This figure also includes revenues accruing to Dubai.

b This is a total UAE figure.

c These figures are estimates for countries such as Oman and Egypt.

Source: The primary sources for these data include the Petroleum Information Foundation, *The Petroleum Economist,* and *The Middle East Economic Digest.* It has been drawn together in J. A. Bill and R. Stookey, *Politics and Petroleum: The Middle East and the United States* (Brunswick, Ohio: King's Court Communications, 1975), p. 128; and Congressional Quarterly, *The Middle East: U.S. Policy, Israel, Oil and the Arabs* (Washington, D.C.: Congressional Quarterly, 1977), p. 138.

Iraq and Saudi Arabia were reluctant participants in any case. The 1973 scenario was quite different. Under the direction of King Faisal, the Saudis took the lead. On 17 October 1973, all the OAPEC countries announced their decision to cut production monthly by 5 percent of the previous month's sales. On 18 October, the Saudis made public their determination to cut their own production by 10 percent. When President Nixon requested $2.5 billion emergency aid for Israel, Saudi Arabia declared a total embargo against oil exports to the United States. Other Arab countries followed the Saudi lead. Although not nearly as shattering as it could have been, the embargo's impact was felt internationally. Available Arab oil fell from 20.8 million barrels a day in October to 15.8 million barrels by December. Saudi crude oil accounted for nearly half of this shortfall. Although countries such as Canada, Nigeria, and Indonesia, as well as non-Arab Iran, picked up some of the slack, "in terms of international trade in crude oil, the net loss was quite considerable — about 14 percent."[32] The possibility of another oil embargo has been a concern of world leaders ever since. The effects of the next one promise to be much more devastating.

This economic reality carries enormous political meaning in international politics. Although the term often used in the American press is *blackmail*, this oil leverage represents the reawakening of the Arab in world politics. There is little reason to believe that the Middle Eastern leaders would hesitate to use their power in what they consider their national self-interest any more than would the leaders of any other nation-state to use its particular resources for its own ends. It is often forgotten, for example, that in the summer of 1973 — just a few months before the oil-exporting countries resorted to "blackmail" — the United States suddenly declared an embargo on soybeans, a temporary policy that threatened to cripple our Japanese allies, for whom we had developed the market in soybeans, now their chief source of protein. Not

---

[32] Robert B. Stobaugh, "The Oil Companies in Crisis," *Daedalus* 104 (Fall 1975):180. This is the best article available on the actual implementation of the embargo. See also Jerome D. Davis, "The Arab Use of Oil," *Cooperation and Conflict* 11 (1976):57–67.

surprisingly, this and similar programs have been an integral part of American foreign economic and political policy for years. And other countries have made use of similar programs. The Middle East will be no exception.

The most explosive of the regional problems upon which oil power will have an effect is the Arab-Israeli issue discussed in the last chapter. There can be little doubt that economic self-interest is a major factor in Israel's substantial loss of support in the world community of nations. There are other reasons for this loss of support as well, of course. But since 1973, it has become increasingly clear that with the exception of support from the United States and, perhaps, the Republic of South Africa, Israel stands quite alone. Sub-Saharan Africa is a good case in point. Israel had spent two decades carefully developing economic and political relations with these countries. "By mid-November, 1973, all African states with the exceptions of Malawi, Lesotho, Swaziland, and Mauritius, had severed their ties with Israel."[33] Although many of these states had already broken relations with Israel before the October War, the decisions had as much to do with economic self-interest as with ideological sympathy.

In the industrialized West, Middle Eastern oil power has also had a perceptible influence. The Atlantic Alliance cracked under the strain of Arab pressure. In November 1973, the European Economic Community drafted a statement demanding that Israel return to its pre-1967 borders and that the rights of the Palestinian refugees be taken into account in any settlement. In subsequent meetings among Western oil-consuming countries, France refused to agree to the recommended multilateral approach and insisted on negotiating its own arms-oil deals with the Arabs. Even the Japanese, always reluc-

[33] Victor T. Le Vine and Timothy Luke, "Africans, Arabs, and the Limits of Realpolitik" (Paper delivered at the Annual Meeting of the Midwest Political Science Association, Chicago, Illinois, 21 April 1977). This is an important and provocative paper that documents well the movement of the OPEC countries out of the "have-not" and into the "have" category of nations. It unfortunately imposes upon the Arabs an expectation that they will somehow act less in their own national interests than do other nation-states. And the authors underestimate the continuing strength of Arab-African relations.

tant to move too far out of the shadow of the United States, took the side of the Arabs in the last weeks of 1973.

In May 1978, the United States Senate approved a controversial arms package recommended by the Carter administration. The package included the sale of fifteen F-15s and seventy-five F-16s to Israel, fifty F-5Es to Egypt, and sixty F-15s to Saudi Arabia. The Israelis and their powerful lobby in Washington chose to oppose the package on the grounds that the sale of F-15s to Saudi Arabia would dangerously shift the balance of power against them in the Middle East. Actually, the showdown was not so much a military issue as a psychopolitical one. The Israelis feared that the Saudi-American connection was becoming so close that their own privileged position with respect to the United States would be jeopardized. In a brutal confrontation between the long invincible Israeli lobby on the one hand and the Carter administration backed by a developing, but low-key, Arab lobby on the other hand, the arms package was approved by a 54–44 vote. Less than a decade ago, Israel could count on an overwhelming, one-sided majority in the United States Senate. Many senators viewed the outcome of the vote as a political watershed in American relations with the Middle East.

There were many reasons for this astonishing result. They included President Sadat's dramatic conciliatory gesture to the Israelis; Prime Minister Begin's intransigent response to Sadat and his aggressive policy concerning Israeli settlements in the occupied territories; the careful political strategy prepared and implemented by the Carter administration; the overreaction and sledgehammer approach of the Israeli lobby; and the genuine concern for the security of Saudi Arabia, a moderate and faithful ally trying to survive in an explosive area. But there is even more than this involved. The Saudi-American relationship has been a close one for forty years. The binding resource has been oil. As we have seen above, Aramco is an all-American consortium. After October 1973, the Saudi-American connection became especially close.

In June 1974, the United States and Saudi Arabia agreed to establish a Joint Commission on Economic Cooperation, which was to promote cooperative programs in all economic areas. Another joint commission was soon set up to promote military cooperation. In short, "It was agreed that Saudi Arabia and the United States will continue to consult closely on all matters of mutual interest."[34] Since 1974 and within the general framework of these joint commissions, the United States and Saudi Arabia have quietly established a number of extremely close economic and military arrangements. They reportedly specify, among other things, that 50 percent of Saudi Arabian annual balance-of-payment surpluses be placed in long-term investments in the United States; that 87 percent of Saudi surplus existing liquid cash be put in long-term bond markets in the United States; that these financial instruments are to carry at least a 7.5 percent rate of interest, but are not marketable to third parties; and that the Saudis can draw on the interest payments to pay for military equipment sold by American suppliers. "In return, Saudi Arabia agreed not to increase the posted price of petroleum by more than five percent in any given year for a period ending on 31 December 1984."[35] In June 1978, a leading authority on Saudi economic affairs estimated that out of $100 billion that Saudi Arabia had invested in the world marketplace, $60 billion rested in dollar obligations of various kinds.[36]

The American-Saudi special relationship is such that it will greatly influence American economic and political policy in the Middle East. As long as the current system of government prevails in Saudi Arabia, the United States is locked into a more evenhanded position on the Arab-Israeli issue. The Israelis sensed this in the 1978 arms package confrontation.

[34] U.S., Department of State, "Text of Joint Statement on Cooperation," *Department of State Bulletin,* 1 July 1974. In this agreement as well as one signed in November 1974 with Iran, the United States indicated that it was not averse to pursuing the bilateral route when it so desired.

[35] This quotation and the other information provided in this paragraph comes from "Secret U.S.–Saudi Pact," *International Currency Review* 9 (13 May 1977):8. This report of the details of the United States–Saudi relationship captures the spirit of the cooperation, if not all the accurate details. The publication of this kind of information throughout 1977 by the *International Currency Review* would seem to reflect the unhappiness of European financiers about the rather exclusive American-Saudi arrangements.

[36] A. J. Meyer, lecture delivered in Tokyo, Japan, 14 June 1978.

Also, as we will see below, this relationship, like the one fashioned with Iran, carries severe implications for the patterns of domestic Middle Eastern politics.

Among other important international relationships that have undergone significant change as a result of shifting oil power and prices, the situation of the least-developed countries of the world deserves brief mention. Much has been written about the fact that the poorer, non-oil-producing countries in Asia, Africa, and Latin America have borne the brunt of the OPEC economic offensive. Although there are numerous important differences among these countries in energy and economic situation, there can be little doubt that they have suffered severely because of the sudden increase in oil prices. Between 1973 and 1974 alone, the cost of the oil imports of these poorer countries increased from \$3.7 billion to \$13.1 billion.[37] And these scarce financial resources have not been recycled back to these countries in the way they have returned to the advanced industrial societies, such as the United States and Great Britain. These nations have also been the victims of indirect economic pressures. Through higher import costs, the new oil prices helped generate increases in the prices of other essential goods and services. This increasingly precarious situation, in which the formerly emerging nations of the Afro-Asian world have begun to sink beneath huge external debts and declining living standards, is fraught with international political danger.[38]

The gravity of this new development in increasing the gap between the haves and have-nots has resulted in a considerable literature, mostly produced by scholars in the industrial Western world. This literature has tended to place the responsibility for the deteriorating situation of the less-developed world squarely at the door of the oil-producing countries, especially

[37] Feraidun Shams B., "Oil-Poor Developing Countries," *Current History* 74 (March 1978) :112.

[38] Within the Middle East itself, Egypt is a case in point. In 1978, it had some \$78 billion in foreign debts. Bankruptcy was avoided in 1977 by extraordinary debt-rescheduling. In 1978, Japan, together with Saudi Arabia and other Arab oil countries, offered about \$1 billion in order to help Egypt avoid default. *New York Times*, 17 June 1978, p. 28.

those in the Middle East.[39] This school of thought has attempted to document its position by focusing on the impact of oil price increases on the trade balances of developing countries and on the nature of the OPEC aid program to these countries.

The United States Senate report referred to above emphasized the fact that "only an estimated $16 billion, or 12 percent of the total accumulated assets of OPEC, have gone directly to the non-oil developing countries."[40] In one periodical, this was referred to as "OPEC's 12% Crumb for Developing World."[41] A related argument criticizes the distribution of the aid that is given, that is, the rich Arab countries' tendency to earmark the overwhelming proportion of their aid for fellow Muslim countries at the expense of the non-Islamic countries of Africa and Asia. In more general terms: "Because of their new found wealth and status, the Arab states have gradually begun to behave much more like the developed First World states and they are forgetting their former fraternity with the Fourth World nations."[42]

This kind of analysis not only distorts a very complex situation by failing to examine all of its facets but also is an impediment to developing a solution to an admittedly serious problem. Our basic argument is that the Middle Eastern oil-exporting countries cannot be considered the primary culprits for the economically precarious and politically explosive state of the world's poorest societies. That responsibility must be shared. In the first place, the dramatic rise in oil prices was only one of many factors fueling the relative economic deterioration of these countries. Among these factors was a major price boom in many basic commodities that began in 1972, eighteen months before the major oil price increase occurred. Prices of commodities exported from industrial countries had

[39] See, for example, U.S., Congress, Senate, Committee on Foreign Relations, Subcommittee on Foreign Economic Policy, Staff Report, *International Debt, The Banks and Foreign Policy* (Washington, D.C.: Government Printing Office, 1977).

[40] Ibid., p. 4.

[41] *Afro-Asian Affairs,* 9 November 1977.

[42] Le Vine and Luke, "Africans, Arabs, and the Limits of Realpolitik," pp. 28–29.

already increased by nearly 50 percent between 1968 and 1973. A recent study estimates that the oil price increases were responsible for less than 30 percent of the deterioration in the trade balances of the developing countries.[43]

The OPEC countries in general and the Middle Eastern members in particular have not been niggardly in their foreign aid programs. Besides bilateral organizations such as the Kuwait Fund for Arab Economic Development (KFAED), the Abu Dhabi Fund for Economic Development, the Saudi Arabian Fund for Development, and the Kuwait Investment Company, there have been numerous multilateral aid programs. These include the Arab Bank for the Economic Development of Africa (ABEDA) along with its Special Arab Aid Fund for Africa (SAAFA), the Islamic Development Bank, the OPEC and OAPEC Special Funds, and the Arab Fund for Economic and Social Development. Between 1973 and 1977, Arab oil-producing countries dispensed over $19 billion in soft loans and grants.[44] When aid is figured as a percentage of gross national product (GNP), the Middle Eastern members of OPEC are contributing approximately 3 percent in aid, while the advanced Western countries average below 0.4 percent.[45] This gap is even more marked when one recognizes that several of the major Middle Eastern OPEC countries have a GNP per capita income much lower than that of the industrialized Western societies and that in cases such as Iran, Algeria, and Iraq, funds are badly needed for domestic development programs. The economic assistance given by the less populated Middle Eastern oil producers, such as Kuwait, Qatar, and the United Arab Emirates, has run as high as 10

[43] See Hossein Askari and John Thomas Cummings, *Oil, OECD, and The Third World: A Vicious Triangle?* (Austin, Tex.: Center for Middle Eastern Studies, 1978), p. 30. This book successfully clarifies and explains the confusing and often misunderstood relationship between the rich oil-exporting countries and the world's poorest societies. In so doing, it is a rare and valuable source.

[44] *Middle East Economic Digest*, 14 April 1978, p. 15.

[45] For an interesting analysis of these comparative aid statistics, see Askari and Cummings, *Oil, OECD, and the Third World*, p. 36. In 1978, it was reported that Japan and the United States were spending only 0.21 and 0.27 percent of their burgeoning gross national products on foreign aid. See *Time*, 12 June 1978, pp. 77–78.

percent of GNP in recent years. The criticisms of OPEC aid policy that emanate from the Western countries are less than convincing in view of these circumstances.

The criticism that Arab and Iranian aid is heavily skewed in favor of fellow Muslim countries is also questionable. Much of the less-developed world does embrace Islam. These neighboring societies are best known to the donors. And should the Arab decision to funnel more assistance to coreligionists and cultural allies be any more surprising than the American decision to favor Western, Christian countries with its Marshall Plan? Despite this partiality, OPEC has expressed deep concern for non-Islamic developing societies. India, for example, has been the second largest recipient of OPEC aid. And there has been a genuine effort to broaden the distribution of aid over time. Between 1975 and 1977, for example, the proportion going to Arab countries declined from 57.6 percent to 40.4 percent.[46]

The international problem of the rich and poor nations is not a new one. Surely, the oil-exporting countries of the Middle East can do more than they already have done to alleviate the problem. But they alone cannot solve the problem. The issue is one that confronts all nations, and only through a worldwide cooperative effort can something fundamental be done about it. As long as the Western industrial powers continue to peg their aid programs well below the 0.7 percent of GNP recommended by the United Nations, there is little reason to believe that their demands that the oil-exporting countries contribute even more than they are already giving will be heeded. If the latter should decide for their own reasons to increase their aid programs even more significantly, the problem would remain, since "collectively they are simply too small a part of the world economy to supply most of the funds needed by the LDC's [less-developed countries]."[47] Unless there is effective cooperation among the developed, developing, and oil-exporting countries, the tensions and imbalances in the international system could easily explode into conflict and violence.

[46] *Middle East Economic Digest,* 14 April 1978, p. 15.
[47] Askari and Cummings, *Oil, OECD, and the Third World,* p. 43.

Petroleum power has thus influenced international politics in many ways. It has altered the foreign policy of the world's great powers and has juggled alliances and realigned political coalitions. While catapulting a fortunate few of the world's traditionally poorest countries into the ranks of the world's richest, it has deepened the already pronounced divisions between those who have most and those who have least. These transformations have been closely intertwined with domestic political policies, which have themselves been influenced by the economic force of oil.

Domestic Political Patterns and Petroleum. Petroleum power has had a decided influence on the form and substance of Middle Eastern political systems. In the first instance, it has sharply propelled the forces of modernization discussed in chapter 1. In so doing, it has heightened the strain on the traditional political systems, while providing them with new and unprecedented opportunities. Most of the leaders of the oil-rich countries have chosen to enlist the expanding oil power to preserve their own positions of ascendancy. The preservation of patrimonialism has taken precedence over the promotion of political development. As part of this process, and because of their desire to improve their countries' positions in the international political arena, Middle Eastern leaders have tended to stress modernization. There is little doubt that this has improved the living conditions of the peoples of these societies, who now have the best homes, schools, hospitals, and transportation and communication facilities in their histories. In turn, their political leaders have all this besides a near monopoly on national political power, buttressed by the most sophisticated police and military organizations possible.

Oil has fortified the traditional in the Middle East. It is not accidental that the last kings are the wealthy kings (with only the partial exceptions of Husayn in Jordan and Hassan in Morocco). For years now, petroleum has artificially dampened the fire of revolution in the area. Internally, the royal patrimonial leaders have used its product to buy time and to bribe middle-class challengers. Regionally, the oil-rich countries have provided badly needed aid to the more radical forces, especially the homeless Palestinians. Resources are needed by everyone and every movement regardless of ideology. Outside of North Africa, only Iraq of the more radical authoritarian-mobilizational regimes has significant petroleum power. In the Middle East overall, the authoritarian-traditional and distributive regimes guided by monarchical leaders control 81 percent of the region's oil reserves (see Table IX.1).

The countervailing trend is much weaker, since only Iraq, Algeria, and Libya of the more radical systems have significant hydrocarbon reserves. Iraq and Algeria require all their resources and more in order to implement ambitious development programs at home. Their support for revolutionary movements in the region is largely limited to the moral variety. Only Libya has the surplus financial reserves to provide substantial material aid to opposition movements throughout the Middle East. And the Qaddafi government has a consistent record of doing so. Although time and the forces of demands for development are on the side of the Libyans, their current waves of support are only ripples swamped by the huge tide of Saudi and shaykhdom funds that wash across the region and out into the international system.

The conservative tilt in the Middle East is reinforced by factors other than the great financial influence that flows from petroleum. Just as we saw in the case of OPEC, there are a large number of shifting alliances and agreements in the Middle East that defy the logic of a simple ideological, political, or economic explanation. Although the basic political fissure is between the traditional and the radical, there are numerous examples of alliances that crisscross this gap. OPEC and OAPEC, which are analyzed above, are only two of the more visible examples of such alliances.

During the 1970s, the Algerian government sent a high-powered team of petroleum experts to Abu Dhabi to assist that country in establishing a modern and effective oil policy. Headed by a competent technocrat of great integrity named Mahmoud Hamra-Krouha (whom the Algerians could ill afford to lose in their own talent-thin oil organization), this Algerian team has been responsible for impressively developing the Abu Dhabi National Oil Company (ADNOC) and for training a number of native Abu Dhabians in petroleum science and technology. At the same time, the Iranians have been sporadically sending a number of their skilled oil technicians to Algeria to help train the Algerians.

In June 1975, after years of bitter ideological conflict and national rivalry, the Shah's traditional regime in Iran reached an accord with the radical mobilizational government in neighboring Iraq. Although many astonished observers predicted that the agreement could not last more than a few months, it remains in effect today. Not long before the accords, the Shah had labeled Iraqi strongman Saddam Husayn "the gangster and savage." Just after the agreement, the Shah described Saddam as "an astonishing, delightful, and imaginative young man." On the other side, Saddam Husayn, who had in the past described the Shah as a "Zionist tyrant," now referred to him as "a great Emperor and brother." In North Africa, Egypt's Sadat and Libya's Qaddafi have had a relationship that has alternated between lukewarm and very cold. Iraq maintains important economic and political ties with the political elite in Abu Dhabi. Syria stepped into the Lebanese civil war, initially on the side of the conservative Christian Arabs there. And Saudi Arabia has provided substantial aid to the Palestinians and more recently has even provided assistance to the radical regime in South Yemen.

In the Middle East, communication chanels remain open, alliances fragment, basic ideological divisions are intersected at innumerable points by temporary coalitions, and patterns of cooperation and conflict shift with the political wind. Fundamental differences concerning political form and policies with respect to change are present but are not always a good basis for predicting future developments. In this sense, OPEC is an excellent microcosm of the Middle Eastern political system. It contains important built-in rivalries and natural coalitions; although these are important to understand, the fact that the membership votes primarily on the basis of the issue at hand results in whirling alliances. Thus, only the system is given; its continued existence and style of organization rest to a great extent upon the flexible nature of its internal patterns of cooperation and conflict. The fact that substantial resources are present and that these resources are controlled in a manner designed to further preservation of the system are two further reasons for the continued existence of traditional patrimonialism in the Middle East. In this kind of system, rapid modernization can be accommodated while political development continues to be retarded.

CONCLUDING THOUGHTS

It remains for us to pull together some of the strands from the preceding chapters and to raise a few fundamental and persistent questions about the Middle Eastern political systems and their viability in the present currents of change. Although most of this book is about the domestic political systems of the area, we have treated at length in the preceding chapter and in this one two transnational phenomena: the never-ending quarrel between the Arab states and Israel, and the tremendous impact on the whole region of the possession of petroleum by some of the states within it. It has become almost impossible to analyze the domestic political structures in Egypt, for example, because those structures inevitably have reflected the urgent foreign policy aspects of Egypt's existence. To mention just a few of the recent interpenetrations of political systems, there are: the recent Syrian and Israeli interventions in Lebanon, the Shah's adventures in Oman and his offer to intervene in Somalia, and the quiet but effective occupation of the Spanish Sahara by Morocco in North Africa. There are the periodic discussions of union — Libya and Egypt, Libya and Tunisia, Egypt and Syria, Egypt and Sudan; there has been discussion of a military pact between Iraq, Iran, and Saudi Arabia. These and other interregional plans are constantly discussed publicly at summit meetings and privately during quiet visits between leaders of the area. The Shah of Iran and King Husayn of Jordan are constantly huddling with one another, for example. Over all this there is poured the gravy of oil money, which, seeping into the political crevices of the area, flavors everything and alters many of the old relationships. It is not possible to predict the exact dimensions of all the changes to come, but come they will.

Oil has bought time for the traditional systems in the Middle East. Without this largess, it is very likely that they would have tumbled into revolution before now. Afghanistan, a traditional regime without oil, was the scene of a radical coup in April 1978. Two months later, the "oil-less" regimes in the two Yemens were shaken by the violent deaths of their leaders. In South Yemen, the violence was the result of a struggle within the elite in which the more radical faction triumphed over the more moderate group. Would the Shah and the Saudi kings have lasted so long without the generosity that the possession of oil permits them to display toward their own inhabitants and their neighbors?

But the oil revolutions produce their own problems. The Shah has not found that all the stresses and strains of his system can be ironed out by financial outlays. His preoccupation with military modernization and economic growth at the expense of social and political development has been only one of many flaws in his system. In 1978, riots and demonstrations against Pahlavi rule spread through Iran's major cities as the Shah fought to steady his shaky throne. In Saudi Arabia, many members of the royal family seem to be bewildered by the huge physical transformation that oil has brought. New cities cannot be built, or educational institutions and their accompanying infrastructures created, without altering much that traditional Saudis would very much like to retain. Saudi Arabia, which now has "underway the most advanced airports and airways systems in world aviation history,"[48] is having a difficult time taking off in the face of traditional winds that continue to carry with them public beheadings of shamed royal family members and flogging sentences for foreigners found trafficking in liquor. The new age they are entering promises to be a most complex and trying one.

To King Farouk was attributed the old cliché that soon there would be only five kings left in the world, those of hearts, spades, clubs, diamonds, and the king of England. In the Middle East, at least, it is possible that the present incumbents will be the last on their thrones. The Saudi case may be something of an exception; the royal family there is so large and

48 *New York Times,* 24 April 1978, p. 5.

monopolizes positions of authority and educational talent so assuredly that it would be difficult for an outsider to assume control. But even in Saudi Arabia some new ruler might prefer to be called president. Precisely this sort of coup took place in Afghanistan in 1973 when the old king (Zahir) was replaced by a president (who was also a close member of the king's own family) — but kingship, though not family domination, was dead.

In Jordan, Husayn's brother is the crown prince, but who knows what political forces would have to be contained to seat him safely and permanently on Husayn's throne? It is unlikely that the Pahlavi dynasty in Iran will survive that much longer in spite of the former Shah's personal shrewdness and political experience; much the same can be said of Hassan in Morocco.

The Arab-Israeli dispute has played a role similar to that of oil in diverting Arab (and especially radical Arab) energies towards Palestine rather than towards other activities, perhaps revolutionary, probably imperialistic, and almost certainly violent. Some of these other activities occurred anyway. The Egyptians were involved in a war in Yemen in the 1960s — their Vietnam, in Nasser's own words. The Syrians even today continue to try to stir up the Kurds in Iraq, and the Iraqis, of course, along with the Libyans, have been the "bad boys" of the neighborhood gang. Had there been no Israel, the Arab world would still be rent with deep ideological and political divisions. There would be a scramble for oil. Possibly Saudi Arabia could have survived some of this, but Kuwait might have long since succumbed to Iraqi power. The Arabs in modern times have always been embarrassed about their family quarrels. Without Israel (or with an accommodation with Israel) it is likely that some and perhaps much of this bickering will increase in intensity. Indeed, it is not too farfetched to say that Israel might ally itself with some Arab state against still another. In 1970, it almost did so when Husayn asked for Israeli help to neutralize Syrian support for the Palestinian guerrillas in Jordan. Jordan is indeed the natural ally, geographically, for any adventure some future Israeli government might embark upon.

Thus, the Arab-Israeli dispute too has retarded natural — be it good or bad — political development in the Middle East by siphoning off the radical energies that otherwise might have produced such development. And the machinations of the United States and the Soviet Union have done little to directly promote political development in the area. The United States has consistently supported the authoritarian-traditional systems of Middle Eastern monarchy to the very end, while the Soviet Union has ideologically zigzagged its way through the area — an area upon which it has always had imperialistic designs. Ironically, both the United States and the Soviet Union have, on the other hand, indirectly encouraged political development in the Middle East. In the case of the United States, such encouragement has been the result of several decades of exposure to American values stressing democratic participation and individual liberties. In the Soviet case, it has stemmed from the impressive record of modernization (especially in Soviet Central Asia) that saw Russia transform itself into a major world power only a few decades after its revolution in 1917. This model forced many Middle Eastern leaders to begin social and political reforms in self-defense against the Soviet challenge to the north.

Assuming that some accommodation comes between Arabs and Israelis, what happens to the Palestinians? As this is being written in 1978 a number of credible scenarios present themselves. First, there is the Camp David accord in which Sadat, whispering that he would never consent, did indeed agree to a separate peace with Israel. Nevertheless, to do this effectively he needs the tacit support of the Saudis, who on the Israeli question have always been somewhat more interested in the status of Jerusalem than in the fate of Palestinians. But the Old City of Jerusalem is not the most difficult problem in the Arab-Israeli dispute. This scenario leaves Syria to dangle on the vine; it would leave the Palestinians even less. Another scenario, and one which would make Sadat's consent less painful, is some face-saving formula that would create a Palestinian "entity" out of the West Bank and Gaza, but without giving the Palestinians the substance of a state that could threaten Israel. This bears a strong resemblance to the Camp David agreement too; in effect Sadat opted for a combination of scenarios. The West Bank would be completely landlocked and without resources. It is already filled with Palestinians; it is hard to believe that an ingathering from the far-flung reaches of the Arab world would give it economic substance and life. Our argument here is that no scenario giving the Palestinians very much is necessarily needed for an Egyptian accommodation with the Israelis.

An interesting possibility (the third scenario) is for the Palestinian "entity," when it comes into existence on the West Bank, to gradually absorb Jordan. The result would be a new Palestine that would contain present-day Jordan as well as the West Bank and Gaza. King Husayn understands this possibility very well; perhaps nothing more complicated than this explains his apparent lack of interest in "recovering" the West Bank or of participating very energetically in the Sadat-Begin negotiations. Currently, the big powers and Israel could prevent this occurrence, but in the long run it becomes more probable. Jordan already contains a very large number of Palestinians, whose attachment to Husayn is not altogether that great.

A fourth scenario would involve a comprehensive peace settlement spurred by a coordinated United States–Soviet policy. This, after all, was precisely what was beginning to develop just before Sadat made his historic trip to Jerusalem in November 1977. However dramatic and courageous Sadat's move was, it effectively destroyed the momentum of the time for a general Geneva peace conference. Now the Geneva alternative seems for the moment to be dead. This scenario would stress the centrality of the Palestinians to any agreement and would almost certainly lead to the establishment of some kind of independent Palestinian state. As the most comprehensive solution, this one would also be the most difficult to implement politically. Still, as it becomes apparent that Sadat and Begin did not solve the whole problem at Camp David, it becomes an increasing possibility.

And, of course, there are many other possible outcomes. Whatever may happen to them, the Palestinians will not continue to wander in the wilderness forever. They will one day have their homeland, their state. But before this transpires, it is likely that there will be much more conflict, violence, and international travail.

The huge influx of oil monies into the Middle East has significantly expanded industrial and commercial activities in the area.[49] One of the social by-products of this quickening process has been the explosive growth of two relatively new classes. The first is a professional middle class, a burgeoning salaried group with a modern higher education. The political elites of the authoritarian-mobilizational regimes are drawn from this class, which challenges monarchy everywhere. A recent example of its rise to power occurred in Afghanistan in 1978 when the remnants of the royal family were destroyed and a former journalist and novelist, Nur Muhammad Taraki, took over as prime minister. The Tarakis are the heirs of the Nassers and the Atatürks.

The second new class movement that has arisen in the current generation is the inevitable labor movement, however poorly organized it may be at any one time. Up to now, labor has not been well organized in the Middle East, except in Israel, Morocco, Algeria, and Bahrain. But this is certain to change. Revolutions are rarely made by industrial workers, but they are often supported and shored up by them. Again, the point is very simple. As the Middle East becomes more urban than rural and more industrial than agricultural, it will generate a new class consciousness that may well be inimical to the present more traditional structures remaining in the area.

The international environment will also change in unpredictable ways. What will be the nature of future American-Soviet rivalry in the area? It need not remain what it is today. What natural political or military ambitions will emanate from within the area? What adventures will tempt future Arab, Iranian, Turkish, or Israeli leaders? We cannot be naive enough to believe that there will be none. What struggles will ensue between the rich and the poor — between both

[49] The 1908–1985 Saudi Five-Year Plan, for example, schedules expenditures of over $140 billion.

nations and individuals? (The Palestinians remain the single greatest poor nation of individuals in the Middle East today. And their presence alone has already nearly brought down two Arab states: Jordan and Lebanon. In Kuwait, their numbers continue to threaten the traditional ruling system.) It is not difficult to imagine the mad scramble for resources, living space, and access to markets by those whose current share of these things is less than that of others.

These struggles may be hastened by ideology. Nationalism is, of course, not dead, even if its Arab variety is much less viable since the year of Nasser's death. But new nationalisms grow quickly to justify struggles against exploiters or imperialists. It is possible to envisage an Egyptian nationalism encouraging adventures in Sudan or perhaps in Libya. It is equally possible to imagine Algerian nationalistic stirrings that might affect its immediate neighbors. Is it impossible to conceive of a permanent Syrian hegemony over Lebanon — a Greater Syria at last — especially one with Israeli blessing? Or, at least in Lebanon, a redistribution of populations along sectarian lines? Again Palestinian nationalism is going to have to be reckoned with, as Begin knew only too well when he pressured his cabinet in the summer of 1978 to drag its heels on a settlement for the West Bank.

And what about the greatest ideology of all, religion? Islam is changing quite obviously, as indeed all religion in the world is doing. But in the Middle East religion has been so tied to the traditional society that the stresses of modernization may well produce explosive results. In the spring of 1978, Iranian university students rioted in Tehran, partially over the presence of women students in their classrooms. There is in Iran, as in other parts of the Middle East, a renascent "born-again" enthusiasm that has kindled many of the youth, including women. But just as the United States is ever more secular in spite of Billy Graham and the Reverend Moon, the Middle East is moving with fits and starts away from the traditional structures of cultural Islam. Nowhere is this more apparent than with respect to the position of women. It staggers the imagination to believe that the traditionalists will be able to hold the line with respect to women's rights in the years to come. We are tempted to rephrase a famous French saying: the more things remain the same, the more they will change. Underneath the murky waters of convention, history, religion, and tradition dart the sparkling facets of change until almost at once the system is no longer the same. The entire notions of family, sex, children, education, employment, marriage, divorce, manners, and culture are in the balance. The changes will be much to cope with for any generation, traditional or otherwise, but they are inevitable.

This is of course the trauma of modernization. And modernization means gaps, divisions, imbalances, and inequalities. Various Middle Eastern nations will differ in the depth and direction of their modernizing processes. This is inevitable in a part of the world where nations as poor as Afghanistan, Pakistan, and Sudan exist alongside countries as wealthy as Saudi Arabia, Iran, and Kuwait. Among the modernizers, those that do so more effectively and with less turmoil will have leverage in a variety of ways over those that have lagged behind.

Today, in spite of Saudi richness and Egyptian dependence upon that richness, the Egyptians largely go their own way; moreover, in making area policy (whether vis-à-vis Israel or otherwise), the Egyptians seem likely to remain among the leaders in the Middle Eastern world. This is true even if an Egyptian leader (Sadat after Camp David) is at any one time very unpopular. And if money talks, it does not convey all messages. A regional neocolonialism may develop in the area as those countries which have modernized most rapidly siphon off, by sweet talk, by technological or cultural threats, or by other such devices, much of the excess riches of such wealthy oil states as Saudi Arabia. It is evident that more tensions and strains may come from all this.

Just as there are significant gaps within and among Middle Eastern societies with respect to the level of modernization, there is yet another level at which the imbalances are even more pronounced and explosive. This is the growing gap between modernization on the one hand and political development on the other. As modernization races further and further out ahead of political development, the potential for political violence and social upheaval increases significantly. New demands, sharpened and heightened by modernization and petroleum wealth, inundate political leaders, who are less and less able to meet them on traditional patrimonial terms. In many ways, the Begins and the Sadats are as ineffective in this respect as are the embattled monarchs of the area.

The technocratic elites that have come to guide the destinies of Middle Eastern countries increasingly decry the lack of "infrastructures" and deplore the multiplication of "bottlenecks" that exist in their systems. In so doing, they become more and more sensitive to economic and technical difficulties, but the problems are partially rooted at quite another level. The cultural, social, and political infrastructures and bottlenecks also require attention. And they are much less susceptible than economic and technical difficulties to manipulation by man.

As the Middle East wearily makes its way to the twenty-first century, we can only suggest that severe overhauling of the extant political systems is very much in order; we do not mean that it is necessarily functionally needed (a value judgment), but rather simply that it seems inevitable. Monarchies are anachronisms and will go the way of all royal flesh. The clichés called socialism and capitalism (the Saudis believe that the possession of oil richness is the product of their capitalism, just as no doubt Qaddafi considers Libyan wealth a product of his own unusual ideological position) will give way to something else, whatever it may be called. There will be ever increasing demands for participation, assuaged by cosmetic and fraudulent symbols. The Middle East is hardly likely to be democratic in the Western sense, nor should it be expected to be so. But much about the Middle East seems outworn, if not obsolete.

The Lebanese communal and sectarian system, so long admired, is in shambles. The revolutions from above (as in Iran) are currently demonstrating their inadequacies. Turkey still is under the spell of nostalgia for Atatürk, and Pakistan continues to stumble along in a ceaseless ballet of civilian demagogues and incompetent generals. The crushing social and economic problems in Egypt increasingly outstrip President Sadat's ability to deal with them. Israel is no exception. It has found no time in its thirty years of life to put together a constitution or even to agree on constitutional principles. It has a miserable electoral law, if the object of such legislation is to produce a responsible majority government. It does not know how to deal with *its* Arabs (those under its control) — even the 40,000 bedouins in the Negev — and it is living in an environment that is steadily growing more Middle Eastern (and hence less Israeli), even if simultaneously the entire Middle East is becoming modernized.

Despite this litany of problems and failures, there is much that holds promise for the future of the Middle East. Vast natural resources are available. They have finally come under the control of the indigenous leaders, who now sometimes direct their utilization in what is considered to be the best interests of the peoples of the area. Partially because of this, the Middle East is moving back towards the center of the world stage. The new generation of political leaders that is taking power in the area is not as ideologically radical as is often thought. Witness the actual policies of President Assad of Syria and Boumedienne of Algeria, or for that matter al-Bakr of Iraq. Nor are the traditional leaders as reactionary as their public images sometimes suggest. Leaders from all political camps in the Middle East have exhibited as much international responsibility as have those from any other region on the globe.

The Middle East is vibrant and alive. It is today a restless, turbulent area at the threshold of enormous alterations in its philosophies, its life-styles, and its distributive justice. It is filled with political fault-lines that can give way to violence as easily as to constructive cooperation. At the center of the struggle are the persistence of continuity and the inevitability of change. The social, economic, and political issues that this book analyzes reflect this conflict between continuity and change in every facet. And its consequences increasingly affect all our lives.

Selected Bibliography

CHAPTER I: POLITICAL DEVELOPMENT AND THE CHALLENGE OF MODERNIZATION

Almond, Gabriel A., and G. Bingham Powell, Jr. *Comparative Politics: System, Process, and Policy.* Boston: Little, Brown and Co., 1978.

Anthony, John Duke. *Arab States of the Lower Gulf.* Washington, D.C.: The Middle East Institute, 1975.

Antoun, Richard, and Iliya Harik, eds. *Rural Politics and Social Change in the Middle East.* Bloomington: Indiana University Press, 1972.

Bill, James A., and Robert L. Hardgrave, Jr. *Comparative Politics: The Quest for Theory.* Columbus, Ohio: Charles E. Merrill, 1973, ch. 2.

Binder, Leonard, James S. Coleman, Joseph LaPalombara, Lucian W. Pye, Sidney Verba, and Myron Weiner. *Crises and Sequences in Political Development.* Princeton, N.J.: Princeton University Press, 1971.

Halpern, Manfred. "Four Contrasting Repertories of Human Relations in Islam." In *Psychological Dimensions of Near Eastern Studies,* ed. L. Carl Brown and Norman Itzkowitz. Princeton, N.J.: The Darwin Press, 1977, pp. 60–102.

Hudson, Michael C. *Arab Politics: The Search for Legitimacy.* New Haven: Yale University Press, 1978.

Landau, Jacob M., ed. *Man, State, and Society in the Contemporary Middle East.* New York: Praeger Publishers, 1972.

Leiden, Carl, ed. *The Conflict of Traditionalism and Modernism in the Muslim Middle East.* Austin: University of Texas Press, 1966.

Masannat, George S., ed. *The Dynamics of Modernization and Social Change: A Reader.* Pacific Palisades, Calif.: Goodyear Publishing Co., 1973.

Moore, Clement Henry. *Politics in North Africa: Algeria, Morocco, and Tunisia.* Boston: Little, Brown and Co., 1970.

Peretz, Don. *The Middle East Today.* 3rd ed. New York: Holt, Rinehart and Winston, 1978.

Roos, Leslie L., and Noralou P. Roos. *Managers of Modernization: Organizations and Elites in Turkey (1950–1969).* Cambridge, Mass.: Harvard University Press, 1971.

Rustow, Dankwart A. *A World of Nations: Problems of Political Modernization.* Washington, D.C.: Brookings Institution, 1967.

Szyliowicz, Joseph S. *Education and Modernization in the Middle East.* Ithaca, N.Y.: Cornell University Press, 1973.

Tachau, Frank, ed. *The Developing Nations: What Path to Modernization?* New York: Dodd, Mead and Co., 1972.

Waterbury, John, and Ragaei El Mallakh. *The Middle East in the Coming Decade.* New York: McGraw-Hill, 1978.

CHAPTER II: ISLAM AND POLITICS

Algar, Hamid. *Religion and State in Iran, 1785–1906.* Berkeley and Los Angeles: University of California Press, 1969.

Arberry, A. J., ed. *Religion in the Middle East.* 2 vols. Cambridge: Cambridge University Press, 1969.

Coulson, N. J. *A History of Islamic Law.* Edinburgh: Edinburgh University Press, 1964.

Gaudefroy-Demombynes, Maurice. *Muslim Institutions.* London: George Allen and Unwin, 1950.

Gilsenan, Michael. *Saint and Sufi in Modern Egypt: An Essay in the Sociology of Religion.* New York: Oxford University Press, 1973.

Hodgson, Marshall G. S. *The Venture of Islam.* 3 vols. Chicago: University of Chicago Press, 1974.

Holt, P. M., Ann K. S. Lambton, and Bernard Lewis. *The Cambridge History of Islam.* 2 vols. Cambridge: Cambridge University Press, 1970.

Keddie, Nikki R., ed. *Scholars, Saints, and Sufis: Muslim Institutions in the Middle East Since 1500.* Berkeley: University of California Press, 1972.

Kerr, Malcolm. *Islamic Reform: The Political and Legal Theories of Muhammad 'Abduh and Rashīd Ridā.* Berkeley: University of California Press, 1961.

Ibn Khaldun. *The Muqaddimah: An Introduction to History.* Translated by Franz Rosenthal. Princeton, N.J.: Princeton University Press, 1967.

Nasr, Seyyed Hossein. *Ideals and Realities of Islam.* London: George Allen and Unwin, 1966.

Rosenthal, Erwin I. J. *Political Thought in Medieval Islam: An Introductory Outline.* Cambridge: Cambridge University Press, 1958.

Smith, Wilfred Cantwell. *Islam in Modern History.* Princeton, N.J.: Princeton University Press, 1957.

Watt, W. Montgomery. *Bell's Introduction to the Qur'ān.* Edinburgh: Edinburgh University Press, 1970.

Williams, John Alden, ed. *Themes of Islamic Civilization.* Berkeley: University of California Press, 1971.

CHAPTER III: THE GENES OF POLITICS:
GROUPS, CLASSES, AND FAMILIES

Barth, Fredrik. *Political Leadership Among Swat Pathans.* London: The Athlone Press, 1959.

Beck, Lois, and Nikki Keddie, eds. *Women in the Muslim World.* Cambridge, Mass.: Harvard University Press, 1978.

Bill, James A. *The Politics of Iran: Groups, Classes, and Modernization.* Columbus, Ohio: Charles E. Merrill, 1972.

————. "Class Analysis and the Dialectics of Modernization in the Middle East." *International Journal of Middle East Studies* 3 (October 1972) : 417–34.

Bodman, Herbert, Jr. *Political Factions in Aleppo, 1760–1826.* Chapel Hill, N.C.: University of North Carolina Press, 1963.

Brown, Kenneth L. *People of Salé: Tradition and Change in a Moroccan City.* Manchester: Manchester University Press, 1976.

Bulliet, Richard W. *The Patricians of Nishapur: A Study in Medieval Islamic Social History.* Cambridge, Mass.: Harvard University Press, 1972.

Eisenstadt, S. N. "Convergence and Divergence of Modern and Modernizing Societies." *International Journal of Middle Eastern Studies* 8 (January 1977) :1–27.

English, Paul Ward. *City and Village in Iran*. Madison: University of Wisconsin Press, 1966.

Fernea, Elizabeth Warnock, and Basima Qattan Bezirgan, eds. *Middle Eastern Muslim Women Speak*. Austin: University of Texas Press, 1977.

Fernea, Robert A. *Shaykh and Effendi: Changing Patterns of Authority Among the El Shabana of Southern Iraq*. Cambridge, Mass.: Harvard University Press, 1970.

Gubser, Peter. *Politics and Change in Al-Karak, Jordan*. New York: Oxford University Press, 1973.

Gulick, John. *The Middle East: An Anthropological Perspective*. Pacific Palisades, Calif.: Goodyear Publishing Co., 1976.

Hussein, Mahmoud. *Class Conflict in Egypt, 1945–1970*. Translated by Michel and Susanne Chirman, A. Ehrenfeld, and K. Brown. New York: Monthly Review Press, 1973.

Khuri, Fuad I. *From Village to Suburb: Order and Change in Greater Beirut*. Chicago: University of Chicago Press, 1975.

Levy, Reuben. *The Social Structure of Islam*. Cambridge: Cambridge University Press, 1957.

Nieuwenhuijze, C. A. O. van. *Social Stratification and the Middle East: An Interpretation*. Leiden: E. J. Brill, 1965.

———. *Commoners, Climbers and Notables*. Leiden: E. J. Brill, 1977.

Patai, Raphael. *Golden River to Golden Road: Society, Culture, and Change in the Middle East*. 3rd ed. Philadelphia: University of Pennsylvania Press, 1969.

Springborg, Robert. "Patterns of Association in the Egyptian Political Elite." In *Political Elites in the Middle East*, ed. George Lenczowski. Washington, D.C.: American Enterprise Institute, 1975.

CHAPTER IV: THE POLITICS OF PATRIMONIAL LEADERSHIP

Andrae, Tor. *Mohammed: The Man and His Faith*. New York: Barnes and Noble, 1935.

Dekmejian, R. Hrair. *Patterns of Political Leadership: Lebanon, Israel, Egypt*. Albany: State University of New York Press, 1975.

Frey, Frederick W. *The Turkish Political Elite*. Cambridge, Mass.: M.I.T. Press, 1965.

Gellner, Ernest. *Saints of the Atlas*. Chicago: University of Chicago Press, 1969.

Guillaume, A. *The Life of Muhammad: A Translation of Ishaq's Sīrat Rasūl Allah*. London: Oxford University Press, 1955.

Lenczowski, George, ed. *Political Elites in the Middle East*. Washington, D.C.: American Enterprise Institute, 1975.

Margoliouth, D. S. *Mohammed and the Rise of Islam*. 3rd ed. New York: G. P. Putnam's Sons, 1905.

Quandt, William B. *Revolution and Political Leadership: Algeria 1954–1968*. Cambridge, Mass.: M.I.T. Press, 1969.

Rustow, Dankwart A. *Philosophers and Kings: Studies in Leadership*. New York: George Braziller, 1970.

Tachau, Frank, ed. *Political Elites and Political Development in the Middle East*. Cambridge, Mass.: Schenkman Publishing Co., 1975.

Vatikiotis, P. J. *The Fatimid Theory of State*. Lahore, Pakistan: Orientalia Publishers, 1957.

Waterbury, John. *The Commander of the Faithful: The Moroccan Political Elite — A Study in Segmented Politics*. New York: Columbia University Press, 1970.

Watt, W. Montgomery. *Muhammad at Medina*. Oxford: The Clarendon Press, 1956.

———. *Islam and the Integration of Society*. London: Routledge and Kegan Paul, 1961.

Weber, Max. *The Theory of Social and Economic Organization*. New York: Oxford University Press, 1947.

Yuval, Elizur, and Eliahu Salpeter. *Who Rules Israel?* New York: Harper & Row, 1973.

CHAPTER V: THE POLITICS OF LEADERS AND CHANGE

Abdel-Malek, Anouar. *Egypt: Military Society*. Translated by Charles Lam Markmann. New York: Vintage Books, 1968.

Bayne, E. A. *Persian Kingship in Transition*. New York: American Universities Field Staff, 1968.

Bill, James A. *The Politics of Iran: Groups, Classes, and Modernization*. Columbus, Ohio: Charles E. Merrill, 1972.

———. "Iran and the Crisis of '78." *Foreign Affairs* 57 (Winter 1978/79): 323–42.

Binder, Leonard. *In a Moment of Enthusiasm: Political Power and the Second Stratum in Egypt*. Chicago: University of Chicago Press, 1978.

Burrell, R. Michael, and Abbas R. Kelidar. *Egypt: The Dilemmas of a Nation, 1970–1977*. Beverly Hills, Calif.: Sage Publications, 1977.

Gran, Peter. *Islamic Roots of Capitalism, Egypt 1760–1840*. Austin: University of Texas Press, 1979.

Heikal, Mohamed. *The Cairo Documents*. Garden City, N.Y.: Doubleday and Co., 1973.

Hussein, Mahmoud. *Class Conflict in Egypt, 1945–1970*. Translated by Michel and Susanne Chirman, A. Ehrenfeld, and K. Brown. New York: Monthly Review Press, 1973.

Karpat, Kemal, et al. *Social Change and Politics in Turkey*. Leiden: E. J. Brill, 1973.

Kinross, Lord. *Atatürk: The Rebirth of a Nation*. London: Weidenfeld and Nicolson, 1964.

Leder, Arnold. *Catalysts of Change: Marxist versus Muslim in a Turkish Community*. Austin: University of Texas Center for Middle Eastern Studies, 1976.

Mayfield, James B. *Rural Politics in Nasser's Egypt*. Austin and London: University of Texas Press, 1971.

Nasser, Gamal Abdel. *Egypt's Liberation: The Philosophy of the Revolution*. Washington, D.C.: Public Affairs Press, 1955.

Özbudun, Ergun. *Social Change and Political Participation in Turkey*. Princeton, N.J.: Princeton University Press, 1976.

Pahlavi, Mohammed Reza Shah. *The White Revolution*. Tehran: Imperial Pahlavi Library, 1967.

Pfaff, Richard H. "Disengagement from Traditionalism in Turkey and Iran." *Western Political Quarterly* 16 (March 1963): 79–98.

Philby, H. St. John. *Arabian Jubilee*. London: Robert Hale, 1954.

————. *Saʿudi Arabia*. London: Ernest Benn, 1955.

el-Sadat, Anwar. *In Search of Identity: An Autobiography*. New York: Harper & Row, 1978.

Tamkoç, Metin. *The Warrior Diplomats*. Salt Lake City: University of Utah Press, 1976.

Weiker, Walter. *Political Tutelage and Democracy in Turkey: The Free Party and Its Aftermath*. Leiden: E. J. Brill, 1973.

Zonis, Marvin. *The Political Elite of Iran*. Princeton, N.J.: Princeton University Press, 1971.

CHAPTER VI: VIOLENCE AND THE MILITARY

Barakat, Halim. *Lebanon in Strife*. Austin: University of Texas Press, 1977.

Be'eri, Eliezer. *Army Officers in Arab Politics and Society*. New York: Frederick A. Praeger, 1970.

Bill, James A. "The Military and Modernization in the Middle East." *Comparative Politics* 2 (October 1969) :41–62.

Bullock, John. *Death of a Country: The Civil War in Lebanon*. London: Weidenfeld and Nicolson, 1977.

Haddad, George M. *Revolutions and Military Rule in the Middle East*. 3 vols. New York: Robert Speller and Sons, 1965–1973.

Harris, George S. "The Role of the Military in Turkish Politics." *Middle East Journal* 19 (Winter and Spring, 1965) :54–66, 169–76.

Havens, Murray C., Carl Leiden, and Karl M. Schmitt. *The Politics of Assassination*. Englewood Cliffs, N.J.: Prentice-Hall, 1970.

Horne, Alistair. *A Savage War of Peace: Algeria 1954–1962*. New York: Viking, 1978.

Hurewitz, J. C. *Middle East Politics: The Military Dimension*. New York: Frederick A. Praeger, 1969.

Leiden, Carl, and Karl M. Schmitt. *The Politics of Violence and Revolution in the Modern World*. Englewood Cliffs, N.J.: Prentice-Hall, 1968.

Perlmutter, Amos. *Politics and the Military in Israel, 1967–1977*. Totowa, N.J.: Frank Cass, 1978.

Vatikiotis, P. J. *The Egyptian Army in Politics*. Bloomington: Indiana University Press, 1961.

————. *Politics and the Military in Jordan*. New York: Frederick A. Praeger, 1967.

Yapp, M. E., ed. *War, Technology and Society in the Middle East*. London: Oxford University Press, 1975.

CHAPTER VII: THE IMPRINT OF IDEOLOGY

Abu Jaber, Kamel S. *The Arab Baʿth Socialist Party: History, Ideology, and Organization*. Syracuse: Syracuse University Press, 1966.

Antonius, George. *The Arab Awakening*. Beirut: Khayat's, 1955.

Binder, Leonard. *The Ideological Revolution in the Middle East*. New York: John Wiley and Sons, 1964.

Cleveland, William L. *The Making of an Arab Nationalist*. Princeton, N.J.: Princeton University Press, 1971.

Cottam, Richard W. *Nationalism in Iran*. Pittsburgh: University of Pittsburgh Press, 1964.

Haim, Sylvia G., ed. *Arab Nationalism: An Anthology*. Berkeley: University of California Press, 1962.

Hanna, Sami A., and George H. Gardner. *Arab Socialism: A Documentary Survey.* Leiden: E. J. Brill, 1969.

Harris, George S. *The Origins of Communism in Turkey.* Stanford: The Hoover Institution, 1967.

Isaac, Rael Jean. *Israel Divided: Ideological Politics in the Jewish State.* Baltimore: Johns Hopkins Press, 1976.

Ismael, Tareq Y. *The Arab Left.* Syracuse: Syracuse University Press, 1976.

Karpat, Kemal H., ed. *Political and Social Thought in the Contemporary Middle East.* New York: Frederick A. Praeger, 1968.

Khadduri, Majid. *Political Trends in the Arab World: The Role of Ideas and Ideals in Politics.* Baltimore: Johns Hopkins Press, 1970.

Quandt, William B., Fuad Jabber, and Ann Mosely Lesch. *The Politics of Palestinian Nationalism.* Berkeley: University of California Press, 1973.

Said, Abdel Moghny. *Arab Socialism.* New York: Barnes and Noble, 1972.

Sharabi, Hisham. *Nationalism and Revolution in the Arab World.* Princeton, N.J.: D. Van Nostrand Co., 1966.

Springborg, Robert. "On the Rise and Fall of Arab Isms." *Australian Outlook* 31 (1977) :92–109.

Tütsch, Hans E. *Facets of Arab Nationalism.* Detroit: Wayne State University Press, 1965.

Yamak, Labib Zuwiyya. *The Syrian Social Nationalist Party: An Ideological Analysis.* Cambridge, Mass.: Harvard University Press, 1966.

Zabih, Sepehr. *The Communist Movement in Iran.* Berkeley: University of California Press, 1966.

CHAPTER VIII: THE ARAB-ISRAELI CONNECTION

Ben-Sasson, H. H., ed. *A History of the Jewish People.* Cambridge, Mass.: Harvard University Press, 1976.

Brecher, Michael. *Decisions in Israel's Foreign Policy.* New Haven: Yale University Press, 1975.

Childers, Erskine B. *The Road to Suez: A Study of Western-Arab Relations.* London: MacGibbon and Kee, 1962.

Elon, Amos. *Herzl.* New York: Holt, Rinehart and Winston, 1975.

Golan, Matti. *The Secret Conversations of Henry Kissinger: Step-by-Step Diplomacy in the Middle East.* New York: Quadrangle/The New York Times Book Co., 1976.

Halpern, Ben. *The Idea of the Jewish State.* 2nd ed. Cambridge, Mass.: Harvard University Press, 1969.

Hirst, David. *The Gun and the Olive Branch: The Roots of Violence in the Middle East.* London: Faber and Faber, 1977.

Khouri, Fred J. *The Arab-Israeli Dilemma.* 2nd ed. Syracuse: Syracuse University Press, 1976.

Lilienthal, Alfred M. *The Zionist Connection: What Price Peace?* New York: Dodd, Mead and Co., 1978.

Luttwak, Edward, and Dan Horowitz. *The Israeli Army.* New York: Harper & Row, 1975

Quandt, William B. *Decade of Decisions: American Policy Toward the Arab-Israeli Conflict, 1967–1976.* Berkeley: University of California Press, 1977.

Rodinson, Maxime. *Israel and the Arabs.* Baltimore: Penguin Books, 1973.

Sachar, Howard M. *A History of Israel from the Rise of Zionism to Our Time.* New York: Alfred A. Knopf, 1976.

el-Sadat, Anwar. *In Search of Identity: An Autobiography.* New York: Harper & Row, 1978.

Safran, Nadav. *Israel: The Embattled Ally.* Cambridge, Mass.: Harvard University Press, 1978.

Sheehan, Edward R. F. *The Arabs, Israelis, and Kissinger.* New York: Reader's Digest Press, 1976.

Stookey, Robert W. *America and the Arab States: An Uneasy Encounter.* New York: John Wiley and Sons, 1975.

CHAPTER IX: THE POWER OF PETROLEUM

Abir, Mordechai. *Oil, Power and Politics.* London: Frank Cass, 1974.

Anthony, John Duke, ed. *The Middle East: Oil, Politics, and Development.* Washington, D.C.: American Enterprise Institute, 1975.

Askari, Hossein, and John Thomas Cummings. *Middle East Economies in the 1970s: A Comparative Approach.* New York: Praeger Publishers, 1976.

———. *Oil, OECD and the Third World: A Vicious Triangle?* Austin: University of Texas Center for Middle Eastern Studies, 1978.

Freedman, Robert O. *Soviet Policy Toward the Middle East Since 1970.* New York: Praeger Publishers, 1975.

Hartshorn, J. E. *Objectives of the Petroleum Exporting Countries.* Nicosia, Cyprus: Middle East Petroleum and Economic Publications, 1978.

Kerr, Malcolm H. *The Arab Cold War.* 3rd ed. London: Oxford University Press, 1971.

Magnus, Ralph H., ed. *Documents on the Middle East.* Washington, D.C.: American Enterprise Institute, 1969.

Mikdashi, Zuhayr. *The Community of Oil Exporting Countries: A Study in Government Cooperation.* Ithaca, N.Y.: Cornell University Press, 1972.

Mosley, Leonard. *Power Play: Oil in the Middle East.* Baltimore: Penguin Books, 1974.

Rustow, Dankwart A., and John F. Mugno. *OPEC: Success and Prospects.* New York: New York University Press, 1976.

Stocking, George W. *Middle East Oil: A Study in Political and Economic Controversy.* Nashville, Tenn.: Vanderbilt University Press, 1970.

Vernon, Raymond, ed. *The Oil Crisis.* New York: W. W. Norton and Co., 1976.

Waterbury, John, and Ragaei El Mallakh. *The Middle East in the Coming Decade.* New York: McGraw-Hill, 1978.

Index

Abbasids, 64, 102, 103, 121, 169
Abdel-Malek, Anouar, 124, 226, 227n
Abduh, Muhammad, 52–53
Abdul Aziz Ibn Saud, King, 173, 179, 181–183, 183n, 301
Abdullah, King (Jordan), 179, 277, 301, 321, 350
Abu Bakr, 42, 137, 138, 138n, 147, 157
Abu Dhabi, 2, 18, 31, 33, 89, 96, 109, 176, 179, 364–366, 380–381, 383, 393–394
Abu Talib, 137, 139
Aden, 108, 238–239, 243, 261, 328
Al-Afghani, Jamal al-din, 51, 52–53, 284
Afghanistan, 17, 20, 21, 30, 32, 33, 48, 70, 78, 238–239, 254–255, 269, 295, 364, 366, 396–397, 399, 402
Aflaq, Michel, 307, 309–311
A'isha, 102, 147
Alawites, 39, 62, 256
Algeria, 13, 14, 17, 21, 30, 32, 34, 35, 78, 126, 176, 221, 245–246, 258, 261, 271, 330, 364, 366–367, 371–372, 376, 380–383, 390, 393, 400, 404
Ali, Imam, 42, 59, 60, 102, 121, 137, 147, 148n, 157, 158, 171, 210
Amer, Abd al-Hakim, 259, 268
Amir Kabir (Mirza Taqi Khan), 154–155
Anglo-Iranian Oil Co., 199, 203, 296, 368, 370
Anjuman, 107, 166n
Aqaba, Gulf of, 143, 328, 331, 338–339
Arab-Israeli conflict, 1, 28, 34, 219, 244, 256, 305, 318–359, 361, 382, 385, 387, 397, 398
Arab Legion, 256, 331, 333
Arab socialism, 305–306, 308–311
Arab Socialist Union, 89, 220, 223, 229, 232, 308
Arafat, Yasir, 324, 342
Asabiyya, 81, 286
al-Askari, Ja'far, 95, 273

al-Assad, Hafez, 39, 256, 265, 330, 358, 404
Assassinations, 273–276
Atatürk, Kemal, 54, 56, 106, 173, 179, 183–196, 197, 197n, 216, 222, 223, 228, 235, 271–272, 285, 290, 293, 296, 297, 403
Ayub Khan, 267–268, 272, 278

Badr, Battle of, 140, 148
Baghdad Pact, 220, 265, 267n, 314
Bahais (Babists), 40, 74
Bahrain, 20, 21, 30, 78, 86, 87, 96, 98, 364, 366, 368, 377, 400
al-Bakr, Gen. Ahmad Hasan, 267, 404
Bakr Sidqi, 265–266
Balfour Declaration, 299, 299n, 321
Bandung Conference, 219–220, 307
al-Banna, Hasan, 46, 52, 60–61, 275–276, 291
Baraka, 41, 145, 152, 158n
Bar-Lev Line, 252n, 334, 345–346
Barmecids, 103, 154
al-Barzani, Shaykh Mulla Mustafa, 247–248
Ba'th, 309–311
Begin, Menahem, 28, 231, 241, 320n, 324, 326, 329, 339n, 341–342, 344, 349, 354n, 356, 358, 386, 399
Ben Bella, Ahmad, 14, 57, 245
Ben Gurion, David, 299, 337
Bernadotte, Count Folke, 241–242, 273, 342–343
Bhutto, Zulfikar Ali, 255, 268
Black Saturday, 239–240, 263
Boumedienne, Houari, 13, 14, 245, 330, 404
Bourgeois middle class, 117, 119, 122, 125, 126
Bourguiba, Habib, 13, 54, 57, 58, 85, 109, 317
Britain (England), 89, 108, 180, 185, 186, 200, 220, 228, 229, 241, 243, 263–265, 294–297, 299, 300–301, 314, 321–322, 326, 335, 337–338, 368, 370, 388

Brotherhoods, 81, 82, 120, 122, 160, 166
Buhrayd, Jamilah, 107–110
Bureaucratic middle class, 117, 119, 121, 126

Camp David, Md., 230, 260, 286, 320n, 324, 327, 329, 348–349, 354–355, 357–358, 398, 399, 402
Carter, Jimmy, 205, 231, 320n, 330, 332n, 343, 354, 362, 381
China, 220, 225–226, 248, 312
Chou En-lai, 219, 224
Class, 111–133
  definition of, 112
  structure, 113, 116, 121, 129
Cleric middle class, 117, 119, 120
Cliques, 15, 26, 75, 77–79, 84, 85, 86, 91, 94
Copts, 40, 73, 287
Coups, 262–270
Cyprus, 238, 253, 319

Dayan, Moshe, 336–339, 341, 351n
Demirel, Suleyman, 195
Dhofar, 180, 248, 254
Diwaniya, 85
Dubai, 109, 110, 364, 366, 383
Dulles, John Foster, 220

Ecevit, Bulent, 195
Egypt, 13, 17, 20, 21, 22, 24, 25, 27, 30, 32, 34, 85, 86, 88, 100, 101, 109, 121, 125, 132, 179, 216–223, 225, 227, 228, 235, 236, 239–240, 249, 251–253, 257–259, 260–264, 278, 280, 291–293, 294n, 301, 306–309, 311, 313, 315, 323n, 324–327, 329–332, 332n, 334, 340, 342, 345–346, 348–350, 353–354, 357, 364, 366, 377, 386, 388n, 395, 403
"Emanation," 151–153, 158, 175, 207, 208, 213
Eshkol, Levi, 339
Ethiopia, 22, 259

Factions, 77, 84, 85, 91, 94
al-Fahd group, 181
Faisal, King (Saudi Arabia) , 31, 183, 239, 321
Family, 91–98, 116, 129–130

Farouk, King, 89, 150, 179, 217, 220, 225, 229, 263, 280–281, 301, 337, 396
al-Fateh, 242
Fatima, 102, 148
France (the French) , 14, 107, 108, 193, 220, 294, 296–298, 301, 314, 326, 334, 337–338, 369, 385
Free Officers, 89, 217, 220

Gallipoli, 185, 187
Gaza Strip, 322, 323n, 332n, 340, 354
Glubb Pasha, 239, 256n, 265
Golan Heights, 253, 326–327, 334, 341, 344–345, 352, 356
Gomaa, Sharawi, 223, 229, 230n
Group, 75–91
  associational, 77–78, 83, 85
  definition, 75n
  formal, 76–77, 80–83, 94, 99
  informal, 76–77, 79, 82–90, 92, 94, 111, 130
  institutional, 77–78, 83
Group-class interaction, 129–133
Guilds, 81–83, 120, 122
Gulbahar Hatun, 104–106

Habash, George, 342
Hadd, 44–45
Hafsa Hatun, 104–105
al-Haq, Zia, 268
Harem, 99, 101
Harun al-Rashid, 102–103, 154, 210
Hashim, clan of, 137, 139, 149
Hassan, King (Morocco) , 134, 163, 170, 173, 252, 270, 392, 397
Hijra (Hegira) , 139, 140
Hoveyda, Amir Abbas, 96, 202
Hurrem Sultan (Roxelana) , 104–106
Husayn, King (the Hashemite) , 181, 242n, 251, 273, 327, 350
Husayn, King (Jordan) , 134, 173, 181, 289, 392, 395, 397, 399
al-Husri, Sati, 292, 303

Ibrahim Pasha, 105, 154
Idris, King (Libya) , 179, 257, 281, 297, 373
Ijtihad, 45, 65
al-Ilah, Abd, 265–266
Imam, 157, 174, 209, 210
India, 40, 84, 179, 180, 225, 239, 255, 267–268, 315, 391

Indonesia, 40, 315, 371, 376, 384
Inönü, Ismet, 179, 187, 189, 193,
    193n, 194, 194n, 195, 196, 196n,
    236
Iqbal, Muhammad, 53–54
Iran, 2, 13, 14, 16, 17, 18, 20, 21, 22,
    24, 30, 31, 33, 34, 63, 64, 65, 68,
    70, 78, 86, 89, 90, 94, 95, 96, 100,
    101, 109, 124, 126, 130, 154, 157,
    163, 169, 170, 176, 179, 196, 199,
    200, 202, 205, 219n, 221, 239,
    246, 247–252, 254–255, 261, 295–
    296, 305, 308, 312–313, 357, 364–
    368, 370–371, 373–376, 380–383,
    388, 390, 394–395, 397, 401–403
Iraq, 2, 13, 17, 18, 21, 22, 30, 32, 35,
    78, 79, 85, 89, 95, 100, 126, 132,
    176, 218, 238–239, 246–248, 251,
    254, 256, 261, 265–267, 301, 305–
    306, 309, 311–313, 321, 353, 364–
    366, 367–368, 370–371, 373–376,
    380–383, 388, 390, 393–397, 404
Israel, 13, 16, 17, 20, 21 28, 29, 30, 38,
    49, 59, 68–69, 135, 220, 221, 226,
    228, 230, 234, 240–244, 251–253,
    256–261, 284, 286n, 288, 300–301,
    313, 318–320, 323–327, 329–332,
    332n, 335–336, 338, 340–341,
    343–346, 346n, 348–354, 356–358,
    384–386, 395, 397–398, 400, 404

Japan, 84, 226, 362, 385, 388n
Jerusalem, 286, 320n, 325, 328, 341,
    349–350, 398, 399
Jordan, 13, 17, 18, 20, 21, 30, 126, 131,
    134, 163, 176, 239, 251, 289, 300,
    301, 306, 323n, 324, 326–327,
    331, 340–341, 392, 395, 399, 401
June War (1967), 221, 260, 268

Karabekir, Kazim, 188, 194
Kassem, Abdel Karim, 54, 247, 266,
    272, 312
al-Kawakibi, Abd al-Rahman, 302
Khadija, 102, 110, 137, 139, 147, 163
Ibn Khaldun, 81, 172, 286
Khalid, King, 134, 183, 270, 330
Kharijites, 59–60
Khayzuran, 102–104
Khomayni, Ayatullah Ruhullah, 206
Kissinger, Henry, 327, 348, 351–353,
    356, 366

Knesset, 69, 329, 349, 365
Krim, Muhammad Bin Abdul,
    238–239, 244–245, 244n, 297
Kurds, 246–248, 249, 256–257, 295
Kuwait, 16–18, 20, 21, 25, 30, 31, 35,
    85, 181, 238, 255, 323n, 327,
    364–366, 368, 371, 373, 380–383,
    390, 397, 401–402

Lebanon, 2, 9, 13, 17, 20, 21, 30, 33,
    36, 39, 79, 83, 88, 89, 90, 91, 125,
    127, 129, 130, 135, 169, 238,
    242n, 252, 255–256, 297, 306,
    319, 323n, 325, 330, 332, 395, 401
Libya, 13, 17, 18, 20, 21, 30, 32, 35,
    58–59, 125, 129, 249, 251, 257,
    261, 281, 287, 297, 301, 330, 353,
    364–366, 371–374, 376, 380–383,
    393, 395, 401
Likud bloc, 28, 356n
Litani River, 325, 332

Makkawi, Nagwa, 108
Mansur, Hasan Ali, 96, 202
Marei family, 88–89, 232
Mecca, 103, 136, 137, 138, 139, 140,
    141, 141n, 142, 143, 149, 181
Medina, 139, 140, 141, 141n, 142, 156
Meir, Golda, 72, 355, 356
Menderes, Adnan, 30, 195, 297
Mexico, 23, 363, 378
Military (Middle Eastern), 249–270
Modernization, 3–6, 9, 10, 12, 14, 15,
    16, 17, 18, 20, 21, 23, 24, 28, 33,
    34, 36, 76, 95, 98, 122, 123, 126,
    127, 128, 132, 214–215, 281, 392,
    402–403
Moghuls, 50–51, 152, 169
Morocco, 13, 17, 18, 21, 30, 78, 79, 80,
    90, 94, 100, 116, 126, 134, 158,
    163, 169, 176, 239, 244, 257, 297,
    327, 364, 366, 392, 395, 397, 400
Moyne, Lord, 241, 273, 343
Muhammad, 40, 42, 92, 102, 110,
    117, 120, 135, 136, 137, 138, 138n,
    139, 140, 141, 141n, 142, 143, 144,
    145, 146, 146n, 147, 147n, 148,
    148n, 149, 150, 155n, 156, 157,
    158, 163, 181, 291, 303, 328
Muhammad V, King (Morocco),
    179, 297
Mujtahid, 45, 65, 157, 209

Musaddiq, Muhammad, 199, 200, 200n, 201, 201n, 203, 296, 370
Muslim Brotherhood, 46, 60–61, 68, 217–218, 275–276, 291, 292, 313

Naguib, Muhammad, 173, 217, 264, 301
Nasir al-Din Shah, 53, 154
Nasser, Gamal Abdel, 14, 54, 61, 88, 89, 173, 179, 216–228, 230–232, 234, 235, 249, 264, 268, 271–272, 276n, 277n, 282n, 286, 289, 294, 300–301, 303, 306n, 310, 314– 316, 324, 325, 333, 337–339, 343, 397, 400, 401
Nasserism, 218, 225n, 283–284, 284n, 305, 306n
National Resurgence party (Iran), 203–204, 206
Negev Desert, 239, 336
Neo-Destour party, 26, 35
Nurbanu Sultan, 106

October War (1973), 28, 256, 258, 268
Oman, 2, 13, 30, 48, 69, 134, 179, 248, 254, 364, 366, 395
OPEC, 361, 365, 371–382, 388–394
Ottomans, 50, 93, 104, 105, 106, 152, 154, 162, 169, 184, 294–295

Pahlavi, Farah Diba, 109, 203
Pahlavi, Muhammad Reza Shah, 14, 36, 96, 134, 157, 165, 173, 179, 196–215, 236, 251, 254–255, 332n, 357, 374, 380–381, 394–396
Pahlavi, Reza Shah, 54, 57, 68, 179, 196, 197, 197n, 198, 203, 295, 295n
Pakistan, 21, 40, 48, 115, 116, 251, 254–255, 267–268, 364, 366, 402, 403
Palestine, 69, 238–242, 244, 256, 299– 301, 306, 319–320, 322, 336, 343, 348, 397
Palestine Liberation Organization, 324, 330, 342–343, 351, 354n, 356, 358
Palestinian Arabs, 1, 36, 39, 107, 133, 286–287, 300, 319, 322–323, 323n, 324, 329–330, 332n, 336, 342, 348–350, 353, 355–356, 358, 385, 393–394, 398–399, 401

Parliaments, 26, 27, 29, 77, 78, 84, 114
Patrimonalism, 150, 151, 152, 153, 155, 156, 158, 160, 161
Persian Gulf, 36, 86, 134
Physical Quality of Life Index (PQLI), 19–23, 36, 215
Political Development, 3, 6–10, 14, 15, 17, 24, 25–29, 34, 35, 36, 76, 95, 126, 127, 128, 132, 214–215, 281, 319
Political elites, 6, 9, 10, 12, 14, 25, 26, 27, 94, 114, 134, 176, 281
Political parties, 26, 27, 29, 77, 78, 114
Power, 112–117

Qabus, Sultan, 134, 180
Qaddafi, Mu'ammar, 13, 257, 278, 287–288, 297, 330, 373, 393–394, 403
Qatar, 16, 20, 21, 30, 31, 364, 366, 371, 383, 390
Qawmiyya, 287, 293, 300
Quran, 41, 99, 111, 121, 284, 291, 328

Rabin, Yitzak, 338–339, 356
Rajal khayr, 165–166
Republican Peoples' party (Turkey), 187, 188, 190, 192, 194n, 195
Resolution, 242, 343–344, 351
Rif Rebellion, 238, 244, 244n

Sa'ada, Antun, 298–300
Sabry, Ali, 89, 229, 230n
Sadat, Anwar, 13, 14, 61, 73, 89, 109, 114, 144, 179, 228, 229, 230n, 231, 233, 235, 236, 260, 268, 276n, 286, 307–308, 313, 320n, 324, 329–330, 343–344, 349, 353, 353n, 358, 386, 394, 398–399, 401
Safavids, 152, 162, 169
al-Said, Nuri, 95, 265–266, 301
Said bin Taymur, Sultan, 179–182
Salah al-Din, 50, 237, 348
Saudi Arabia, 2, 13, 16, 17, 20, 21, 30, 33, 34, 78, 85, 86, 126, 127, 134, 163, 169, 170, 176, 239, 254, 257, 301, 319, 328, 330, 332n, 345, 348, 357, 363–366, 368, 371– 376, 379–384, 386–387, 394–397, 402

SAVAK, 201, 203, 204, 206, 250
Sharaf, Sami, 223, 229
Sharjah, 89, 110, 364, 366
Sharm el-Shaykh, 328, 331, 338, 340
Sharon, Ariel, 331, 345, 354n
Shi'i Muslims, 39, 40, 45–46, 65, 247
Sinai, 259–260, 323n, 326–328, 334, 338–340, 342, 344–346, 352, 352n, 354, 356
Soviet Central Asia, 40, 398
Soviet Union, 17, 18, 34, 220, 253–254, 259–261, 311–315, 329–330, 334, 342, 346, 350–351, 365, 367, 398
Sudan, 2, 13, 17, 21, 30, 32, 40, 239, 248, 251, 259, 267, 333, 401, 402
Suez Canal, 220, 252, 263–264, 294, 327, 329, 337, 340, 341–342, 345, 352
Sufi Orders, 46, 160, 166
Suleyman I, 104–106, 154
Sunni Muslims, 39, 40, 45–46, 65
Suwaydi, Ahmad, 96
Syria, 13, 17, 20, 21, 22, 30, 32, 35, 39, 62, 79, 126, 132, 137, 218, 221, 238–239, 251, 253, 256, 261, 264–265, 271, 295, 297–299, 300, 301, 305–306, 311–313, 323n, 324, 326–327, 330–334, 340, 342, 352–353, 358, 364, 366, 377, 395, 398, 401, 404

Tariqa, 55, 82
Ibn Taymiyyah, Ahmad, 60
Tikka Khan, 268
Tudeh party, 199, 200, 203
Tunisia, 13, 17, 18, 20, 21, 26, 30, 32, 33, 34, 35, 109, 125, 132, 221, 255, 257, 271, 297, 300, 364, 366, 395
Turkey, 13, 17, 18, 20, 21, 22, 24, 27, 29, 30, 33, 34, 55–56, 64, 70, 78, 86, 93, 125, 132, 135, 174–175, 179, 186, 187, 190, 191, 195, 197, 221, 222, 236, 246, 251, 253–255, 271, 284, 293, 295–297, 305, 364, 366, 403

Uhud, Battle of, 140, 148
Ulema, 47–48, 66, 118, 120, 121, 126
Umar, 63, 147, 148n
Umayyad Dynasty, 42, 102

United Arab Emirates, 16, 18, 20, 21, 30, 31, 371, 381, 383, 390
United Arab Republic, 220, 221, 301
United Nations, 331, 338–339, 341, 343, 349–351
United States, 18, 34, 84, 108, 260, 288, 314–315, 329–330, 332n, 334, 343, 345–346, 350–352, 354, 357, 360–362, 365–368, 374, 382, 384, 387–388, 398
Uthman, 138, 147, 148

Vatan Society, 184
Vazirs, 118, 119, 130, 161
Veil, 99, 100, 101, 107

Wafd party, 88, 217, 294
Wataniyya, 286, 293–294, 305
Weizmann, Ezer, 299, 339, 354n
West Bank, 322, 323n, 326–327, 332n, 341, 348, 354, 356
White revolution (Iran), 201–203, 207, 270, 305
Women, position of, 55, 57, 66, 98–111, 401
World War I, 185, 187, 293–297, 312, 321, 360
World War II, 239, 296–297, 314, 317, 322

Yahya Khan, Agha, 268, 272
Yazid, 42
Young Turks, 184, 185, 187, 189, 194, 295
Yemen, 17, 20–21, 30, 32–33, 48, 69, 100, 102, 104, 143, 163, 221, 228, 248, 255, 258, 261, 290, 301
Yemen, People's Republic of, 21, 32, 243, 394, 396

Zaghlul, Sa'd, 294
Zahir Shah, 57, 179, 397
Za'im, 88
Zakat, 43
Zayid, Shaykh, 96, 109, 110, 176
Zionism, 240n, 299, 299n, 300, 318, 320, 350
Ziyarid, 115
Zoroastrians, 40, 74
Zubayda, 102–104